Scott Foresman

Roget's Student
Thesaurus

Editorial Offices: Glenview, Illinois • Parsippany, New Jersey • New York, New York
Sales Offices: Reading, Massachusetts • Duluth, Georgia • Glenview, Illinois
Carrollton, Texas • Ontario, California

ISBN 0-673-65138-X

This book also appears under the title *Writer's Thesaurus.*

Acknowledgments and credits appear on pages 534 through 536.

Library of Congress CIP information is available upon request from the publisher.

6 7 8 9 10 11 12 - DOC - 04 03 02 01

Table of Contents

To Parents

Young people like to share with others what they know, what they see, what they feel, and what they imagine. As they mature, they need to express themselves with increasing competence in spoken and written communication. Scott Foresman's *Roget's Student Thesaurus* helps students build their vocabularies and improve their writing skills, at the same time encouraging them to enjoy the world of words they first discovered as young children.

This thesaurus is a resource for determining distinctions among words whose meanings are similar or related. In addition, *Roget's Student Thesaurus* shows students why successful writers choose certain words, and it gives tips to help students improve their own writing.

The entry words were carefully chosen by teachers and editors for their usefulness to students in the middle and upper grades. The synonyms included in the entries expand the student writer's stock of words. Most entry words include a large list of synonyms in order to capture the widest possible variety of meanings. For example, synonyms listed for the entry word *eager* range from *enthusiastic, impatient,* and *anxious* to *keen* and the informal *gung-ho.* For the entry word *argue,* there are eleven synonyms, including some idioms, such as *to lock horns* and *to be at loggerheads.*

The thesaurus presents information in ways designed to appeal to students. Each entry word is defined in easy-to-understand language and shown in an example sentence. Synonyms for the entry words are also accompanied by short definitions and example sentences. Antonyms are included when appropriate, as well as cross-references to words with related meanings. Colorful illustrations not only help students learn, but make learning more fun.

Various aspects of English-language usage and history are included, as well as occasional famous quotations that show words in context. Features unique to this book are briefly described on the next page.

▼••• **AROUND THE WORLD** provides examples of words, phrases, concepts, and expressions from many cultures and languages.

▼••• **HAVE YOU HEARD . . .?** illustrates words in the context of commonly heard expressions.

▼••• **IDIOMS** are singled out to help students understand phrases in which the meaning cannot be understood from the literal meanings of the words, as in "bring home the bacon" or "put one's foot down."

▼••• **VERB PLUS** gives students another category of idioms—phrases that take on a new meaning when another word is added to a verb, as in "break down" or "break in."

▼••• **WORDS AT PLAY** presents amusing verses and rhymes for student enjoyment.

▼••• **WRITER'S CHOICE** provides brief excerpts from works of well-known and respected writers. The examples show effective word choice and point out why a particular word is the right one for the situation.

▼••• **WATCH IT!** offers helpful hints for using words, or, in some cases, for when to avoid using them.

▼••• **WORD STORY** gives fascinating historical background about certain words.

▼••• **WORD POOL** provides a vocabulary-building list of words that, although not synonyms, are related in some way.

▼••• **WRITING TIP** offers helpful "how-to's," such as how to use euphemisms to make ideas sound better, or how to avoid overused words and clichés.

▼••• **NOTABLE QUOTABLE** shows synonyms employed in famous or striking quotations from distinguished speakers and writers.

▼••• **WORD WORKSHOP** demonstrates the use of synonyms in revising writing to make it livelier and more effective.

Skill with language confers many benefits on young people. We offer this book as a powerful aid in reaching that goal.

Introduction

Celebrated Gymnast
Retains Trophy

Notorious Forgery Suspect
Hangs on to Claim of Innocence

Illustrious Artist
Saves Magazines
For Illustration Ideas

Noted Critic Reserves
Comment on New Book
By Popular Writer

Distinguished Ambassador
Withholds Support of Treaty

Prominent Business Executives
Agree to Hold Questions
On Plans to Move Company

Think about the headlines on the opposite page. Each one says something very different, yet, if you consider the words, you'll discover that in all of the headlines someone famous keeps or holds back something.

The words *celebrated, illustrious, noted, notorious, distinguished,* and *prominent* all have meanings similar to the meaning of *famous.* Yet each word has a slightly different meaning that sets it apart from *famous.* For example, *distinguished* means famous and admired, but, in contrast, *notorious* means famous for doing something bad. Words with similar meanings are called *synonyms.*

As a further example, consider the word *keep.* It means to have for a long time, to hold, or to hold back. Notice the synonyms for *keep* in the headlines*: retains, saves, reserves, hangs on to, holds,* and *withholds.*

Words are powerful, and using them well helps you communicate with others when you speak and when you write. The English language includes a wealth of words you can use to express ideas effectively and precisely. This book is a thesaurus, a book of words. It is organized so that you can easily find words with similar or related meanings.

Although synonyms have almost the same meaning, the differences among words are important because they enable you to say and write exactly what you mean. Your thesaurus can show you just the word you need. It can help you avoid repeating the same word to the point of boredom. It can even introduce you to new words.

A thesaurus sometimes provides examples of words with opposite meanings, called *antonyms.* In addition, you will find some cross-references to words with related meanings and a number of interesting stories about how certain words came into the English language.

Although the thesaurus is a marvelous resource, you won't be able to throw your dictionary away. For one thing, a thesaurus doesn't include all of the words in most dictionaries, and, for another, it doesn't give every meaning for the words that are included.

This thesaurus has some special features you won't find in a dictionary. Among these are features that show expressions from around the world, examples of words often confused because they look alike, and samples from the works of well-known writers that show effective use of language.

Understanding a Thesaurus Entry

Use the entry for *foolish* on the opposite page to learn about the information included in the different parts of a thesaurus entry.

- The entry word *foolish* is shown in large type at the left of the page. What word appears in small type just below the entry word? What information does this word provide?

- Look at the paragraph next to the entry for *foolish*. The first sentence gives a definition. What meaning of *foolish* is found in this word study?

- Notice the example printed in italic type after the meaning, to show how the word can be used in a sentence. Every entry word will have at least one example sentence.

- What synonyms are listed for *foolish?*

- Cross-references show other words listed in the thesaurus that have related meanings. What entry would you see to find a word suggesting lack of intelligence?

- Remember that antonyms are words with opposite meanings. What antonyms are listed for *foolish?*

- Special features in this thesaurus provide a variety of additional kinds of information related to the entry word or its synonyms. Here you see a sample Word Pool feature listing a number of the more unusual synonyms for *foolish.*

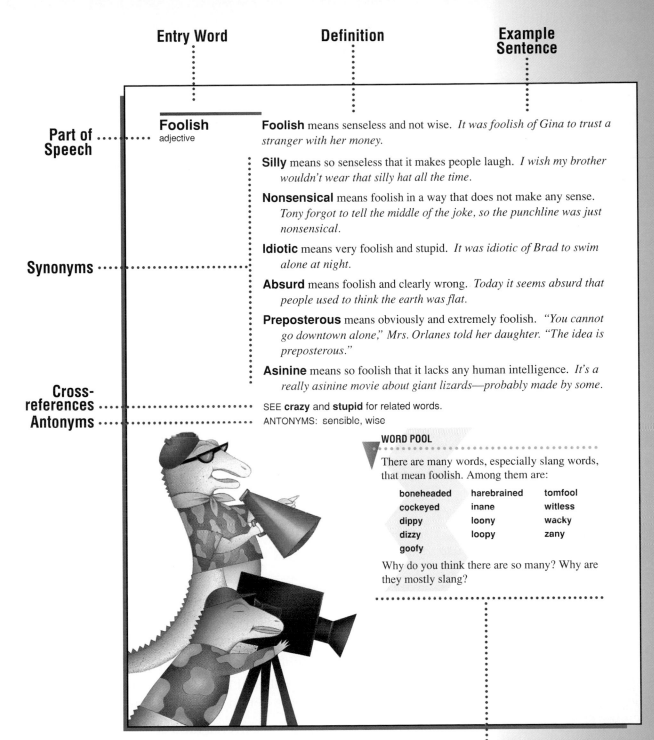

Entry Word

Definition

Example Sentence

Part of Speech

Foolish
adjective

Foolish means senseless and not wise. *It was foolish of Gina to trust a stranger with her money.*

Silly means so senseless that it makes people laugh. *I wish my brother wouldn't wear that silly hat all the time.*

Nonsensical means foolish in a way that does not make any sense. *Tony forgot to tell the middle of the joke, so the punchline was just nonsensical.*

Synonyms

Idiotic means very foolish and stupid. *It was idiotic of Brad to swim alone at night.*

Absurd means foolish and clearly wrong. *Today it seems absurd that people used to think the earth was flat.*

Preposterous means obviously and extremely foolish. *"You cannot go downtown alone," Mrs. Orlanes told her daughter. "The idea is preposterous."*

Asinine means so foolish that it lacks any human intelligence. *It's a really asinine movie about giant lizards—probably made by some.*

Cross-references SEE **crazy** and **stupid** for related words.
Antonyms ANTONYMS: sensible, wise

WORD POOL

There are many words, especially slang words, that mean foolish. Among them are:

boneheaded	harebrained	tomfool
cockeyed	inane	witless
dippy	loony	wacky
dizzy	loopy	zany
goofy		

Why do you think there are so many? Why are they mostly slang?

Additional Information or Comments

9

Choosing Synonyms

Gymnast Places in Three Events

Lincoln Johnson was the Hoover Gymnast Club's star in the
meet on Friday. He placed in three of the six events. He was ~~good~~! *outstanding*

The meet began with the floor exercise event. Linc, as he is
called by his friends, got off to a ~~good~~ start. His routine included *fine*
tumbling, and he ~~did~~ a perfect back flip. He did a ~~good~~ job of ~~doing~~ *accomplished* *superior* *executing*
some handsprings, too, and ended up with first place.

Linc took second place for the routine he ~~did~~ on the rings. The *performed*
third big event for Linc was the parallel bars. All the time he spent
practicing paid off when he ~~did~~ a number of difficult movements on *achieved*
the two long wooden bars. In this event, Linc again took first place.
He certainly had a ~~good~~ day. *first-rate*

Clarice, who is Linc's classmate, wrote this report. Notice the changes she made before putting it in for the class newsletter.

Clarice thought that she had used the word *did* too often. She knew she could use her thesaurus to find words with similar meanings.

In the entry for *do*, Clarice discovered the synonyms *perform*, *accomplish*, *achieve*, *execute*, *fulfill*, and *carry out*. Notice the four words she used in place of *did*. You will find these synonyms on page 124 of this thesaurus.

Clarice noticed she had used the word *good* three times, and she thought *good* was too weak to describe how well Linc had performed. She turned to *G* to find the entry word for *good*. This comment with the word study convinced her to look for more exact words: "People often use *good* when another word would be more precise and more interesting."

A list of cross-references included this line: "See **excellent** for words that mean extremely good." When she turned to *excellent*, Clarice discovered these synonyms: *first-rate, fine, first-class, superior, outstanding,* and *exceptional*. Which ones did she use as substitutes for *good*? *Excellent* and its synonyms are on page 149 of this book.

Why Are There So Many Synonyms?

Perhaps you have been wondering why we have two, three, or more words that mean almost the same thing. One reason is that words came into English from many other languages.

Let's take a look at three synonyms: *calm, quiet,* and *cool*.

Calm means not excited or emotional. It comes from an Italian word meaning "time for rest." That word comes from a Greek word meaning "heat of the day."

Quiet means calm and without much excitement or noise. This word comes from a Latin word meaning "at rest."

Cool often means somewhat cold. It also can mean not excited or upset. This word comes from an old English word meaning "cool." It was used in the same ways as *cool* is used today.

• What do you think is the reason for the connection between the Italian and Greek words that *calm* comes from?

• What does it mean to be hot-tempered? Can you connect this idea to the word *cool* when it is used to mean not excited?

Features in Your Thesaurus

Every thesaurus lists synonyms and antonyms, but this thesaurus has some special features that will help you improve your vocabulary and your writing. Browse through your thesaurus to find these features. Notice that they provide additional information about words and comments on language. The more you know about words, the better you will be able to communicate with others at speaking and writing.

One of the special features is shown below. Other features are illustrated on the pages that follow. A Features Index on page 526 will help you find where these features appear in your thesaurus.

AROUND THE WORLD

This feature gives you words, phrases, or proverbs from many cultures and languages. The example below accompanies the entry for *friend*.

AROUND THE WORLD: Friendship

A friend in need is a friend indeed.
— **English proverb**

A good friend is revealed on a bad day.
—**Turkish proverb**

On the day of poverty you know who is a true friend.
— **Ghanaian proverb**

He who helps you in need is a true friend.
— **Swahili proverb** (East Africa)

Know a friend when you are in trouble.
— **Tamil proverb** (India)

- Compare the five statements about friendship. What idea is communicated in all of the different sayings from around the world?

HAVE YOU HEARD...?

This feature lets you in on the full meaning of familiar phrases and sayings. The example below is from the entry for *beg*.

HAVE YOU HEARD...?

You may have heard the saying "Beggars can't be choosers." This means that if you are asking someone's help, you have to accept whatever help they give you. If you are unwilling to take what is offered, you may get nothing at all.

A similar idea is in the saying "Don't look a gift horse in the mouth." A horse's teeth show how old it is, and thus how good a gift the horse is. But if you show that you are judging the quality of someone's gift, you may not get it after all.

• Who would you expect to use these sayings, a person giving something or a person getting something?

IDIOMS

There are many phrases in English with meanings that can't be understood from the ordinary meanings of words. These phrases are called *idioms*, and you will find idioms throughout your thesaurus.

Sometimes an entry contains so many synonyms that they are put into a separate feature. This one comes from the entry for *bother*.

IDIOMS

There are so many idioms meaning "to bother someone" that we do not have space to give example sentences for them. Here is a list of some of them. Can you think of others?

drive someone up the wall	**get under someone's skin**
get in someone's hair	**give someone a pain**
get on someone's nerves	**put someone's back up**
get someone's goat	**set someone's teeth on edge**

• Why do you think there are so many ?

VERB PLUS
• • • • • • • • • •

This feature introduces you to some of the many special phrases in English that combine a verb with one other word. Such a verb phrase is a kind of idiom because the words used together don't have the meaning you might expect from the separate words.

This Verb Plus comes from the entry for *act*.

- Which of the verb phrases would you use to say that someone was behaving mischievously?

- Which phrase would you use to say that someone was substituting for another?

14

WORDS AT PLAY
· · · · · · · · · · · ·

This feature presents rhymes and humorous verses to show that words amuse and entertain.

Enjoy the lines about "Fat Albert" from the entry for *about*.

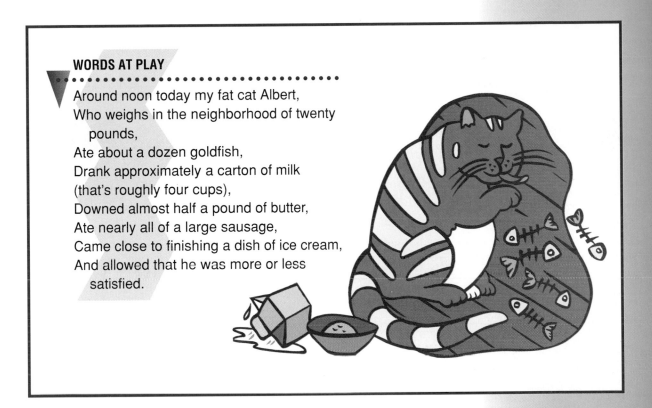

WORDS AT PLAY
· ·

Around noon today my fat cat Albert,
Who weighs in the neighborhood of twenty
    pounds,
Ate about a dozen goldfish,
Drank approximately a carton of milk
(that's roughly four cups),
Downed almost half a pound of butter,
Ate nearly all of a large sausage,
Came close to finishing a dish of ice cream,
And allowed that he was more or less
    satisfied.

- The following synonyms are listed with *about: around, approximately, roughly, almost, nearly, close to, in the neighborhood of,* and *more or less*. Find all of them in the verse.

- Do you think that using all these synonyms in one verse makes the verse funnier? How?

WRITER'S CHOICE

Writers of books you enjoy reading are good at using just the right words. This feature offers examples from the works of well-known and respected authors, examples that illustrate why some words are better choices than others. Brief comments explain why particular words are effective.

Read the sentence about the wolf's eyes from an award-winning book by Jean Craighead George and the comment that explains why *scanned* is an effective word in this context.

WRITER'S CHOICE

The great wolf's eyes softened at the sight of the little wolves, then quickly hardened into brittle yellow jewels as he scanned the flat tundra.

—Jean Craighead George, *Julie of the Wolves*

Why *scanned?* The wild wolf needs to feed and protect himself and the little wolves. He looks quickly to see if there is anything that he can hunt or that he may have to fight. Because tundra is flat and treeless, it is easy to see anything important there right away.

• This Writer's Choice feature accompanies the entry word *watch*. Why do you think *scanned* is a better choice than *watched* would have been?

WATCH IT!

This feature gives you hints about using words. Sometimes two words sound alike but mean different things. Other words have added meanings that may make a word insulting to a group of people. The example below appears with the entry for *cheat*.

WATCH IT !

Gyp is a word that many people use without knowing that it is an insult. *Gyp* is short for *Gypsy*. People who did business with Gypsies had a prejudice that the Gypsies would cheat them. So *gyp* came to mean "cheat." It remains an insult and an expression of prejudice. Since there are so many other words meaning "cheat," it's a good idea not to use *gyp*.

- Why is it a good idea to avoid using the word *gyp?*

WORD STORY

This feature tells you stories. The stories are about how words came into our language. The example below comes from the entry for *ashamed*.

WORD STORY

Mortify comes from two Latin words meaning "to make dead." Did you ever hear someone say, "I was so ashamed, I wished I could die"?

- *Mortified* is one of the synonyms for *ashamed*. What does the Word Story tell you about the meaning of the synonym?

WORD POOL

This feature adds words to the words in the synonym list. The Word Pool words are not more synonyms. They are words related to the main idea of the entry. The example below is from the entry for *enclose.*

WORD POOL

There are many other verbs that mean to shut someone or something in. Often these words are also nouns that mean an enclosure. You *fence* a horse inside a *fence,* and you *pen* a pig inside a *pen.* The words below are not synonyms of each other, but they share the meaning "to enclose."

cage	hedge	coop
jail	corral	pen
fence	stable	

- Are all of these verbs also nouns?
- Many of these words suggest farming. Why do you think that is?

NOTABLE QUOTABLE

This feature shows you synonyms used in interesting ways, by interesting writers, to say interesting things. The example below is from the entry for *because.*

> "Education is our passport to the future, for tomorrow belongs to those who prepare for it today."
> — Malcolm X
> (1925–1965)

- Do you think the quotation would sound as good if it used *because* instead of *for?*

WRITING TIP
· · · · · · · · · ·
This feature helps you with various hints to improve your writing. The example below is from the entry for *wonderful*.

WRITING TIP: Connotations
· ·

Connotations are the ideas or feelings that a word suggests without exactly meaning them. At many places in this book, we say that a word suggests something. Those suggestions are connotations. Connotations help us to choose one synonym instead of another. The two synonyms may mean the same thing while suggesting different things.

The synonyms for *wonderful* have many different connotations. Some people use *wonderful* over and over. Other people use the synonyms, without being careful about the connotations. A cake may be wonderful, but it probably isn't marvelous; cakes aren't hard to believe. A prize may be fabulous, but it probably isn't awesome; prizes don't often have great power or size.

Good writers think about the connotations of the words they use. At times, when you read good writing, you feel that it makes you excited in ways that are hard to understand. Often that excitement comes from the power of suggestion. Be careful about the connotations of the words you use, and the success of your writing may be phenomenal.

- How do connotations help you choose synonyms?
- Why is a cake probably not marvelous?

WORD WORKSHOP

This feature puts synonyms to work so that you can see how much they help. The example below is from the entry for *great*.

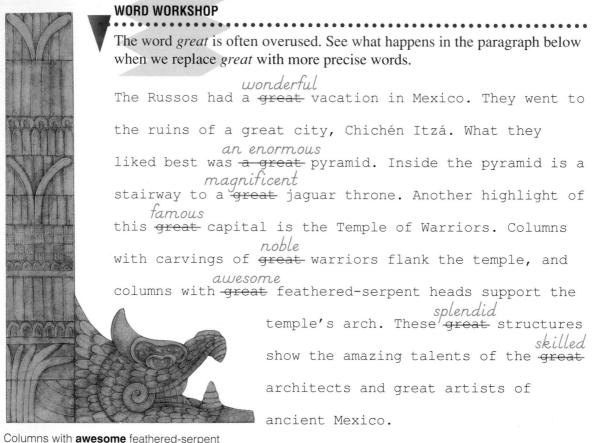

WORD WORKSHOP

The word *great* is often overused. See what happens in the paragraph below when we replace *great* with more precise words.

The Russos had a ~~great~~ *wonderful* vacation in Mexico. They went to the ruins of a great city, Chichén Itzá. What they liked best was ~~a great~~ *an enormous* pyramid. Inside the pyramid is a stairway to a ~~great~~ *magnificent* jaguar throne. Another highlight of this ~~great~~ *famous* capital is the Temple of Warriors. Columns with carvings of ~~great~~ *noble* warriors flank the temple, and columns with ~~great~~ *awesome* feathered-serpent heads support the temple's arch. These ~~great~~ *splendid* structures show the amazing talents of the ~~great~~ *skilled* architects and great artists of ancient Mexico.

Columns with **awesome** feathered-serpent heads support the temple's arch.

- The synonyms replacing *great* come from other entries. Which ones?
- Why do you think these synonyms were used?

Entries

A collection of entry words, their synonyms, and their antonyms

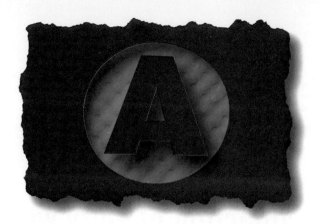

Ability
noun

Ability means the power to do something well. *Renee's ability to make her own clothes has saved her a lot of money.*

Talent means an inborn ability. *Julio's drumming shows real musical talent.*

Capacity can mean ability. *Bob has a great capacity for foreign languages and speaks three.*

Facility can mean ability. *Anne's facility in math has impressed all her teachers.*

Skill means an ability gotten by means of training and practice. *Michiko's skill in cooking has improved over the years.*

Competence means the skill to do a certain job or task. *Piloting an airplane requires a high degree of competence.*

Aptitude means talent combined with interest. *John's aptitude with engines led to a career as a mechanic.*

Capability means ability, for one thing in particular or for life in general. *Someone of Mark's capability can easily handle a wide variety of jobs.*

Knack means an aptitude for doing something easily. *Alice has a knack with tools and enjoys making home repairs.*

Know-how is an informal word meaning practical ability. *It will take a lot of know-how to get that old car running again.*

About
adverb

About means somewhere near in number, size, or time. *The population of the United States is about two hundred fifty million. Jaime is about six feet tall. The school bus usually gets to the corner at about 7:45.*

Around can mean about. *I usually wake up around 6:30. Around thirty people live in Julia's building.*

Approximately means as nearly as you can estimate. *On a clear night, a person can see approximately 3,000 stars without using a telescope.*

Roughly can mean about. It emphasizes that the estimate is not precise. *It takes roughly four hours to drive from Boston to New York City.*

Almost means about, but not quite. *It's almost time for the bell to ring.*

Close to and **nearly** mean almost. *"Let's go! It's close to ten o'clock," called Joe impatiently. "Wait just a minute. I'm nearly ready," answered his brother.*

In the neighborhood of means about or somewhere near in size or amount. *Counting all my part-time jobs, I earned in the neighborhood of four hundred dollars last summer.*

More or less means about. It emphasizes that the estimate could be too large or too small. *The house costs eighty-five thousand, more or less.*

SEE **estimate** and **measure** for related words.

WORDS AT PLAY

Around noon today my fat cat Albert,
Who weighs in the neighborhood of twenty
    pounds,
Ate about a dozen goldfish,
Drank approximately a carton of milk
(that's roughly four cups),
Downed almost half a pound of butter,
Ate nearly all of a large sausage,
Came close to finishing a dish of ice cream,
And allowed that he was more or less
    satisfied.

23

Accompany
verb

Accompany means to go along with someone or something. *Lightning and thunder often accompany heavy rain.*

Attend can mean to go along with someone in order to assist. *Attended by two secretaries, the head of the company arrived at the meeting.*

Escort means to go along with someone on official business, or as someone's date. *The President is escorted by Secret Service agents.*

Convoy means to accompany a ship or other vehicle in order to protect it. *Three warships convoyed the oil tankers through the Persian Gulf.*

Chaperon means to go along with and supervise young people. *Four parents and two teachers will chaperon the seventh-grade dance.*

Act
verb

Act means to do something. *The firefighters acted quickly to smother the flames.*

Behave means to act in a certain way. *The children behaved very nicely when their grandparents were here.*

Work can mean to act in the proper way. *This radio hasn't worked since I dropped it.*

Perform can mean to act. *The plane performed perfectly on its test flight.*

The dogs sometimes **act up** when they are left alone too long.

Function means to act. It is often used when one person or thing is doing the job of another. *The landlord also functions as janitor in this building.*

VERB PLUS

Sometimes when a word is added to a verb, it creates a phrase that has special meaning. Here are some phrases with **act**:

Act for means to do something in place of someone else. *My mother is acting for her boss, who is out sick.*

Act on means to accept or follow. *Tina acted on your advice and stopped seeing that boy.*

Act up means to behave badly. *The dogs sometimes act up when they are left alone too long.*

Adapt
verb

Adapt means to change something or someone so as to suit a need. *Bill had to adapt to sharing his room when baby Albert was born.*

Adjust means to change something to a better position or fit. *You can adjust the seat of the car if you are cramped.*

Accommodate can mean to adapt. *The Chens accommodated to their new country quite quickly.*

Conform means to act so as to suit rules or standards. *I don't want to be friends with Becky if that means conforming to her ideas of how to dress.*

SEE **change** for related words.

WATCH IT!

Adapt and **adopt** look a lot alike, but they have entirely different meanings. *Adapt* means to change to make suitable. *Adopt* means to take as your own. If you like someone's plan, you *adopt* it. If you don't like it as it is, you *adapt* it.

Admit
verb

Admit means to make something known or say that something is true, especially when you don't really want to. *I have to admit your costume is funnier than mine.*

Acknowledge means almost the same as admit, but is used especially about information that has been kept back until then. *Tiffany acknowledges that she borrowed your book and forgot to tell you.*

Confess means to admit something bad that you have done. *Larry confessed to his aunt that he fell asleep when he should have been cleaning the basement.*

Own up to is an idiom meaning to confess. *Blair owned up to having started the argument.*

Get something off your chest is an idiom meaning to confess completely. *Let me get the whole story off my chest.*

Make a clean breast of is an idiom meaning to confess completely. *Rod made a clean breast of his part in the practical joke.*

ANTONYM: deny

Adult
adjective

Adult means fully grown and developed. *Children are not admitted to this movie without a parent or adult guardian.*

Grown-up means adult, but is used especially in contrast to something childish. *Now that Chris has a job, his parents hope he'll think about money in grown-up ways.*

Mature means fully grown and developed, especially mentally. *Mi-Ok is more mature and self-controlled than many older girls.*

Full-grown means fully grown and developed, especially physically. *A young hyena is no match for a full-grown lion.*

ANTONYMS: childish, immature

Advance
verb

Advance means to go forward or to cause something to go forward. *Flood waters are advancing toward the town, and rain continues to fall. Halfway through the chess game, Milos advanced his queen to threaten my king.*

Proceed means to go forward again after stopping. *Once the stalled car had been towed away, traffic could proceed.*

Progress can mean to go forward toward some desirable goal. *The neighborhood cleanup has progressed halfway down this block.*

Move ahead means to go in front of someone or something. *The racehorse started slowly, but moved ahead at the second turn.*

Make headway means to go forward. *The sailors made little headway rowing against the strong current.*

Press on means to go forward in spite of difficulties. *The explorers pressed on through the wilderness and finally sighted a river.*

ANTONYMS: retreat, withdraw

Advantage
noun

Advantage means anything that helps you get what you want, or anything that is in your favor. *Tall people have an advantage in playing basketball.*

Benefit means anything that does you good or that is good to have. *One of the benefits of taking shop classes is that you can save money by making simple repairs yourself.*

CONTINUED ON THE NEXT PAGE

Profit can mean benefit. *"What profit is there in keeping magazines you don't read?" asked Marty's father.*

Gain means anything you get that is valuable or good to have. *Sylvia's biggest gain from summer school is knowing how to study better.*

Ace in the hole is an idiom meaning a secret, strong advantage. *The detective's ace in the hole was a videotape of the crime.*

ANTONYMS: disadvantage, drawback

Afraid
adjective

Afraid means feeling fear. It is always used after the noun it modifies. *Some people are afraid of heights.*

Frightened means suddenly made afraid. *The frightened driver hit the brakes too hard, and the car skidded.*

Scared means the same as afraid but is less formal. *Padma's little brother is scared of firecrackers.*

Fearful can mean afraid. It suggests that someone is often afraid. *Joe is a fearful guy and doesn't like rough games.*

Alarmed means feeling fear and worry because of a danger. *Everyone in the neighborhood was alarmed by the huge fire.*

Terrified means feeling great fear and dread. *The terrified villagers fled from the volcano's burning lava and hot gases.*

Petrified can mean feeling fear so strong that it makes you unable to move or think. *When the earthquake struck, I was too petrified to get out of the house.*

Get or **have cold feet** is an idiom meaning to become or be afraid. *People tell me I should sing in public, but I get cold feet whenever I think about it.*

SEE **fear**, **scare**, and **terrifying** for related words.
ANTONYMS: fearless, unafraid

The **terrified** villagers fled from the volcano's burning lava and hot gases.

27

Alert
adjective

Alert means ready for whatever may happen. *Because Althea was alert, she was able to stop the car in time to avoid an accident.*

Watchful means paying close and careful attention, in case of emergency or danger. *The guard dog in the drugstore is very watchful and barks at any little sound.*

Vigilant means on guard, careful, and prepared to deal with danger. *The neighborhood watch system encourages local residents to be vigilant.*

Wide-awake can mean alert, especially to opportunities for gain. *Kevin is wide-awake to every chance to earn more money.*

Observant means quick to notice things. *An observant farmhand found the first traces of five-thousand-year-old buildings when he was plowing the north pasture.*

Attentive means paying careful attention. *Since his grandfather's stroke, Joseph has been attentive to the sick man's every need.*

Keep your eye on the ball and **stay on your toes** are idioms meaning to be alert. These idioms come from sports. They are used more generally, however. *The former senator lost the election because he failed to keep his eye on the ball in Washington. The reporter stayed on her toes and got an exclusive interview with the newly elected senator.*

SEE **careful** for related words.
ANTONYM: inattentive

The neighborhood watch system encourages local residents to be **vigilant.**

Alone
adjective

Alone means away from others, or being the only one. *Laraine is alone in the house every afternoon until her mother gets home from work.*

Unaccompanied means alone, often by choice. *After his unaccompanied performance, the saxophonist will play several songs with our studio orchestra.*

Isolated means alone and cut off from others. *Jana feels less isolated now that she is in a class with other hearing-impaired children who can sign.*

CONTINUED ON THE NEXT PAGE

Single-handed means done by one person. *This bookshelf is Chuck's first single-handed carpentry project.*

Solo can mean single-handed. *She completed her solo voyage around the world in just over two years.*

By yourself means alone. *After Aunt Ingrid died, my Uncle Gustaf lived by himself for many years.*

SEE **lonely** and **single** for related words.

Amount
noun

Amount means the figure you get when you add up all the things that you are measuring or counting. *Sherry was surprised at the amount of the grocery bill.*

Quantity means an amount. *The fruit punch contains only a small quantity of sugar.*

Number means the figure you get when you count a group of people or things. *The number of goats in Saada's father's herd grew by twelve that spring.*

Sum can mean the figure you get when you add a group of numbers together. *Six is the sum of four and two.*

Total means sum. *I have a five-dollar bill and two ones—a total of seven dollars.*

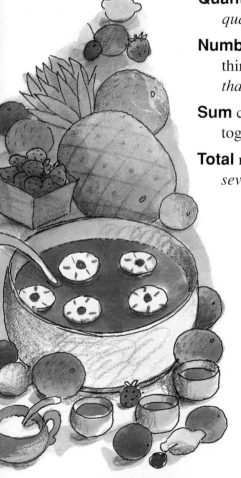

The fruit punch contains only a small **quantity** of sugar.

> **WATCH IT!**
>
> **Amount** can mean how many or how much. **Number** means only how many. You can speak of an amount of milk or an amount of beans, but you wouldn't speak of a number of milk.
>
> **Less** means how much. **Fewer** means how many. How much milk? Less. How many beans? Fewer.
>
> People are often careless in the way they use *less* and *fewer*. If you see an advertisement for a food with less calories, the writer was careless. Think how strange it would sound the other way—if the ad said, "Fewer Fat!"

Ancient
adjective

Ancient means very old. It is generally used to describe things, but can be used to describe people. *Workers digging for the highway have come upon an ancient Native American city.*

Antique means of former times. It always describes things. *In the back of the resale store, Joleen found an antique telephone.*

Old-fashioned means out of date in style, working, thinking, or behaving. *I told my mom not to buy those old-fashioned shoes, but she went ahead and did it anyway.*

Archaic means not used since a very long time ago. *Elisabeth enjoyed the old poem, but Mr. Allen had to explain some of the archaic words in it.*

Obsolete means no longer in use. It is often used about machines. *Kenny's computer is obsolete—they don't even make it anymore.*

Prehistoric means from the time before there was written history. *In the cave, Floyd and Vera found stone blades and other prehistoric tools.*

SEE **old** for related words.

WRITING TIP: Archaic and Obsolete Language

Fashions, hairstyles, and models of cars change over time. Language does too. Words that once were common can become obsolete as our civilization changes. Such words are often labeled "archaic" in a dictionary. You will come across these words in literature written a long time ago. And writers still use some of these words in stories about olden times. You may have read *thee, quoth, befell, doth,* and *hast.*

When you write, you will want to avoid archaic words unless you are creating a story about a long time ago. If, for example, you are writing about a knight in the Middle Ages who rescues a maiden in distress, you might use the word *damsel* in referring to the girl. And you might have your hero call the wicked knight a *varlet.*

The dragon showed its **ire** and might by breathing fire at the knight.

Anger
noun

Anger means a strong feeling of being annoyed or mad. *In his anger, Spike tore up the letter.*

Indignation means anger caused by injustice or disgraceful acts. *Susanna felt indignation at how badly Bonnie had behaved.*

Wrath means great anger. *The team played so sloppily that the coach stormed off the field in wrath.*

Ire means great anger. It is a formal word, often used in stories and poetry. *The dragon showed its ire and might by breathing fire at the knight.*

Rage means loud, violent anger. *Hissing with rage, the mountain lion defended her cubs.*

Fury means wild rage that is out of control. *Dave was in such a fury that he could barely speak.*

SEE **cross** and **mad** for related words.

AROUND THE WORLD: Anger

To spend the night in anger is better than to spend it in repentance.
— **Senegalese proverb**

There is no disease like anger.
— **Gujarati proverb** (India)

Even an ant gets angry.
— **Spanish proverb**

Announce
verb

Announce means to make something known to the public. *The manager called a press conference to announce that the team had traded two pitchers.*

Proclaim is a formal word that means to announce officially. *Mexico proclaimed its independence from Spain in 1821.*

Publish can mean to make something very widely known. *Once the charges of corruption have been published, there will be little anyone can do to stop the investigation.*

Broadcast means to make something widely known by radio or television. *Warnings of the approaching hurricane were broadcast to residents of the coast.*

Advertise means to make something known to the public by paying for it. *The sale was advertised in the local newspaper.*

Publicize means to make something known to as many people as possible. *The kids publicized their car wash by standing near the road with signs.*

SEE **state** and **tell** for related words.

The kids **publicized** their car wash by standing near the road with signs.

32

Answer
verb

Answer means to say or write something in response to a question or request. *Ernesto is the only one who answered the fourth question correctly.*

Reply means to answer. It is a somewhat more formal word and may suggest thoroughness and thoughtfulness. *The store manager replied to Aunt Delva's complaint with a careful and detailed explanation.*

Respond means to answer by words or by actions. *The students responded to the news of the hurricane by collecting money for the victims.*

Retort means to give a sharp, quick, and often defensive answer. *When I told the foreign tourist she had unusual clothes, she retorted, "So do you, where I come from."*

HAVE YOU HEARD...?

You may have seen "R.S.V.P." written on an invitation you received. It stands for a phrase in French, "Répondez, s'il vous plaît" (rā pon′dā sēl vü plā′), which means "respond, please." When an invitation says R.S.V.P., it means that you should call or write the person who sent it and say whether you will accept.

Appearance
noun

Appearance means the way that someone or something looks. *With its fresh mud wall and new straw roofs, the African village had a prosperous appearance.*

Look can mean appearance. *Jeremy has the healthy look of someone who works outdoors.*

Air can mean appearance. It often suggests an appearance that causes a feeling. *There was a certain air of mystery about the deserted old house.*

Aspect can mean someone's or something's usual appearance. *The security guard has a watchful aspect.*

Argue
verb

Argue means to disagree strongly and give reasons for your opinion. *Sandy argued with the umpire who called her out at second base.*

Dispute can mean to argue loudly or at length. *The neighbors are disputing about how late it's OK to play music.*

Squabble means to dispute over something seemingly unimportant. *The children squabbled about who should be first in line.*

Bicker means to squabble continually. *The twins bicker about who gets to choose TV programs.*

Spat means to argue, with some hurt feelings. *The girls are spatting because Janey told on Maria.*

Quarrel means to dispute angrily. *We heard Dave and Chuck quarrel and then saw them wrestle on the ground.*

Wrangle means to quarrel. It suggests a lot of anger. *The drivers wrangled bitterly, each saying that the other caused the accident.*

Feud means to quarrel fiercely for a long time, especially one group with another. *Ranchers feuded with farmers about land uses.*

Lock horns is an idiom meaning to argue or to come into conflict. *Dad and the garage owner locked horns over the size of the bill.*

Be at loggerheads is an idiom meaning to disagree very strongly. *Mom and I are constantly at loggerheads over how late I can stay out on school nights.*

Split hairs is an idiom meaning to argue about small matters, using ideas that lack common sense. *"Not washing the silverware because you said you'd do the dishes is really splitting hairs, Emily!" complained her sister.*

SEE **fight** and **objection** for related words.
ANTONYM: agree

WORD STORY

What are *loggerheads,* anyway? In old times, sailors heated tar for repairing ships in long-handled cups called loggerheads. During naval battles, they used the loggerheads to throw hot tar at each other. When two ships were close enough for this to happen, they were "at loggerheads."

Ashamed
adjective

Ashamed means feeling painfully unhappy with yourself, especially because you have done something wrong or foolish. *Eric was deeply ashamed when his mother found out that he had failed the test.*

Humiliated means ashamed in front of other people. *Lynn felt humiliated because she had to wear a hand-me-down dress to the party.*

Embarrassed means painfully unhappy, self-conscious, and insecure. *Mark was embarrassed when he realized he was the only guest wearing a costume at the party.*

Sheepish means ashamed, awkward, and shy. *The waiter looked so sheepish after he dropped our dinners that it was hard to stay angry.*

Abashed means shy, embarrassed, and somewhat ashamed. It suggests that some event suddenly produced the feeling. *The coatroom attendant was abashed when she brought someone the wrong coat.*

Mortified means badly humiliated. It may suggest that the person also feels anger. *When my brother shows my baby pictures to his grown-up friends, I feel mortified.*

SEE **shame** and **sorry** for related words.
ANTONYM: proud

Mark was **embarrassed** when he realized he was the only guest wearing a costume at the party.

WORD STORY

Mortify comes from two Latin words meaning "to make dead." Did you ever hear someone say, "I was so ashamed, I wished I could die"?

Ask
verb

Ask means to try to get information by using words. *Ask Marcy where she got that great jacket.*

Inquire means to ask in order to get detailed information. *Yukio inquired about the hours that the video rental store is open.*

Query means to ask about something, especially in a way that expresses doubt. *Reporters queried the politician's explanation of where the money came from.*

Quiz means to ask questions about what has been learned. *Our science teacher always quizzes us on last night's homework.*

Question means to ask over and over again, in a systematic way. *The police questioned several suspects about the bank robbery.*

Interrogate means to ask someone many questions for a long time. *When we've interrogated the spy, we'll know who helped her get the code book.*

ANTONYMS: answer, reply

Attack
verb

Attack means to begin fighting someone or something with actions or words. *A mother bear may attack anyone who gets close to her cubs. A group of parents has attacked the plan to close the schools early.*

Assault means to attack suddenly, usually with weapons. *The enemy assaulted our fort with bombs and cannons.*

Charge can mean to attack by a sudden rush. *An elephant opens its ears wide when it charges.*

Storm can mean to attack a place suddenly, usually as a group. *Allied armies stormed the Normandy beaches in 1944.*

Raid means to attack suddenly and then leave. *Guerrillas raided the towns across the border.*

Light into is an idiom that means to attack, especially with words. *Tomás lit into me for losing our concert tickets.*

CONTINUED ON THE NEXT PAGE

Sail into is an idiom that means to attack. *With fists flying, Batman sailed into the band of gangsters.*

Gang up on is an idiom that means to attack as a group. *The crooks ganged up on the police officer.*

SEE **fight** for related words.
ANTONYM: defend

Avoid
verb

Avoid means to stay away from something or someone. *Darnell avoided the poison ivy by staying on the path.*

Escape can mean to avoid or get away from something or someone. *By going to the mountains we were able to escape the fierce heat in the city.*

Shun means to avoid carefully at all times, because of strong feelings. *Gloria is shy and shuns attention.*

Give a wide berth to and **steer clear of** are idioms meaning to avoid. *The other animals give lions a wide berth. Even a lion, however, steers clear of a rhinoceros.*

Give, show, or **turn a cold shoulder** are idioms that mean to avoid someone. *Katie really likes Niral, but he's been giving her the cold shoulder.*

SEE **escape, evade,** and **flee** for related words.
ANTONYM: confront

The other animals **give lions a wide berth.**

WORD STORY

Give a wide berth to and *steer clear of* are both idioms taken from talk about ships. A place where a ship ties up to a wharf is called a berth. A big ship needs a wide berth. When two ships pass, it is a good idea to steer them so that they clear each other by a large distance, because ships cannot change direction or stop quickly.

Awkward
adjective

Awkward means lacking grace, skill, or ease in action or manner. *Since Nancy broke up with Derek, he acts in a really awkward way whenever they meet. Willie sprained her wrist playing volleyball, so it's awkward for her to write.*

Clumsy means stiff and likely to bump into things or drop them. *Tad is so clumsy, I believe he can trip over his own feet while he's sitting down.*

Inept can mean unskilled or clumsy. *"I remembered your party, but I forgot your address," is a completely inept excuse.*

Uncoordinated means clumsy in a way that looks as if the parts of the body are not working together. *Sid looks uncoordinated when he walks, but he's amazing on the basketball court.*

Heavy-handed means awkward and forced. It is used more often about something said than about something done. *Sam's heavy-handed attempt at a joke was just plain embarrassing.*

Gauche means socially awkward. *Did Edna realize how gauche it was to eat while she was dancing?*

Gawky means uncoordinated. *Terry has grown so fast this year that she will be gawky for a while.*

All thumbs is an idiom that means very clumsy, especially in working with one's hands. *If I weren't all thumbs, I would sew on the button myself.*

ANTONYM: graceful

WORDS AT PLAY
. . . .

There is a young man named Dubose,
So clumsy, as everyone knows,
   He is really all thumbs.
      "But," as he tells his chums,
"It's better than being all toes!"

B

Bad
adjective

Bad means not good or not as it ought to be. *Carmen's first shot was bad, but her second went into the bull's-eye.*

Unsatisfactory means not good enough. *The end of this movie is unsatisfactory because it doesn't show what happened to the hero.*

Poor can mean not good in quality. *The singer gave a poor performance because she was suffering from a cold.*

Coarse can mean poor. *The food at the diner is cheap but coarse.*

Inferior means worse than others or worse than it should be. *Medical knowledge a century ago was very much inferior to what it is today.*

Second-rate and **substandard** mean inferior, especially compared to others. *The angry customer called it a second-rate restaurant, but the owner insisted nothing was substandard.*

SEE **naughty, terrible,** and **wicked** for related words.
ANTONYMS: good, fine, excellent

Carmen's first shot was **bad,** but her second went into the bull's-eye.

Bear
verb

Bear means to put up with pain or discomfort. *There's not much to do about a sunburn but bear it.*

Stand can mean the same as bear, but it is more informal. *I don't know how the neighbors stand all that racket from upstairs.*

Suffer can mean to bear something that cannot be helped. *Lauren ate too much pepperoni, onion, and olive pizza, and now she's suffering the consequences.*

Endure can mean to put up with pain or discomfort, often for a long time. It suggests strength of mind or body. *The first people to reach North America had to endure a journey on foot across Arctic lands from Asia.*

Take can mean the same as endure, but it is more informal. *The new troops took everything the enemy threw at them without retreating.*

Abide means to endure. It is mostly used with "not," often about personal feelings or opinions. *Ashley can't abide the way those kids talk about clothes all the time.*

Tolerate can mean to bear and even accept something. It suggests patience and willingness to change. *Kazuo has learned to tolerate his braces, and they don't bother him now.*

Swallow can mean to bear something without responding to it. *Elena swallowed Nora's rudeness because she didn't want to quarrel.*

VERB PLUS

Sometimes when a word is added to a verb, it creates a phrase that has special meaning. Here are some phrases with **bear:**

Bear down means to try especially hard. *With the bases loaded and no outs, Tammy bore down and struck out the next three batters.*

Bear on means to be logically related. *The price of fuel bears on the costs of airplane tickets.*

Bear out means to support the truth of something else. *Ian's story bears out Sandra's.*

José and his friends spend Saturday mornings **beating** conga drums at the Caribbean Cultural Center.

Beat
verb

Beat means to hit over and over. *José and his friends spend Saturday mornings beating conga drums at the Caribbean Cultural Center.*

Hammer can mean to beat. *"Where are they?" cried Shirley, hammering on the door with her fists.*

Pound means to hit hard, over and over. *Winds howled, and waves pounded the little ship.*

Bang can mean to beat noisily. *Liza's little sister loves to bang on pots and pans.*

Batter means to pound something hard enough to cause damage. *In the Middle Ages, cities had walls that attacking armies tried to batter down.*

Spank means to beat with an open hand or a flat object. *There's no need to spank your dog when housebreaking it.*

Paddle can mean to spank. It is a somewhat informal word. *"You're too big to paddle," Mr. Troop told the boys, "so you're grounded for a month."*

Thrash means to beat as a punishment. *The blacksmith's apprentice got thrashed after he nearly set the forge on fire.*

SEE **hit** for related words.

Beautiful
adjective

Beauty is in the eye of the beholder.
— Margaret Wolfe
   Hungerford
   (1855–1897)

Beautiful means very pleasing to the senses or the mind. *These beautiful rugs were made by hand in Turkey 100 years ago, but they still look almost like new.*

Pretty means pleasing to see or hear. It is often used to describe girls and women. *Mariko looks really pretty in that hat.*

Handsome means pleasing to see. It is often used instead of *beautiful* or *pretty* to describe a man or boy. *Candace thinks Mr. Walking Bear, the science teacher, is awfully handsome.*

Good-looking means handsome or pretty. *My mother always tells my father how good-looking he is because she knows it makes him feel good.*

Lovely means especially beautiful and fine. *The rose garden in the park is so lovely, I could stay there for hours.*

Gorgeous means very fancy or colorful. *Dust from the volcano makes sunsets gorgeous everywhere.*

Stunning means strikingly beautiful. *The model in this picture wears a stunning silk evening gown.*

Elegant means beautiful and graceful. It suggests careful attention. *While Grandpa cooks the holiday turkey, Grandma makes the table elegant with candles and flowers.*

ANTONYMS: ugly, unattractive

Because
conjunction

Education is our passport to the future, for tomorrow belongs to those who prepare for it today.
— Malcolm X
   (1925–1965)

Because means for the reason mentioned. *Lyle is late tonight, because he missed the bus.*

Since can mean because. It is used when the cause is explained before the effect. *Since Lyle missed the bus, he is late tonight.*

For means because. This meaning is used mostly in writing. *The people rejoice tonight, for the long war has ended.*

So means with the effect mentioned, or for the purpose mentioned. *Tawana washed the dishes, so you don't have to.*

As a result means with the effect mentioned. *Mickey went around the corner too fast, and as a result the bike skidded.*

Beg
verb

Beg means to ask with deep feeling for something. *Running Bear begged to go on the hunt with his brother.*

Entreat means to beg in order to persuade someone. *Conservationists have been entreating the state government not to dam this river for several years.*

Plead can mean to beg repeatedly or to make an urgent appeal. *Mrs. Turner pleaded with the social worker to help her family.*

Petition means to ask earnestly, especially in a formal request. *The student council petitioned the principal for a relaxed dress code during the heat wave.*

Beseech means to beg or ask seriously. It is a formal word, not often used today except in stories and poems. *Beseeching the bandits for mercy, the villagers wept and screamed.*

Implore means to beg with very deep feeling. *Joan of Arc implored the prince of France to let her lead his soldiers in battle.*

SEE **request** and **urge** for related words.

HAVE YOU HEARD...?

You may have heard the saying "Beggars can't be choosers." This means that if you are asking someone's help, you have to accept whatever help they give you. If you are unwilling to take what is offered, you may get nothing at all.

A similar idea is in the saying "Don't look a gift horse in the mouth." A horse's teeth show how old it is, and thus how good a gift the horse is. But if you show that you are judging the quality of someone's gift, you may not get it after all.

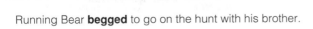

Running Bear **begged** to go on the hunt with his brother.

Beginning
noun

Beginning means the time when something first happens or first exists. *The Declaration of Independence marked the beginning of the United States.*

Start can mean a beginning. *Jason led the sack race from start to finish.*

Creation means the act of making something that did not exist before. *Since the creation of the Cafeteria Committee, we've had better desserts.*

Dawn can mean a beginning, especially the earliest part of a beginning. *World War II marked the dawn of the atomic age.*

Rise can mean a beginning, especially one that happens gradually. *Parents and police have prevented the rise of gangs here.*

Opening can mean a beginning, especially of a story, music, or other works of art. *The opening of the musical, with its great song and fabulous dancers, really grabbed Mike's attention.*

Introduction can mean a beginning in common use. *Since the introduction of the microwave, cooking habits have changed greatly.*

SEE **start** for related words.
ANTONYMS: conclusion, end, finish

Belief
noun

Belief means an idea that someone holds to be true. *It is Joanna's belief that Willard sent her that valentine.*

Trust means belief that someone or something will do what is expected. It suggests expecting good things. *"And this be our motto," wrote Francis Scott Key, "'In God is our trust.'"*

Confidence means trust. It suggests sureness based on experience. *Mr. Anagnos has such confidence in Peter that he lets him help the mechanics work on cars.*

Reliance means trust. It suggests trust in a particular result or accomplishment. *Owen has complete reliance on his skill with a cane and feels no need for a dog guide.*

Dependence can mean trust. It suggests a need for whatever is trusted. *The sick man feels great dependence on the volunteers who bring him meals every day.*

44

CONTINUED ON THE NEXT PAGE

Conviction can mean a belief of which someone is firmly convinced. *The family shares the conviction that education is the ticket to a better life.*

Faith means a very strong, unquestioning belief. *Rev. Martin Luther King, Jr., spoke of his faith in freedom and justice.*

SEE **idea** and **opinion** for related words.
ANTONYMS: disbelief, doubt, mistrust

Bend
verb

Bend means to change shape, or make something change shape. *The snow is so heavy that it bends the tree branches almost to the ground.*

Curve means to go out of a straight line, or to make something go out of a straight line. *Kiesha lives in the building where the road curves around the park.*

Twist can mean to bend. It suggests something that bends many times. *These Native American baskets are made of twisted grass with feathers and beads worked in.*

Curl means to twist into many circles. *Natalia can peel an apple so that the skin curls off in one long piece.*

Turn can mean to change direction by curving. *When you get to the corner, turn left, and the bodega is three doors down.*

Wind means to turn back and forth several times. *The river winds between low green hills.*

The river **winds** between low green hills.

ANTONYM: straighten

45

Best
adjective

Best means better than all others. *Six Ponies is the best weaver in the village, so everyone wants one of her blankets.*

Star means best. *Michael is the star player on the wheelchair basketball team.*

Supreme can mean best. *Today's no-hitter was the supreme event of Marla's summer.*

Superlative is a formal word that means best. *The contest judges praised Manuel's enchiladas as "superlative."*

Matchless means so much better than others that there is no equal. *The princess wore a matchless necklace of gold.*

Top and **tops** can mean best. **Tops** is slang. *Even if Gavi weren't the school's top debater, he'd still be tops with Leilani.*

SEE **excellent** for related words.
ANTONYM: worst

The princess wore a **matchless** necklace of gold.

WORD STORY

Many words that mean "of the best kind" begin with *top* or *top-*. Some of these are *top-drawer*, *topflight*, and *top-notch*. Like *top* and *tops*, they suggest that the best things have high quality and are above all others. Why do you think that people feel this way? Can you think of other examples?

Big
adjective

Big means more than the usual size, number, or amount. *Since Ramona is big for her age, she can wear her mother's old coat.*

Large means big. It often describes the extent or amount of something. *Will the auditorium be large enough for the championship rally?*

Great means large and out of the ordinary. *Great crowds came out for the parade welcoming the soldiers home.*

CONTINUED ON THE NEXT PAGE

This fossil shark had **sizable** jaws.

Bulky can mean big and awkward because of its size. *The duffel bag with the softball equipment in it is too bulky to fit in a locker.*

Sizable means fairly big. It is a somewhat formal word, often used for understatement. *This fossil shark had sizable jaws.*

Considerable can mean sizable. *Having her cast autographed by a soap opera star gave Dorann considerable satisfaction.*

Goodly can mean sizable. *Thirty dollars is a goodly sum of money to pay for a Halloween costume.*

SEE **huge** for related words.
ANTONYMS: little, small, tiny

Blame
verb

Blame means to hold someone responsible for something that has gone wrong. *Lucia feels she gets blamed for things that her brothers and sisters do.*

Accuse means to state that you blame someone. It can be done privately or publicly. *Travis accused me of starting the rumor.*

Charge can mean to accuse. It is commonly used for public, legal accusations. *Health inspectors charged the restaurant with having a dirty kitchen.*

Indict means to accuse. It is used especially for the legal process of bringing someone to trial. *Because the main witness did not appear, the accused robber could not be indicted.*

Denounce can mean to accuse someone in a very public, formal way. *During the 1950s, many Americans were denounced as Communists.*

Throw the first stone is an idiom that means to be the first to say that someone has done wrong. It is a quotation from the Bible. *Considering how messy your room is, you're in no position to throw the first stone at your sister.*

SEE **criticize** and **scold** for related words.

Bother
verb

Bother means to cause someone to be nervous, impatient, and angry. *It bothers Mrs. Moore that people try to help her just because she uses a cane.*

Annoy means to make someone rather angry, especially by a series of actions. *Every time Tova hears how good-looking her brother is, she gets more annoyed.*

Disturb can mean to bother someone. It suggests an interruption of previous calm. *Don't disturb Emilio while he's doing his math.*

Pester means to bother someone by repeated actions or requests. *Edie pestered her brother all week to let her wear his school jacket to the mall.*

Hassle is an informal word meaning to pester. *I'm sorry to hassle you, but I need the blouse by this weekend.*

Harass is a formal word meaning to bother someone repeatedly. *Tenants told the court that the landlord had harassed them by shutting off the heat and water.*

Nag means to pester someone by criticizing. It suggests an effort to make someone do something that he or she doesn't want to do. *When Dad started working nights, he nagged us a lot about helping Mom with dinner and the dishes.*

Bug can mean to bother someone. This meaning of the word is slang. *It bugs me when people play music too loud.*

Tease means to bother someone on purpose, as a joke. *I teased Kip about losing the game, and now he's mad at me.*

SEE **worried** for related words.
ANTONYMS: calm, comfort

IDIOMS
There are so many idioms meaning "to bother someone" that we do not have space to give example sentences for them. Here is a list of some of them. Can you think of others?

drive someone up the wall	get under someone's skin
get in someone's hair	give someone a pain
get on someone's nerves	put someone's back up
get someone's goat	set someone's teeth on edge

Why are there so many, do you think?

48

Brag
verb

Brag means to praise yourself, what you've done, or what you own. *"I caught a fish this big," bragged Denise happily.*

Boast means to brag. It is a somewhat more formal word, suggesting less obvious pride. *The city boasts of its good weather and beautiful scenery.*

Crow can mean to brag openly and loudly, in triumph. *The winning soccer team crowed about how well they played, and gave themselves a cheer.*

Gloat means to feel great satisfaction, often over someone else's misfortune. *We gloated when the sixth grade was kept in during recess because they were so noisy.*

Blow your own horn is an idiom meaning to brag. *Even though we all go to Lara for help at the computer, she never blows her own horn about it.*

SEE **praise** for related words.

"I caught a fish this big," **bragged** Denise happily.

Brave
adjective

Brave means showing no fear in a dangerous or difficult situation. *Sheila is brave enough to tell her friends that smoking is stupid.*

Courageous means brave and strong in spirit. A courageous person chooses to do what is right even when it is difficult or dangerous. *Two courageous boys rescued my brother when he fell through the ice.*

Fearless means having no fear. *That fearless cat is playing with a huge dog.*

Unafraid means having no fear. *On the day of the big test, Ellen was unafraid because she had studied hard.*

Bold means willing and eager to face danger and take risks. *Bold Mr. Kuzma is a high-rise construction worker.*

Daring means willing and eager to face danger and take risks. *The daring pilots thrilled the crowd with their stunts at the air show.*

Heroic means showing unusual bravery in accomplishing great deeds. Heroic people often put themselves in danger to help others. *Emilio's efforts to save the animals in the burning house were heroic.*

Gallant means fearless and eager to show one's bravery. *In this movie, a gallant sea captain rescues Rosalinda from pirates.*

Valiant means very brave in facing danger or trying to reach a goal. *Despite the valiant efforts of Chief Joseph, the Nez Percé people were forced to give up their land.*

Spunky is an informal word meaning courageous. *The spunky little chickadee is driving the bigger birds from the feeder.*

ANTONYMS: cowardly, fearful

The **spunky** little chickadee is driving the bigger birds from the feeder.

> ## WORD POOL
>
> There are many words for the quality shown by someone who is brave.
>
> | | | |
> |---|---|---|
> | bravery | gallantry | nerve |
> | boldness | guts | pluck |
> | courage | heart | spunk |
> | daring | heroism | valor |

Break
verb

The flowerpot **shattered** when it fell to the sidewalk.

Break means to come apart suddenly or to force something to come apart. *The point on this pencil keeps breaking.*

Crack means to break, but not into pieces. *The Liberty Bell in Philadelphia cracked in 1835 during a funeral.*

Shatter means to break into many pieces. *The flowerpot shattered when it fell to the sidewalk.*

Fracture means to crack something hard, such as a bone. *Kim fractured her collarbone when she fell.*

Smash means to break forcefully. *The store alarm went off when someone smashed the window.*

Split means to break or divide into parts. *Abraham Lincoln was called "Railsplitter" because in his youth he split logs for fence rails.*

Splinter means to break into long, thin, sharp pieces. *The wooden door splintered under the blows of the firefighter's axe.*

Crumble means to break into crumbs or other small pieces. *Rita crumbled a cracker into her chili.*

SEE **cut** and **tear** for related words.
ANTONYMS: fix, mend, repair

▼ VERB PLUS
....

Sometimes when a word is added to a verb, it creates a phrase that has special meaning. Here are some phrases with **break:**

Break down can mean to stop working. *The furnace broke down, and it's freezing in here.* It can also mean to begin to cry. *Tyler breaks down whenever he speaks of his dead dog.*

Break in can mean to prepare for use. *You can break in your jeans by washing them a couple of times.* It can also mean to interrupt. *I wasn't done with my story when Marla broke in with hers.*

Break out can mean to begin suddenly. *A fire broke out in the paint factory.* It can also mean to have pimples. *Mike's skin is starting to break out.*

Break up can mean to separate. *Joe and Gina broke up for a while, but they're back together again.* It can also mean to start laughing. *Sue loves that joke, but she breaks up whenever she tries to tell it.*

Bright
adjective

Bright means giving much light. *The sun is so bright that Nicole is wearing sunglasses.*

Shiny means reflecting much light. *The shiny new dime makes the old one look dull.*

Brilliant means very bright. *The concert stage is in brilliant light so everyone can see the musicians.*

Beaming means sending off beams of light, or seeming to do so. *The beaming headlights of the car showed a deer on the highway. Dad's beaming smile told us how much he liked his present.*

Radiant means full of light, or seeming to be so. *In the city aquarium, the radiant tanks hold colorful fish. Paolo's eyes were radiant with happiness.*

Luminous can mean giving steady, clear light. *This clock has luminous hands, so you can tell time at night.*

Sunny means bright with sunshine. *If it's sunny tomorrow, we'll go to the beach.*

Glowing means shining with warm soft light. *A glowing fire makes a room cozy.*

Gleaming means bright amid dark surroundings. *At the back of the dusty old store, Alicia spotted a gleaming silver teapot.*

Sparkling means flashing very brightly. *After the storm, the wet trees were sparkling with sunlit raindrops.*

Glittering means sparkling. *Ayo stared at the glittering jewels on the crown in the museum.*

Dazzling means bright enough to hurt the eyes. *The light from a camera flashbulb is dazzling.*

Glaring means dazzling. *We came out of the movie theater into glaring July daylight.*

SEE **flash** and **shine** for related words.
ANTONYMS: dark, dim, dull

Many trees were **burned** in the forest fire.

Burn
verb

Burn means to injure or damage by heat. *Many trees were burned in the forest fire.*

Singe means to burn very slightly. *Margo got the fire extinguisher so fast that the desk was barely singed.*

Scorch means to burn a surface slightly, but enough to show damage. *Tim scorched the sleeve of his shirt because the iron was too hot.*

Sear means to burn the surface. *People sometimes sear meat over a high flame and then roast it at a lower temperature.*

Char means to burn something enough that it turns black. *The fire charred the wooden walls of the cabin.*

IDIOMS

Burn is a key word in many idioms. Here are some of them:

Burn your bridges behind you means to leave yourself no way back, or to make sure that your choice is final. *Quitting his job was one thing, but Rick really burned his bridges behind him when he insulted his boss.*

Burn the candle at both ends means to use up time or energy very quickly. *You're going out for the basketball team and the school play? That's burning the candle at both ends!*

Burn the midnight oil means to study or work very hard, especially late at night. *With her law exams coming up, Aunt Doneeta expects to burn the midnight oil all this month.*

53

Busy
adjective

Busy means working steadily, with many things to do. *Mom was busy in the garden all morning.*

Hard-working means ready and willing to work hard. *Jaime is so hard-working that his delivery business has been a great success.*

Industrious means hard-working and always busy. It is a more formal word than *hard-working.* *This company is looking for industrious workers.*

Diligent means thoroughly and carefully busy, especially in doing a particular thing. *Mara is diligent in practicing ice-skating.*

Active can mean working hard or with energy. *Since my grandfather retired from his job, he has become active as a hospital volunteer.*

Bustling means busy in a noisy, hurried way. It is often used to describe places where work is done. *Since the highway came through, Stockton has turned into a bustling factory town.*

ANTONYM: idle

WRITING TIP: Cliché

If you want to say that someone is very busy, you will probably think of some phrases right away. "Busy as a bee" is one. "Busy as a beaver" is another. Each of these phrases is a cliché (klē shā′). A cliché is a phrase that has been used so often that everyone knows it, such as "not for a million dollars," or "not with a ten-foot pole." Many clichés are comparisons, such as "mad as a wet hen" and "old as the hills." Some phrases have become clichés recently: "no problem" and "do your own thing." If everybody says it, it's a cliché.

When you are writing, clichés can be good or bad. They are useful when you are writing your first version, because they help you keep going. It's a good idea to take them out when you revise, though. Clichés are dull. Everyone has heard them before, so they won't keep your reader interested. Clichés are also not precise. Because they can be used at almost any time, they don't say something exact about one particular time. A synonym is often more interesting and more precise. For instance, if someone spends hours every day learning to play the guitar, that person is *diligent*—not "busy as a bee."

Call
verb

Call means to ask or order someone to come. *Mom called me in to dinner.*

Invite means to ask someone to come, especially to a social event. *The Wangs have invited Pedro to Arthur's birthday party.*

Summon means to order someone to come, especially to an official event. *Helga was summoned to testify at the trial.*

Hail can mean to call someone. *The detective hailed a taxi.*

Assemble means to call or bring a group together. *Trumpeter Walker Reddins has assembled the members of his great band once more.*

Convene is a formal word that can mean to call together for a meeting. *The President will convene his cabinet to discuss the trade deficit.*

The detective **hailed** a taxi.

55

Calm
adjective

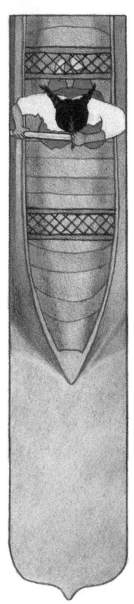

The canoe slid easily through the **placid** water.

Calm means not excited or emotional. *I like the way Ms. Andrews stays calm, even when others are upset.*

Quiet means calm and without much excitement or noise. *Jerold likes to take a walk early in the morning when the streets are quiet.*

Peaceful means quiet and full of peace. *The mountain looks peaceful, but inside is boiling lava that may someday erupt.*

Cool can mean not excited or upset. This meaning of the word is informal. *One reason Gilda is a good speaker is that she stays cool under pressure.*

Tranquil means very calm or very quiet. *The warm sun and gentle breeze made for a very tranquil day.*

Collected means not excited even at a time of disturbance or danger. *When the accident happened, Vicki was the only one collected enough to get the license number.*

Placid means pleasantly calm and peaceful. *The canoe slid easily through the placid water.*

Serene means tranquil. It suggests a mental or physical distance from excitement or care. *Max took comfort from the serene manner of his sick grandmother when he visited her in the hospital.*

SEE **comfort** and **quiet** for related words.
ANTONYMS: disturbed, excited, upset

WRITING TIP: Emphasis by Repetition

"Calm, cool, and collected" is a familiar way of saying that someone is entirely calm. Since the words are synonyms, why use all three? For one thing, they all start with the same sound, so the alliteration makes the phrase interesting. (See **power** for a Writing Tip on alliteration.) Also, they provide emphasis by repetition. If you wanted to say there was absolutely nothing in a box, you might write that it was "completely and utterly empty." The repetition lets your reader understand how important it is that the box is empty.

You need to be careful with this method, however. In most cases, repetition doesn't add much. "The trees are high and tall" is just wordy. Use repetition only when you really mean to emphasize an idea—and don't use it too often even that way, or your reader may get tired of it.

Care
noun

Care means an unhappy, nervous feeling, with fear of pain or loss. *After weeks of struggle and care, the refugees have escaped from the fighting.*

Concern can mean an uneasy feeling because something or someone important to you is in trouble. *Marcia's parents feel a lot of concern because she wants to quit school.*

Worry means repeated, nervous thought about possible pain or loss. *Our worry about Billy Don's safety turned to anger when he strolled in two hours late.*

Anxiety means strong worry and fear. *Every time Coach Petrangelis tells us how important this next game is, my anxiety gets worse.*

Tension can mean worry and emotional upset, especially lasting a long time and using up much strength. *After the tension of waiting for the audition, White Bird felt that actually performing was almost easy.*

Strain can mean tension. *The staff in the hospital emergency room are under serious strain much of the time.*

Distress means sorrow or pain that contains much anxiety. *Her cat's illness caused Kate great distress.*

SEE **worried** for related words.
ANTONYM: indifference

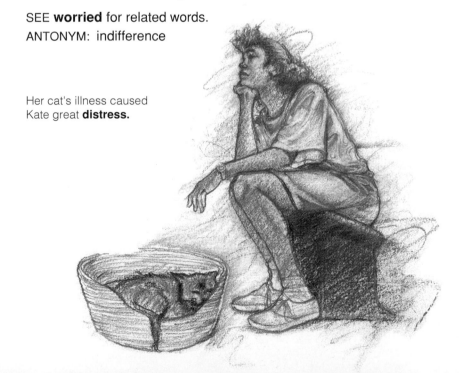

Her cat's illness caused Kate great **distress.**

Careful
adjective

Careful means paying close attention to what you say and do. *I feel safe in the car with Mrs. Gomez, who is a very careful driver.*

Cautious means careful to avoid danger. *Pia has been very cautious about riding her bike in the street after seeing the bike safety movie.*

Wary means very careful and expecting danger. *Mice have to be wary of cats and owls.*

Guarded can mean cautious. It is used especially to describe someone's way of talking. *The scientists are very guarded about their invention, and they say it needs more tests.*

Deliberate can mean careful and thorough. *Mr. Tyler spread the tar on the roof in a deliberate, unhurried fashion.*

SEE **alert** for related words.
ANTONYMS: careless, negligent, thoughtless

Careless
adjective

Careless means not paying attention to what you say or do. *Tom was careless, and now his shoes are all wet.*

Thoughtless means not thinking before doing or saying something. *Those thoughtless girls talk loudly while everyone else is trying to study.*

Unthinking means thoughtless. *Mr. Foster was embarrassed by his unthinking expectation that the electrician would be a man.*

Heedless is a somewhat formal word meaning careless. *Heedless of the possibility of extinction, hunters killed more and more elephants for their ivory.*

Inconsiderate means thoughtless of other people's feelings. *Taking a parking space reserved for the disabled isn't just inconsiderate, it's illegal.*

Reckless means not thinking about possible danger. *Reckless driving frequently causes accidents.*

Rash means dangerously careless, often because of haste. *Maryanne now regrets her rash decision to quit school.*

ANTONYMS: careful, cautious

Carry
verb

Carry means to hold something while moving from one place to another. *Anna carries her books in a purple backpack.*

Convey is a formal word meaning to carry. *The local transit system conveys thousands of passengers into the business district every day.*

Tote is an informal word meaning to carry. *On the days she has baton practice, Shirley has to tote her uniform and equipment to school.*

Pack can mean to carry. This meaning is informal. *The sheriff warned the cowboys not to pack their guns in town.*

Transport means to carry something in a ship, plane, or other vehicle. *Cities typically developed near rivers, which provided the most economical way to transport goods and materials.*

Cart means to carry, in a cart or otherwise. *Nashota's father will use his van to cart the cans and bottles to the recycling center.*

Haul means to carry or to drag. It suggests moving something heavy. *It took two hours to haul the sofa up to Grandma's apartment.*

Lug means to haul. *Sid says it's called luggage because you have to lug it.*

Bear means to carry something very heavy. *Glaciers bear dirt and stone across the land, dumping their rocky load when they melt.*

HAVE YOU HEARD...?

You may have heard people say that doing something is like "carrying coals to Newcastle." This means that it is completely unnecessary. Newcastle is short for Newcastle upon Tyne, an English city on the Tyne river. The city has been a center of coal mining for hundreds of years. No one needs to carry pieces of coal to a place where there is already plenty.

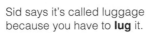

Sid says it's called luggage because you have to **lug** it.

Catch
verb

Catch means to get hold of someone or something moving. *Chelsea throws the Frisbee, and her dog catches it.*

Trap means to catch and keep hold of an animal or a person. *The cattle rustlers were trapped in a canyon by the posse.*

Capture means to get by force. *Scientists have captured a huge snake.*

Take can mean to capture. *"You'll never take me alive!" shouted the rebel leader.*

Seize means to take suddenly and by force. *The owl has seized a mouse and is carrying it back to her owlets.*

Grab and **snatch** mean to seize. These words are often used when the seizing is done directly by a person or animal. *When two players from the other team grabbed Tony, he dropped the football, but Gershon snatched it up and ran for fifteen yards.*

Arrest means to take someone to a police station as a prisoner. *People arrested by the police must be informed of their legal rights.*

SEE **get** and **take** for related words.
ANTONYMS: free, let go, release

Scientists have **captured** a huge snake.

HAVE YOU HEARD...?

You may have heard people say that something has been done "catch as catch can." This means in any way possible, by whatever methods worked. *When the basement flooded, we moved everything upstairs catch as catch can, and now we have to get it all organized again.*

If the phrase sounds a bit odd, that is because it's about 600 years old, from a time when English was different from its modern form.

Cause
verb

Cause means to make something happen. *Last fall's hurricane caused extensive damage along the Atlantic coast.*

Produce can mean to cause. *A bee sting produces pain and swelling.*

Occasion means to cause. It is used to refer especially to events or actions. *Lamar's good grades have occasioned much praise from his family.*

Generate means to bring into existence. *The sun's light generates heat on Earth. News of the huge snake generated a lot of excitement around town.*

Effect is a formal word meaning to cause something to occur. *Modern inventions such as television have effected many changes in the way people spend their evenings.*

Bring about and **give rise to** mean to cause. *The neighborhood committee has brought about many local improvements. This success may give rise to committees in other neighborhoods.*

Lead to means to be the cause of something, at least in part. *Forgetting to change a car's oil can lead to major engine trouble.*

SEE **happen** for related words.

News of the huge snake **generated** a lot of excitement around town.

WATCH IT!

The verb **effect** means to make something happen, and it is often confused with the verb **affect,** which means to change someone or something. *When the city effected changes in bus schedules, some neighborhoods were affected more than others.* Remember, when you *effect* a change, you *affect* a situation.

61

Celebrate
verb

Celebrate means to note a special day with proper activities. *Mexicans proudly celebrate their independence with two days of colorful fiestas.*

Commemorate means to show respect for a memory, often on a special day. *In January, the United States commemorates the birth of Rev. Martin Luther King, Jr.*

Observe can mean to show respect on a particular day. *The Jewish faith observes Yom Kippur with fasting and prayer.*

Keep can mean to observe or to celebrate. *The Larsens keep Thanksgiving by having a family reunion—all 68 of them.*

Honor can mean to show respect, often at a particular time. *At this morning's ceremony, the city will honor those firefighters who have died in the line of duty.*

ANTONYM: ignore

Center
noun

Center means a point equally distant from each side or end. It is often used to mean the most important point of activity. *There was a bowl of oranges in the center of the table. Jorge was the center of attention as he described his trip to Puerto Rico.*

Middle means the central or halfway part of something. *Ms. Gustavson is the one in the middle of the photograph. The bell rang when Kenneth was right in the middle of a story.*

Heart can mean the innermost or most important part of something. *Public buildings like the City Hall and the Board of Education are often in the heart of the city.*

Hub can mean the center of activity. *After school, the Youth Center is the hub of our neighborhood.*

Focus can mean hub. *On market day, the village square is the focus of trade for miles around.*

Core can mean the central or most important part of something. *The core of Nadia's problems at school is that her family needs her to help so much at home.*

Nucleus means a central part of something, around which the rest is formed. *Lifting weights and jogging is the nucleus of Kazuko's exercise plans.*

Change
verb

Change means to make or become different. *Jermayne changes her nail polish every couple of days. Inside its case, the pupa changes to a butterfly.*

Alter means to change slightly. It suggests limited change of a particular sort. *The pilot altered her flight plan to avoid a bad thunderstorm.*

Modify means to change partially for a specific reason. *Barry modified the ending of his report to include the latest news.*

Vary means to change in a number of ways. It suggests change for the sake of difference, or change according to circumstances. *The form of government varies from country to country.*

Turn can mean to change. It often describes change in color or form. *The sun turned Alan's face red. Water turns to steam when it boils.*

Diversify is a formal word meaning to vary. *The toy company will diversify its business by making clothes and candy.*

Turn over a new leaf is an idiom meaning to change completely and make a fresh start. *After the holidays, Mrs. O'Malley says she will turn over a new leaf and start to diet and exercise.*

SEE **adapt** and **turn into** (at **turn**) for related words.

Inside its case, the pupa **changes** to a butterfly.

IDIOMS

Change is a key word in several idioms. Here are some of them:

Change hands means to go from one owner to another. *The gas station changed hands twice in one year before Mr. Ortega bought it.*

Change off means to take turns. *Mariolet and I change off doing the dishes and setting the table.*

Change your tune means to say something very different from before. *Cassie thinks she's a better cook than I am, but she'll change her tune when she tastes my barbecue.*

63

Characteristic
noun

Characteristic means something that is part of a person's or thing's special nature. *Large size is the most obvious characteristic of the Saint Bernard dog.*

Trait means a characteristic. It is used about people, not things. *The one trait that really bothers Ryan's friends is his impatience.*

Mark can mean something that shows what a person or thing is like. *Quincy has all the marks of a promising musician.*

Hallmark can mean a characteristic that is a sure sign of someone's or something's nature. *Courage is the hallmark of every war hero.*

Earmark can mean hallmark. *The earmark of Jill's drawing is her skill with shading.*

Idiosyncrasy means something about a person that is quite unusual. *Wearing all her glasses at once is just one of Ms. Hurston's little idiosyncrasies.*

SEE **disposition** and **quality** for related words.

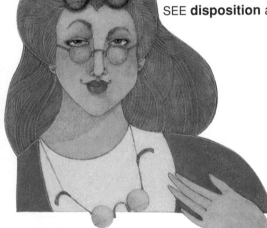

Wearing all her glasses at once is just one of Ms. Hurston's little **idiosyncrasies.**

WORD STORY

Hallmark originally meant an official stamp guaranteeing the purity of gold and silver objects. It comes from Goldsmith's *Hall*, London, and the identifying *mark* put on the object.

Earmark originally meant a *mark* made on the *ear* of an animal to show who owns it.

Cheap
adjective

Cheap means low in price. *Fruit is cheaper in summer than winter.*

Inexpensive means not high in price. It usually describes something good. *We dined at a pleasant, inexpensive Italian restaurant.*

Reasonable can mean inexpensive and fairly priced. *Ten dollars for an hour's canoe rental seemed very reasonable.*

Economical means giving good value for money. *Our neighborhood grocery is high-priced, but the more economical stores are far away.*

CONTINUED ON THE NEXT PAGE

Dirt-cheap means extremely low in price. *"In this part of town," joked the real estate agent, "land is dirt-cheap."*

Dime a dozen is an idiom meaning common, extremely low in price, and worth very little. *Even though Dad says cookies like these are a dime a dozen, he's eaten plenty of them.*

SEE **discount** for related words.
ANTONYMS: costly, expensive

Cheat
verb

Cheat means to do something dishonest while hoping others won't notice. *Anyone who cheats on this test will fail.*

Trick means to cheat by misleading or fooling someone. *Outlaws tricked the rancher and sold him his own hay.*

Swindle means to cheat someone, usually out of money. *The company was swindled out of $18,000 by a trusted employee.*

Defraud means to cheat someone of money, property, or rights. It suggests deliberate crime on a large scale. *Many families have been defrauded of their savings by people selling shares in a false gold mine.*

Short-change means to cheat someone by giving less change from a purchase than is due. *When Milly counted her money, she realized that the clerk had short-changed her.*

Sucker and **take** are slang words meaning to cheat. *Dad says the man suckered him into buying the car and took him for two grand!*

Gyp is a slang word meaning to cheat. *I thought it was a gold chain, but I was gypped.*

SEE **deceive** for related words.

When Milly counted her money, she realized that the clerk had **short-changed** her.

WATCH IT!

Gyp is a word that many people use without knowing that it is an insult. *Gyp* is short for *Gypsy*. People who did business with Gypsies had a prejudice that the Gypsies would cheat them. So *gyp* came to mean "cheat." It remains an insult and an expression of prejudice. Since there are so many other words meaning "cheat," it's a good idea not to use *gyp*.

Check
verb

Check means to hold something back or to keep something within limits. *Dense jungle growth checked the explorer's progress.*

Control can mean to check. *Dick finally controlled his excitement and told the good news to his friends.*

Restrain means to limit action or to prevent someone from doing something. *The cast on Tina's foot restrains her movements. She walks the dog on a leash now to restrain him from chasing cars.*

Curb means to hold back or limit, especially by some particular method. *I curb my desire to talk during assembly by taking notes.*

Rein can mean to hold back, the way a horse is held back by reins. *"If you don't rein your spending, Karl, you can't expect to save money," warned his uncle.*

Choose
verb

Choose means to decide to do or take something. *Nestor chose to give his report on the life of Manuel Quezon y Molina, first president of the Philippine Commonwealth.*

Pick means to choose from many things just what you want. *Robin picked the gray kitten because it was the liveliest of the four.*

Select means to choose from many things after thinking carefully. *"We're only going to rent one movie, Deke, so be sure about the one you select," his mother advised.*

Prefer means to like something better than something else. *My folks want Grandma to stay with us, but she prefers having her own home.*

Elect means to choose, especially by voting for a person. *United States citizens elect a President every four years. When my family went fishing at dawn, I elected to stay in bed.*

Pick out means to choose with extra care. *Mr. Johnson picked out the biggest catfish in the tank.*

Single out means to choose one person or thing in particular. *Some girls singled out the drummer as their favorite and screamed whenever he sang.*

SEE **decide** for related words.
ANTONYM: reject

Clear
adjective

Clear means easy to hear, see, or understand. *Latrice speaks in a clear voice. We had a clear view of the stage from our seats. Clive gave a clear explanation of the causes of air pollution.*

Distinct can mean clear. *There is a distinct possibility of a transit strike this year.*

Plain can mean clear. *It is plain that Ron is the best boxer for his age at the gym.*

Obvious means especially clear. *In this video game, there are three obvious traps and several hidden ones.*

Apparent means possible to know from what is seen and heard. *From the big grin that spread over her face, it was apparent that she liked her birthday present.*

Evident means easy to know from what is seen and heard. *John blushed and mumbled, making it evident that he was embarrassed.*

Prominent can mean easy to see. *With his new telescope, Galileo found prominent spots on the sun.*

Conspicuous means hard not to see. *The mountains are conspicuous from miles away.*

SEE **definite** for related words.
ANTONYM: unclear

The mountains are **conspicuous** from miles away.

Climb
verb

The squirrels **climb** the pole to get the birdseed.

Climb means to move upward, most often by using feet or hands or both. *The squirrels climb the pole to get the birdseed.*

Ascend means to move upward toward the highest point. *The Japanese mountaineers will try to ascend one of the highest peaks in the Andes.*

Mount means to go up or climb up. *Mrs. Vargas slowly mounted the stairs to her apartment.*

Scale can mean to climb up or over. *Red Shirt scaled a snow-covered pine tree to look for caribou.*

Clamber means to climb with difficulty, using both hands and feet. *Clambering over the roof in her heavy equipment, the firefighter reached the burning timbers and chopped them away.*

Scramble means to climb where climbing is especially hard and awkward. It may suggest climbing on all fours. *An otter will scramble up a steep, muddy riverbank and slide down again, over and over, just for fun.*

Shin means to climb a pole or something like a pole by holding tight with your arms and legs and pulling yourself up a little at a time. *"Jake, please shin up that pole and get our kite string loose," begged his little brother.*

Shinny means to shin. *Meka shinnied up the palm tree and came down with a large, ripe coconut.*

SEE **rise** for related words.
ANTONYM: descend

WORD STORY

Sometimes there are two words that are almost the same and have the same meaning, such as *shin* and *shinny*. Some other pairs like this are *electric/electrical*, *round/around*, and *special/especial*. Words often have more than one form. Usually, one word in a pair like this stops being used. Sometimes, however, there are enough people using each of the two words that they both survive. Can you think of other pairs like these?

Clothes
noun

Clothes means covering for a person's body. *Miguel has grown so much he needs new clothes.*

Clothing means clothes. It is a slightly more formal word. *New-to-You Fashion Shop sells both women's and men's clothing.*

Wear can mean clothing. It is usually used about categories of clothing. *Mom works in the children's wear department, but next week she is being transferred to sportswear.*

Duds is an informal word that means clothes. *"Mighty fancy duds, Elliott," said my English teacher, who thinks he's funny.*

Dress can mean clothing of a particular type. *It's a softball game and a picnic dinner, so casual dress will be fine.*

Garb means clothes, often the kind used in a certain type of work or of an unusual kind. *People in the armed forces wear military garb.*

Wardrobe means all the clothes a person has. *Most of Ray's wardrobe came from his older brothers.*

Outfit can mean clothes that go together. *Mom has a plaid skirt and a red blouse that she wears as an outfit with her velvet blazer.*

Uniform means the clothes worn by some special group while at work. *When Aunt Phyllis goes to her Army Reserve training, she looks strong and proud in her uniform.*

poncho

sarong

kimono

caftan

parka

AROUND THE WORLD: Clothing

burnoose (North Africa and the Middle East)
caftan (Turkey and Egypt)
cheongsam (China)
dashiki (Africa)
kilt (Scotland)
kimono (Japan)
muu-muu (Hawaii)
parka (Alaska, NE Asia)
poncho (South America)
sari (India)
sarong (Malaysia)
serape (Mexico)

Cold
adjective

Cold means having or feeling no warmth. *"Waiter, this soup is cold," announced Mr. Simpson.*

Cool means somewhat cold, in a pleasant and comfortable way. *It's cooler in Serafina's room, where there's a breeze.*

Chilly means unpleasantly cold. *Although Spain is usually sunny, winter temperatures can be quite chilly.*

Freezing can mean so cold that people are very uncomfortable. *Mr. Harris called the landlord to say the apartment is freezing.*

Frigid mean's very cold. *Polar bears live in frigid Arctic regions.*

Wintry means cold, like winter. *The air conditioning makes it wintry in that theater.*

Frosty means cold enough to see your breath. *On frosty days, water vapor condenses and becomes visible in the air.*

Icy and **glacial** mean extremely cold, like ice. *In my dream, the man in the black cloak took my hand in his icy grasp. He led me through glacial darkness to a room silver with moonlight.*

Polar bears live in
frigid Arctic regions.

ANTONYMS: hot, warm

Color
noun

Color means one of the sensations produced in the eye by light. *At sunset the clouds change color: white, orange, gold, then gray.*

Hue means color. It is used mostly in poems and stories. *Under the pagoda stood a slender maiden in a robe of many hues.*

Shade can mean a color slightly different either in darkness or lightness. *The many shades of green in plants all show the presence of chlorophyll.*

Tone can mean a shade. *Vita's shoes and belt are in tones of yellow.*

CONTINUED ON THE NEXT PAGE

Tint means a shade, especially a light or pale one. *When my grandmother left the beauty shop, her normally white hair had a blue tint to it.*

Tinge means a slight tint. *When the neon sign goes on across the street, the walls in this room take on a purple tinge.*

▼ HAVE YOU HEARD...?
· ·

You may have heard people say that something is "a horse of a different color." This means that it is very much unlike something else, to which it has been compared. Often it suggests that the "horse of a different color" is harder to do, or to deal with, or less likely to succeed. *"I can strike Danny out any time, but Peg is a horse of a different color," said George.*

Come
verb

Come means to get to a place. *We've been waiting here for almost half an hour, but the bus hasn't come yet.*

Arrive means to get to a place, especially after a trip of some length. *Gene leaves the farm at 7:30 and arrives at school at 8:45.*

Reach means to get to a place, especially after much effort. *Settlers reached the southern tip of South America about 8,000 years ago.*

Gain can mean to get to a place, especially after much effort. *By traveling at night, the refugees gained the border safely.*

Attain means to get to a place, especially after much effort. *It took the spacecraft* Voyager *twelve years to attain the orbit of Neptune.*

Land means to get from water or air to a place on land. *Mario's plane landed on time. Mrs. Suzuki landed the boat and lowered the sail.*

Show up and **turn up** mean to come to a place. They suggest that there was a strong possibility of not coming. *We knew that Ginny might show up at the dance, but we were really surprised when Vanessa turned up as well.*

Make an appearance means to come to an event but not stay. *James's father and stepmother barely made an appearance at his graduation party.*

ANTONYM: leave

Comfort
verb

The chimpanzee **soothes** her baby by hugging it until it is quiet.

Comfort means to make someone feel better who is in pain or upset. *The nurse comforted Tina's parents and told them the burn was minor.*

Soothe means to comfort. *The chimpanzee soothes her baby by hugging it until it is quiet.*

Console is a more formal word meaning to comfort at a time of sadness. *Mr. Sullivan tried to console the weeping boy.*

Reassure means to calm someone who is worried or afraid. *Darnell reassured his sister that their quarrel wasn't serious.*

Relieve means to reduce pain or trouble. *The pharmacist told Mrs. Dengas that a heating pad might relieve her sore shoulder.*

Cheer up means to help someone feel happier. *While Sophie had to stay home with pneumonia, her grandfather telephoned every day to cheer her up.*

Take a load off someone's mind is an idiom that means to make someone feel better by removing a reason for worry. *When the letter carrier found my wallet, it took a load off my mind.*

SEE **calm** and **quiet** for related words.
ANTONYMS: bother, distress

Comfortable
adjective

Comfortable means giving or feeling comfort and pleasure. *Andrew wants to keep his old sneakers because they're so comfortable.*

Comfy is an informal word meaning comfortable. *Doesn't Buster look comfy, curled up in the sunlight?*

Relaxing means giving peace and comfort. *After driving her bus all day, Mom likes to spend a relaxing half hour with the paper before starting dinner.*

Cozy means comfortable, warm, and giving or feeling friendly happiness. *Half asleep in the cozy tepee, Two Baskets listened to the prairie wind howling.*

Snug means comfortable and sheltered, usually in a small space. *The finches have a snug little nest in that old oak tree.*

Easy can mean comfortable and free from care or worry. *It will be a while before Lucy feels easy moving about on crutches.*

CONTINUED ON THE NEXT PAGE

WRITING TIP: Rhyme Time

Why do people say "snug as a bug in a rug" to mean very safe and comfortable? A rug does have many openings the right size for a small insect to hide in—but this is not the main reason. And the picture that the phrase creates is a cute one—who wouldn't feel friendly toward a cozy bug?—but this is not the main reason. The main reason people keep using this phrase is because it rhymes, like "hot shot" and "no pain, no gain." Rhyme pleases the ear and gets attention. This is why it is used so much in advertising: it helps the message stick in the mind.

Even if you are not writing a poem, you can use rhyming phrases to sound livelier and more interesting. Rhyme can make your writing more exciting, more inviting.

Command
verb

Command means to tell someone officially to do something. *The Emperor of Persia commanded his armies to conquer the cities of Greece.*

Order can mean to tell someone forcefully to do something. *If kids act up, Mr. Tyler orders them to behave or get detention.*

Direct means to tell someone officially to do something. It is not so strong a word as *command*. *The police officer directed Mr. Cornell to show his driver's license.*

Instruct can mean to tell someone to do something. *Bertha's parents have instructed her to call whenever she will be late.*

Dictate can mean to give specific orders that must be obeyed. *In a democracy, no one can dictate to the people how they should vote.*

Tell can mean to give someone an order in an informal way. *Freddie, tell your brother to get ready for bed.*

Ask can mean to give someone an order in a polite way. *Mom asked me to set the table for supper.*

SEE **persuade** and **urge** for related words.

73

Common
adjective

Common means happening often or often met with. *"It's just a common cold," Dr. Wu told Jerome.*

Ordinary means like most others. *Since the note was written on ordinary paper, the police concentrated on tracing its rare purple ink.*

Typical and **standard** mean ordinary. They suggest something happening or done many times. *It's typical of Lorraine to be late, and her standard excuse is that the bus got stuck in traffic.*

Average can mean like most others. It is often used with numbers. *On an average day, the store sells two dozen sponges.*

Normal means like most others. It suggests that this is a good way to be. *It is normal for people to want to be liked and respected.*

Everyday means happening or met with every day. *Rice, eaten only occasionally by many Americans, is an everyday food in Asia.*

Familiar means well-known and often met with. *It's a familiar story: Kimberly quit school but couldn't find a job, and now her life's going nowhere.*

Popular can mean widespread and done, had, or known by many people. *Grandpa and Grandma like to do popular dances from years ago.*

Run-of-the-mill means ordinary and not very good. *They replaced Juana's favorite comedy with a run-of-the-mill game show.*

SEE **general** and **usual** for related words.

ANTONYMS: exceptional, extraordinary, rare, uncommon

Grandpa and Grandma like to do **popular** dances from years ago.

A brave **company** of Pilgrims landed at Plymouth in 1620.

Company
noun

Company means a group of people who are together for some reason. *A brave company of Pilgrims landed at Plymouth in 1620.*

Band means a small group of people who stay together for a special purpose. *Derrick and a band of other boys lift weights in the gym after school.*

Party can mean a group of people who are together for a short time. *The waiter says that big table is reserved for a party of eight.*

Gang can mean a group of friends who often do things together. *Mr. Timkins goes bowling on Thursdays with a gang from his office.*

Team means a group of people playing or working together. *The Clemente School debating team won the city championship.*

Crew can mean a group of people who work together. *After the storm, a crew from the power company repaired the downed lines.*

Troop means a group of people, often a large group, who move or act together. *Sharon's Girl Scout troop is collecting blankets for the homeless.*

Troupe means a group of performers. *The bottom acrobat had the weight of the whole troupe on his shoulders.*

SEE **crowd** for related words.

75

Complain
verb

The umpire tried to calm the **squawking** manager.

Complain means to say that something is not the way it should be, and that you are unhappy about it. *Mrs. Baylor complained to the landlord about the lack of heat in the apartment.*

Grumble means to complain in a growling, angry way. *The sailors grumbled about the food until the captain threatened not to give them any.*

Whine means to complain in a sad voice, especially about unimportant things. *My brother often whines about having to go to bed.*

Gripe is an informal word that can mean to complain in a continuous, annoying way. *Rob gripes about the hard work on his paper route, but he likes the money.*

Squawk is a slang word that means to complain loudly about something. *The umpire tried to calm the squawking manager.*

Kvetch is a slang word meaning to complain steadily. *If Rasia found money, she'd kvetch about having to pick it up.*

Moan and groan means to complain bitterly. It suggests too much complaining. *Coach says no more moaning and groaning about early practice, or it will start with a three-mile run.*

SEE **objection** for related words.

> **WORD STORY**
>
> *Kvetch* comes from Yiddish, a language combining old German and Hebrew and spoken by Jews of Eastern and Central Europe. Other words from Yiddish include *bagel, chutzpah, lox, mensch, nosh,* and *shtick.* You can find these words in your dictionary.

Complicated
adjective

Complicated means very difficult to understand because of many parts. *Dimitri likes complicated jigsaw puzzles with hundred of pieces.*

Complex means having many parts and therefore not easy to understand. *A complex set of instructions came with the new VCR.*

Intricate means having many closely interconnected parts and therefore not easy to understand. *In medical school Uncle Miguel is learning the intricate systems of the human body.*

CONTINUED ON THE NEXT PAGE

Involved can mean very intricate and therefore hard to understand. *This mystery is so involved, I can't even remember who got killed!*

Tangled means very complicated or involved, like a messy ball of string. *It took twenty minutes to sort out Ralph's tangled account of the accident.*

Elaborate means made with great care, filled with detail, and quite complex. *Engineers may spend many months designing an elaborate computer circuit.*

SEE **hard** for related words.
ANTONYM: simple

Engineers may spend many months designing an **elaborate** computer circuit.

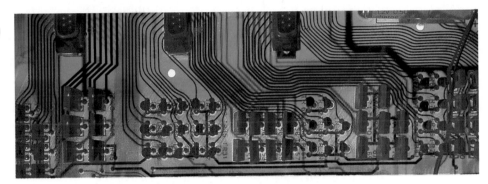

Condition
noun

Condition means the general way something or someone is. *The condition of the town grew much worse when two more factories closed.*

State means a way something or someone is. It suggests attention to some particular way. *The reporters questioned the doctors about the President's state of health after the operation.*

Circumstance means a condition that has an effect on something or someone. *The police said that under the circumstances—an icy road and a broken stoplight—both drivers were very lucky.*

Situation means a set of circumstances, considered in relation to one person or thing. *Joel's in an awkward situation—he's promised to go to two parties at the same time.*

Status can mean condition, especially at a particular time. *What is the status of Anne Red Deer's science project? Is she nearly finished?*

Shape can mean status. *The survivors were in very bad shape after two weeks in a lifeboat.*

77

Confirm
verb

Confirm means to show that something is true and to remove all doubt about it. *Earl's failure to come to practice confirms that he doesn't really want to be on the cheerleading squad.*

Prove means to show the truth of something, especially by presenting arguments or evidence. *Liam proved his story of having met the star by showing the autograph he had gotten.*

Verify means to show that something is correct and accurate. *Publishers make great efforts to verify the facts in textbooks.*

Substantiate is a formal word meaning to show that something is true with solid evidence. *The defense attorney told the jury she would substantiate her client's alibi with documents.*

Authenticate means to show or declare that something is true or genuine. *Mrs. Ichemi has agreed to buy the doll after it is authenticated as an antique by an expert.*

Corroborate means to support the truth of something. It is a formal word often used about public events. *Photographs corroborating reports of a UFO failed to develop.*

Bear out means to support the truth of something. *Over and over, experiments bear out Einstein's theory of relativity.*

ANTONYMS: contradict, deny, disprove

HAVE YOU HEARD…?

You may have heard people say that "the exception proves the rule." The meaning of this proverb has changed with time. The proverb used to mean that an exception *tests* a rule. If there was an exception, then the rule might not be a good or true one. You can find this meaning of *prove* in your dictionary. And a place to test new weapons is still called a "proving ground."

Gradually, however, the use of *prove* meaning "confirm" became more common than "test." People still know the proverb, but now they use it to mean that an exception shows that a rule is good or true. Because the rule works, people are saying, it is not weakened by an exception.

Confused
adjective

Confused means unable to think clearly or act correctly. *Alan's directions got us so confused that we arrived more than an hour late.*

Bewildered means confused, especially by many parts or items. *On his first day at the big school, Luis was bewildered by all the long halls and doors and hurrying students.*

Puzzled means unsure or unable to understand. *The ranger was puzzled by the strange tracks he found.*

Perplexed is a formal word that means very puzzled. *Perplexed by the new disease attacking the sheep, the vet sent for experts from the university.*

Baffled means completely puzzled. *In World War II, Navajo soldiers left the enemy baffled when they sent radio messages in a code based on the Navajo language.*

Muddled and **befuddled** mean confused. *When repair crews closed the expressway, traffic got completely muddled. The befuddled drivers clogged all nearby roads.*

The ranger was **puzzled** by the strange tracks he found.

Mixed up means confused. *Our waiter got mixed up and brought baked potatoes instead of the rice we had ordered.*

WORD POOL

Here are some words for a confusing situation. These are not synonyms but related words. If there is confusion in your mind about what they mean, look them up in your dictionary.

anarchy	disarray	tangle
bedlam	disorder	turmoil
chaos	jumble	uproar
clutter	mess	

Conquer
verb

Conquer means to defeat someone or something by great effort. *Scientists are attempting to conquer cancer.*

Overpower means to conquer completely by great strength. *Pirates overpowered our ship.*

Overwhelm means to conquer completely by great strength. *The attacking force greatly outnumbered the brave defenders and easily overwhelmed them.*

Vanquish is a formal word that means to defeat someone. *The Ashanti vanquished many nearby West African peoples during the 1700s.*

Subdue is a formal word that means to bring under control. *The rodeo rider was able to rope and subdue the calf within half a minute.*

Rout means to defeat and cause to flee. *During World War II, British forces routed the German army in the battle of El Alamein.*

Overthrow means to take away power by defeating it. *Rebels tried to overthrow the government and seize control for themselves.*

SEE **defeat** and **victory** for related words.

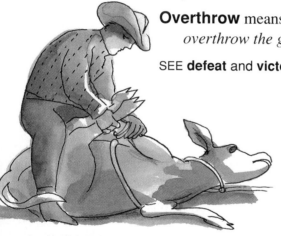

The rodeo rider was able to rope and **subdue** the calf within half a minute.

WORD STORY

You probably have noticed that many words meaning "to conquer" begin with the prefix *over-*. See if your dictionary has these: *overbear, overcome, overthrow, overturn, overwhelm.*

Why do you think these words contain *over-?* There is probably a connection with the way we say that a winning side comes out "on top."

Consider
verb

Consider means to think carefully about something before making a decision. *Sal's mother is considering a second job to help pay for the house.*

Contemplate means to consider something for a long time. *If Ray is seriously contemplating a career in the Navy, he should talk to a recruiter.*

CONTINUED ON THE NEXT PAGE

Study can mean to consider something fully and in detail. *The new library plan is being studied to ensure complete wheelchair access.*

Weigh can mean to think very carefully about something. This is a formal meaning. *Judge Liotta instructed the jury to weigh all the evidence before reaching a verdict.*

Mull over means to consider. *I'm still mulling over what to do for my science project.*

Take into account and **keep in mind** mean to include something particular in your thinking. *Ralph tries to take into account that his grandparents grew up without TV, but it is hard to keep in mind how much life has changed for them.*

SEE **decide, imagine, plan,** and **think** for related words.
ANTONYMS: disregard, ignore

Consult
verb

Consult means to talk with someone in order to make a decision. *Reggie and Marta will consult with Mr. Goldman about the drama club's next play.*

Confer means to talk in order to exchange ideas or information. *The President conferred with the Secretary of State for almost two hours this morning.*

Negotiate means to talk in order to come to an agreement. *The government of the United States has declared that it will not negotiate with terrorists.*

Parley means to hold discussions about a peace agreement, especially with an enemy. *After parleying for several days, the Crow and Blackfoot leaders agreed that both tribes would share the valley hunting grounds.*

Deliberate is a formal word that means to confer about something and consider various points of view. *The School Board is deliberating whether to close Sullivan Junior High or to make the expensive repairs that are needed.*

SEE **discuss** for related words.

The solar system **comprises** one star, nine planets, dozens of moons, and thousands of comets and asteroids.

Contain
verb

Contain means to have something inside. *Janet lives in a building that contains ninety-seven apartments.*

Hold can mean to contain. *Our football stadium holds 50,000 people.*

Include means to have as a part or parts. *Mr. Palencia sold us the mirrors for half price, including the frames.*

Accommodate means to hold conveniently or comfortably. *Sam's car accommodates only four people, but it uses very little gas.*

Comprise means to include all the parts that make up a whole. *The solar system comprises one star, nine planets, dozens of moons, and thousands of comets and asteroids.*

Keep in means not to let out. *Joey knew that if he did not bring in his homework, he would be kept in after school.*

WATCH IT!

Comprise and **compose** are used in similar sentences, but they have quite different meanings. *Compose* means to make up. *Comprise* means to include. Parts *compose* a whole. The whole *comprises* the parts. And see what happens in the passive voice. The whole *is composed **of*** the parts. A part *is comprised **in*** the whole.

You are not the first person to find this confusing—and you won't be the last.

Continue
verb

Continue means to go on. *World War II continued from 1939 until the defeat of Germany and Japan in 1945.*

Last means to continue. *The parade lasted for an hour and a half.*

Remain and **linger** can mean to continue. *Lisbet remains in poor health, with a cough that has been lingering for weeks now.*

Persist can mean to last for a long time. *The weather service expects the drought to persist all summer.*

Endure is a formal word meaning to last for a long time, especially when it is hard to do so. *Although they now live thousands of miles apart, the two women's friendship has endured since their schooldays in Moscow forty years ago.*

Keep on means to continue. *George kept on getting taller until he was nearly twenty.*

Hold on means to continue. It suggests effort or difficulty. *Once nearly extinct, the whooping crane still holds on, and its numbers are growing slowly.*

ANTONYMS: cease, stop

Control
noun

Control means the ability to direct or guide people or events. *The governor announced that the forest fires are now under control.*

Power can mean control. *Marilynn has the power to make my day with one smile.*

Authority means control, often of a particular sort. *A police officer has the authority to arrest people.*

Command can mean a position of control. *The pilot is in command of the airplane during a flight.*

Mastery means control, especially complete control. *With total mastery, the tightrope artist rode his bicycle on the high wire.*

With total **mastery,** the tightrope artist rode his bicycle on the high wire.

83

Copy
noun

The drawing is an **imitation** of the Mona Lisa, by Leonardo da Vinci.

Copy means something that is made to look like something else. *Mrs. Dobey gave Nan a copy of the pattern for the blouse.*

Duplicate means an exact copy. *Did you have a duplicate of your key made yet?*

Facsimile and **replica** mean a duplicate. *The church has a window that is a facsimile of one in Poland. A second replica is being made now for a church in San Francisco.*

Reproduction can mean a copy, often in a different form. *The art museum sells reproductions of this bronze sculpture made in Nigeria about 700 years ago.*

Carbon copy means an exact copy made by using carbon paper. *"Type this letter with three carbon copies, please," requested Mrs. Varga.* Nowadays, carbon paper is almost never used, and the phrase is almost always used to mean something very similar. *Sally is a carbon copy of her mother at that age.*

Imitation can mean a copy, usually not as good as the thing it is like. *The drawing is an imitation of the Mona Lisa, by Leonardo da Vinci.*

Counterfeit means a copy that is meant to cheat people. *The reason Dolores got that stylish designer-label bag so cheap is that it's a counterfeit.*

Clone can mean an imitation. This meaning is slang. *The group's new album, <u>Less of the Same</u>, is just a clone of their last one.*

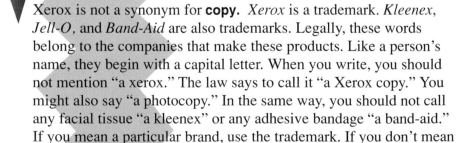

WATCH IT!

Xerox is not a synonym for **copy.** *Xerox* is a trademark. *Kleenex, Jell-O,* and *Band-Aid* are also trademarks. Legally, these words belong to the companies that make these products. Like a person's name, they begin with a capital letter. When you write, you should not mention "a xerox." The law says to call it "a Xerox copy." You might also say "a photocopy." In the same way, you should not call any facial tissue "a kleenex" or any adhesive bandage "a band-aid." If you mean a particular brand, use the trademark. If you don't mean a particular brand, use a more general word or phrase.

Correct
adjective

Correct means just as it should be, having the facts and without mistakes or faults. *Jon got the correct information from an encyclopedia.*

Right can mean correct. *My watch stopped; I don't know the right time.*

Accurate means very correct. It suggests carefulness with details. *Accurate measurements of the earth's surface are now made by lasers.*

Precise means accurate. *Sylvia gave us precise instructions.*

True can mean accurate. *Mr. McBride's scorecards are a true record of the team's games.*

Exact means perfectly accurate. It can suggest that something matches another in every way. *The two history books agree on the exact words of the letter.*

ANTONYMS: false, inaccurate, incorrect, wrong

WRITING TIP: Using Precise Language

Suppose you are helping an auto mechanic in a garage. "Bring me that tool," she asks.

"Which one?" you wonder.

"The number six socket wrench," she adds.

It's easier to repair cars when you have the right tool, the precise tool you need for the job. It's also easier to communicate when you use precise language. Have you ever written a book report with language like this?

```
This is a good book because it has an inter-
esting character and an interesting plot.
```

You can say a lot more by being precise:

```
This suspenseful historical novel tells the
story of how two teenage sisters and their
musician father are rescued from slavery by
the famous Harriet Tubman.
```

Using precise language can also help you avoid wordiness. For example, you don't need to write "just as it should be, having the facts and without mistakes or faults" when you can write "correct."

Cost
noun

Cost means what is paid for something. *I'd love to buy that skirt, but I can't afford the cost.*

Expense means the amount of money spent on something. *The committee wanted to have a live band at the school dance, but the principal disapproved of the expense.*

Expenditure can mean expense. *The state's expenditures on highway repairs have been larger than expected.*

Fare means the money that a person pays to ride on a commercial vehicle. *Andrew lost his bus fare and had to walk to school.*

Dues mean the money that a person pays to belong to a group. *Mom says that it is worth paying union dues because of the pay raises and other benefits she receives.*

Rent means the money that someone pays for the use of property. *I asked to borrow Abigail's skates, but she tried to charge me rent!*

Toll means money paid for a right or privilege, especially travel on a road or bridge. *My father has a job collecting tolls at the new bridge.*

SEE **price** for related words.

Crazy
adjective

Crazy means senseless and foolish. *Whose crazy idea was it to walk all the way home?*

Lunatic means crazy. *It's lunatic to go out in the rain with no hat or umbrella.*

Mad means very crazy and possibly dangerous. *Mr. Brady may look like a mad scientist, but he's actually a lot of fun to talk to.*

Mr. Brady may look like a **mad** scientist, but he's actually a lot of fun to talk to.

CONTINUED ON THE NEXT PAGE

Insane means mentally ill and not legally responsible. *The murderer was declared not guilty because he was insane, and he was sent to a mental hospital instead of prison.*

Loony is an informal word that means crazy and silly. *The movie has a loony plot about a dog who can read.*

SEE **foolish, hysterical,** and **peculiar** for related words.
ANTONYMS: rational, sane

WATCH IT!

There are many words that we use to describe people and things that are strange, abnormal, senseless, or just plain silly. You and your friends might call each other "crazy" or names like that and then laugh together about them. But it is not polite to use *crazy, mad, lunatic,* or *loony* in describing sick people. *Insane* is used for legal purposes. Otherwise the phrase to use is "mentally ill."

Create
verb

Create means to bring something into being. *The Johnsons created a study area for their children by putting a large table and some book-shelves in one corner of the dining room.*

Invent means to think up something completely new and bring it into being. *Thomas Edison invented the phonograph in 1877.*

Originate means to start new ideas or methods. *The ancient Greeks originated the concept of democracy.*

Devise means to invent, especially in a clever way. *Using two boards, Manuel devised a ramp to get Elena's wheelchair up the steps.*

Concoct can mean to make up something, especially a story. *As Tatum explained how her turtle laid its eggs on her homework, Mrs. Donnell wondered at her student's ability to concoct such a tale.*

Think up means to have an idea. *Tom thought up a great way to raise money for our school club.*

Dream up means to have an idea. *Clara dreamed up a solution to the lack of closet space in our apartment.*

SEE **make** for related words.

Crime
noun

Crime means an act that breaks a law. *Why are television shows so full of crimes?*

Offense means an act that breaks a law, or an act that many people think is bad. *Driving a car with a broken rear light is a minor offense, so the police officer wrote a warning ticket.*

Wrong can mean an offense. *I think Peter has done me a wrong, but he refuses to apologize.*

Misdeed is a formal word that means an offense. *The prosecutor urged the jury not to let the criminal's misdeeds go unpunished.*

Sin means an act that breaks a religious law. *The Ten Commandments forbid sins such as killing, stealing, and lying.*

Villainy is a formal or literary word meaning very wicked, harmful behavior. *The memory of Nazi villainy remains strong half a century after World War II.*

Misdemeanor is a legal term meaning a minor crime. *Speeding is a misdemeanor.*

Felony is a legal term meaning a major crime. *People in prison for certain felonies lose their right to vote.*

Malpractice means a crime against a client, especially by a doctor. *Dr. Lu's records convinced the jury that there had been no malpractice.*

Criminal
noun

Criminal means a person who breaks the law. It suggests a person who breaks many laws. *The judge sentenced the criminal to five years in prison for stealing cars.*

Crook can mean a person who breaks the law often. This meaning is informal. *The police recovered the money from the robbery, but the crooks got away.*

Outlaw means a criminal. It suggests a criminal of old times. *Robin Hood, the legendary outlaw, robbed the rich and gave to the poor.*

Bandit means a person who robs people, especially as one of a group. It suggests a criminal of old times. *Bandits stopped the stagecoach and ordered the passengers to hand over all their money.*

CONTINUED ON THE NEXT PAGE

A band of **desperadoes** invaded the little Western town.

Desperado means a bold, reckless criminal, especially of old times. *A band of desperadoes invaded the little Western town.*

Hoodlum means a criminal, especially one who is likely to hurt people. *A group of hoodlums is responsible for the series of assaults on subway passengers.*

Thug means a hoodlum. *The film of the riot showed thugs smashing windows and overturning cars.*

Gangster means a person who belongs to an organized group of criminals. *The judge was accused of accepting money from gangsters.*

Mobster means a gangster. *Mobsters smuggle illegal drugs into the United States.*

Racketeer means a gangster who uses threats of violence to get money. *Racketeers threatened to ruin the business unless its owners paid them a thousand dollars every week.*

SEE **steal** and **thief** for related words.

WRITER'S CHOICE

When my father was about ten years old a group of bandits attacked our house. There had been a very poor harvest that year, and bandits had already attacked several homes. . . . It was night when the bandits came.

—Huynh Quang Nhuong, *The Land I Lost*

Why *bandit?* When the author's father was a boy in Vietnam, the family lived in a small village. At this time, groups of robbers roamed the land, and they were especially bad during years of poor harvest because there wasn't enough food to go around. Because they robbed in groups, in old times, the author calls them bandits.

Criticize
verb

Criticize means to point out what is wrong with someone or something. *I hate to go to the movies with Pete because he criticizes everything he sees.*

Condemn means to criticize strongly and openly. *Everyone condemns cruelty to animals.*

Censure is a formal word meaning to criticize. It is used most often about public affairs. *Representative Guthrie was censured by her own party for mishandling public funds.*

Knock can mean to criticize. This meaning is informal. *Travis says he quit the swimming team because Coach Bronson always knocks him instead of helping.*

Find fault means to look for what is wrong and point it out. *I asked Don to read my report because he's so good at finding fault.*

SEE **blame, objection,** and **scold** for related words.
ANTONYMS: compliment, praise

Cross
adjective

Cross means in a bad mood. *Oliver had been carrying the drum for an hour, and he was feeling cross.*

Cranky and **crabby** mean becoming angry easily and grumbling about everything. *Margo woke up cranky this morning. After she had breakfast and walked to school, she felt less crabby.*

Irritable, touchy, and **disagreeable** mean easily annoyed. *Mr. Dunda's bad headaches make him irritable. He's never touchy except when he's in pain. Even then, he tries not to be disagreeable.*

Grumpy and **grouchy** mean bad-tempered and complaining. *After three days of camping in the rain, the scouts are getting grumpy. Once the sun comes out, they'll forget how grouchy they were.*

Ornery means bad-tempered or difficult. *That ornery dog in the junkyard growls at everyone who goes by.*

Disgruntled means discontented and in a bad mood for a reason. *The disgruntled customer returned the faulty radio to the store.*

SEE **anger** and **mad** for related words.
ANTONYMS: good-natured, pleasant

Crowd
noun

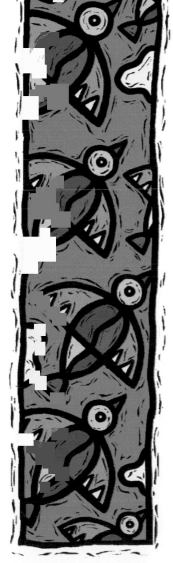

A group of birds
is called a **flock.**

Crowd means a large group of people together. *Huge crowds filled the Colosseum in ancient Rome to watch the gladiators.*

Mob means a crowd, especially a noisy and violent one. *The mob made so much noise that the governor returned to her helicopter.*

Multitude means a very large crowd. *At his funeral, a multitude of people poured into the streets to honor the Italian composer Verdi.*

Flock can mean a crowd. *A flock of preschoolers came running out the door of the daycare center.*

Swarm can mean a crowd moving together. *Every weekday morning and evening, swarms of commuters pour through the train station.*

Drove can mean a swarm. *Shoppers eager to take advantage of the sale turned up in droves.*

Throng means a crowd. It suggests that people are moving and pushing around. *Throngs of happy citizens poured into the streets to celebrate the end of World War II.*

Horde means a rough crowd of people. *A horde of angry customers demanded their money back.*

SEE **company** for related words.

WORD POOL

Flock, swarm, and *drove* are all words that mean a group of animals of some kind: a flock of sheep or birds, a swarm of insects, a drove of cattle. Many groups of animals have particular names of their own. Although these names were in use hundreds of years ago, many of them are not used today.

clowder of cats	gang of elk	rag of colts
charm of finches	knot of toads	school of fish
dray of squirrels	labor of moles	shrewdness of apes
drift of hogs	leap of leopards	skulk of foxes
exaltation of larks	nest of rabbits	tribe of goats
flight of swallows	pace of asses	watch of nightingales
gaggle of geese	pride of lions	wedge of swans

Cruel
adjective

Cruel means willing to give or see pain. *Even before the Civil War, some Southerners believed keeping people in slavery was cruel.*

Vicious can mean deliberately cruel. *Black Beauty was badly treated by his vicious owner.*

Brutal and **inhumane** mean very cruel and lacking human feeling. *When we hear of the brutal things done in war, we can hardly believe that people were so inhumane.*

Merciless means completely lacking in mercy. *The king's tax collectors went about their business in merciless fashion.*

Pitiless means merciless. *The pitiless slaughter of whales went on for years and years.*

Ruthless means merciless and brutal. *Josef Stalin was a ruthless dictator who had millions of people killed.*

Cold-blooded can mean calmly cruel. *The cold-blooded gangsters showed no sense of guilt in court.*

SEE **fierce** and **unkind** for related words.
ANTONYMS: kind, merciful

Cry
verb

Cry means to shed tears. *In every part of the refugee camp, sick and hungry children were crying.*

Weep means to cry. It is a slightly more formal word. *The music was so beautiful that some members of the audience wept.*

Sob means to cry with short, quick breaths. *Glenn sobbed as he searched the park for his lost watch.*

Bawl means to cry loudly. *The lost child in the supermarket bawled until his mother found him.*

Wail means to cry with long moans. *My grandmother started to wail as they lowered the coffin into the ground.*

Blubber means to cry with many tears and much noise. *It's embarrassing, but every time I see Lassie Come Home, I blubber.*

Whimper means to cry with low, whining sounds. *Everett whimpered when he looked in the mirror and saw his blemishes.*

SEE **misery, pain, sad,** and **sorrow** for related words.

Curious
adjective

Curious means eager to know more. *The bear is curious about the possibility of getting honey from the beehive.*

Inquiring means interested in many subjects and eager to learn about them. *The ancient Greeks were famous for their inquiring minds.*

Inquisitive means extremely curious, especially about other people's lives. *Norma is quite inquisitive; she always asks where I went and who was with me.*

Prying means inquisitive in an unpleasant way. *"Would it be a prying question if I asked how you got that black eye?" Tim asked Jackie.*

Nosy is an informal word that means prying. *The nosy neighbor always comes past when we get the mail.*

Snoopy is an informal word that means prying in a sneaky way. *For a week, the snoopy reporter concealed herself in a bush next to the candidate's house.*

ANTONYM: uninterested

WORD STORY

Snoopy comes from a Dutch word meaning "to eat in secret." Snooping is something you try to do in secret too.

The bear is **curious** about the possibility of getting honey from the beehive.

93

Cut
verb

Lightning from the storm last night **split** that tree.

Cut means to divide or remove with something sharp. *Vanya cut several slices of bread from the freshly baked loaf.* *"Please cut that baked chicken recipe out of the paper, Hollis," requested her mother.*

Carve means to cut something by moving a knife back and forth through it. *Aunt Kathleen carved the turkey last Thanksgiving.*

Slice means to carve. *The man at the deli counter sliced half a pound of roast beef for me.*

Split means to cut, usually from end to end. *Lightning from the storm last night split that tree.*

Saw means to cut with short back-and-forth strokes. *The carpenter sawed boards for the roof of the house.*

Chop means to cut something by hitting it with a sharp tool. *Mom chopped the fallen tree branches into firewood.*

Dissect means to cut open an animal or plant for scientific research. *Mrs. Kessler will show the class how to dissect earthworms.*

Butcher can mean to cut an animal into parts for food. *Mr. Sampson butchers the deer that the hunters bring home.*

Trim means to cut off parts that are not needed or are not neat. *Mom trims the extra fat from the steak before cooking it.*

Clip means to remove most of something, using shears, scissors, or clippers. *We clip our cat's nails to keep him from scratching the furniture.*

Snip means to cut something off with small, quick strokes. *Because the vase was short, I snipped several inches off the flower stalks.*

Shave means to cut off hair with a razor. *Erica loves to rub her hand along her father's smooth face after he has shaved.*

Shear can mean to cut wool off a sheep. *Sam found that wool just sheared from the sheep was pretty rough.*

Prune can mean to cut branches off a bush or tree. *Pruning young trees makes them bear more fruit.*

Amputate means to cut off a part of the body. *The soldier's leg, badly wounded in battle, had to be amputated.*

CONTINUED ON THE NEXT PAGE

Sometimes when a word is added to a verb, it creates a phrase that has special meaning. Here are some phrases with **cut:**

Cut down can mean to take less or use less of something. *My dentist says to cut down on sweets.*

Cut off can mean to stop or block. *"Hurry!" cried the sheriff. "We can cut off those rustlers at the mountain pass."*

Cut out can mean to stop doing something. *"I told you to cut out that arguing," said Mr. Jones.*

Cut up can mean to hurt someone's feelings. *She was badly cut up by his insults.*

Cute
adjective

Cute means pleasing or good-looking. It is a general word used to show liking and approval. *The kittens were all so cute I had a hard time deciding which one I wanted.*

Attractive means interesting and pleasing to look at. *Benito's apartment is very attractive.*

Appealing means attractive and enjoyable. *Dusty says her new stepfather has a very appealing personality.*

Amusing means pleasantly entertaining and interesting. *I like spending time with Chantal because she is amusing.*

Charming means pleasant and fascinating. *Princess Diana is famous for her smile, which is both shy and charming.*

Adorable can mean very attractive. This meaning is informal. *Wet, my terrier looks like a drowned rat; dry, she's adorable.*

Enchanting means very charming. *The Mendozas find their first grandchild totally enchanting.*

SEE **beautiful** and **nice** for related words.

You may think that toads look horrible,
But toads find other toads adorable.

Dainty
adjective

Dainty means pretty and small. *In the Middle Ages, women had dainty prayer books that fit into the palms of their hands.*

Delicate means pretty in a way that is weak, thin, or light. *Aunt Kay has a favorite delicate seashell that she keeps high out of reach.*

Fine can mean with many small parts and needing very precise skill. *This model of the school, ten inches tall, has many fine details.*

Exquisite means beautiful and with many small parts. *The old dress was trimmed with lace as exquisite and delicate as a spider's web.*

ANTONYMS: coarse, crude

Damp
adjective

Damp means slightly wet, often in an unpleasant way. *Miguel's palms and forehead were damp, and his sore throat was getting worse.*

Moist means slightly wet, often in a pleasant way. *In the flower shop, the air smells of rich, moist soil.*

Humid means having a lot of moisture in the air. *We left fingerprints on everything we touched that humid afternoon.*

Muggy means hot and humid. *The day was muggy, and my shirt kept sticking to my back.*

Clammy means damp and cold. *Snakes look clammy, but in fact they're as dry as humans.*

Dank means damp all the time. *Deanna ruined her stamp collection by storing it in that dank basement—all the glue stuck!*

SEE **wet** for related words.

Danger
noun

Danger means a chance of harm or injury. *Road signs warn drivers of danger ahead.*

Risk means a chance of harm or loss. *Lynn wonders if the view would be worth the risk of the climb.*

Jeopardy is a somewhat formal word that means danger or risk. *Hundreds of lives were put in jeopardy when the jet airplane lost its left engine.*

Hazard means a likely cause of injury or misfortune. *The hazards of mining include cave-ins, explosions, and flooding.*

Threat can mean a possible cause of injury or misfortune. *The weather forecaster warned of the threat of a statewide blizzard.*

Menace means a threat. *"To somebody on crutches," Lars explained, "stairs can be a real menace."*

Peril means great danger that is difficult to avoid. *The house was in great peril as the tornado approached.*

SEE **dangerous** and **harm** for related words.
ANTONYM: safety

The house was in great **peril** as the tornado approached.

Dangerous
adjective

Dangerous means likely to cause injury or harm. *Yelling insults at a superhero is a dangerous thing for a movie villain to do.*

Unsafe means dangerous. *Bilal could see that the leaky boat was unsafe.*

Risky means involving a chance of injury or harm. *Sarah doesn't ride her bike after dark because it's risky.*

Hazardous and **perilous** mean full of danger. *The winding mountain roads were hazardous, and darkness made them especially perilous.*

Precarious means with a chance of danger at any time. *The mountain goat stands in a precarious position at the edge of a cliff.*

On thin ice is an idiom that means in a dangerous situation. *"If you keep talking back to me," T. J.'s mother warned, "you're on thin ice for sure!"*

SEE **danger** and **harm** for related words.
ANTONYMS: harmless, safe

The mountain goat stands in a **precarious** position at the edge of a cliff.

Dark
adjective

Dark means with little or no light. *As winter approaches, the days grow dark earlier.*

Shadowy means dark with shadows. *The path under the trees was shadowy and cool.*

Dusky means in twilight or as if in twilight. *The dog trotted down the dusky road as the light faded from the sky.*

Dim means so dark that things cannot be seen clearly. *Olga stumbled over a locked chest in the dim hall.*

Gloomy and **somber** mean dark and cheerless. *Poor and lonely, the poet left his gloomy room and walked the somber winter streets.*

Pitch-dark and **pitch-black** mean with no light at all. *Mina woke in the pitch-dark forest and groped for her flashlight. The moon had been bright when she went to sleep, but now the sky was full of pitch-black clouds.*

SEE **dim** for related words.
ANTONYMS: bright, light

WRITER'S CHOICE

It seemed to Thomas as though they had waited for hours. He couldn't see a foot in front of him where he lay in the trees surrounding the clearing. He was not to talk, nor could he move very much. This scaring of the Darrows wasn't at all like he had imagined it earlier, when it was still day. Now he was chilled through to the bone, lying low on his stomach in the pitch-black night. He couldn't see his father where he, too, lay in wait, a short distance away.

—Virginia Hamilton, *The House of Dies Drear*

Why *pitch-black?* Thomas, his father, and some others are lying in the woods at night, hoping to scare the Darrow brothers out of committing a crime. The plan depends on surprise, so Thomas and the others have no light with them. Even if there are stars and a moon, the trees shut them out, making the night seem without any light at all.

Dead
adjective

Dead means no longer alive. *My cat Midnight sometimes brings home dead birds.*

Deceased means recently dead. *Reverend Bledsoe reminded the family about their deceased grandfather's many good deeds.*

Departed is a euphemism for dead. *Folktales often tell how the spirits of the departed linger in familiar places.* See the Writing Tip below.

Late can mean dead, usually within living memory. *"We gather here today to honor the late Mayor," said Rabbi Bronstein, "and to keep her memory alive."*

Lifeless means with no signs of life. *The lifeless bodies of hundreds of sea birds lay in the oil spill.*

Extinct means all dead. It refers to an entire species or larger group. *Dinosaurs have been extinct for millions of years.*

ANTONYMS: alive, live

WRITING TIP: Euphemism

Euphemism (yü′fə miz′əm) comes from Greek words meaning "good speaking." Euphemisms are words used to make ideas sound better. For example, some people find death too disturbing to speak of directly. Many gentler words and phrases can replace direct words like *die*. Some of these euphemisms are *pass, pass away, pass on,* and *breathe one's last.* Others, which push away sadness with humor, include *kick the bucket, bite the dust, buy the farm,* and *push up the daisies.* Another group of euphemisms has a religious content: *go to one's reward, awake to life immortal,* and *meet one's Maker.*

When you write, think about your reader. If you are writing a letter to a friend or relative about someone who has died, the gentler word or phrase is probably more suitable. On the other hand, if you are writing a report on the Civil War, the direct word or phrase may be the better choice. You may also want to think about your subject. It might be fine to write or say humorously, "Oh well, another great idea just bit the dust," but you would not want to use that kind of language about a real person.

What other ideas do people often use euphemisms for?

Deal
noun

Deal means an arrangement for trade or exchange. This meaning is informal. *Lucy thought that trading three cat's-eye marbles for a circus ticket was a pretty good deal.*

Bargain means a deal. *William Penn made a fair bargain with the Indians, who remained friendly to the colonists.*

Transaction is a formal word meaning a deal. *Selling his services to a Northern shipbuilding company was the first legal transaction Frederick Douglass had ever made.*

Agreement means an arrangement to act in certain ways. *I thought we had an agreement: you'd vacuum and do the bathroom, and I'd do the laundry and wash the kitchen floor.*

Understanding can mean an agreement, usually an unwritten one. *Cyril and Toby have an understanding: if Cyril leaves Toby's things alone, Toby will leave Cyril's things alone.*

Contract means a legal agreement. *The third baseman has signed a contract for a total of $6,000,000.*

Compact and **pact** are formal words that mean an agreement, especially a political one. *The two senators entered into a compact to support each other for reelection. Several environmental groups, however, made a pact to oppose those two senators.*

Accord is a formal word that can mean a compact. *In 1818 the United States and Great Britain reached an accord permitting citizens of both countries to settle and trade in the Oregon region.*

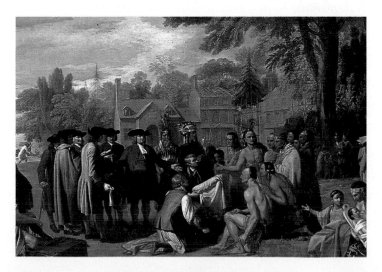

William Penn made a fair **bargain** with the Indians, who remained friendly to the colonists.

Deceive
verb

Deceive means to make someone believe something that is not true. *Denise deceived us by saying she had made the sweater she bought.*

Mislead can mean to deceive. *The ads try to mislead people by making cigarettes seem healthy.*

Fool can mean to deceive in a harmless or joking way. *César fooled us into thinking he really could play the clarinet.*

Bluff means to deceive, especially by pretending to have confidence. *Despite her doubts, Kiyo managed to bluff her way through the interview.*

Hoax means to deceive. It suggests a mischievous trick. *The newspaper hoaxed its readers with an April Fool's story that Australia was drifting northwards.*

Pull the wool over someone's eyes is an idiom meaning to deceive someone. *The salesman really pulled the wool over Rene's eyes when he told her this jacket was of high quality.*

Pull someone's leg is an idiom that means to hoax. *I think Ed was just pulling your leg when he claimed to know karate.*

SEE **cheat** and **trick** for related words.

Decide
verb

Decide means to make up your mind. *It was such a hot day that we decided to go to the city swimming pool.*

Determine means to decide firmly, often from several choices. *Jolene is still trying to determine which hairdo looks best on her.*

Resolve means to decide firmly. *In Gone with the Wind, a starving Scarlett O'Hara resolved never to go hungry again.*

Conclude can mean to decide after thinking it over. *The police concluded that the driver who caused the accident had been drinking.*

Settle means to decide finally. *Bella thinks Sally should settle on a ponytail.*

Rule can mean to decide publicly and with authority. *The referee ruled that the ball was out of bounds.*

SEE **choose** for related words.

CONTINUED ON THE NEXT PAGE

President Harry Truman

You may have heard someone say that "the buck stops here." The person who says this means that he or she is the person who decides about something and takes responsibility for it. President Harry Truman is famous for using this phrase to show that as head of the United States government, he had to decide what to do for the country.

More than a hundred years ago, people playing cards used a coin or other marker to show whose turn it was to deal the cards. This marker was called a *buck,* and it moved around the table as people took turns. Where the buck stopped, that player was responsible for the next deal. "Passing the buck" is still used to mean trying to avoid responsibility for deciding.

Decorate
verb

Decorate means to make something look good by adding things to it. *Liam's classroom was decorated with flags from all the countries that once were home to the students' families.*

Ornament means to decorate. *Earl ornaments his hat with all kinds of buttons.*

Adorn is a formal word meaning to decorate. *Archaeologists have discovered ancient paintings adorning the walls of caves.*

Beautify means to make something more beautiful. *Reverend Samson asked everyone to help beautify the chapel by painting the walls and polishing the brass.*

Trim can mean to decorate, especially around the outside or the edges. *Her aunt and her grandmother have been trimming Bea's wedding dress for months.*

Garnish means to decorate something, especially food. *In the Middle Ages, cooks garnished foods with marigolds and roses.*

Decrease
verb

Decrease means to make or become less. *Gabriel's mother suggested he decrease the salt in the meat loaf next time.*

Lessen means to decrease. *As she spoke, Sachie's anxiety about her report began to lessen.*

Diminish means to decrease. *Dawn Flower's fever diminished, and she began to feel better.*

Reduce means to make less. *A nutritionist gave a lecture to the sixth and seventh graders about reducing fat and sugar in their diets.*

Dwindle means to become less. *As winter wore on, the supply of hay for the livestock began to dwindle.*

Taper means to become less, especially in a gradual but steady way. *The number of robberies has tapered off since we started the neighborhood watch.*

Cut back means to reduce. *Dahlia rattled her piggy bank and figured she'd have to cut back her spending on movies.*

SEE **shorten** and **shrink** for related words.
ANTONYMS: add, increase

Defeat
verb

Defeat means to win against someone in a game or fight. *Our basketball team was defeated by a score of 64 to 62.*

Beat can mean to defeat. *Many scientists believe that with enough time and research, we can beat AIDS.*

Best can mean to defeat. *Bested in the 100-yard dash, Willie won the mile race.*

Trounce can mean to defeat completely. *The mayor trounced his opponent in the election.*

Lick and **whip** can mean to defeat completely. These meanings are informal. *Pedro has licked his problems with math, and now he helps other kids whip their problems.*

SEE **conquer** and **victory** for related words.

Defect
noun

Defect means a part that is wrong with something. *The first sweater Bruce knitted had a few defects.*

Fault means a defect. *A fault in the wiring plunged the hotel into darkness.*

Imperfection can mean a defect. *There is a slight imperfection in the corner of this rug.*

Flaw means a small defect, especially a small crack or opening. *Closely examining the telescope, Bruce discovered a tiny flaw in one lens.*

Blemish means a defect that isn't serious but looks bad. *The hot pan left a blemish on the tabletop.*

Glitch is a slang word that means a defect preventing something from working right. *The glitch in the school intercom probably won't be fixed until next week.*

Bug can mean a defect that prevents something from working properly. This meaning is informal. *Mateo's computer program has a bug in it that stops the printer.*

WORD STORY
Glitch comes from a Yiddish word that means "slip" or "skid." When something develops a glitch, it's as if it slips out of the way it should be going.

The first sweater Bruce knitted had a few **defects.**

Definite
adjective

Definite means clear and exact. *"Molly needs a definite answer: will you buy her guitar or not?" asked Jim.*

Clear-cut can mean definite. *Daley has a clear-cut choice—he can apologize, or he can forget about coming to my party.*

Distinct can mean definite and unmistakable. *Since Jonah had played the game before, he had a distinct advantage over me.*

Decided means definite and unquestionable. *Georgia's smile faded, and her eyes took on a look of decided annoyance.*

Explicit means clearly and fully stated. *Sonya gave us explicit directions for getting to her house.*

SEE **clear** and **correct** for related words.

Sonya gave us **explicit** directions for getting to her house.

Deliberate
adjective

Deliberate means done on purpose after careful thought. *It was a mistake, not a deliberate lie.*

Intentional means deliberate. It emphasizes the purpose. *Mr. McKinnon gave the class a letter with six intentional mistakes for them to correct.*

Intended means planned. It is commonly used to describe effects or results. *The intended effect of the park is to suggest a Japanese garden.*

Voluntary means done by free choice. *Today, all United States military service is voluntary.*

Calculated can mean done on purpose. It emphasizes planning. *Beatriz remained silent in a calculated effort to attract attention.*

SEE **careful** and **plan** for related words.

Delicious
adjective

Delicious means very pleasing and satisfying, especially to the senses of taste and smell. *This pie is delicious.*

Luscious means sweet and rich in taste. *The luscious fresh raspberries were served with whipped cream.*

Scrumptious is an informal word that means delicious. *Ladonna's mom gave us oatmeal cookies, and they were scrumptious.*

Yummy is an informal word that means delicious. *"Ooh, that looks yummy," Garland said, as his mother spread icing on the cake.*

Delectable is a somewhat formal word that means delicious. *This banana cream pie is a delight to the eye and delectable to the tongue.*

SEE **tasty** for related words.

WORD STORY

Delicious, luscious, and *delectable* all come from a Latin word meaning "to attract." So do *delight, delicacy,* and *delicatessen.* Because these words came into English at different times and in different ways, they developed various meanings. *Luscious,* for example, probably started as a short way of saying *delicious.* When the sound changed, it got its own idea, of rich sweetness. If word history had a motto, it might be, "Out of one, many."

Descend
verb

Descend means to come down. *Rob can descend the hill in his wheelchair faster than we can walk down.*

Drop can mean to go down suddenly. *Salina rushed back to get her jacket because the temperature had dropped 20 degrees during the night.*

Land can mean to descend from the sky. *The plane had to land suddenly when a passenger became ill during the flight.*

Sink means to descend slowly or gradually. *Christy's chin sank onto her chest as she learned the disappointing news.*

Dive can mean to go down suddenly. *We saw the falcon dive at its prey.*

Take a nosedive means to descend quickly at a steep angle, head first. *The jet took a nosedive, but the pilot got the engine started again and leveled off the aircraft.*

SEE **fall** for related words.
ANTONYMS: ascend, rise

We saw the falcon **dive** at its prey.

Describe
verb

Describe means to tell about someone or something. *In her report, Ramona described the natural beauty of the Grand Canyon.*

Portray can mean to describe. *In <u>Uncle Tom's Cabin</u>, Harriet Beecher Stowe portrayed life under slavery.*

Characterize means to describe the special qualities of someone or something. *Dachshunds are characterized by short legs and a long body.*

Represent can mean to describe, often in an untruthful way. *The man at the door represented himself as a fire inspector, but he left quickly when Mrs. Luna asked him for identification.*

Detail means to describe something fully, telling even the smallest facts. *Mr. Moravcik will detail for us what math assignments are due this week.*

CONTINUED ON THE NEXT PAGE

In your writing, details will help to describe the sights, sounds, and feelings you want to communicate. Specific words portray a scene so that your readers can picture it in their minds. If you want to describe a rich person's living room, you can show it as immense by using details such as vast windows that stretch its entire length and overlook a city skyline. To describe a cozy kitchen, you can mention bright curtains at windows overlooking a well-tended flower garden.

Characters also become clearer as you choose details to describe them. For example, you might describe one character as teen-aged, size six, with a sunburn, wearing a pony-tail and glasses. A character described as middle-aged, scrawny, balding, with bad teeth and a sneering smile comes across as a very different person.

Deserve
verb

Deserve means to be worthy of something, either good or bad, in return for something you have done. *Principal di Leo said our class deserved a lot of credit for our work on the science fair.*

Earn can mean to deserve. *If Brenda wants to be debate captain, she'll have to earn it.*

Rate can mean to deserve. This meaning is informal. *Andrea and I think your sketch rates a first prize.*

Merit is a formal word that means to deserve. *Felipe's work with the neighborhood youth center merits special recognition.*

Warrant is a formal word that can mean to deserve. It suggests that there is good reason for something. *When the band won a first in the state competition, the teachers felt this warranted a special concert.*

SEE **value** for related words.

> " Those who deny freedom to others deserve it not for themselves. "
>
> — Abraham Lincoln (1809–1865)

Destroy
verb

Destroy means to put an end to something, often by breaking or pulling it to pieces. *The buffalo stampede destroyed the cornfield.*

Demolish means to smash to pieces. *An earthquake can demolish buildings.*

Wreck means to break something so completely that it cannot be fixed. *During last night's storm, lightning wrecked the gas station sign.*

Ruin means to make something worthless or useless. *If Paul doesn't stop sliding around in the dirt like that, he's going to ruin his jeans.*

Spoil means to ruin. *We should take the rug out of the basement before the damp floor spoils it.*

Annihilate means to destroy so completely that nothing remains. *The rockets annihilated the village.*

Devastate means to destroy completely. It suggests a large area of destruction. *The hurricane devastated thousands of acres of the sugar cane crop.*

Tear down means to demolish. *Mr. Lu's company will tear down the old barn and build a theater there.*

Wipe out means to annihilate. *Lava from the volcano wiped out the trees and buildings on the north side of the island.*

SEE **break** and **harm** for related words.
ANTONYMS: create, make

The buffalo stampede **destroyed** the cornfield.

Different
adjective

Different means not alike. *Edgar and Edwin try hard to be different, because they don't want to be known as "the twins."*

Various means different. It is used when there are many different things. *Every morning, Babur opens his family's shop and sets out the thirty baskets of various spices.*

Miscellaneous means of many sorts, not all the same. It may suggest no effort to choose. *My sister collects only clear marbles, but she keeps some miscellaneous ones to trade.*

Varied means of many sorts. It suggests that the differences are planned. *Good nutrition means eating varied wholesome foods, not just your favorites.*

Diverse means varied. *Sue reads books on many diverse subjects.*

Mixed means of many kinds combined together. *Connie thinks "Mixed Nuts" would be a good name for our comedy act.*

Assorted means mixed. *I always choose assorted jellybean flavors because I can never decide on just one flavor.*

ANTONYMS: alike, identical, same, similar

 WATCH IT !

Various and **varied** look alike, but they have different meanings. Consider the sentence: "This restaurant offers a *varied* menu." This sentence emphasizes that the differences are planned. But the sentence "The leaves turn *various* colors in the fall" emphasizes the many different kinds of colors.

The leaves turn **various** colors in the fall.

Dig
verb

Dig means to make a hole in the ground. *The map says to dig for the treasure under the big oak tree.*

Excavate is a formal word that means to dig. *The tour guide explained how workers excavated the Erie Canal using only hand tools.*

Unearth means to dig up. *The Wilson's dog Rocket buries bones in the yard and unearths them weeks later.*

Mine means to dig something valuable out of the earth. *People have mined tin and copper for thousands of years.*

Tunnel means to dig an underground passage. *The prisoners tried to tunnel their way under the dungeon walls.*

Burrow means to dig. It usually describes an animal. *The prairie dog peered out of the hole where it was burrowing.*

Dim
adjective

Dim means not easy to see, hear, or understand. *Principal Robertson's voice was so dim on the intercom that we didn't hear him announce the assembly.*

Unclear can mean hard to understand. *The reasons why his team hasn't won a game are unclear to Quincy.*

Indistinct means too dim to tell for sure. *The indistinct face in the yearbook photograph is either Alejandro or Lester.*

Obscure means hard to see or understand. *The lawyers argued about an obscure legal question.*

Vague means not sharp or precise. *Irma's memories of her grandparents are vague.*

Blurred means having vague outlines or edges. *No one understands the blurred drawings on the cave wall.*

Fuzzy can mean blurred. *If I don't have my glasses on, even big signs look fuzzy.*

Faint means dim and hardly noticeable. *"I can't read this handout," said Tammy. "The words are too faint."*

SEE **dark** for related words.
ANTONYMS: bright, clear, definite, distinct

The diver **plunged** into the still water of the lake.

Dip
verb

Dip means to stick something into a liquid and take it out right away. *Elena dipped a spoon into the stew to get a taste.*

Dunk means to dip. It is used about food. *Mr. Vargas dunked his doughnut in his coffee.*

Douse means to wet something by sticking it into a liquid. *David doused the bread in batter and laid it in the frying pan.*

Submerge means to go under or put under the surface of a liquid for a while. *When the river is high, the basements on this side of town become submerged.*

Plunge means to submerge suddenly and forcefully. *The diver plunged into the still water of the lake.*

Soak can mean to put something into a liquid and leave it there for a while. *Before cooking dried beans, you should soak them in water overnight.*

Steep means to soak, especially in order to transfer a flavor. *My stepfather steeps his tea a long time.*

Dirty
adjective

Dirty means not clean. *Our dog Max was too dirty to be allowed inside the car.*

Soiled means made dirty. *Andre's soiled shirt couldn't be cleaned, so he used it as a rag.*

Filthy means extremely dirty. *Dad told Terry to wash his filthy hands outside and not in the clean sink.*

Grimy means filthy. *Ethan and Jonathon tried to peek through the grimy window of the old barn.*

Grubby means filthy. *Kate felt grubby after two days without a shower.*

Foul can mean so dirty that it is disgusting. *The soldiers pushed the prisoners into a foul, stinking dungeon.*

Smudged means marked with streaks of dirt. *The police noticed that the carpet was smudged where something had been dragged across it.*

Stained means marked with a color that will not wash out. *We're hoping to sell the stained white chair at the yard sale.*

Dingy means dirty looking, especially from long use. *The old tomcat likes to curl up on the dingy blanket in the alley.*

Polluted means dirty and dangerous to use. *Mona drinks bottled water because her parents think the city water is polluted.*

SEE **pollute** and **stain** for related words.
ANTONYM: clean

Disappear
verb

Disappear means to go from sight. *Arlene turned off the TV, and the picture disappeared.*

Vanish means to disappear, usually suddenly and often mysteriously. *The magician will now make her assistant vanish from the stage.*

Evaporate can mean to disappear the way water does when it turns to vapor. *The bad feelings between Lana and Crystal evaporated when Lana broke her arm.*

Fade can mean to disappear slowly. *As the sun rises, stars fade away.*

ANTONYM: appear

Disappoint
verb

Disappoint means not to keep a promise to someone. *Curtis promised to play with his sisters and won't disappoint them.*

Fail can mean to be of no use when needed. *The flashlight failed because the batteries were too old.*

Betray can mean to hurt someone who trusts you, on purpose. *When Babette heard what Alyx had said about her, she felt betrayed.*

Let down can mean to disappoint or hurt the feelings of someone who trusts you. *We were very hopeful that this drug would stop the fungus, but it has let us down.*

Disaster
noun

Disaster means something very bad that happens suddenly. *Disasters such as the 1989 San Francisco earthquake remind us of nature's awesome power.*

Calamity means a disaster that causes great damage or suffering. *The oil spill was a calamity that should never have happened.*

Catastrophe means a huge disaster with terribly destructive effects. *It will be years before the city recovers from the catastrophe of the hurricane.*

Tragedy can mean an event that causes great sadness. *The long war in Vietnam was a tragedy for millions of people.*

Blow can mean a sudden event that causes sadness or distress. *The firing of the football coach was a great blow to the team.*

Shock can mean a sudden event that causes fear or grief. *The shock of waking up in a burning house caused Enrique to have nightmares for months.*

Disasters such as the 1989 San Francisco earthquake remind us of nature's awesome power.

WORD STORY

Disaster comes from an old French word meaning "unfavorable star." Long ago, many people believed that bad things were caused by unfavorable positions of the stars and other heavenly bodies. Some people still do.

Discount
adjective

Discount means costing less than the regular or listed price. *The Tombas got a discount fare because they took a late-night flight.*

Reduced means lower in price than before. *Arnetta bought her heavy coat at a reduced price in February.*

Cut-rate means sold at lowered prices, but it also suggests that the value of the item may not be good. *This cut-rate skirt came apart when Rita washed it, so it was no bargain.*

Budget can mean sold at low prices that help save money. *Tori says this budget shampoo is as good as more expensive brands.*

Wholesale can mean sold at the prices that store owners pay for merchandise. *The Friedkins got their sofa at a factory outlet store for the wholesale price.*

On sale means sold at lowered prices. *Everything in the store was on sale that day.*

Marked down means on sale. *All these marked down tapes cost only five dollars.*

Everything in the store was **on sale** that day.

SEE **cheap** for related words.

116

Discouraged
adjective

Discouraged means having lost courage, confidence, or enthusiasm. *Sharon became discouraged when she found that all the tapes she wanted were sold.*

Downhearted means discouraged. *We were downhearted when our dog, Mugsy, didn't come home for the third night in a row.*

Dejected means discouraged. *Not making the football team left Ricardo dejected.*

Downcast can mean downhearted. *Loud Thunder, returning empty-handed from another hunt, was downcast.*

Disheartened means discouraged enough to lose hope. It suggests sadness that lasts for a while. *The whole town has been disheartened by the layoffs at the auto plant.*

Dismayed means discouraged and afraid. *The candidate was dismayed when the polls showed her far behind.*

Down in the dumps is an idiom that means downhearted. *Ray has been down in the dumps since Dana broke up with him.*

SEE **hopeless** and **sad** for related words.
ANTONYMS: encouraged, heartened

Sharon became **discouraged** when she found that all the tapes she wanted were sold.

WORD STORY

You have probably noticed that several words and phrases meaning "discouraged" begin with *down*. In fact, the word *down* itself can mean discouraged: *Chris is feeling down because he didn't make the team.*

Why do you think that *down* and *down-* are used this way? There is probably a connection with the way we speak of "low spirits" or "the depths of despair."

Discuss
verb

Discuss means to talk about something, hearing several opinions. *The neighborhood store owners met last night to discuss the problem of vacant buildings.*

Debate can mean to discuss something in a formal way, with each person taking a turn to speak and reply. *Jesse and Kayla will debate what should be done about air pollution.*

Kick around is an informal phrase that can mean to discuss something in order to think it through. *At the meeting we'll kick around some theme ideas for the dance.*

Talk turkey is an idiom that means to discuss something in a serious, honest way. *Mr. Cruz and the mechanic talked turkey about how much the car repairs would cost.*

Chew the fat and **shoot the breeze** are idioms that mean to discuss whatever comes to mind in a casual, friendly way. *After work, Mom likes to sit and chew the fat with the other mail carriers. On weekends, she goes over and shoots the breeze with Aunt Casey.*

SEE **consult** for related words.

Dishonest
adjective

Dishonest means willing to lie, cheat, or steal. *A dishonest accountant stole $4,000 from the business.*

Crooked can mean dishonest. It expresses contempt. *That man was so crooked his own dog didn't trust him.*

Deceitful means willing to deceive. *Voters will not elect someone they believe is deceitful.*

Lying means not telling the truth. *The lying witness tried to mislead the jury.*

Untruthful can mean not telling the truth. *Since she is known to have been untruthful many times in the past, people tend not to believe her.*

Corrupt is a formal word that means dishonest, usually for money. It is often used about people in public life. *The FBI videotaped the corrupt judge accepting a bribe.*

ANTONYMS: honest, truthful

Dislike
noun

Dislike means a feeling of not liking someone or something. *Teresa has a real dislike for long bus rides.*

Distaste means a strong dislike. *Tanya's distaste for cold weather is even stronger now than when she first came to Chicago.*

Disgust means an extreme dislike of something physically unpleasant. *The smell of the garbage truck filled us with disgust.*

Disfavor is a formal word that means a mild dislike. *A suggestion to convert the village fishponds into rice fields met with general disfavor.*

Displeasure is another formal word that means a slight anger or dislike. *Frowning with displeasure, the empress rejected the architects' plans for the summer palace.*

Disapproval means dislike of something because it is bad. *The students showed their disapproval of the movie by protesting outside the theater.*

SEE **hate** for related words.
ANTONYM: fondness

The smell of the garbage truck filled us with **disgust.**

Disloyal
adjective

Disloyal means betraying and not faithful. *Hernán has many friends because he is never disloyal to them.*

Faithless means disloyal. It is a somewhat formal word, usually found in books. *Benedict Arnold was faithless to the American Revolutionary cause.*

Treacherous and **traitorous** are formal words that mean disloyal, especially to your country. *The treacherous scientist passed secret plans to the enemy. He was put in jail when his traitorous activities were discovered.*

Double-crossing is an informal word that means disloyal, especially to a friend or partner. *When their business broke up, Mrs. Prescott accused her partner of being a double-crossing thief.*

Two-timing is a slang word that means double-crossing. *When Fingers Flynn vanished with all the loot, the other robbers called him a two-timing rat.*

ANTONYMS: faithful, loyal, true

Dismiss
verb

Dismiss can mean to get rid of a worker. *After ten years with the company, the bus driver was dismissed.*

Discharge can mean to dismiss a worker, usually for a good reason. *Maureen was afraid to tell her parents she'd been discharged from her job for being late too often.*

Fire can mean to dismiss a worker suddenly. This meaning is informal. *Late Friday afternoon, six people in the print shop were fired.*

Lay off means to dismiss a worker, often for a specific period of time. *Mrs. Turner was laid off from her job last month, but she hopes to be rehired soon.*

ANTONYMS: employ, hire

Display
noun

Display means something arranged to be seen. *The store window display has dummies in bathing suits and sunglasses.*

Show means display. *Ms. Olivia Worthington will be judge of this year's flower show.*

Exhibit means a display meant to be seen by many people. *Mason designed the library's exhibit for Black History Month.*

Exhibition means a large public exhibit with many parts. *There will be an exhibition of martial arts in the park fieldhouse Saturday.*

Fair means a large exhibition, especially of agricultural or other products. *Spain hosted both the Olympics and a world's fair in 1992.*

Exposition means a very large exhibition, usually with exhibits from many different places. *The World's Columbian Exposition took place in Chicago in 1893.*

Spectacle can mean a public show, especially a very fancy one. *The Olympics always begin and end with an enormous spectacle.*

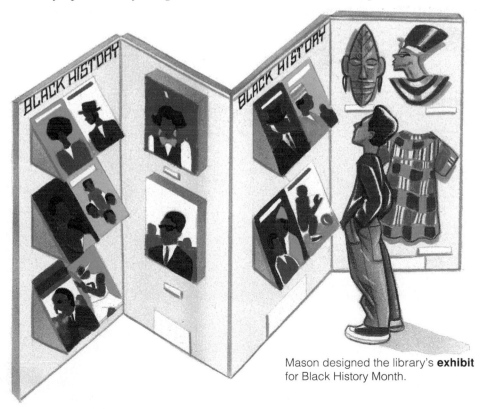

Mason designed the library's **exhibit** for Black History Month.

Disposition
noun

Disposition means a person's typical way of thinking and feeling. *Eddie has an easygoing disposition and seldom worries about anything.*

Temperament means a person's disposition, combined with typical physical and emotional qualities. *Darlene is loud and bossy and has an argumentative temperament.*

Personality means the combination of everything that makes a person different from others. *Mr. Phillips thinks LaToya's personality is perfect for volunteering at the foster home.*

Character can mean a person's typical sense of right and wrong. *Gavin must be really upset; complaining like that is so out of character for him.*

Nature can mean disposition. *It's just not Dwight's nature to be a leader.*

SEE **characteristic** and **quality** for related words.

Distant
adjective

Distant means a long way off. *After the wagon train made camp, Eliza walked to the edge of the circle and studied the distant mountains.*

Far means distant. *Three riders approached the ranch from the far end of the valley.*

Faraway means very distant. *Iris enjoys reading novels about faraway places.*

CONTINUED ON THE NEXT PAGE

After the wagon train made camp, Eliza walked to the edge of the circle and studied the **distant** mountains.

Far-off means faraway. *"This, Consuela, is a picture of your great-grandfather taken in far-off Spain," said her mother.*

Outlying means located at a distance from the center of something. *Children from outlying farms ride the schoolbus into town.*

Remote means very far away in space or time. *Modern telescopes receive light from remote parts of the universe.*

ANTONYMS: close, near

Distribute
verb

Distribute means to give out. *Mr. Raincloud distributed the hay to his six horses.*

Dispense means to distribute. It suggests a measured amount. *The relief workers will dispense food and blankets as soon as they reach the refugee camp.*

Issue means to make available many similar items. *Darryl thinks the Post Office should issue Michael Jackson stamps.*

Hand out means to distribute, especially from hand to hand. *"Danny, will you please hand out shop safety rules?" asked Mr. Montroy.*

Pass out means to hand out. *Cerise has an after-school job passing out ads for a florist.*

Deal out can mean to distribute. It suggests taking turns. *Standing at the grill, Ms. Escobar dealt out hamburgers to everyone in line.*

SEE **share** for related words.
ANTONYM: gather

WORD STORY

Dispense comes from a Latin word meaning "to weigh." In old times, money was made of precious metals like gold and silver. To know how much money was worth, people had to weigh it. You can see a connection to the same Latin word in *expense* and *compensation*. In English, *dispense* is used about distributing all sorts of things, but it still suggests a measured or weighed amount.

Do
verb

Do means to take a piece of work and finish it. *"Have you done all your homework yet?" Jimmy asked his brother.*

Perform means to do something that needs training and practice. *Dr. Gomez will perform several operations today.*

Accomplish means to do something that needs time and effort. *Miriam accomplished a great deal of work last week because she didn't go out at all.*

Achieve means to succeed in doing something important or difficult. *Rebecca knew that if she practiced extra hard she'd achieve a place on the gymnastics team.*

Execute means to do something already decided on. *The astronauts executed all the experiments planned for their mission.*

Fulfill is a formal word that means to do something expected. *"Travis has carefully fulfilled all his responsibilities as a laboratory assistant," said the letter of recommendation.*

Carry out means to do all of something, step by step. *The police carried out a thorough search for the missing jewels.*

WRITER'S CHOICE
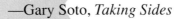

For the coach, watching his players was as exhausting as playing. He ran up and down the court, shouting plays through cupped hands and slapping a clipboard against his thighs when a play was executed poorly.

—Gary Soto, *Taking Sides*

Why *execute?* Because basketball players don't just make up all their plays as they go along. They learn certain plays from their coach and decide how to use them in games. Then they execute these plays— sometimes successfully, sometimes poorly.

Doubt
noun

Doubt means a feeling of not believing something or not being sure. *Ashley has made up her mind and doesn't feel any doubts.*

Uncertainty means a feeling of not being sure. *After a moment's uncertainty, Nestor recognized the path back to his family's farm.*

Suspicion means a feeling of not trusting someone. *The car moving down the dark alley with its lights off raised Deena's suspicion.*

Mistrust means suspicion. *The way Colin avoided answering questions filled Leroy with mistrust.*

Distrust means strong suspicion or a serious lack of trust. *Jim glared at the old pirate with a sullen look of distrust.*

Misgiving means a feeling of doubt that something will succeed. *Desmond had misgivings as he crossed the stream by stepping from rock to rock.*

Disbelief means a feeling of not believing or refusing to believe. *Mrs. Griswold listened to their excuses with open disbelief.*

Skepticism means unwillingness to believe or trust. *David feels some skepticism about the account his excited cousin gave of the accident.*

Take something with a grain of salt is an idiom that means to have doubt about something. *DeWayne tells so many extraordinary stories that I tend to take them all with a grain of salt.*

ANTONYM: belief

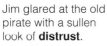

Jim glared at the old pirate with a sullen look of **distrust**.

Drink
verb

Drink means to swallow liquid. *The pool of water was so filthy that even animals wouldn't drink there.*

Sip means to drink slowly, a small amount at a time. *Thomas sipped the hot chocolate to avoid burning his mouth.*

Guzzle means to drink greedily, one swallow right after another. *Matthew tipped back his head and guzzled the juice straight from the bottle.*

Drain can mean to drink from a container until it is empty. *Tonya was so thirsty she drained the entire carton of milk.*

Gulp means to drink quickly. *Mr. Banas gulped his coffee and ran for the bus.*

Imbibe is a formal word that means to drink in. It is now used mostly to compare other activities to drinking. *Tina is at computer school now, imbibing knowledge like a sponge.*

Dry
adjective

Dry means without water. *Hank got soaked in the rain and was glad to put on dry clothes.*

Arid means getting little rain for a long time. It is used about land. *The Pueblo people have learned how to survive in the arid American desert.*

Parched means very dry and hot. *After weeks of drought, dust blew over the parched fields.*

Dehydrated means with the water taken out. *There were only a few dehydrated shreds of flesh remaining on the dead cow's bones.*

Withered means dry and lifeless. *Mrs. Paulson keeps a withered rose from her wedding bouquet in a glass case.*

ANTONYM: wet

Dull
adjective

Dull means not interesting. *Since Julian finds basketball dull, he passed up free tickets to the game.*

Uninteresting means too common and ordinary to hold your interest. *Delcie yawned and wondered how a movie about giant mutant killer beavers could be so uninteresting.*

Boring means so dull that it makes you unhappy. *It was such a boring TV show that Pauline turned it off halfway through.*

Tiresome means dull and making you tired. *Mrs. Goosewing spent a tiresome afternoon cleaning windows.*

Monotonous can mean boring and always the same. *Huong swayed back and forth to the monotonous rhythm of the train.*

Tedious means monotonous and long. *Yvonne complained that braiding her sister's hair was a tedious job.*

Dreary means dull and gloomy. *The movie opens in a dreary alley.*

Humdrum means dull and lacking variety. *Mr. Timmons felt that his life had become humdrum, so he planned an exciting vacation in Alaska.*

ANTONYMS: exciting, fascinating, interesting

WORDS AT PLAY

There was a young man of Siberia
Whose life became dreary and drearier
He tried bareback riding,
Sky diving, hang gliding
Then said, "I think boredom's superior!"

127

Eager
adjective

Eager means wanting something very much or looking forward to doing it. *Eager to apply for jobs, hundreds of people lined up for hours.*

Keen can mean eager and filled with enthusiasm. *Bounding from their kennels, Mr. Frobisher's restless hounds were keen to run.*

Anxious can mean eager but worried that something may go wrong. *James was anxious to buy the bike before his grandmother changed her mind.*

Impatient means eager and unwilling to wait for something. *Jane gulped down her dinner because she was impatient to leave for baton practice.*

Enthusiastic means eager and excited. *Matsue raced down the soccer field to the enthusiastic cheers of the fans.*

Gung-ho is an informal word that means extremely enthusiastic. *It is Austin's first computer class, and he is gung-ho to start.*

ANTONYMS: indifferent, reluctant

WRITER'S CHOICE

Then as the wagon came closer and closer, Poppa waved and Mr. Whitfield's laugh reached us almost before the sound of the horse's hooves. We stood motionless in the fierce sunlight, ready with our practiced smiles and greetings, eager to welcome our new neighbors.

—Pam Conrad, *Prairie Songs*

Why *eager?* It's the Nebraska frontier. Houses are miles apart. The nearest town is half a day's ride. People want neighbors very much: for company, help, and safety. When they hear that neighbors will be coming, the settlers look forward to welcoming them. The settlers are so eager, they even practice saying hello.

Earth
noun

Earth means the planet on which we live. *"The earth is our home,"* *Ms. Solomon said to her class, "neither playground nor junkyard."*

World means earth. It is used to mean all the planet's people and their cultures. *The Olympic Games bring the world's athletes together.*

Globe can mean earth, especially its round shape. *A hundred years ago, who could have imagined that people would ever circle the globe in airplanes?*

WATCH IT!

Some people feel that **earth** should *always* be capitalized, but others disagree. Everyone does agree on one rule: when you write about the earth in relation to other planets, you should capitalize it, along with the names of the other planets. *Venus and Earth are closer to the sun than Jupiter is.*

Ease
noun

Ease means freedom from worry or trouble. *"This powerful but lightweight vacuum cleaner will provide you with hours of ease," the salesman declared sincerely.*

Comfort can mean the absence of pain, need, or worry. *Since he grew up very poor, Mr. Chin has worked hard to live in comfort.*

Rest can mean a time free from activity or disturbance. *The girls carried the bags upstairs, took a short rest, then put the groceries away.*

Relaxation can mean rest while at ease and enjoying yourself. *Dilip likes to read for relaxation, and Mariko likes to listen to records.*

Leisure means free time to do what you like. *After school, Marcus does homework and helps his father in the shop, so he has little leisure time to watch TV.*

The life of Riley is an idiom that means a life of ease, comfort, and luxury. *Inez plans to marry a rich man and live the life of Riley.*

ANTONYM: discomfort

Easy
adjective

Easy means not hard to do or use. *"If putting this contraption together is so easy," said Greg, "why don't you do it yourself?" This puzzle is too easy and not much fun.*

Simple means not hard to understand or do. *Ana's recipe for flan is so simple that I had no trouble using it.*

Effortless means needing little strength or energy. *"The more you practice, Zanna, the more effortless your singing will be," said Mrs. Turk.*

Uncomplicated means not hard to understand. *The plot of this book is uncomplicated, but the writing is hard to read.*

Plain means not hard to understand. *It's plain from the graceful way she moves that Alexa is a dancer.*

Light can mean not hard to do or bear. *Since Mr. Shea has been in the hospital, our reading assignments have been really light.*

ANTONYMS: difficult, hard

WRITER'S CHOICE

Rusty followed her around to the passenger side. Her mother made a cup with her hands.

"For you to step into," she explained. . . .

She stepped on them gingerly and hauled herself up to the seat. Her mother ran to the other side and pulled herself effortlessly into the driver's seat. Rusty watched as she swiftly lowered her hand toward the three gear levers. The van gave a shudder and her mother pushed off the hand brake.

—Michelle Magorian, *Back Home*

Why *effortlessly?* The girl, Rusty, has to step into her mother's boosting hands in order to haul herself up into the high seat of a delivery van. Rusty's mother, however, has now been driving the van for months, and she swings herself up into the driver's seat as if the climb took no special strength or energy.

Eat
verb

The mouse has **nibbled** the cheese.

Eat means to swallow food. *Chip's family eats breakfast early.*

Consume can mean to use up an amount of food. *A crowd at a ball game can consume many thousands of hot dogs.*

Devour means to eat hungrily or greedily. *Most sharks devour their prey whole.*

Feed can mean to eat. It is used mostly for animals. *Every year about this time, flocks of wild turkeys sweep through the woods east of town to feed on the berries.*

Graze means to eat grass. *Bison once grazed on these prairies.*

Dine means to eat dinner. *The Riveras celebrated Beto's high school graduation by dining at their favorite restaurant.*

Nibble means to eat in small bites. *The mouse has nibbled the cheese.*

Gobble means to eat quickly, in large bites or gulps. *The way Frankie gobbles her popcorn, it's gone before the movie even starts.*

Feast means to eat a large, special meal. *The family feasted on roast turkey and all the trimmings at Grandma's and Grandpa's 40th anniversary party.*

Snack and **nosh** mean to eat between meals. *Homework makes Larry hungry, so he snacks on tostadas. Mom prefers us to nosh on fruit.*

IDIOMS

Eat is a key word in many idioms. Here are some of them:

Eat crow means to admit you are wrong in a humiliating way. *Megan insisted that her volleyball team couldn't lose, but she'll have to eat crow now that our team has the trophy.*

Eat high on (or **off**) **the hog** means to feast or to live in a grand style. *Uncle Mike keeps playing the lottery because he says he'd like to eat high on the hog just once in his life.*

Eat your words means to take back something you've said and to admit that it was wrong. *People who said the Wright Brothers' airplanes would never fly ate their words in the end.*

Eat out of someone's hand means to trust someone fully, or to believe or obey someone without question. *Sean is so good with children that he'll soon have his day camp group eating out of his hand.*

Economical
adjective

Economical means careful to avoid waste, especially of money. *Mrs. Quang, who buys rice only in large quantities, is an economical shopper.*

Thrifty means economical. *"You may not like wearing your sister's old coat, Chelsea, but we need to be as thrifty as we can," said her mom.*

Sparing is a formal word that means economical. It is often used about things other than money. *If people are not sparing in their use of fossil fuels, the earth's climate may change greatly.*

Saving means careful to save money. *When Jim really wants something special, he can become very saving in his ways.*

ANTONYMS: extravagant, wasteful

WATCH IT!

Economical and **economic** look as if they should mean the same thing—but they don't. *Economical* means careful with money. *The smaller car uses less gasoline and will be a more economical choice than the big one.* *Economic* means involving money or any of the things it buys. *Economic problems are on voters' minds this year.*

For words that look alike and *do* mean the same thing, see the Word Story at **climb**.

Edge
noun

Edge means the line or place where something ends. *Zena planted marigolds around the edges of the class garden.*

Margin means an area next to an edge. *The Department of Parks wants to build a stone path on the margin of the fishpond.*

Rim means the edge of something round. *The rims of these plates are decorated with flowers.*

Border means an edge or the area along the edge. *The white linen tablecloth had pink daisies embroidered all around the border.*

Boundary means an edge of a place or the area along the edge. *When the two countries merged, the boundary lines between them were left off the new maps.*

Brim means the inner part of a rim. *Shantiah watched the tiny green fly swim around the brim of her cup.*

CONTINUED ON THE NEXT PAGE

Brink means the top edge of something steep. *Standing at the brink of the Grand Canyon, the tourists took photos of each other.*

Circumference means the outside of a circle or sphere. *An NBA basketball is about thirty inches in circumference.*

Perimeter means the outer boundary of a shape or area. *"Sergeant Hernandez, post sentries around the perimeter of the camp!" ordered the captain.*

Effect
noun

Effect means something that happens because of something else. *One effect of the very cold weather was a great increase in the amount of heating fuel consumed.*

Result means an effect, especially a particular event. *As a result of the newspaper's support for her, Mrs. Estevez won the mayoral election.*

Outcome means an effect, especially one that happens at the end of many events. *The outcome of the trial is still in doubt.*

Consequence means an effect, especially one that has several causes or happens a while after the cause. *As a consequence of walking in the woods wearing shorts, Mario got poison ivy on his legs.*

ANTONYM: cause

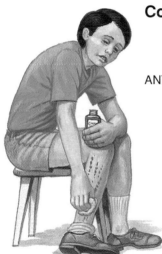

As a **consequence** of walking in the woods wearing shorts, Mario got poison ivy on his legs.

AROUND THE WORLD: Living with Consequences

You've made your bed, now lie in it.
— **English proverb**

You have cooked the broth, now eat it.
— **German proverb**

He who eats the honey must expect the sting of the bees.
— **Egyptian proverb**

Beans grow where beans are planted.
— **Korean proverb**

You reap what you sow.
— **English proverb**

There is no catching fish in dry clothes.
— **Portuguese proverb**

Effort
noun

Effort means a use of strength and energy in hope of doing something. *Kerri practices every day in an effort to perfect her volleyball serve.*

Attempt means an effort, but not always a strong one. *Mr. Paxton asked the chorus to make one more attempt at the song before rehearsal ended.*

Try means an attempt. *Sonia's first try at knitting a scarf didn't get very far.*

Endeavor means a serious effort over time. *Carmen's endeavor to improve her typing speed was successful.*

Stab can mean an attempt, often a brief or casual one. *Sheila took a stab at the video game but gave up quickly.*

Crack, shot, and **whack** can mean an attempt. These meanings are informal. *After Orville took his first shot at making potato salad, Earl had a crack at cooking hot dogs. Later, Billy Joe took a whack at cleaning up the kitchen.*

Mr. Paxton asked the chorus to make one more **attempt** at the song before rehearsal ended.

Elementary
adjective

Elementary means first and simplest. *Rona is learning how to use tools in her elementary carpentry class.*

Primary means first. *In the primary grades, schoolchildren learn to read and write.*

Basic means first and necessary for everything that follows. *A basic part of judo is learning how to fall.*

Fundamental means basic. It emphasizes how necessary something is. *The most fundamental part of cooking is using fresh, good-quality ingredients.*

Introductory means said or done first, to help with what follows. *Marlon's first day of work began with an introductory film about the company.*

Preliminary means said or done first. *Before the trial began, Judge Carver made preliminary remarks to the jury.*

ANTONYM: advanced

Eloquent
adjective

Eloquent means able to speak or write gracefully and persuasively. *Mrs. Ling's eloquent speeches convinced many of her neighbors to vote for her as assemblywoman.*

Fluent can mean able to speak in a smooth, easy way. *Spending summers with his grandparents in Puerto Rico has made George fluent in Spanish as well as English.*

Vocal can mean able and eager to speak freely. *At the meeting with the landlord, several tenants were extremely vocal about problems.*

Silver-tongued means very eloquent in speaking. *"You always know how to get around me, you silver-tongued rascal," Mom said to Dad as she kissed him.*

Articulate can mean able to speak or write clearly and easily. *Jaime doesn't speak up often, but he's very articulate when he does.*

Glib means speaking cleverly and persuasively, but not necessarily truthfully or knowledgeably. *Maurice gave a glib answer to the question, and we got past the gate.*

ANTONYM: tongue-tied

Embarrassed
adjective

Embarrassed means uneasy, self-conscious, and insecure. *Midge was terribly embarrassed when Jeff told everyone at the party that she didn't want to be there.*

Abashed means embarrassed, especially when the feeling comes suddenly. *Hillary was more abashed than hurt when she walked into the glass door.*

Fazed means confused and disturbed. It is an informal word, mostly used with "not." *Luisa is not fazed by having lost the election, and she will run again.*

Flustered means confused and nervous. *Boos from the fans got the pitcher flustered, and he walked the next two batters.*

Disconcerted means flustered. It is a formal word. *Disconcerted by criticism in the newspapers, the opera singer canceled the rest of his performances.*

Discombobulated is an informal word that means completely confused, nervous, and upset. *When the famous movie star winked at the coatroom attendant, she got so discombobulated that she gave him the wrong coat.*

SEE **ashamed** and **confused** for related words.

Emblem
noun

Emblem means a picture that stands for something else. *Julia's running club uses a picture of a lightning bolt as the emblem on their jackets.*

Symbol means a thing that stands for something else. *The bald eagle is a symbol of the United States. In China, the dragon was a symbol of the Emperor's power.*

Sign can mean a mark, picture, or thing that stands for something else. *Miss Belhuomini's diamond ring is a sign that she is engaged to be married.*

Token can mean a mark, picture, or thing that stands for something else. *The company gave Mr. Fitzroy a watch as a token of gratitude for his thirty years of service in the shipping room.*

CONTINUED ON THE NEXT PAGE

Badge means something a person wears to give information about that person. *The sheriff threw his badge in the dust and rode out of town forever.*

Insignia means something a person wears to give information about that person. *Now that Aunt Ruby has been promoted to sergeant, her uniform gets a third stripe as an insignia.*

In China, the dragon was a **symbol** of the Emperor's power.

AROUND THE WORLD: Emblems

Islam

Peace

Olympic Games

Judaism

Kenya

Emergency
noun

Emergency means a sudden and dangerous situation that calls for quick action. *The Kims had an emergency last night—Myung had an asthma attack and had to go to the hospital.*

Crisis can mean a dangerous situation, especially the most dangerous part of a story or set of events. *The crisis in the movie came when all six of the explorers fell into the river.*

Predicament means a difficult or dangerous situation that is hard to get out of. *Trapped in a burning building, the hero is in a terrible predicament.*

Crunch and **pinch** can mean an emergency. These meanings are informal. *"We're in a severe financial crunch," said Mr. Charles, pacing the office floor, "and we have to pay the bills soon." "We've gotten out of similar pinches in the past," responded his partner. "Something will turn up before the end of the month."*

Empty
adjective

Empty means with nothing in it. *The pig snuffled hungrily at the bottom of the empty apple barrel.*

Vacant means with nothing on it or in it. It is mostly used to describe places. *Bag in hand, Agatha climbed the steps and read the sign: "Room Vacant, Breakfast Included. Inquire Within."*

Blank means with nothing on it. It is used mostly to describe surfaces. *They've painted over the graffiti in the alley, so now all the garage doors are blank.*

Hollow means empty inside. *I thought this was a solid chocolate rabbit, but it's a hollow one.*

Bare can mean empty, especially on the surface. *By November, many trees have bare branches.*

ANTONYM: full

Enclose
verb

Enclose means to shut something in on all sides. *Vinu's father enclosed their field with a thorn fence.*

Surround means to enclose. *The soldiers moved quietly to surround the enemy camp.*

Envelop can mean to enclose. It suggests being wrapped or covered. *As her grandfather read, Oona sank back on the pillow, enveloped by her big quilt and the smell of cookies baking.*

Encircle means to form a circle around something. *Members of the tribe encircled the old storyteller, moving in closer to hear her words.*

Blockade means to keep everything from going in or out of a place. *During the Civil War, Union ships blockaded southern ports.*

Besiege means to surround a city or fort in order to capture it. *For nine days, Shawnee braves besieged Boonesborough, hoping to defeat Daniel Boone.*

SEE **limit** and **lock** for related words.

As her grandfather read, Oona sank back on the pillow, **enveloped** by her big quilt and the smell of cookies baking.

WORD POOL

There are many other verbs that mean to shut someone or something in. Often these words are also nouns that mean an enclosure. You *fence* a horse inside a *fence*, and you *pen* a pig inside a *pen*. The words below are not synonyms of each other, but they share the meaning "to enclose."

cage	hedge
coop	jail
corral	pen
fence	stable

Encourage
verb

Encourage means to help someone gain courage or confidence. *The basketball coach's praise encouraged Rafael to try out for the team.*

Inspire means to fill someone with courage or confidence. *Mrs. Chernoff's success in night school inspired her husband to learn English there too.*

Hearten means to encourage and make happier. *After weeks of nasty weather, it was heartening to see the sun yesterday.*

Cheer on means to encourage someone by yelling. *The scout troop cheered on their team in the tug-of-war.*

Root for means to cheer on. *"If I have to root for anybody,"* Lucy said, *"I'm rooting for the guys who lost the last time."*

SEE **urge** for related words.
ANTONYMS: discourage, dishearten

End
verb

End means to come to the last part of something or bring it to its last part. *This story begins and ends on a ranch in Wyoming. When an argument starts, Fran tries to end it at once.*

Finish means to end what you started to do. It indicates that the entire job has been done. *The first three runners finished the race very close together.*

CONTINUED ON THE NEXT PAGE

The first three runners **finished** the race very close together.

140

Complete means to finish. *Jeron must complete his homework before he can watch TV.*

Conclude is a formal word that means to end. *The company president concluded his report to the stockholders by resigning his position.*

Terminate is a formal word that means to end. *The city will terminate ferry service when the new bridge opens.*

Close can mean to bring something to its last part. *The band will close its concert with "The Stars and Stripes Forever" march.*

Wind up can mean to end. *Miles didn't take the directions and wound up getting lost.*

Wrap up can mean to end. *The TV talk show host wrapped up the program by thanking his guests for appearing.*

SEE **last** and **stop** for related words.
ANTONYMS: begin, start

Enemy
noun

Enemy means someone who hates someone or something. *The enemies of civil rights tried to keep African Americans from voting. The United States and Japan were enemies in World War II.*

Foe means an enemy. It is used mostly in books. *The famous detective and his criminal foe stood face to face at last!*

Archenemy means a main or special enemy. *In this computer game, your archenemy is the Zork, who can wipe out your score.*

Invader means an enemy who enters a country by force. *As the invaders approached our city, we could see the flash of their guns and missiles against the sky.*

SEE **fight** and **opponent** for related words.
ANTONYMS: ally, friend

WORD STORY

Enemy comes from a Latin word meaning "friend." How can this be true? The Latin word began with the letters *ami-*. You can see the same letters in *amigo* and *amiable*. If you wanted to say that someone was not your friend, you might call that person your "un-amigo." Try saying that several times fast, and you'll see where *enemy* came from.

Jonas's grandparents **immigrated** to the United States in the 1920s.

Enter
verb

Enter means to go into or come into a place, or to join an activity. *Mrs. Goosewing says that it's bad manners to enter her office without knocking. How many people have entered the dance contest?*

Immigrate means to come into a country or a region to live there. *Jonas's grandparents immigrated to the United States in the 1920s.*

Trespass means to enter someone's property illegally. *Ms. Knuba caught two men trespassing on school grounds last night.*

Intrude means to enter where you are not welcome. *Amelia says JoLynne tries to intrude on our conversations, but I think she's just trying to be friendly.*

Invade means to enter by force, as an enemy. *The armies of Attila the Hun invaded Italy in A.D. 452.*

Set foot in is an idiom that means to enter. It is mostly used with "not" or "never." *How can Mr. Wynn say it's a bad restaurant when he's never set foot in the place?*

ANTONYMS: exit, leave

WATCH IT!

Immigrate means to come into a country to live. **Emigrate** means to leave a country to go live in another country. *The Akbars emigrated from Pakistan and immigrated to the United States.*

Erase
verb

Erase means to remove by rubbing or as if by rubbing. *Juan erased the misspelled word and rewrote it correctly.*

Delete means to remove something written. *The computer's DEL key deletes the last letter you typed.*

Obliterate is a formal word that means to remove all trace of something. *Bombs obliterated many buildings in the city.*

Wipe out means to destroy completely as if by rubbing. *All footprints at the scene of the crime were wiped out by the heavy rain.*

Blot out means to remove all trace of something as if by putting ink blots on it. *Dark clouds blotted out the sun.*

Escape
verb

Escape means to get away or to get out. *Thanks to the smoke alarm, all the residents of the apartment escaped the fire. The canary escaped from its cage and has been flying around the house all afternoon.*

Elude means to escape in a clever way. *The rebels eluded government troops by dressing as wealthy tourists.*

Break out can mean to escape from being locked up, often by using force. *Taking several guards as hostages, six prisoners broke out of the state penitentiary.*

Fly the coop is an idiom that means to escape from being or feeling locked up. *"Gracious!" Mrs. Tingle exclaimed at the open cage door, "Our hamster appears to have flown the coop!"*

Give someone the slip is an idiom that means to escape, especially in a clever way. *When he saw the knotted sheets dangling from the window, Sheriff Logan knew that Smitty O'Rourke had given him the slip again.*

Throw someone off the scent is an idiom that means to escape pursuit, especially in a clever way. *Jim entered the movie theater and at once left by another door, throwing the dark stranger off his scent.*

SEE **avoid, evade,** and **flee** for related words.

Especially
adverb

Especially means more than others or in a special way. *Luis likes to eat fruit, especially papaya. Mary Ann was especially glad to see Philip, since he had been away all summer.*

Particularly means especially. *"I hate getting out of bed," Minh yawned, "particularly on dark, rainy days like this."*

Specifically means with attention to a single item or detail. *Isabel wants to be a nurse, specifically to help old people.*

Primarily means more than others or mainly. *Hilary's mother is primarily a children's doctor, but she sees grownups on occasion.*

Principally means more than others or mainly. *On vacation, Mr. Shelby is principally interested in fishing.*

In particular means especially. *Carly loves to shop, in particular for new clothes.*

Above all means more than anything else. *Luther likes acting class a lot, above all because he's learning sign language.*

Estimate
verb

Estimate means to form an opinion about the size, weight, amount, or value of something. *Evon estimates that he has about 125 marbles in the jar.*

Value means to estimate the worth of something in money. *The store values this baseball card at twenty dollars, but I got it at a show for sixteen.*

Appraise can mean to give an expert judgment about the money value of something. *The painting was appraised by the museum staff at four thousand dollars.*

Evaluate means to judge the value or quality of something. *The coach will evaluate our skills before deciding who may join the wrestling team.*

Rate means to evaluate. *The Azteca is rated as one of the best restaurants in town.*

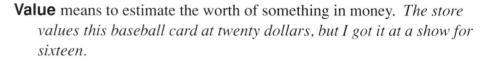

Evon **estimates** that he has about 125 marbles in the jar.

CONTINUED ON THE NEXT PAGE

144

Assess means to estimate the value of property for tax purposes. *The county has assessed this house at ninety thousand dollars.*

Guesstimate means to make an imprecise estimate. It is an informal word. *Joy guesstimates that she has spent hundreds of hours learning to use her computer.*

SEE **measure** for related words.

Evade
verb

Evade means to get away from someone or something by trickery or cleverness. *By changing her name, her clothes, and her car, Ms. Craig managed to evade the private investigator.*

Dodge can mean to evade. It suggests twisting aside to get out of the way. *The quarterback dodged questions after the game by staying in the shower until the reporters left.*

Duck can mean to dodge. *The candidate ducked all requests for a debate, claiming to be too busy.*

Sidestep can mean to get away from something, as if by stepping out of the way. *Fabian managed to sidestep questions about his filthy jeans by going in the back door.*

SEE **avoid** and **escape** for related words.

WRITER'S CHOICE

I liked gym about as much as I liked cooking. Besides, I got enough exercise ducking and dodging the Shephards' Great Dane. I had been running from the dog for almost two years now, ever since we moved in next door to the Shephards.

—Johnniece Marshall Wilson, *Poor Girl, Rich Girl*

Why *ducking* and *dodging?* These two words together describe the kind of back-and-forth motion that this girl uses to avoid the dog. The repeated *d* sound makes these words a natural pair, like *push* and *pull.* The sound also suggests that this girl isn't seriously worried about being attacked by the neighbors' dog.

Event
noun

Event means something that happens, especially if it has some importance. *If we can get a famous speaker, like the mayor, she will make this year's graduation a real event.*

Incident means something that happens, especially something not very important. *Compared to Sandy's other problems, misplacing her glasses was a minor incident.*

Occurrence means something that happens, especially something not very important. *It seems to me, Ben, that forgetting to make your bed has become a daily occurrence.*

Circumstance can mean an event. *It was an unlucky circumstance that the rain began just as the block party started.*

Episode means an event, or a series of related events. It is often used in discussing stories. *In this week's episode, the heroine rescues the hero from several terrible predicaments.*

Evidence
noun

Evidence means something that shows what is true and what is not true. *The footprints are evidence that someone crossed the lawn.*

Clue means something that suggests what may be true. *Since none of us could guess what Emily was holding behind her back, she gave us a clue.*

Testimony means a statement that is used as evidence, especially in court. *Mrs. Daniels gave testimony that Steve and Sammy were at home when the store windows were broken.*

Affidavit means a written statement that a person swears is true. *The lawyer wanted everyone invoved in the accident to sign an affidavit.*

SEE **confirm** for related words.

Examine
verb

Examine means to look at something carefully in order to find out about it. *The dentist will examine Sari's teeth for cavities.*

Inspect means to examine something, especially officially. *The immigration officer inspected the Miklos family's papers, and then welcomed them to the United States of America.*

CONTINUED ON THE NEXT PAGE

Scan can mean to look something over closely. *Jinella scanned the footprints with a magnifying glass.*

Study can mean to examine thoroughly. *Gregory studied the bus schedule again, wondering if his grandmother had missed a connection somewhere.*

Check can mean to look at something in order to see if it is all right. *Kay needs a ride tomorrow because her mom has to have their car's brakes checked.*

Scrutinize means to examine very thoroughly. *Salina scrutinized the dress for twenty minutes before deciding to buy it.*

SEE **look into** (at **look**) and **search** for related words.

Jinella **scanned** the footprints with a magnifying glass.

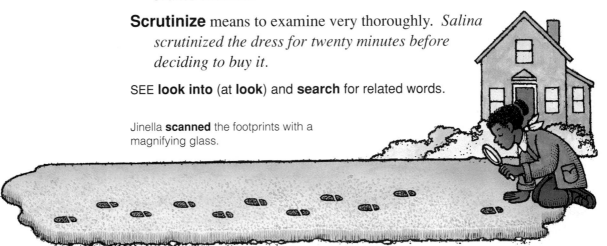

WATCH IT!
. . . .

Some words can mean contradictory things. **Scan** can mean to look over closely. *The programmer will have to scan the computer printout line by line in order to figure out what has gone wrong.* Or *scan* can mean to look over quickly. *Toni scanned the morning headlines, hoping to find some good news.*

Another word like this is **gauge,** which can mean to measure carefully. *"This month," said Ms. Ramirez, "the class will gauge weather conditions, such as rainfall and windspeed, as accurately as possible."* Or *gauge* can mean to estimate. *Dad gauged our travel time as two hours, but it was more like three.*

Biweekly is a particularly confusing word. It can mean happening once every two weeks. *The instructions are to run this ad biweekly.* Or *biweekly* can mean happening twice a week. *The instructions are to run this ad biweekly.* Should the ad appear every two weeks or two times a week?

Example
noun

Example means one thing or person that shows what others are like. *"On your left," said our guide, "is a perfect example of French armor from the Middle Ages."*

Instance means an example. *George Washington and Dwight Eisenhower are instances of generals who became President.*

Case means an example. It is often used for an event, or for someone's life. *The farmer recalled a case several years ago of a fox attacking his chickens.*

Illustration can mean an example used to explain something. *"Today," said Mr. Blau, "we will focus on manufacturing states, using Ohio as an illustration."*

Sample means a part that shows what the whole is like. *Gary asked for a sample of the chocolate cherry ice cream before buying a cone.*

Specimen means one thing taken and used to show what others are like. *Jamie's class went on a trip to collect specimens of pond life.*

Jamie's class went on a trip to collect **specimens** of pond life.

Excel
verb

Excel means to do better than others. *Betty excelled the whole sixth grade in pre-algebra.*

Outdo means to excel. *Mateo outdid his cousins in the swimming race.*

Surpass is a formal word that means to excel. *For years, chess players from the Soviet Union surpassed all others.*

Outshine can mean to do a lot better than others. *Leonardo da Vinci outshone his contemporaries in many areas of achievement.*

Go one better is an idiom that means to excel. *Ramón took a prize in art, but César went him one better and took two prizes.*

Run rings around is an idiom that means to excel easily. *Give Kenny a guitar, and he will run rings around anybody in town.*

SEE **conquer** and **defeat** for related words.

Excellent
adjective

Excellent means having very high quality. *When it was Barry's turn to cook dinner, he made excellent tacos.*

First-rate means excellent. *Suit Yourself sells first-rate clothing.*

Fine and **first-class** mean excellent. *"Why, Daniel, this drawing isn't just good, it's fine!" the art teacher cried. "You're becoming a first-class artist!"*

Superior means having very high quality, especially compared to others. *"Now that you have seen the others," Mr. Bartholomew murmured, "I will show you a truly superior diamond."*

Outstanding means so excellent as to stand out from others. *You have to be an outstanding athlete to be considered for the Olympic team.*

Exceptional means very outstanding of its kind. *The teacher said that Stan's composition showed exceptional writing ability.*

SEE **best** and **wonderful** for related words.
ANTONYMS: bad, poor, terrible

WRITING TIP: Slang

There are lots of slang words that mean "excellent." For some reason, people create new ways to express this idea faster than for almost any other idea. Here are just a few of them:

bad	cool	fab	keen	righteous
boss	dandy	groovy	neat	swell
chill	dynamite	icy	nifty	tough

Slang is more commonly found in conversation than in writing. Why? For one thing, many people feel that slang is not appropriate in most writing. In talking with your friends, *icy* and *bad* may be perfectly fine. Yet they will not do to praise a novel in a book report.

For another thing, slang gets old very quickly. Some of the words in this list may already be so out of date that you have never heard them used to mean excellent. When you see in this book or in your dictionary that a word is slang, be careful about using it in your writing. In dialogue, slang can help suggest a character through conversation, but in description, it can make your story sound old very quickly.

Excessive
adjective

Excessive means more than is right, more than is necessary, or more than makes sense. *Making a hundred posters for the school art fair is excessive; we need only ten.*

Extravagant can mean excessive and uncontrolled. *Commercials often make extravagant claims, but to say this soda will make you smarter is really too much.*

Superfluous means too much and not wanted. *I try to weed out the superfluous commas in my essays.*

Unreasonable can mean excessive. *Jen thinks it's unreasonable of Ms. Lochrie to expect us to write a report by Wednesday.*

Immoderate means more than makes sense. *It's the kind of movie where everyone drives at immoderate speeds.*

ANTONYM: inadequate

Excitement
noun

Excitement means strong and active feelings, usually with much sound and motion. *The crowd roared with excitement when the teams ran onto the field.*

Commotion means a noisy and excited disturbance. *The gerbil caused a commotion in the classroom when it escaped from its cage.*

Hurly-burly means a noisy and excited disturbance. *When BillyBob first came to Atlanta, the hurly-burly of city life amazed him.*

Fuss means a lot of bother and excitement, usually about something unimportant. *"All right," said the police officer, "what's all this fuss about a missing flowerpot?"*

Flutter can mean confused excitement. *It's Grandpa's first date in forty years, so he's in a flutter.*

Bustle means busy and noisy activity. *Amid much bustle, the Senior Citizen's Club unloaded the truck and set up tents.*

Stir can mean confused excitement. *The school board's suggestion that classes be held year-round has created a stir in the community.*

SEE **noise** for related words.

Excuse
noun

Excuse means a reason that you give for why you should not be blamed. It may be true or false. *Shannon's only excuse for not feeding the dog was that she forgot.*

Alibi can mean an excuse. *"Late and dirty—what's your alibi this time, Sam?" his mother asked.*

Justification can mean a good excuse. It suggests that the excuse is true. *As a justification for wanting a bigger allowance, Theo made a careful list of his weekly expenses.*

Defense can mean an excuse. It suggests a serious or public statement. *"My client's defense is that she didn't know she had picked up somebody else's bag," the lawyer declared.*

SEE **reason** for related words.

Exercise
noun

Exercise means repeated activity that increases strength, endurance, and skill. *Jan and Lou get exercise by skating two miles every day.*

Training can mean the development of strength, endurance, and skill by exercise. *Jenny's former gym teacher went into training for the Pan American Games.*

Workout means a period of exercise. *Tina ran a mile during her workout this morning.*

Calisthenics and **aerobics** are kinds of exercise. Calisthenics especially increases strength and gracefulness; aerobics especially increases endurance. *Ricki does slow calisthenics to get warmed up and then fast aerobics to raise her pulse.*

WORD STORY

Calisthenics comes from two old Greek words meaning "beauty" and "strength." The ancient Greeks, who created the Olympic Games, felt that the athletic body was the most beautiful body.

Jan and Lou get **exercise** by skating two miles every day.

151

Shortages of food and **snowballing** popular discontent contributed to the breakup of the Soviet Union in 1991.

Expand
verb

Expand means to become larger. *The United States expanded greatly with the Louisiana Purchase.*

Swell means to become larger by puffing up. *Nelson sprained his wrist, and it's swelling rapidly.*

Bulge means to swell out. *See the hamster's cheeks bulge with food.*

Balloon means to become larger quickly. *The number of applications to the music program ballooned when Ms. Selkirk said she would teach this year.*

Mushroom means to become larger quickly. *The number of robberies in the neighborhood has mushroomed since the police foot patrol stopped.*

Widen means to become larger across. *The street widens just before it meets the highway.*

Snowball can mean to expand faster and faster. It suggests something out of control. *Shortages of food and snowballing popular discontent contributed to the breakup of the Soviet Union in 1991.*

SEE **increase** and **lengthen** for related words.
ANTONYM: shrink

Expect
verb

Expect means to believe that something will probably happen. *I expect to see Sally after school today.*

Anticipate means to expect. It often suggests something you are pleased about. *Clara anticipates a call from her grandparents on her birthday.*

Hope means to expect and wish for something. *Julio hopes to get his driver's license next month.*

Foresee means to expect. It often suggests a special ability to figure out what will happen. *When the guys decided to keep the money they found, only Darren foresaw that it would bring them a great deal of trouble.*

Bargain for is an idiom that means to expect. *Linda found high school more of a change than she had bargained for.*

Look forward to is an idiom that means to expect with eager pleasure. *Tim always looks forward to weekends with his dad.*

SEE **forecast** for related words.

Expel
verb

Expel means to require someone to leave, often as a punishment. *No one was expelled from our school this year, but three people were suspended.*

Eject means to force out or drive out. *For throwing bottles onto the field, the fans were ejected from the stadium.*

Oust means to eject. *Corruption and brutality have provoked the people into ousting the president and his military advisors.*

Bounce can mean to eject. This meaning is slang. *Kevin and Lance got bounced from the library for talking too loud—but they still had to write their reports.*

Evict means to force legally out of a house or land. *"Pay the rent immediately or I'll have you evicted!" shouted the landlord, waving his arms angrily.*

Kick out is an idiom that means to expel. *Carla was kicked out of camp for climbing the water tower.*

Expensive
adjective

Expensive means costing a lot of money. *Luis decided not to buy those expensive sneakers.*

Costly can mean expensive. *Dad gave Mom a bottle of costly perfume for her birthday.*

High can mean expensive. *Mr. and Mrs. Parks like the apartment, but the rent is too high for their budget.*

Overpriced means costing more than it is worth. *Gina says those tropical fish are really overpriced.*

Steep can mean very expensive. *The little grocery on the corner had steep prices compared to the supermarket.*

Sky-high can mean very expensive. *I can't believe anyone pays these sky-high rates for a motel room.*

Cost an arm and a leg is an idiom that means something is extremely expensive. *Marnie wants a computer with a color monitor, but they cost an arm and a leg.*

SEE **valuable** for related words.
ANTONYMS: cheap, inexpensive

Experience
verb

Experience means to have something happen to you. *Our team has experienced some bad luck this year, but we played fairly well for much of the season.*

Undergo means to experience something, often something unpleasant. *Mario has to undergo a serious operation to repair the damage to his arm.*

Feel can mean to experience. *Yoko felt great sadness when her best friend moved to California.*

Have can mean to experience. *Kerry had an accident on her bike last weekend.*

Suffer can mean to experience something unpleasant. *The President of the PTA suffered defeat in her bid for re-election.*

Sustain can mean to suffer. *Mrs. Restrepo's house sustained minor damage during the flood.*

Expert
adjective

Expert means knowing most of what there is to know about something. *It takes expert training for a dog to become really obedient.*

Accomplished can mean expert, especially at doing something particular. *As a performer, Mozart was a child prodigy, but it took him years to become an accomplished composer.*

Experienced means knowing a lot about something from doing it many times. *An experienced leader will take the Scout troop on the hike.*

Skilled means able to do something well because of knowledge and practice. *José is a skilled typist who can keyboard fifty words a minute.*

Skillful means able to do something well because of knowledge and practice. *Jill's mother is skillful enough to make most of her own dresses.*

Masterful can mean very skillful. *Hannah made a masterful over-the-shoulder catch to save the ball game.*

Proficient means skilled and able to do something successfully. *Familiar with computers since fifth grade, Frank was proficient at debugging programs.*

SEE **ability** for related words.
ANTONYMS: incompetent, inexperienced, unskilled

An **experienced** leader will take the Scout troop on the hike.

Explain
verb

Explain means to make something easier to understand by talking or writing about it. *This book explains the background of the war in Vietnam.*

Interpret means to explain the meaning of something. *Rob interprets the movie as a comedy, but Tara thinks it was serious.*

Clarify means to make something clearer and easier to understand. *Celia could not understand the diagram and asked the teacher to clarify it.*

Spell out means to give a careful, detailed, and easy to understand explanation. *Roger had trouble setting the VCR until Marissa spelled out the process for him, one step at a time.*

ANTONYMS: confuse, misinterpret

HAVE YOU HEARD...?

You may have heard people say that someone has "shed light on the question." This means to provide information about a subject, especially a subject in doubt—as if shining a light into darkness. *"My next witness," said Ms. Ortega, "can shed some light on the question of the defendant's whereabouts at that time."*

Explode
verb

Explode means to break into bits suddenly with a loud noise. *The fuel tank exploded and destroyed the space shuttle.*

Burst can mean to explode. *The kitten was so startled when the balloon burst that she climbed up the curtains.*

Blast can mean to make something explode. *Many rocks had to be blasted to build this tunnel.*

Detonate means to blast. *Workers detonated the dynamite, and the old hotel collapsed.*

Blow up means to explode. *Prick the potatoes with a fork so that they don't blow up in the microwave.*

Go off means to explode. *Uncle Ted lost a finger as a boy because a firecracker went off in his hand.*

Extra
adjective

Extra means more than usual or more than necessary. *Every student should bring an extra pencil to the exam. Rodney always carries extra batteries for his tape player.*

Spare can mean extra. It suggests that something will probably not be needed. *Ms. Healy checks her spare tire every few weeks.*

Surplus means extra. It suggests that there is a lot more of something than necessary. *The bakery sends its surplus bread to the church's shelter for the homeless.*

Additional means added to something else. *"Will you stop now," asked the TV host, "or risk all your prizes for an additional five thousand dollars?"*

Supplementary means additional. It suggests adding enough to be complete or satisfactory. *After Lynn's broken leg healed, she had six weeks of supplementary therapy to strengthen it.*

Ms. Healy checks her **spare** tire every few weeks.

WRITING TIP: Regionalisms

In Louisiana, especially in New Orleans, when people give something extra, they say it is "for lagniappe" (pronounced lan yap′ or lan′yap). *After we paid the bill, the waiter brought us each a candy for lagniappe.* The word *lagniappe* comes through Spanish from a Peruvian Indian word meaning "gift."

Every region has words and phrases that are more common there than in the rest of the country. These can be very useful when you want to tell a story that happens in a particular setting, not just any place. For example, also in New Orleans, "poor boy" is the name for a kind of sandwich that in other parts of the country is called a "grinder," "hero," "hoagy," or "sub." Which word do you use?

You might want to start a list of regionalisms to use in your writing.

Fad
noun

Fad means something that attracts popular attention, but not for long. *The fad at my school last year was unmatched shoes or socks, but nobody dresses that way now.*

Fashion can mean a popular way of doing something or a popular kind of clothing. *Ms. Greenberg says that recycling will never go out of fashion.*

Style means fashion. *Rima always knows about the new hair styles before anyone else.*

Rage can mean a very strong fad. *Leather jackets suddenly became all the rage.*

Craze means a strong but brief popular interest in something. *Many people thought rock music would be just a craze, but it's certainly here to stay.*

Mania can mean a craze. *Yogurt & More was founded when the mania for frozen yogurt first started.*

Failure
noun

Failure means someone or something that does not do well. *The sidewalk sale was a failure because it rained all day.*

Flop can mean a failure, especially of something that is meant for people to like. *The movie cost thirty million dollars to make, but it was a terrible flop!*

Washout can mean a disappointing failure. *As a pitcher, Carole was a washout, so she switched to third base and played well all summer.*

CONTINUED ON THE NEXT PAGE

Dud can mean someone or something that fails to function. *Saul's new computer game was a dud, but the store promised to replace it.*

Bust can mean something that fails completely, like a bankrupt business. *With hardly any rain this year, the corn crop was a bust.*

Fiasco means a complete failure. *Chip's breadmaking was a fiasco because he forgot to put yeast in the dough.*

Flash in the pan is an idiom that means something successful at first but eventually a failure. *The team's early success was a flash in the pan, and they went on to lose most of their games.*

ANTONYM: success

WORD STORY

Fiasco comes from an Italian word that means "bottle." *To make a bottle* is an Italian idiom that means to fail totally. No one, including the Italians, knows why it has this meaning.

Fair
adjective

Fair means right and not favoring one person over another. *"It's not fair!" cried Darcy. "They're calling all the fouls against our team!"*

Just means fair, based upon rules or laws. *Miguel thought his punishment was just, so he didn't complain.*

Impartial means not favoring one person or side over another. *The lawyers questioned the members of the jury to be sure they were impartial.*

Evenhanded means impartial. *Ms. Pellas asked us to write an evenhanded report on the dispute between the workers and the factory owner.*

Unbiased means trying to be completely fair. *After listening to both sides of the controversy, Judge Vorhees wrote an unbiased opinion that was fair to everyone.*

Equitable means fair and treating everyone with equal justice. *My dad helped fight for equitable treatment of African Americans in the 1950s and '60s.*

ANTONYMS: biased, unfair, unjust

My dad helped fight for **equitable** treatment of African Americans in the 1950s and '60s.

Fake
adjective

Fake means not real, but intended to seem real. *Some fake furs look almost genuine.*

Imitation means fake. *Sarah bought an imitation diamond necklace at a yard sale and later learned the diamonds were real!*

Phony is an informal word that means fake. *The spy spoke in a phony German accent.*

Counterfeit means made to look real in order to cheat people. *Elora found a fifty-dollar bill, but it turned out to be counterfeit.*

False can mean not real. *The robber wore a false mustache, but it looked silly on him.*

Artificial can mean not real. It describes something that has been made by effort and is used instead of something natural. Something artificial is not usually intended to fool anyone into thinking it is genuine. *Rafael doesn't drink diet soda because he doesn't like the taste of artificial sweeteners.*

Synthetic can mean artificial. *Mr. Shapiro says that synthetic fuels are important because people may run out of natural fuels some day.*

ANTONYMS: authentic, genuine, real

Fall
verb

Fall means to come down suddenly, often out of control. *All the books fell off Marla's desk. Rain has been falling all day.*

Drop means to fall or to let something fall. *At the sound of shots, the soldiers dropped to the ground. "All right, Lefty, drop the gun!" said the sheriff.*

Collapse can mean to fall down or fall apart. *Only the strongest earthquakes actually cause buildings to collapse.*

Tumble means to fall in a helpless way. *Lloyd slipped and tumbled into the snow.*

Slump means to fall heavily, unable to resist. *Hassan's camel tried weakly to rise but slumped back onto the sand.*

Pitch can mean to fall very suddenly forward. *When Rena slipped, she pitched onto the grass.*

CONTINUED ON THE NEXT PAGE

Topple means to fall as a result of becoming unsteady. *We made a tower of empty boxes, but it toppled.*

Cascade means to fall in a waterfall or like a waterfall. *Luz has beautiful dark hair that cascades down her back.*

Plummet means to fall straight down or descend rapidly. *The pilot, dangling from his parachute, watched his burning plane plummet to the ground below.*

Keel over means to fall over suddenly, usually unconscious. *I saw Calbert start to faint, but I couldn't catch him before he keeled over.*

SEE **descend** for related words.
ANTONYMS: rise, ascend

We made a tower of empty boxes, but it **toppled.**

IDIOMS

Fall is a key word in many idioms. Here are some of them:

Fall flat means to fail, especially to fail at pleasing. *Davey's magic act fell flat when everyone saw him hide the card.*

Fall down on the job means to fail at a responsibility. *The third time I forgot to take out the garbage, Mom accused me of falling down on the job.*

Fall off the face of the earth means to vanish without explanation. *This rock group made two great albums in the eighties, then fell off the face of the earth.*

Fall short means to fail to reach what is needed or expected. *This year's PTA blood drive fell short of its goal by seven pints.*

Familiar
adjective

Familiar means very friendly and able to share ideas and feelings like members of the same family. *The Burches and Seebergs have become familiar since they set up a car pool together.*

Chummy is an informal word that means very friendly, as chums are. *Jerome and Carl got really chummy during the hockey season.*

Intimate means completely familiar. *Iris has become intimate with one of the women she reads to at the nursing home.*

Close can mean intimate. *Max couldn't believe that his close friend Baram would be moving soon.*

Inseparable means so intimate that they seem to be always together. *Conchita and Lisa have been inseparable since they learned how much they both love horses.*

SEE **friend** and **friendly** for related words.
ANTONYM: formal

Famous
adjective

Famous means well-known and interesting to many people. *Marlene likes to read biographies of famous entertainers.*

Noted means well-known, especially for a particular skill or accomplishment. *Marie Curie was a noted scientist who won two Nobel prizes.*

Celebrated means well-known and popular. *Jamal's mother is the dentist of celebrated TV star Lance Dawson.*

Prominent means well-known and important. *Prominent business leaders support the new airport.*

Distinguished means well-known and admired because of outstanding qualities or work. *Many distinguished black writers lived in Harlem during the 1920s.*

Renowned means distinguished. *Renowned for her beautiful singing voice, Alice Weekes will give three concerts in the park this weekend.*

Eminent means renowned. It particularly suggests being outstanding. *Thomas Edison and Alexander Graham Bell were eminent American inventors.*

CONTINUED ON THE NEXT PAGE

This statue was made by the **illustrious** Italian sculptor Donatello.

Illustrious means outstanding and very famous for a long time. *This statue was made by the illustrious Italian sculptor Donatello.*

Notorious means famous for doing something bad. *Lake Silverset is notorious for its mosquitoes.*

ANTONYMS: obscure, unknown

WRITER'S CHOICE

This is Tiger Moran, perhaps not the best-known hoodlum of his era but definitely one of the shrewdest. Said to have amassed a fortune equivalent to that of the notorious Al Capone, this rumrunner and bank-stickup artist suddenly disappeared from public view in August 1930.

—Walter Dean Myers, *The Mouse Rap*

Why *notorious?* Unlike Tiger Moran, Al Capone was well-known and interesting to many people. Unlike other famous people, Capone was famous for bad deeds.

Fat
adjective

The **portly** gentleman walked slowly, carrying his cane.

Fat means having too much body weight. *Last winter our dog Roxanne got much less exercise, ate all day long, and got fat.*

Overweight means weighing more than is normal for your height and age. *The doctor told Melissa that she is 15 pounds overweight.*

Stout means fat and big. *Because Grandpa is stout, he's always asked to play Santa Claus at Christmastime.*

Pudgy means fat and short. *Amy's little brother may be pudgy now, but I bet he grows up to be as tall and slender as Amy.*

Chubby means round and soft. It is used especially to describe babies and children. *Kyle held his sister's chubby hands while his father changed her diaper.*

Plump means likably chubby. *Quite slender in her twenties, Elaine became plump in her forties.*

Portly means stout, solid, and dignified. *The portly gentleman walked slowly, carrying his cane.*

Obese means extremely fat. *Scientists are still not sure why some people become obese.*

ANTONYMS: skinny, slender, thin

Fear
noun

> " The only thing we have to fear is fear itself. "
>
> — **Franklin D. Roosevelt**
> **(1882–1945)**

Fear means the feeling of being scared. *Jon won't go to the pool with us because of his fear of water.*

Fright means sudden fear. *"Oh, Billy, you gave me such a fright, jumping out like that!" said his mother, laughing.*

Alarm means fright caused by danger. *Alarm filled the passengers' faces when the bus skidded on the wet highway.*

Dread means great fear of something that may happen. *After a week of rain, people by the river live in dread of a flood.*

Panic means fear so great that it causes unreasonable, frantic activity. *In the movie, people fled in panic from the giant insects.*

Terror means very great fear. *Word of the approaching forest fire spread terror through the town.*

CONTINUED ON THE NEXT PAGE

Horror means terror. *Pam tries to hide it, but she has a real horror of dogs.*

Phobia means a deep, senseless fear of something in particular. *Mr. Collins lives on the ground floor because he has a phobia about heights.*

SEE **afraid, scare,** and **terrifying** for related words.
ANTONYMS: bravery, courage

WORD POOL

English is the largest language in the world, with many more than half a million words. One reason it grew so large is that English is always ready to create words. Many of these words are formed by putting together words from other languages. For instance, all these phobias—and many more— were named by combining the Greek name for the thing feared with the word *phobia*.

ailurophobia (fear of cats)
ballistophobia (fear of bullets)
clinophobia (fear of going to bed)
doraphobia (fear of fur)
eisoptrophobia (fear of mirrors)
gephyrophobia (fear of bridges)
harpaxophobia (fear of robbers)
ichthyophobia (fear of fish)
kakorraphiaphobia (fear of failure)
linonophobia (fear of string)
logophobia (fear of words)

myxophobia (fear of slime)
nephophobia (fear of clouds)
oikophobia (fear of home)
phronemophobia (fear of thinking)
rhabdophobia (fear of magic)
sciophobia (fear of shadows)
triskaidekaphobia (fear of thirteen)
teratophobia (fear of monsters)
xenophobia (fear of strangers)
zelophobia (fear of jealousy)

Feeling
noun

Feeling means a state of mind, such as anger, happiness, sadness, or fear. *Pilar was suddenly overcome by a strong feeling of homesickness as she looked at the photographs of her friends back home in Mexico City.*

Emotion means a strong feeling. It is not used to show feeling, but to describe it calmly. *Paige could barely control her emotions when she learned she had won the contest.*

Sense can mean a feeling, especially one that is not directly based on facts. *"I have a strong sense that we're being watched," said Tiye.*

Sensation can mean a sense. *Kevin gets a strange sensation of peacefulness whenever he sees his boyhood home.*

Sentiment can mean a feeling, especially a tender or noble one. *Everyone was touched when Grandma and Grandpa shared their sentiments at their fiftieth anniversary party.*

Passion means a very strong feeling. *Ana argued with great passion that she should be allowed to go to the same high school as her brothers.*

Mood means a feeling, especially one that lasts for a while. *After bowling that winning game, Dai was in a great mood all evening.*

Fierce
adjective

Fierce means ready and willing to fight. It suggests anger and desire to cause injury. *The Vikings were fierce warriors.*

Ferocious means very fierce. It is used mostly about animals. *The grizzly bear became ferocious when she saw someone too close to her cubs.*

Savage means fierce, uncontrolled, and uncivilized. *Drawing his cutlass, the savage pirate demanded the ship's treasure.*

Vicious can mean fierce by nature, without reason. *The vicious little dog ran onto the sidewalk barking loudly.*

Bloodthirsty means fierce and eager to kill. *Smaller dinosaurs fled from the bloodthirsty allosaurus.*

SEE **cruel** for related words.
ANTONYM: gentle

The **vicious** little dog ran onto the sidewalk barking loudly.

Fight
verb

Fight means to oppose someone or something with actions or words. *My grandfather fought in the Second World War. Our congresswoman is fighting the plan to dump chemicals outside town.*

Struggle means to fight with difficulty. *African Americans have long struggled against injustice and hatred.*

Battle means to fight for a long period of time. *To cross the bay, the swimmers battled the waves and tide.*

Combat means to fight something strongly. *The nurse explained to Joshua that shots are very important in combating disease.*

War means to fight very strongly for a very long time. *The warring nations finally signed a peace treaty after many months of fighting.*

Come to blows is an idiom that means to get into a fight. *The two cowboys came to blows over the price of the horse.*

SEE **argue, attack,** and **oppose** for related words.

Find
verb

Find means to come upon something. *This morning, Bess found a set of keys on the street.*

Discover means to find something that has not been known or that has been hidden. *Many explorers tried to discover the source of the Nile River.*

Detect means to notice or discover. *Abby detected a buzzing sound coming from the car engine.*

Locate can mean to find the position of someone or something. *I couldn't locate the street on the map, so Mom pulled over and asked a police officer for directions.*

Spot can mean to locate. *Luis tried to spot his sister in the crowd.*

Pinpoint means to locate exactly. *X rays pinpointed the site of the tumor.*

Run across means to find something or meet someone, usually by accident. *I ran across some old pictures of my grandparents yesterday.*

ANTONYMS: lose, misplace

Firm
adjective

Firm means with your mind made up and not about to change. *Penny's folks are very firm about not letting her break curfew.*

Determined means firm. It suggests keeping to a choice or plan in spite of questions or problems. *Determined to catch one of the caribou, the wolf followed the herd.*

Resolved means firm. It suggests a serious decision, made in spite of real problems. *Henry is resolved that he will make the basketball team despite his height.*

Rigid means very firm, perhaps more than is wise. *The restaurant has a rigid requirement that men wear ties and jackets.*

Inflexible means firm when change might be a good thing. *Mr. Leland's a great coach, but he's inflexible about our not skipping practice.*

Adamant means totally firm. *The witness was adamant in her testimony that she heard two shots.*

SEE **stubborn** for related words.

Determined to catch one of the caribou, the wolf followed the herd.

Fit
adjective

Fit means right for something. *Sometimes that cat acts as if its food weren't fit to eat.*

Proper means right for a particular situation or occasion. *Is this the proper dress to wear to the party?*

Suitable means proper. *Now that Mr. Lee is used to his wheelchair, he needs to find a suitable apartment.*

Appropriate means right for a particular situation. It often suggests good manners and thoughtfulness. *"Your aunt is helping to pay for your school, Delia, so it's appropriate to send her regular letters," said her mom.*

Becoming means right, expecially for someone of a particular sort or someone with a special job. *"Caitlin, your constant giggling is not becoming to someone your age," Grandfather complained.*

Apt can mean proper. *With a few apt words, Major Foxx convinced the general to send reinforcements.*

SEE **correct** for related words.
ANTONYMS: inappropriate, unsuitable

Flash
verb

Flash means to give out a sudden, brief light. *The light from the lighthouse flashed regularly every five seconds.*

Blink can mean to flash repeatedly. *The blinking neon sign across the street keeps changing the colors in Angela's room.*

Sparkle can mean to flash repeatedly and very brightly. *Yolanda's earrings sparkle when she turns her head.*

Glitter means to sparkle. *When mom wears her party dress with the sequins, she glitters all over.*

Twinkle means to flash repeatedly, with very brief light and dark periods. *It was a beautiful summer night, and the stars twinkled overhead.*

Flicker means to give out an unsteady, uneven light. *A cold wind rushed through the castle courtyard, making the torches flicker.*

Glimmer means to flicker softly or faintly. *Tyrone likes to watch the fireflies glimmer in the park at night.*

SEE **bright** and **shine** for related words.

Flee
verb

Flee means to go away in a hurry. *Outnumbered and low on supplies, the troops fled.*

Fly can mean to flee. It is used in more formal ways. *General Bolívar was forced to fly Venezuela in 1814, but within a few years he won its freedom from Spain.*

Bolt can mean to run away as fast as possible. *When no one was looking, the suspect bolted from the police station.*

Abscond means to go away suddenly and secretly, usually with something valuable. *Who would have expected quiet Mrs. Parker to abscond with fifty thousand dollars?*

Take to your heels means to run away. *From the porch, we watched the picnickers take to their heels when the rain began.*

SEE **avoid, escape,** and **evade** for related words.

Flexible
adjective

Flexible means bending easily without breaking. *Why is toast so much less flexible than bread?*

Elastic means able to bend or stretch easily and then return to its original shape. *These casual slacks feature roomy pleats and a comfortable elastic waistband.*

Springy means elastic. It suggests a rapid, strong return to the original shape. *"The wood for your bow," said Eagle Watching, "must be springy and with no flaw."*

Pliable means very flexible. *Mr. Mann is using some thick, pliable wire to unclog the bathroom sink.*

Resilient means springy. *The Nortons want to buy a firm, resilient mattress for Carol's bed.*

Supple means flexible. It is often used to describe people. *In order to be a good gymnast, you have to be strong and supple.*

SEE **bend** for related words.
ANTONYMS: inflexible, rigid, stiff

Flow
verb

Flow means to move in a current. *More than two hundred tributaries flow into the Amazon River.*

Pour means to flow steadily. *A crowd gathered to watch as smoke poured from the burning restaurant.*

Stream means to flow strongly. *Water streamed from the open hydrant.*

Gush means to flow suddenly and in large amounts. *Arthur stared in awe as oil gushed from his family's land.*

Spurt means to flow out with squirting force. *Water spurted from the broken pipe.*

Well can mean to flow steadily from a place, like water rising in a well. *When smoke began welling out of the fireplace, Rafael realized he had forgotten to open the flue.*

Fly
verb

Fly means to move through the air by using wings. *Rita watched nervously as the yellow jacket flew around her can of root beer.*

Wing can mean to fly. It is used mostly about living things. *The swallows return each spring, after winging thousands of miles from the south.*

Soar means to fly upward or very high. *We watched as the eagle soared above the lake.*

Flap can mean to fly with large movements of the wings. *A flock of crows flapped over the farmhouse and then landed in the field.*

Flutter can mean to move the wings quickly but not strongly. *The pigeons fluttered when Juan walked by, but they did not fly away.*

Flit means to fly by fluttering, usually a short distance. *Easily escaping the cat, the birds flit from branch to branch.*

Hover means to stay in one place in the air. *The hummingbird hovers at the flower while it drinks nectar.*

The hummingbird **hovers** at the flower while it drinks nectar.

Follow
verb

Follow means to move in the same direction as someone or something. *The wolves follow the caribou, hoping to catch one.*

Chase means to follow fast and try to catch. *The Shermans' dog is locked in their yard because otherwise she chases cars.*

Pursue means to chase. It is a formal word. *Detective Garcia is now pursuing the car used in the robbery.*

Track and **trail** mean to follow by marks or sound or smell. *"The bandits are only hours ahead of us," said the sheriff, "so their hoof-prints will be easy to track." The posse trailed the bandits to the Bar None Ranch.*

Shadow can mean to follow closely and secretly. *The crooks shadowed the bank messenger, but he noticed them and got away.*

Tail means to follow closely and secretly. *If we tail the spy to her hideout, we may learn how she gets information.*

Tag after means to follow closely and constantly. It suggests that the follower is unwanted. *My sister has her own friends now, and she doesn't tag after me anymore.*

Fond
adjective

Fond means feeling love or a strong liking, or showing such a feeling. *Marla is fond of horses. Dad welcomed Mom home from her business trip with a fond hug.*

Affectionate means fond. It suggests familiarity and closeness. *Mrs. Salvado and Mrs. Erskine are old friends, and their affectionate teasing has gone on for years.*

Tender can mean fond. It suggests kindness toward someone who needs care. *With a tender smile, Celia took the hand of her baby brother, who was still learning to walk.*

Warm can mean fond. It suggests enthusiasm. *Everyone in school gave Mrs. Uchiyama a warm welcome on her first day back after having her baby.*

Devoted means very fond and loyal. *Conrad is devoted to science fiction and reads it whenever he can.*

Foolish
adjective

Foolish means senseless and not wise. *It was foolish of Gina to trust a stranger with her money.*

Silly means so senseless that it makes people laugh. *I wish my brother wouldn't wear that silly hat all the time.*

Nonsensical means foolish in a way that does not make any sense. *Tony forgot to tell the middle of the joke, so the punchline was just nonsensical.*

Idiotic means very foolish and stupid. *It was idiotic of Brad to swim alone at night.*

Absurd means foolish and clearly wrong. *Today it seems absurd that people used to think the earth was flat.*

Preposterous means obviously and extremely foolish. *"You cannot go downtown alone," Mrs. Orlanes told her daughter. "The idea is preposterous."*

Asinine means so foolish that it lacks any human intelligence. *It's a really asinine movie about giant lizards—probably made by some.*

SEE **crazy** and **stupid** for related words.
ANTONYMS: sensible, wise

It's a really **asinine** movie about giant lizards—probably made by some.

▼ **WORD POOL**

There are many words, especially slang words, that mean foolish. Among them are:

boneheaded	harebrained	tomfool
cockeyed	inane	witless
dippy	loony	wacky
dizzy	loopy	zany
goofy		

Why do you think there are so many? Why are they mostly slang?

Forbid
verb

Forbid means to refuse to allow something. *Joetta's dad forbids her to hang around with any gang.*

Prohibit means to forbid by law or official rule. *Many companies prohibit smoking in the workplace.*

Ban means to prohibit. *Dictators usually ban any criticism of their governments.*

Bar can mean to prohibit. It is used especially about refusal to allow entry. *Hunting is barred in this wildlife refuge.*

Veto can mean to forbid, officially or personally. *The President has vetoed six bills this year.*

Rule out means forbid, especially in a general way for a good reason. *The doctor rules out all sports for Augustin until his sprained ankle is completely better.*

SEE **prevent** for related words.
ANTONYMS: allow, permit

Force
verb

Force means to use power to get someone to do something, usually unwillingly. *The dictator forced the newspaper to stop publishing.*

Make can mean to force. *"You can't make me believe that!" George said. "I know Alonzo's not a liar!"*

Drive can mean to force. *"Turn that noise down," Linda's father shouted up the stairs, "or you'll drive us all crazy!"*

Compel means to force, especially unwillingly. *When Mr. Twodeer lost his job, he was compelled to sell his house.*

Impel means to force. It suggests giving a reason or a desire to do something. *Doubts about the suspect's story impelled the detective to search for more evidence.*

Coerce means to compel, often by means of threats. *"I don't want you to feel coerced, but—if you don't eat your vegetables, there'll be no TV for you tonight," said Grandma.*

SEE **persuade** and **urge** for related words.

CONTINUED ON THE NEXT PAGE

Forecast
verb

Forecast means to tell what is going to happen. It suggests the use of scientific methods. *No one believed the Weather Bureau when it forecast heavy snow in May.*

Predict means to forecast. It can be used to describe any method of knowing the future. *This sports columnist predicts that the Houston Astros will win the pennant.*

Foretell means to forecast. It suggests that scientific methods are not used. *Rosa's violin teacher foretells a concert career for her.*

Prophesy means to foretell. *Owen is saving money for a new bike, but I prophesy he'll spend it on computer games first.*

Foresee means to know what is going to happen. It suggests knowing a long time in advance. *Few people foresaw how quickly the Soviet Union would come to an end.*

SEE **expect** and **warn** for related words.

No one believed the Weather Bureau when it **forecast** heavy snow in May.

Formal
adjective

Formal means according to accepted ideas of public good manners. *The principal sent each graduate a formal letter of congratulations.*

Courtly means having manners suitable for a royal court. *The peasant boy made such a courtly speech to the queen that she made him her page.*

Refined means extremely polite and in no way coarse or unpleasant. *Mr. Garcia is so very refined that he always stands up when a woman enters the room.*

Cultivated can mean refined. *"If I were not a cultivated lady," said Priscilla, "I should call you a bad name, sir!"*

Well-bred means taught good manners in childhood. *Charmayne got the job because she's smart and well-bred.*

Chivalrous means having manners suitable for a knight of the Middle Ages. It is used about men. *It is chivalrous of Hank to take the blame, but Marcy actually wrote the note.*

SEE **polite** for related words.
ANTONYM: casual

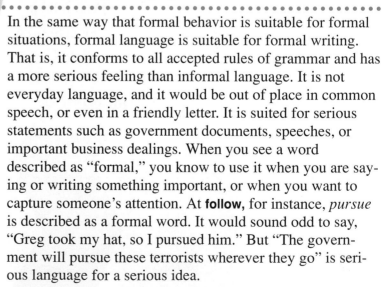

WRITING TIP: Formal Language

In the same way that formal behavior is suitable for formal situations, formal language is suitable for formal writing. That is, it conforms to all accepted rules of grammar and has a more serious feeling than informal language. It is not everyday language, and it would be out of place in common speech, or even in a friendly letter. It is suited for serious statements such as government documents, speeches, or important business dealings. When you see a word described as "formal," you know to use it when you are saying or writing something important, or when you want to capture someone's attention. At **follow,** for instance, *pursue* is described as a formal word. It would sound odd to say, "Greg took my hat, so I pursued him." But "The government will pursue these terrorists wherever they go" is serious language for a serious idea.

Fragile
adjective

Fragile means easily broken or damaged. *On moving day, Mr. Nygren insisted on carrying his mother's fragile old vase by hand.*

Breakable means able to be broken. *Luis is careful to put eggs and other breakable items at the top of the grocery bag.*

Frail can mean easily broken. *The frail legs of the antique table could not support the weight of the clock.*

Delicate can mean very easily broken. *"This one is my favorite," Michael said, carefully holding up a delicate glass unicorn.*

Brittle means hard, but easily broken. *Exercise and calcium-rich foods can help people keep from developing brittle bones as they get older.*

SEE **weak** for related words.
ANTONYMS: durable, sturdy, tough

On moving day, Mr. Nygren insisted on carrying his mother's **fragile** old vase by hand.

WRITER'S CHOICE

Forty, fifty, even sixty below zero—actual temperature, not windchill—seems to change everything. Steel becomes brittle and breaks, shatters; breath taken straight into the throat will freeze the lining and burst blood vessels; eyes exposed too long will freeze; fingers and toes freeze, turn black, and break off. These are all known, normal parts of intense cold.

—Gary Paulsen, *Woodsong*

Why *brittle?* At such low temperatures, steel is still hard and strong, but it may break if something hits it. *Brittle* shows both qualities of the metal in this condition.

Frank
adjective

Frank means saying exactly what is on your mind. *Laurie and Tim had a frank discussion about dating other people.*

Sincere means true to a person's real thoughts and feelings. *James offered Coach Hidalgo his sincere apologies for being late to practice so often.*

Direct can mean frank, without trying to hide or change anything. *"I'll be direct," said Enya. "That wallpaper looks terrible!"*

Straight can mean direct. *After the accident, Sam wanted straight answers about his injured knee.*

Straightforward means frank and clear. *Xavier's straightforward admission that he had lost the book made his parents a little less angry.*

Open can mean frank and sincere. *Although he reads lips well, Charlie has an open preference for friends who know sign language.*

Candid means honestly truthful, no matter what. *Bronwyn was utterly candid and said she just hated the whole idea.*

Blunt can mean a bit too frank, without being careful of others' feelings. *Grandpa tends to be a little blunt in his opinions of the neighbors.*

Make no bones about something means to be frank about it. *Dimitri made no bones about the fact that he trusted his wife's judgment more than his own.*

SEE **honest** and **trust** for related words.
ANTONYM: evasive

WRITING TIP: Be Direct

Good writing is straightforward; you say what you mean directly instead of beating around the bush.

It's better, for instance, to say

> "forgot" than "failed to recall,"
> "create" than "cause to be,"
> "distrusts" than "does not have confidence in,"
> "completed" than "carried through to the conclusion."

After its flipper healed, they **released** the turtle.

Free
verb

Free means to let out of prison, slavery, or any kind of burden. *Three students helped Ms. Wyandotte free her car after the snowplow covered it.*

Release can mean to free. *After its flipper healed, they released the turtle.*

Deliver can mean to release. *Delivered from slavery by an 1828 New York State law, Sojourner Truth became one of the most famous women of her time.*

Liberate means to free. It is often used about public events. *In 1991, Kuwait was liberated from Iraqi rule after months of war.*

Emancipate is a formal word that means to free. *In 1861, millions of people in Russia became free when Czar Alexander II emancipated the serfs.*

Turn loose means to free. It suggests letting go from a leash, a cage, or something like them. *"Play time," Hilda said, pushing open the gate and turning loose the excited colt.*

SEE **liberty** for related words
ANTONYM: imprison

Friend
noun

Friend means someone you like and who likes you. *Colleen's friends gave her a surprise birthday party.*

Comrade means a friend with whom you share things. *Gwen and her comrades in her Girl Scout troop are planning a trip to the zoo.*

Companion means a close friend who accompanies a person. *"Miss Hale and I take this trip every year," Miss Alexander explained, introducing her companion.*

Sidekick is an informal word that means companion. *"Well, Jed," Prairie Pete told his sidekick, "seems we've cleaned up this old town."*

Pal means a friend and companion. *"Be a pal," Myron begged, "and ask her if she likes me."*

Buddy is an informal word that means a close friend. *Ken and his buddy Yuji are almost like brothers.*

Amigo means a close friend who understands you well. *"Let's go, amigo," said David, grabbing his skateboard and Damian's arm.*

Playmate means a person you play with often. *When my kid brother and his playmates are around, I try to be someplace else.*

SEE **familiar** and **friendly** for related words.
ANTONYMS: enemy, foe

AROUND THE WORLD: Friendship

A friend in need is a friend indeed.
— **English proverb**

A good friend is revealed on a bad day.
—**Turkish proverb**

On the day of poverty you know who is a true friend.
— **Ghanaian proverb**

He who helps you in need is a true friend.
— **Swahili proverb** (East Africa)

Know a friend when you are in trouble.
— **Tamil proverb** (India)

Friendly
adjective

Friendly means pleasant and acting like a friend. *William Penn stayed on friendly terms with the Indians of Pennsylvania.*

Cordial means friendly, hearty, and warm. *The speaker received a cordial greeting from the principal, who was once her English teacher.*

Genial means friendly and cheerful. *Mr. Cheng welcomed us to the store with a genial smile.*

Sociable means friendly and fond of company. *Uncle Leon is a sociable man who loves conversation and parties.*

Neighborly means friendly to the neighbors. *It was neighborly of the Rasmussens to bring over dinner when Dad was so sick.*

Agreeable, good-natured, and **likable** all mean pleasant to other people and easy to like. *Agreeable people like Lisa seem to make everyone around them good-natured too. Mom says I'll have more friends if I try to be more likable, but that's easier to say than do.*

Amiable means friendly, agreeable, and courteous to others. *Ms. Stanley is so amiable that she sells a lot of cars.*

SEE **familiar, nice, polite,** and **thoughtful** for related words.
ANTONYMS: belligerent, unfriendly

Uncle Leon is a **sociable** man who loves conversation and parties.

Frown
verb

Frown means to wrinkle your forehead to show anger, disapproval, or deep thought. *Vance knew by the way his mother frowned that he had let her down.*

Scowl means to lower your eyebrows and turn down your mouth in order to show anger. *"You expect this court to believe you?" asked the District Attorney, scowling at the witness.*

Glare can mean to stare fiercely and angrily. *Crazy Horse glared at the soldiers as they crowded about him.*

Pout means to push out your lips to show displeasure or anger. *"All right, stop pouting—we'll do it your way," Mary told Mark.*

Glower means to scowl and glare. *The wrestler shouted defiance and glowered into the TV camera.*

Full
adjective

Full means holding as much as possible. *I hate it when the bus is so full it goes past without stopping.*

Crowded means filled with people. *Cheers for the soldiers on parade came from the crowded sidewalks.*

Packed and **jam-packed** mean filled tightly. *On July 4 the beaches will be packed. It will take hours to get to the beach, because the roads are all jam-packed.*

Stuffed means filled so tightly that it's hard to get things out. *"Roger, this washing machine is stuffed with your towels," said his mother.*

Jammed means filled more tightly than something should be. *They forced their way into the elevator, even though it was already jammed with people.*

CONTINUED ON THE NEXT PAGE

I hate it when the bus is so **full** it goes past without stopping.

182

Crammed means filled more tightly than something should be. *A sewer opening crammed with paper and plastic caused the street to fill with water.*

Chock-full means filled so tightly that no more will fit in. *"Chock-full of jokes—a laugh riot!" says this ad for the movie.*

ANTONYM: empty

WORD STORY

Many words are combined with *full* to show that something is complete, strong, or of the greatest possible size or extent. Someone with a *"full-blown* case of chicken pox" probably has a face covered with blisters. A *"full-bodied* cup of tea" is strong tea, with much flavor. A *"full-fledged* bird" has grown all its feathers.

Full-fledged is also used in more general ways. A "full-fledged lawyer" has completed law school, passed the bar, and found employment as a lawyer. What might qualify someone as a "full-fledged writer" or a "full-fledged doctor"?

Fun
noun

Fun means activity that gives pleasure and excitement. *The whole Ortiz family had fun at the carnival and dance.*

Amusement means any interesting and pleasant activity. *Anita began drawing cartoons as an amusement, but now she works hard at them.*

Pastime means amusement. *Bill's favorite pastime is reading.*

Entertainment means an activity that gives pleasure to an audience. *Professional wrestling is a popular entertainment.*

Play means anything you do for enjoyment with your body or your mind. *Since chores take up all morning, summer afternoon is Mercedes' time for play.*

Recreation is any activity done in order to relax, especially after school or work. *Softball, volleyball, and bicycling are Graham's favorite forms of recreation.*

Hobby means a favorite amusement, done often and regularly. *Nanna Chigi makes such beautiful needlework, it is hard to believe this is only a hobby.*

SEE **game** and **happy** for related words.

Funny
adjective

Funny means causing people to laugh or to be amused. *"This toy is really funny," Sylvia said. "You squeeze its nose and it honks."*

Amusing means mildly funny. *Jean told the class that <u>Chloris and the Creeps</u> might not make them laugh out loud, but it was amusing.*

Witty means funny in a clever way. *Kieran always makes these witty remarks with a perfectly straight face.*

Laughable means funny. It often suggests laughter that makes fun of someone. *Tom's prediction that his team will win first place is laughable.*

Humorous means meant to be funny. *Casey enjoys watching humorous movies from long ago.*

Comic means funny in a happy way. *Hilary delivered the last line with a hiccup and a comic grin.*

Comical means funny. It often suggests that something was not meant to be funny. *The look on Pat's face when she swallowed her gum was comical.*

Hilarious means very funny. *Ida thought the book was hilarious, but her big sister said it was childish.*

Ridiculous means so foolish that it is funny. *The movie has one ridiculous scene with twenty people in a tiny room.*

SEE **humor, joke,** and **laugh** for related words.
ANTONYMS: grave, serious

WORDS AT PLAY

If you seek ways of saying "humorous,"
Your choice of words is numerous.
You also have a wealth of various
Expressions for "hilarious."
And synonyms for "comical"?
The number's astronomical!

Casey enjoys watching **humorous** movies from long ago.

Gadget
noun

Gadget means a small, useful tool having a special purpose. *Dad sends away for every gadget he sees advertised on TV.*

Widget is an informal word that means a gadget. *Ronald's knife has a nail file, scissors, and six other widgets on it.*

Gizmo is a slang word that means a gadget. *We need a gizmo for the sink to catch stuff before it goes down the drain.*

Contraption is an informal word that means an odd, complicated gadget or machine. *Mr. Sotomayor rigged up a contraption that he attached to the window to scare pigeons.*

SEE **tool** for related words.

WORD POOL

People have made up many words to mean any gadget or device for which they can't think of the right name. These words are all meant to sound funny. The ones you know probably depend on where your parents and grandparents grew up; the words change over time too.

dingus	dojigger	thingumabob
doodad	gigamaree	thingumajig
doohickey	hootmalalie	whatchmacallit

Mr. Sotomayor rigged up a **contraption** that he attached to the window to scare pigeons.

185

Game
noun

Game means anything played for fun. *Annette is a whiz at every kind of electronic game.*

Sport means any physical activity done for enjoyment, especially one with special rules. *Baseball was Tommy's favorite sport, until he discovered hockey.*

Athletics means games that use the body's strength, speed, or skill. *The math team has complained that the school newspaper neglects them in favor of covering athletics.*

Contest means a test of skill to see who wins. *Raquel beat Todd in their bubble-blowing contest.*

Competition can mean a contest. *First prize in the tango competition goes to Mr. and Mrs. Rojas.*

SEE **fun** and **happy** for related words.

Gather
verb

Gather means to bring or come together. *Silvie gathered all the lab instruments and put them away.*

Collect means to gather, especially for a particular reason. *The lawyer worked hard collecting evidence to get his client acquitted. Trang made some money collecting bottles to recycle.*

Accumulate means to gather gradually. *Roxy has used her baby-sitting money to accumulate all of the Gorgeous Lizard CDs.*

Congregate means to come together into a crowd. *By 7:00 that morning, people had already begun to congregate at the ticket office.*

Round up means to bring together scattered things or people. *When it was time to leave, the teachers rounded up students from all over the museum.*

SEE **call** for related words.

When it was time to leave, the teachers **rounded up** students from all over the museum.

General
adjective

General means for everyone or everything. *A G-rated movie is suitable for a general audience.*

Universal means general. It emphasizes how widely something exists or happens. *There was universal relief when the Civil War finally ended.*

Global can mean universal. *The astronauts' plight was a matter of global concern.*

Public means for all the people. *The public schools get their money from taxes.*

Widespread can mean existing in many places, among many people. *In our neighborhood there is widespread interest in lowering taxes.*

Far-reaching means very widespread in effect. *The discovery of antibiotics was a far-reaching advance in the control of disease.*

Extensive means far-reaching. *Extensive investigation of the scandal has led several board members to resign.*

Sweeping can mean far-reaching. It is used when something might be limited but actually is broad. *When the new president took office, she made sweeping changes in government.*

SEE **common** and **usual** for related words.

Generous
adjective

Generous means willing and eager to share. *Mr. Peterson's students like him because he is generous with his time and attention.*

Charitable means generous to those in need. *Mr. and Mrs. Wu do a lot of charitable work at the hospital.*

Bighearted means generous and kind. *It was bighearted of Faith to give her lunch to that lost dog.*

Liberal means generous. It suggests giving freely and in large amounts. *All the Rodriguez kids get liberal weekly allowances.*

Lavish means extremely liberal. *Every year the whole family gets together for a lavish holiday dinner.*

SEE **gift** for related words.
ANTONYMS: miserly, stingy

Gentle
adjective

Gentle means smooth and light and quiet, not forceful or sudden or upsetting. *Fujio closed his eyes as a gentle breeze ruffled his hair.*

Soft can mean gentle. *Sissy sang to the crying baby in a soft voice.*

Tender can mean gentle and kind. *The tender touch of Owen's hands soothed his frightened puppy.*

Mild means gentle and calm. *Matt has a mild manner but a strong will.*

Meek means gentle and patient, not quick to anger. *"Be careful," Cynthia warned her new friend. "My cat looks meek, but she's a real tiger."*

Balmy means gentle, pleasant, and refreshing. *"Expect balmy weather this morning," the radio announcer said, "but carry an umbrella for later."*

SEE **calm** for related words.
ANTONYMS: harsh, rough, violent

Get
verb

Get means to have something that you did not have before. *Linc gets a letter every week from his father, who works overseas.*

Obtain means to get something by an effort. *After weeks of practice, Rita obtained her driver's license on the first try.*

Secure can mean to obtain, especially when there is a chance of not getting something. *Danny secured tickets for the concert by waiting in line all night.*

Acquire means to get and own, usually after much effort. *After years of hard work and saving, the Loneros were finally able to acquire their own home.*

Receive means to get something that has been given or sent or handed to you. *Harold received a black eye in the fight.*

Fetch means to go and get something. *Wait here while I run and fetch my glasses.*

Win can mean to get something by effort, skill, or luck. *Lucia won the respect of the crowd for standing up to the bully.*

CONTINUED ON THE NEXT PAGE

Earn means to get something by working for it. *Wendy earns her allowance by taking out the garbage every day.*

Gain can mean to get something worth having. *"Now Jackson gains control of the basketball and races down the court!" the sportscaster cried.*

SEE **catch** and **recover** for related words.

▼ **VERB PLUS**

Sometimes when a word is added to a verb, it creates a phrase that has special meaning. Here are some phrases with **get:**

Get along means to be friendly. *I get along with most of the kids in my class.*

Get away with means to escape punishment for something. *The bandits got away with the robbery by hiding in the old mine.*

Get to means to be allowed to. *"You don't get to order me around just because you're older!" protested Dick to his sister.*

Gift
noun

Gift means something that is given without expecting anything back. *David brought Liz a graduation gift.*

Present means a gift. *The other teachers are giving Mrs. Tanner presents because she's going to have a baby.*

Contribution means a gift, usually of money, to an organization that receives many gifts. *The American Cancer Society uses contributions to fund research.*

Donation means a contribution. *The shelter's lunches are a donation from the local supermarket.*

Legacy means something given by an ancestor, especially in a will. *Tony received a legacy of one thousand dollars when his uncle died.*

SEE **generous** for related words.

David brought Liz a graduation **gift**.

Give
verb

Give means to let someone else have something that was yours. *Mrs. Foster gives ten dollars every month to her church.*

SEE **distribute** and **gift** for related words.

Give is used in phrases that have special meanings. Each of these phrases has its own set of synonyms.

give away

Give away means to let a secret become known. *The game show host accidentally gave away the correct answer.*

Reveal means to make something known. *Derek's accent reveals that he grew up in Jamaica.*

Betray means to let a secret become known to an enemy. *The spy betrayed the general's plans to the enemy.*

Let the cat out of the bag and **spill the beans** are idioms that mean to let a secret become known. *Juana knows all about the surprise party because somebody let the cat out of the bag. George claims he didn't spill the beans about the party.*

give out

Give out means to come to an end. It suggests that something has been used up. *Because Ray is out of training, his strength gives out if he plays hard.*

Fail can mean to give out or to be not enough. *When the wind failed, the sailboat could not go forward.*

Expire means to come to an end. *My library card has expired, so I'm going to get it renewed.*

Lapse can mean to come to an end, especially because something has not been used or renewed. *My magazine subscription has lapsed.*

CONTINUED ON THE NEXT PAGE

190

give up

Give up means to stop doing something. *Whatever dangers he faced, Tall Pine did not give up his journey.*

Quit means to give up. *Mr. Murphy had to quit painting the steps when it got dark.*

Surrender means to stop resisting or fighting. It often means to lose control of something by stopping. *France surrendered its claim to Canada in 1763.*

Yield can mean to surrender. *After decades of struggle, the British finally yielded India its independence.*

Relinquish means to let someone else have control or ownership of something. *"It's time you relinquished the computer to someone else, Liang," said Mrs. McGee.*

Throw in the towel is an idiom that means to stop fighting for something. *When a third burger joint opened in their block, the Stopfels threw in the towel and closed their coffee shop.*

Whatever dangers he faced, Tall Pine did not **give up** his journey.

191

Go
verb

Go means to move. *Let's go outside and play ball. Oh my, just look at that horse go!*

SEE **hurry, run,** and **walk** for related words.

Go is used in phrases that have special meanings. Each of these phrases has its own set of synonyms.

go around

Go around means to move from place to place. *The night guard goes around the building checking for trouble.*

Stray means to leave the correct path or to move without purpose. *If a sheep strays from the herd, the dog chases it back.*

Wander means to move here and there without purpose. *Moustafa wandered until the caravan found him.*

Roam means to wander. It often suggests long distances. *A pack of stray dogs has roamed the neighborhood for weeks.*

Rove and **range** mean to roam. *Ms. Alberts roved all over the Pacific Northwest on her vacation this summer. She ranged throughout New England last year.*

Ramble means to wander, especially on foot. It suggests a happy, peaceful time. *Joe and Kamal rambled over the hill and back.*

Gallivant means to go around looking for fun. *"I don't want you gallivanting around the neighborhood when your homework's not done, young man!" said Steve's mother firmly.*

If a sheep **strays** from the herd, the dog chases it back.

go away

Go away means to move from a place. *Vinny's mother said she had a headache, and we should all go away, please.*

Leave means to go away from someplace or from someone. *Carlos left his friends and went on alone.*

Depart is a formal word that means to leave. *The outraged ambassador departed, angrily threatening war.*

Withdraw can mean to leave, often because you have to. *Told by police to go or be arrested, the demonstrators withdrew.*

CONTINUED ON THE NEXT PAGE

Retreat means to withdraw. *We had to retreat before the enemy forces.*

Quit can mean to leave. *Lucius will have to quit the football team if his grades don't improve.*

Desert means to leave when it is wrong to leave. *The sailors deserted the sinking ship and its passengers.*

Abandon can mean to leave suddenly. It suggests going away from a problem with no thought of returning. *Last week, three cars were abandoned in the vacant lot.*

Vamoose is an informal word that means to leave very quickly and suddenly. *When the dog charged, the squirrels vamoosed.*

go over

Go over means to do something again and again in order to learn it. *The band went over the song three times before Jenny got the words right.*

Practice means to go over. *Miles has been practicing the "invisible thread" magic trick all week.*

Rehearse means to practice a play or other performance by doing it again and again. *Toyia makes dinner on Thursdays because her mom rehearses with the choir that night.*

Review means to read again or study again in order to be sure of learning. *Mrs. Gamba had her class review fractions on Friday.*

Repeat means to do something again, especially to say something a second time. *Kate repeated the directions to be sure she knew where to go.*

Good

adjective

Good has many meanings. They all share feelings of approval and satisfaction. *I had a good meal at that diner—tasty and not expensive. Marceea is a good soccer player. It was good of you to help me with the dishes last night.*

People often use *good* when another word would be more precise and more interesting. Because there are so many synonyms for *good* at various places in this book, they are not listed here. Find the idea you want to describe in the list below, and then see that set of synonyms.

SEE **beautiful** for words that mean pleasing to the senses.
SEE **correct** for words that mean right or having no mistakes.
SEE **excellent** for words that mean extremely good.
SEE **fair** for words that mean just and honest.
SEE **grand** for words that mean dignified or impressive.
SEE **kind** for words that describe people who are pleasant and nice.
SEE **useful** for words that mean good for a particular purpose.
SEE **well** for words that mean in good health.
SEE **wonderful** for words that mean very fine.

ANTONYM: bad

WORD WORKSHOP

The word *good* is often overused. See what happens in the paragraph below when we replace *good* with more precise words.

Some of my friends and I thought it would be a good

idea to start a band. For beginners, I think we're

excellent
~~good~~ musicians. Our drummer, Michael, has a *precise* ~~good~~ sense

of rhythm. Jennifer, our lead singer, has a *lovely* ~~good~~

voice. And José has a *useful* ~~good~~ knowledge of music. Once we

performed before our friends and parents, hoping for

good reviews. Our friends said, "*Awesome* ~~Good~~ band," but our

parents just said, "Loud."

The Grand Canyon at sunrise is a **splendid** sight.

Grand
adjective

Grand means large, fine-looking, and impressive. *Downtown by the river there are several grand hotels.*

Magnificent means grand in a richly ornamental or colorful way. *The French king Louis XIV built a magnificent palace at Versailles.*

Splendid means magnificent. *The Grand Canyon at sunrise is a splendid sight.*

Glorious means especially magnificent and exciting. *The concert will end in a glorious fireworks display.*

Majestic means grand and very dignified. *The inauguration of a President is a majestic event.*

Noble can mean grand in a powerful, admirable way. *The picture shows a noble mountain landscape.*

SEE **beautiful, excellent,** and **wonderful** for related words.
ANTONYMS: small, unimpressive

Gratify
verb

Gratify means to satisfy someone's wishes. *We gratified Sandra's curiosity and told her the whole story.*

Indulge means to yield to someone's wishes in order to please. *The grandparents tended to indulge their granddaughter too much.*

Pamper means to indulge someone too much. *They pamper their poodle—he has enough toys for five dogs.*

Spoil can mean to indulge someone, especially a child, so much that he or she may become selfish. *Too much attention can spoil a child.*

Humor can mean to give in to someone's demands or whims. *The baby is sick, so we try to humor him.*

195

Great
adjective

Great has many meanings. They all share feelings of importance and impressiveness. *Great baseball players are honored in the Baseball Hall of Fame. Amelia Earhart was a great aviator.*

People often use *great* when another word would be more precise and more interesting. Because there are so many synonyms for *great* at various places in this book, they are not listed here. Find the idea you want to describe in the list below and then see that set of synonyms.

SEE **big** and **huge** for words that mean above average in size.
SEE **excellent** for words that mean extremely good.
SEE **expert** for words that mean skillful or very well trained.
SEE **famous** for words that mean widely known.
SEE **grand** for words that mean dignified or impressive.
SEE **wonderful** for words that mean very fine.

WORD WORKSHOP

The word *great* is often overused. See what happens in the paragraph below when we replace *great* with more precise words.

The Russos had a ~~great~~ *wonderful* vacation in Mexico. They went to

the ruins of a great city, Chichén Itzá. What they

liked best was ~~a great~~ *an enormous* pyramid. Inside the pyramid is a

stairway to a ~~great~~ *magnificent* jaguar throne. Another highlight of

this ~~great~~ *famous* capital is the Temple of Warriors. Columns

with carvings of ~~great~~ *noble* warriors flank the temple, and

columns with ~~great~~ *awesome* feathered-serpent heads support the

temple's arch. These ~~great~~ *splendid* structures

show the amazing talents of the ~~great~~ *skilled*

architects and great artists of

ancient Mexico.

Columns with **awesome** feathered-serpent heads support the temple's arch.

196

Greedy
adjective

> "The love of money is the root of all evil."
>
> — New Testament (I Timothy, 6:10)

Greedy means wanting a whole lot of something. *Stacey was so greedy that he ate all the leftover enchiladas.*

Selfish means caring too much about yourself and what you have or want. *Alan is so selfish that he refuses to donate any of his games to needy kids—even games he never plays with.*

Grasping means greedy. It suggests unkindness and possible dishonesty. *The grasping storekeeper tried to cheat the new settlers.*

Grabby means greedy. It suggests forceful selfishness. *"If you're not grabby, Harry, how did you get so much candy?" asked Graciela.*

Envious means resentful that someone else has what you want. *Joanne was envious of Marcia's sweater and was sure it would look better on her.*

Jealous can mean envious. *The puppy was jealous of the new baby for a while, but now they're playmates.*

ANTONYM: generous

Grip
verb

Grip means to hold firmly with the hand or hands. *Gripping the bat nervously, Rory stepped into the batter's box.*

Grasp means to grip tightly. *Consuela grasped the railing as she walked up the dark stairs.*

Clutch means to grasp. *The tiny girl clutched her doll and wouldn't let go.*

Clench can mean to grasp. *Clenching his hat in both hands, Juwon went down the windy alley.*

Clasp can mean to hold tightly with the hands or arms. *"Gold!" shrieked the pirate, clasping the treasure to him.*

SEE **catch** for related words.

HAVE YOU HEARD...?

You may have heard the expression "grasping at straws." To grasp at straws means to try to get out of trouble by methods that are very unlikely to succeed. It comes from the saying "A drowning person will grasp at straws." Floating straw cannot help a person stay afloat, but someone in real trouble will try anything.

197

Group
noun

Group means a number of people, animals, or things. *A group of fans stayed after the show, hoping to get autographs.*

Bundle means a group of items tied or wrapped up. *Bryan tied his dirty shirts into a bundle and headed for the Laundromat.*

Bunch means a group of things of one kind, held or growing together. *"While you're out, pick up a bunch of ripe bananas, please," Mrs. Schiller asked her son.*

Cluster means items of one kind forming a small, tight group. *Those clusters of flowers attract the butterflies.*

Clump means cluster. *Clumps of weeds are sprouting in the cracks in the sidewalk.*

Lot means a number of similar items, thought of as one large item. *This lot of grapefruit came from Texas, and those two lots came from Florida.*

Set means a group of things that belong together. *These dishes are sold as a set, so you can't buy only a couple.*

Batch can mean a group, especially of items made at one time. *Serafina and Bart baked four batches of cookies for the party.*

SEE **company** and **crowd** for related words.

WORD STORY

Batch comes from *bake*. In the same way that you see a sight, think a thought, or do a deed, people used to bake a batch. Any group of baked items was a batch. People still use the word for baked goods, but now it's used for a lot of other things too.

Those **clusters** of flowers attract the butterflies.

Grow
verb

Flowers **develop** from buds into full bloom.

Grow means to increase in size or amount. *The singer's fame grew with every album.*

Develop means to grow and change gradually. *Flowers develop from buds into full bloom.*

Evolve means to develop over a long time, with many stages. *Our knowledge of the solar system has evolved over hundreds of years.*

Mature means to become completely grown. It suggests fulfillment. *Lara has matured a great deal during her years in the Navy.*

Ripen means to mature. *When the grain has ripened, the people of Soyan's village begin the harvest.*

Sprout means to start growing. *Etta put some carrot tops in water, and they've sprouted.*

Bud can mean to show signs of becoming or developing. *Ms. Hendrix says my drawings show I'm a budding artist.*

SEE **increase** for related words.
ANTONYMS: decrease, shrink

Guard
verb

Guard means to keep someone or something safe. *Secret Service agents guard the President at all times.*

Defend means to guard, especially from an attack. *Ute warriors gathered to defend their village against the Navajo.*

Protect means to guard, especially from danger. *Jorge wears goggles while welding in order to protect his eyes.*

Shield means to protect. *Sondra wears a cap with a long bill to shield her face from the sun.*

Shelter means to protect. *In very cold weather, the church is open at night to shelter the homeless.*

Cover can mean to guard. *The sheriff told his deputies to cover him as he went after the rustlers.*

SEE **look after** (at **look**) and **shelter** for related words.

Guess
verb

Guess means to form an opinion without really knowing the facts. *"Guess who was with Doreen at the mall this weekend!" exclaimed Alison.*

Suppose means to believe without knowing for sure. *Chita didn't come out to play, so I suppose she went somewhere with her mother.*

Assume means to suppose or to take something for granted. *Tony assumes he'll be a plumber like his dad.*

Presume means to assume. *You can't presume that Mrs. Lawson will quit skydiving just because she's sixty-five now.*

Theorize means to suggest explanations based on observation and reasoning. *Scientists theorize that the universe began in a Big Bang, billions of years ago.*

Reckon is an informal word that means to suppose. *"I reckon that stranger is the man they're looking for in Wyoming," said the marshal.*

"Dr. Livingstone, I **presume**?"

Have a hunch is a phrase that means to guess without any facts at all. *Stavros has a hunch that the missing lambs have gone up the mountain.*

HAVE YOU HEARD...?

"Dr. Livingstone, I presume?"

Who said this? Why? David Livingstone was a noted missionary and explorer in Africa. Henry M. Stanley, a correspondent for the New York *Herald,* was sent in 1869 by the newspaper's publisher in search of Livingstone, who was on an expedition to seek the sources of the Nile River. After a long and very difficult journey, Stanley finally found Livingstone in 1871. This is what he said when they met.

Guide
verb

Guide means to show the way to a place by actually going there. *People with severely impaired vision may have dogs that are trained to guide them around.*

Conduct can mean to guide. *Several teachers conducted our school group on a trip to the automobile assembly plant.*

Lead means to show the way by going with or ahead of someone. *When the lights went out during the storm, Mrs. Tucker helped lead the patients down the corridor.*

Direct can mean to show or tell the way. *Ted was lost downtown until a woman directed him to the central library.*

Steer can mean to direct someone, or to make something go in a particular direction. *When we moved in, our new neighbor steered us to the cheapest grocery store.*

Pilot can mean to steer. *Kai dreams of piloting jet airplanes someday.*

Usher means to guide someone, especially to or from a door. *Students ushered the audience to their seats for the band concert.*

Shepherd can mean to guide or direct, especially away from danger. *When the tornado neared the town, teachers shepherded the pupils downstairs to the shelter.*

SEE **command** and **manage** for related words.

WORDS AT PLAY

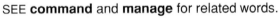

If you need something that will guide you
Faithfully to what's inside you,
A book will do, but it's more fun
To go and get a skeleton.

Just dress it up and call it Jones,
And you can learn about your bones.
Then when you know how bones should go,
From top of head to little toe,
Then you can carefully deposit
Your skeleton within your closet.

Habit
noun

Habit means a repeated action. *Skip has a bad habit of biting his fingernails.*

Custom means a repeated action, especially one that is common to many people. *It is an American custom to eat turkey on Thanksgiving.*

Practice can mean a habit. It suggests that a person has chosen to act this way. *Dad's practice of reading the newspaper at breakfast makes it a quiet meal.*

Routine means a method of doing something that is the same each time. *The launch of a space shuttle follows a strict routine.*

Usage can mean a custom, especially one involving use of words. *"Ain't" is not approved in educated usage.*

SEE **usual** for related words.

It is an American **custom** to eat turkey on Thanksgiving.

The way people use language is partly controlled by custom. Like other customs—of food, or clothes, or manners—the customs of language change gradually. New ones grow, and old ones pass away. Most people at any particular time share a set of language customs. The shared customs are called *usage*.

The usage of educated speakers and writers sets the pattern that people try to follow when using language publicly, officially, or for business. This general usage contains many customs that are taught as rules, such as "Don't say *ain't*" and "Don't split infinitives." Many groups have usage that is common in the group but different from the usage of other groups. For instance, people in England often say "Not to worry" when people in the United States would say "Don't worry." People who know a language well can change their usage to suit various situations.

When you speak, and even more when you write, keep usage in mind. What are you using language for? Who will hear it or read it? Try to use words in the best way for your purpose. In school or for school, educated usage is always a good idea.

Happen
verb

Happen means to take place. *"What happened at school today?" asked Sam's mother.*

Chance means to happen for no clear reason. *Janos chanced to run into an old friend at the mall.*

Occur means to happen. It is used mostly about specific events. *The 1989 San Francisco earthquake occurred during the World Series.*

Befall means to happen or happen to someone, and often refers to something unfortunate. It is used mostly in poetry and stories. *Terrible storms befell the Arctic explorers.*

Come about means to happen. *People wondered how the accident had come about.*

Come to pass means to happen. It is found more often in writing than in speech. *It may come to pass that no candidate gets a majority of votes.*

SEE **cause** for related words.

Happy
adjective

Happy means feeling good and being pleased. *Hernando is a lot happier in school now that he has grown taller.*

Cheerful means happy in an active, open way. *Anna always has a cheerful word for everyone.*

Glad means feeling pleasure because of something good. *Grace was glad that she could bring home a good mark to show her parents.*

Delighted means very pleased with something. *Duc was delighted to meet his grandparents for the first time.*

Lighthearted means happy and without any worries. *After school is over, everyone feels lighthearted and ready for summer fun.*

Merry means laughing and full of fun. *In the evening the merry sailors would dance on deck and sing rollicking songs of pirates and dragons and storms at sea.*

Jolly means cheerful and friendly. *The travelers welcomed the sight of the inn and its jolly host.*

Perky means happy and lively. *When I come home, I see Pepper's perky little face in the window.*

Blithe means cheerful. *Even when everyone else is worried, Erin always stays blithe.*

On cloud nine and **in seventh heaven** are idioms for very happy. *It's a week since Portia made the cheerleading squad, but she's still on cloud nine. Her brother is in seventh heaven, since it means he'll get to go to all the football games.*

SEE **fun** and **joy** for related words.
ANTONYMS: depressed, sad, unhappy

HAVE YOU HEARD...?

You may have heard someone described as "happy as a clam." How did this expression come into our language? It's not at all clear, until you've heard the full expression, "happy as a clam at high tide." Since people dig for clams at low tide, a clam at high tide would be happy to be left alone. The reason clams are gathered only during low tide is that they live in mud flats, which are covered by water at high tide.

Hard
adjective

Hard means needing a lot of work or effort. *Making a cherry pie was harder than Sandi expected.*

Difficult means not easy to do or figure out. *Chuck keeps practicing the difficult dance that his teacher taught him.*

Tough can mean very hard. *Hauling the fallen tree branches out of the yard was a tough job.*

Laborious means requiring a great amount of effort. *After laborious weight training, Robert has gained 20 pounds.*

Uphill can mean difficult and laborious. *Unless the parents help, the principal told her audience, improving conditions at the school will be an uphill battle.*

Backbreaking means extremely hard. *Loading the dinosaur skeleton onto the trucks was backbreaking work.*

Troublesome can mean hard and tiring. *Since he was no longer able to cook for himself, Mr. Dozier found living alone troublesome.*

Strenuous can mean requiring great effort. *The trip to Echo Cliffs will be a strenuous hike.*

SEE **complicated** for related words.
ANTONYMS: easy, effortless, simple

Loading the dinosaur skeleton onto the trucks was **backbreaking** work.

Harm
verb

Harm means to cause pain or injury to someone or something. *To make sure that the animals are not harmed, the area has been designated a wildlife preserve.*

Hurt means to wound someone or something. *Nestor hurt his wrist playing football.*

Injure means to hurt. *Mrs. Wang took the injured dog to a vet.*

Damage means to harm something in a way that lessens its value. *Damaged by water stains, this antique book isn't worth much.*

Mar means to spoil the appearance of something. *A cigarette burn marred the surface of the table.*

Blemish means to mar. *This bush is blemished where insects have chewed the leaves.*

Impair means to injure by weakening gradually. *Lack of exercise can impair your health.*

SEE **break** and **destroy** for related words.
ANTONYMS: aid, benefit, help

Hate
verb

Hate means to dislike someone or something intensely. *Margaret hates being called handicapped.*

Detest means to feel strong dislike and look down on someone or something. *Why do I have to try on clothes that I detest?*

Despise means to look down on and scorn someone or something. *"I despise the drug dealers who've taken over our block," said Mrs. Taylor. "We must get organized and fight them."*

Loathe means to feel disgust for someone or something. *Susan loathes beets.*

Abhor means to feel total dislike, disgust, and horror. *The Mullers abhorred the violent movie and left before it ended.*

Abominate is a formal word that means to hate very strongly and with outrage. *Most people abominate terrorists.*

SEE **dislike** for related words.
ANTONYM: love

Neal still **holds** the city record for the five-mile wheelchair race.

Have
verb

Have means to be the one to whom something belongs. *"Do you have a backpack I can borrow for our hiking trip?"* Sam asked Terry.

Hold can mean to have, especially for a while. *Neal still holds the city record for the five-mile wheelchair race.*

Own means to have something completely, especially by legal right. *Mr. Gonzalez owns two apartment buildings.*

Possess means to own. *"I would give all I possess,"* said Captain Tuckahoe, *"to see that island again."*

SEE **keep** for related words.
ANTONYM: lack

IDIOMS

Sometimes different idioms say the same thing.

Have your cake and eat it too and **have it both ways** mean to get the benefit of two opposite ideas or ways of acting at the same time.

Buy the ticket or save your money, but you can't have your cake and eat it too.

Greg wants it both ways: he dates other girls, but he wants Sharon to date just him.

Don't cry over spilled milk and **it's water under the bridge** mean not to worry about things in the past that you can't change.

"You broke the vase? No use crying over spilled milk," said Grandma.

"Oh, you missed the field trip, Lindsay? Well, it's water under the bridge. You can go next year," said Mr. James.

Healthy
adjective

Healthy means in good condition of body and mind and free of disease. *Children who don't get enough to eat are never really healthy.*

Well can mean healthy, especially when someone has been sick or might be. *Mom goes to work even if she doesn't feel well.*

Fit can mean healthy and strong. *After his operation, Jarel exercised carefully until he was fit again.*

Robust means healthy, strong, and full of energy. *Only someone as robust as Maria could be both in dance club and on the track team.*

Sound means perfectly healthy. *Since Mr. Carberry quit smoking twenty-five years ago, his lungs are now completely sound.*

In the pink is an idiom that means sound. *Rover had worms last month, but he's in the pink now.*

SEE **strong** for related words.
ANTONYMS: ill, sick, unhealthy

AROUND THE WORLD: Health

To a healthy person, everything seems healthy.
— **Russian proverb**

Health is better than wealth.
— **English proverb**

He who has health has hope, and he who has hope has everything.
— **Arabic proverb**

Heavy
adjective

Heavy means weighing a lot. *Dolores took a heavy load of laundry to the basement washing machine.*

Weighty means heavy. *The mail carrier brings our letters, but weighty packages come by special truck.*

Hefty is an informal word that means heavy. *George helped his mother by carrying the three hefty baskets of apples to the back porch.*

Massive means heavy, big, and solid. *Even with two others helping, Kazuo was unable to budge the massive boulder from the yard.*

CONTINUED ON THE NEXT PAGE

Mrs. Washington waved to Betsy from the controls of her **ponderous** steamroller.

Ponderous is a formal word that means heavy and large or massive. *Mrs. Washington waved to Betsy from the controls of her ponderous steamroller.*

Cumbersome means heavy and hard to move. *The cumbersome meteorite was finally brought into the museum hall.*

Leaden can mean hard to move, feeling heavy as lead. *After thirty pull-ups, Hank's arms were leaden.*

ANTONYMS: airy, light

Help
verb

Help means to do part of the work that someone else has to do. *"Jack, help your father bring up the groceries," said Uncle Tim.*

Aid means to help, especially by providing something needed by someone. *The research has been aided by a gift of a computer.*

Assist means to help someone do something by working with her or him. *Terralynn assists Mrs. Feldman with cooking in exchange for sewing lessons.*

Lend a hand is an idiom that means to help someone do something. *Mr. Aponte lent Dad and me a hand with moving the sofa to the other side of the room.*

ANTONYMS: hinder, obstruct

Hesitate
verb

Hesitate means to stop and wait before doing something because you have not made up your mind to do it. *Mr. Bryce hesitated before driving onto the busy highway.*

Waver can mean to hesitate. *Loranne's hearing impairment has never made her waver in her determination to be an actress.*

Falter means to hesitate or stop what you are doing because of doubts. *Amanda wanted to ask the singer for his autograph, but she faltered when she saw the crowd around him.*

Dither means to hesitate nervously and excitedly. *If Momma doesn't stop dithering about whether or not we can afford the new apartment, we won't get it.*

Think twice is an idiom that means to hesitate. It suggests questioning a decision already made. *Dad suggested to Sally that she think twice before spending all her allowance on candy.*

Hem and haw is an idiom that means to hesitate. It suggests avoiding stating a decision. *When Bruce asked MeiMei to the dance, she hemmed and hawed before saying no.*

SEE **hold** for related words.

HAVE YOU HEARD...?

Have you ever heard someone say, "He who hesitates is lost"? This means that someone who takes too much time to decide and act on that decision may miss an opportunity, or may fail to escape from danger.

Hide
verb

Hide means to put out of sight. *We quickly hid the birthday present we were making for Mom when we heard her at the front door.*

Conceal means to hide something on purpose so that it won't be found. *Ugo conceals his comic books, but I always find them.*

Camouflage means to hide something by giving it a false appearance. *This caterpillar's dull colors let it camouflage itself as a twig.*

Stash is an informal word that means to hide something for safekeeping or future use. *The main witness against the gang has been stashed in a hotel someplace by the police.*

CONTINUED ON THE NEXT PAGE

Cache means to store in a safe hiding place. *The explorers cached their supplies at base camp before venturing out onto the ice.*

Bury can mean to hide something by covering it. *When Tana saw the teacher coming, she quickly buried Michelle's note under her books.*

Cover up means to keep something bad from being known. *Company officials covered up the factory's pollution of the nearby river.*

Hole up means to hide yourself. *For her vacation, Ms. Frye holed up in her apartment, sleeping late and taking life easy.*

ANTONYMS: expose, reveal, show

WRITING TIP: Using Vivid Words

A plan *hidden* in secrecy, or a plan *veiled* in secrecy— which description seems more vivid to you? The word *veil* calls up images of a piece of material worn to protect or hide the face. You can almost see the veiled plan. Other words meaning "to hide something from sight" include *cloak, mask,* and *screen.* All of these are also the names of things that are used to conceal or cover, and, like *veil,* they can be used to create vivid descriptions.

High
adjective

High means a long way up. With this meaning, it describes things, such as buildings or mountains, but not people. *This ancient town is surrounded by high walls.*

Tall means high. It describes both people and things. *Just being tall won't get a person on the basketball team.*

Towering means very high. *Looking up at the towering redwoods, Carita almost lost her balance.*

Lofty is a formal word that means very high. It describes things. *The loftiest peak in the world is Mount Everest, on the Tibet-Nepal border.*

Steep means high and almost straight up. *Mountain goats scramble up steep rock and ice with almost unbelievable speed.*

ANTONYM: low

If I were a millionaire, I would **engage** a butler and a driver and a cook and a gardener.

Hire
verb

Hire means to give someone a job. *That waiter can't even carry a tray —I wonder who hired him?*

Employ means to hire. It suggests a steady job. *Mr. Kim's dry cleaning business employs six people now.*

Engage can mean to employ. With this meaning, it is a formal word. *If I were a millionaire, I would engage a butler and a driver and a cook and a gardener.*

Appoint means to name someone for a job or a task. *We've decided to appoint Mary to the poster committee.*

Assign can mean to appoint. It suggests that the job or task is a duty. *"Each of you," Ms. Gonzales told her class, "will be assigned to lead classroom discussion once this month."*

Take on means to hire. *The Morgan farm is taking on extra hands this summer to pick apples.*

ANTONYMS: dismiss, fire

Hit
verb

Hit means to give a forceful blow to someone or something. *Kerwin hit the nail with a hammer.*

Strike means to hit. *Redwing's canoe was severely damaged when it struck a rock.*

Slap means to hit with an open hand. *Uncle Reuben slapped his knee and laughed when I told him that joke.*

Clap can mean to slap. *Nina's friends rushed up to clap her on the back when she finished her gymnastics routine.*

Because there are so many words that mean to hit, we have space only to list them. Some are slang or informal; your dictionary identifies these. The main difference among most of these words is in their sound, not their meaning. So find a few that sound right, look them up in your dictionary, and see which one is right for your sentence.

bash	**clout**	**paste**	**sock**
bat	**club**	**punch**	**swat**
belt	**cuff**	**slug**	**thump**
clobber	**knock**	**smack**	**wallop**

SEE **beat** for related words.

IDIOMS

Hit is a key word in many idioms. Here are some of them:

Hit below the belt means to attack someone unfairly. *When the newspaper published the senator's private mail, she said that was hitting below the belt.*

Hit the ceiling means to get really angry. *When the landlord shut off the heat, the tenants all hit the ceiling.*

Hit the nail on the head means to get something just right. *Mrs. Luria really hit the nail on the head when she said this neighborhood needs more parks, not more parking lots.*

Hit the jackpot means to win a big prize. *Marcus really hit the jackpot — he won a $100 gift certificate in the raffle at our school fair.*

Hit the hay means to go to bed. *"I think it's time for you to hit the hay, Cissie," said Mr. Welsh to his yawning daughter.*

Hold
verb

Hold means to keep something inside. *Harold's backpack can't hold all those books.*

Hold is also used in phrases that have special meanings. Each of these phrases has its own set of synonyms.

hold out

Hold out means to make something available for someone to take. *The principal held out the promise of a pizza party for the class that sold the most raffle tickets.*

Offer means to hold out, especially as a gift. *Adrian offered the guests some cake.*

Present can mean to make available, especially in a formal way. *In her lecture, Dr. Ruíz will present a summary of Aztec civilization.*

Submit can mean to present something for others to judge. *Cordell has submitted his cartoons to the school paper.*

Extend can mean to hold out. It is used mostly about feelings, wishes, or other ideas, not about things. *RuthAnn sent a note to Mrs. Lu, extending her sympathy during Mr. Lu's illness.*

hold up

Hold up can mean to keep something from happening or moving at the expected time. *The parade is holding up traffic on Perkins Avenue.*

Delay means to move something back to a later time. *We will have to delay dinner until Sherry gets home.*

Postpone means to delay. *The baseball game was postponed because of rain.*

Put off means to delay. *Dawanda put off her trip to California when she got sick.*

Table can mean to delay. *The Senate has tabled the discussion of the tax bill until further notice.*

Shelve can mean to delay. *We shelved our plans for a holiday trip this year because the car needs an expensive tune-up.*

CONTINUED ON THE NEXT PAGE

When workers found a weird glowing stone, digging was **suspended.**

Suspend can mean to stop something for a while. *When workers found a weird glowing stone, digging was suspended.*

Adjourn is a somewhat formal word that means to put off until a future meeting. *"This court is adjourned until nine o'clock tomorrow morning," said Judge Melton.*

Put on the back burner is an idiom that means to delay until some uncertain time. *Mr. Gupta's plans to open his own bowling alley have been put on the back burner.*

WORD STORY

Put something on the back burner is an idiom that comes from cooking. Pots that have to be stirred go on the stove's front burners. People put pots that are cooking slowly and don't need attention on the back of the stove.

hold with

Hold with means to feel that something is a good thing to do or a good idea. *Eunice's parents don't hold with her using lipstick or nail polish.*

Endorse can mean to hold with. It suggests a public statement. *Business leaders have endorsed the new tax law.*

Favor can mean to hold with. This word is often used about plans, projects, and ideas. *Sly favors his mom's plan to go to computer school.*

Support can mean to favor. This word is often used about plans, ideas, and political groups. *Most Abolitionists also supported the founding of the Republican Party.*

Approve of can mean to hold with. *My grandmother doesn't approve of short skirts on young women.*

215

Holy
adjective

Holy means coming from God or close to God. *Adam and his family observe all the high holy days.*

Sacred means holy. *The signers of the Declaration of Independence pledged "our lives, our fortunes, and our sacred honor."*

Divine means holy. *Kings once claimed to rule by divine right.*

Blessed means holy and having God's favor. *The birth of a baby is often called a "blessed event."*

Saintly means very good and close to God, like a saint. *My saintly aunt has never said a harsh word to anyone in her entire life.*

Sanctified means set apart as holy. *The land behind the new church will be sanctified as a cemetery.*

Hallowed means honored as holy. *For Muslims, Mecca is a hallowed city.*

SEE **religious** for related words.

HAVE YOU HEARD...?

You may have heard people refer to something as a "sacred cow." Cows are held to be sacred by members of the Hindu religion. This phrase has come to mean something that cannot be attacked or even criticized or discussed. *Communism was a sacred cow in the Soviet Union.*

Honest
adjective

Honest means not stealing, cheating, or lying. *We chose Ting-Wei for class treasurer because we need a really honest person.*

Truthful means telling the facts, not lying. *"Be truthful, Sesha—does this skirt look good on me?" asked her sister.*

Honorable means knowing and doing what is right. *An honorable scientist like Dr. Blake wouldn't dream of stealing an invention!*

Upright can mean honest and good. *Tom might still be getting in trouble if his boxing coach weren't such a strong, upright man.*

Trustworthy means honest and keeping your word. *Everyone in the movie thinks she's trustworthy, so it's easy for her to steal the plans.*

SEE **frank** and **trust** for related words.
ANTONYM: dishonest

"Honesty's the best policy."

— **Miguel de Cervantes (1547–1616)**

Hopeless
adjective

Hopeless means without any feeling that something good will happen. *Mr. Cho sat in his looted store and felt more hopeless than ever before in his life.*

Desperate means hopeless and reckless. *The mountain climbers made a desperate effort to get back to camp through the raging storm.*

Despondent means hopeless and deeply sad. *Mrs. Streeter became despondent after the death of her husband.*

Pessimistic means ready to believe that bad things will happen. *Patrick is too pessimistic even to try asking Barbara out.*

Defeatist means expecting to lose. *"I don't want to hear any more defeatist talk. We are going to go out there and win!" Coach Banion shouted at her team.*

SEE **discouraged** and **sad** for related words.
ANTONYMS: confident, hopeful

Hostile
adjective

The Vikings were a **warlike** people who raided far and wide.

Hostile means being an enemy and fighting or ready to fight. *I don't like to play tennis with her because she gets hostile.*

Quarrelsome means quick to quarrel. *When we complained about his junk-filled yard, the man next door became rude and quarrelsome.*

Aggressive means likely to attack and begin a fight. *At night, the used car lot is guarded by aggressive dogs who rush at the fence when anybody comes near.*

Warlike means ready and eager for war. *The Vikings were a warlike people who raided far and wide.*

Belligerent can mean aggressive and eager to fight. *Belligerent politicians nearly caused a war between the two nations.*

Pugnacious means eager to fight and fond of fighting. *Ted likes boxing, but personally he's not pugnacious at all.*

On bad terms is an idiom that means hostile. It suggests that fighting is very possible but not happening. *Uncle Jonas has been on bad terms with the family since he refused to let them sell the farm.*

SEE **argue, attack, fight,** and **oppose** for related words.
ANTONYMS: agreeable, friendly

217

Hot
adjective

Hot means having or giving off much heat. *It was a very hot day for April. "Don't let the baby touch that hot stove, Alan!" shouted Mrs. Jones in alarm.*

Burning can mean very hot, as if on fire. *Last night Eleanor was burning with fever, but she's much better now.*

Fiery means hot as fire or full of fire. *When Grandfather worked on the railroad, he shoveled coal into a fiery furnace for hours on end.*

Blazing means burning brightly. *The sun is blazing, so bring a hat.*

Sultry means hot and damp and sticky. *Spreading hot tar over a roof on a sultry day like this is hard work.*

Sweltering means very unpleasantly hot. *It was sweltering in the apartment even after we opened the windows.*

Torrid and **scorching** mean extremely hot from very strong sunlight. *The torrid weather in late August caused scorching temperatures throughout the week of the county fair.*

ANTONYMS: cold, freezing

The **torrid** weather in late August caused **scorching** temperatures throughout the week of the county fair.

Huge
adjective

Huge means very big. *A huge oak tree in the park blew down in the storm last night.*

Enormous means much larger than normal. *We're celebrating the hundredth anniversary of the founding of the town with an enormous parade and picnic.*

Immense means so big that it's hard to measure. *An immense flood spread over the valley.*

Giant means much larger than other things of the same kind. *That's the Happy Cow Dairy with the giant milk carton on the roof.*

Gigantic means giant. *At the county fair, Richie saw a gigantic pumpkin weighing 150 pounds.*

Vast means covering a very wide area. *The Great Plains form a vast region east of the Rocky Mountains.*

Colossal means tremendously large. *The colossal head of Washington on Mount Rushmore is as high as a five-story building.*

Mammoth means colossal. *Mammoth Cave has miles of passages and is hundreds of feet deep.*

Titanic means colossal. *The river is held back by a titanic dam, seven hundred feet high.*

SEE **big** and **heavy** for related words.
ANTONYMS: little, small, tiny

Richie saw a **gigantic** pumpkin weighing 150 pounds.

219

Humble
adjective

Humble means not proud or conceited. *In the story, the humble little tailor ends up a multimillionaire.*

Meek can mean humble and not wanting to call attention to yourself. *The class bully was meek as a lamb after the principal called his parents.*

Modest means humble. *Elena is so modest that few people realize she has already had modeling jobs.*

Lowly can mean humble and not feeling that you are as good as others. *It's a movie about a lowly usher who rescues a famous actor from kidnappers.*

Plain can mean without pride and not claiming to be special. *"We're just plain folks," said Ms. Watkins, "and winning the lottery won't change that."*

Simple can mean plain. *The simple fisherman would take no reward for rescuing the drowning children.*

Humor
noun

Humor means the quality of being funny. *"I fail to see the humor in your silly pranks, George," said Mr. Johnson.*

Wit can mean humor that is clever and full of ideas. *"Your paper is full of wit, Rosalie, but the organization still needs work," said Ms. Rivera.*

Comedy can mean the humor of something that happens. *We laughed when Ted dropped his jacket in a puddle, but he just couldn't see the comedy in it.*

Sarcasm can mean unfriendly humor that comes from saying or writing the opposite of what is really meant. *You know, Bryce's sarcasm isn't really funny.*

Irony can mean humor that comes from hidden meanings. *Tova can put you down with such irony that you can't be sure she meant it.*

Satire means humor that comes from mocking something or someone. *Mr. Foster is an interesting teacher because he uses a lot of satire and is always making fun of the history he teaches.*

CONTINUED ON THE NEXT PAGE

Lance the Wonder Horse and His Electric Pineapple is a book of delightful **absurdity.**

Absurdity can mean humor of a foolish, unreasonable kind. *Lance the Wonder Horse and His Electric Pineapple is a book of delightful absurdity.*

Whimsy can mean humor that is odd and imaginative, with much make-believe. *Calvin and Hobbes has whimsy, violence, and friendship, so it's very popular.*

SEE **funny, joke,** and **laugh** for related words.

WRITING TIP: Sarcasm or Irony?

Sarcasm is easy to use and easy to understand. It is just saying the opposite of what you mean, for unfriendly humor. *Bill sure is a genius.*

Irony is using words to hide a meaning, possibly a negative one. In contrast to sarcasm, irony is not direct. It leaves us wondering: did you mean this, or that? *Bill has a very interesting mind.*

Hurry
verb

Hurry means to move faster. *"You'll have to hurry if you want to catch the bus, Karla," said her sister.*

Rush means to move with speed or force. *The rushing crowds leaving the station almost knocked Kendra down.*

Hasten means to move quickly to do something. *Barb hastened to wash the dishes so she could go bowling.*

Speed means to go very fast. *Late for class, Harvey sped around the corner and ran right into Mr. Ornaf's mop and bucket.*

Race can mean to speed. *Workers are racing to repair the bridge before rush hour tomorrow.*

Hustle means to move quickly and with energy. *Greg hustled during basketball practice, trying shots from all around the court.*

Accelerate means to go faster. It is often used about machines and in science. *Coming out of the curve, the racing cars accelerated down the straightaway.*

Shake a leg is an idiom that means to hurry. *"Shake a leg, Kiyoshi, we're all waiting!" called Anne.*

Step on it is an idiom that means to hurry. *"The bees are gaining on us, Bob, so I suggest you step on it," said Professor Todd.*

Get a move on is an idiom that means to hurry. *"If we want to get a good seat at the game, we'd better get a move on," said Dad.*

SEE **eager, quick,** and **run** for related words.
ANTONYMS: delay, slow

AROUND THE WORLD: Haste

Haste makes waste.
— **English proverb**

The hasty man loses his crop.
— **Tamil proverb** (India)

Haste is only good for catching flies.
— **Arabic proverb**

You walk too fast, walk two times.
— **Jamaican proverb**

Hut
noun

The Escobar family rented a **cabin** near Yellowstone National Park for a week.

Hut means a small house. Huts usually have only one or two rooms. They are made from natural materials. *Jomo Kenyatta, first prime minister of Kenya, was born in a thatched hut near Nairobi.*

Cabin means a hut. Cabins are usually built of wood. *The Escobar family rented a cabin near Yellowstone National Park for a week.*

Shed means a small building for keeping things in. A shed is usually smaller than a hut. *Dirk took a shovel and a hoe from the tool shed.*

Shack means a hut or a shed. It suggests that the structure is poorly built out of poor materials. *In some of the world's largest cities, many people have only cardboard shacks for homes.*

Shanty means a roughly built hut or cabin. *During the gold rush years, miners lived a rough life in tents and shanty towns.*

Lodge can mean a small house, especially one used for a short time. *Aunt Patsy and Uncle Fred spent last weekend at a fishing lodge in the mountains.*

Hysterical
adjective

Hysterical means so excited that the emotion is impossible to control or stop. *Hysterical fans tried to get past the police and march with their world champion team in the victory parade.*

Raging means out of control because of anger or as if angry. *A raging blizzard has closed roads and airports in three states.*

Raving can mean raging or too excited to think. *After failing to capture the pirates, the sailors were afraid to face their raving captain.*

Delirious can mean extremely excited and out of control, especially with joy. *At the winning candidate's headquarters, her supporters are delirious at their victory.*

Berserk means completely out of control with anger. *The company president went berserk and fired all the computer programmers.*

SEE **crazy** for related words.

Idea
noun

Idea means a mental picture or plan. *In the empty apartment, Pauline was forming an idea of where to put the furniture and all her plants.*

Notion means an idea. *"I'm not sure why," Irene remarked, "but I have a notion the new secretary won't stay long."*

Thought means an idea about something. *Reporters asked for Representative Lopez's thoughts on how to prevent more bank failures.*

Inspiration can mean a sudden, very good idea. *"I don't know what to do for the science fair," Jerry told his father, "but I'm hoping for an inspiration."*

Brainstorm means inspiration. *The advertising department has had a brainstorm: a new way of packaging!*

Concept means a general idea of something. *This drawing shows an architect's concept of the new office building.*

Impression can mean an idea that is not very clear. *Jenny had the impression that the shabbily dressed woman was watching her for some reason.*

SEE **belief, feeling,** and **opinion** for related words.

HAVE YOU HEARD...?

You may have heard someone who has solved a problem say, "Eureka!" *Eureka* (yù rē′kə) is a Greek word that means "I have found it." According to legend, the ancient Greek scientist Archimedes solved an important problem while taking a bath. He was so pleased with his discovery that he ran into the street shouting "Eureka! Eureka!"

Ignorant
adjective

Ignorant means without knowledge. *Joey fixed the rabbits' breakfast, ignorant of the fact that his rabbits had escaped from the hutch.*

Illiterate means unable to read and write. *Just because Mr. Thom is illiterate doesn't mean he's stupid.*

Uneducated means without schooling. *Although uneducated, Mrs. Daley has relied on charm and natural intelligence to become a successful saleswoman.*

Unaware and **unsuspecting** mean without knowledge of what is going on. *Unaware of the bomb in the suitcase, the unsuspecting pilot prepared for takeoff.*

Unacquainted and **unfamiliar** mean without knowledge of something or someone in particular. *Someone who is unacquainted with a country's customs and unfamiliar with its language shouldn't travel alone.*

In the dark means ignorant. *When the school year began, Luis was completely in the dark about algebra.*

ANTONYMS: educated, informed, knowledgeable

Imaginary
adjective

Imaginary means existing only in the imagination. *Dad had to apologize after he sat on my little brother's imaginary friend.*

Unreal means imaginary. *The things that happen in dreams are unreal but interesting.*

Fictitious means made up. *Tarzan isn't a real person; he's purely fictitious.*

Invented can mean fictitious. *"I want the truth, Harold, not some invented excuse," said his father.*

Fantastic can mean showing great imagination. It is often used for something odd or strange. *The cartoon character Calvin often finds fantastic creatures under his bed.*

Fanciful can mean showing much imagination. *Ramona's fanciful illustrations are the best thing in our school paper.*

Ramona's **fanciful** illustrations are the best thing in our school paper.

SEE **imagine** and **pretend** for related words.
ANTONYMS: actual, real

Imagine
verb

Imagine means to form a mental picture of something. *Lying on her bunk, Corporal D'Annunzio imagined the parade she'd get for coming home a hero.*

Visualize means to imagine. *"Visualize a cabin in the woods," said Dr. Wright to his audience, "a gathering darkness, heavy rain."*

Envision means to imagine. *Louise envisioned herself wearing high heels and falling flat on her face.*

Picture can mean to imagine. *Here in the cold, it is hard to picture Grandma and Uncle Tomás in the hot sunshine.*

Fancy means to imagine. It is often used to suggest something unrealistic or improbable. *Although the cape was too long, Jeffrey could easily fancy himself to be Superman.*

Conceive means to think up an idea and give it form by picturing it. *The prisoners conceived a daring daylight escape plan.*

Daydream means to spend time playing with mental pictures. *John likes to daydream about winning a lot of money and traveling around the world.*

SEE **imaginary** and **pretend** for related words.

Imitate
verb

Imitate means to try to be, look, or sound like something or someone else. *Monica can imitate the calls of the birds in the forest near her home.*

Copy can mean to imitate. *After her sister's friends went home, Regina tried to copy their style of dancing.*

Impersonate can mean to imitate a person's voice, style, and appearance, pretending to be that person. *That actor can impersonate the President perfectly.*

Mimic means to make fun of someone or something by imitating. *Boys on the team often mimic the coach's high voice, but only when he's not around.*

CONTINUED ON THE NEXT PAGE

66 No man ever yet became great by imitation. 99

— **Samuel Johnson (1709–1784)**

226

Many people **do impressions of** Elvis nowadays.

Mock can mean to mimic. It implies ridicule or cruelty. *The clown stood behind the ringmaster, mocking his gestures.*

Do an impression of means to impersonate, usually as entertainment for an audience. *Many people do impressions of Elvis nowadays.*

SEE **pretend** for related words.

Important
adjective

Important means mattering a lot or making a big difference. *Getting a new job is really important to Luann's mom.*

Major means important, especially more important than others. *The steel mill used to be a major employer in this town.*

Significant means important, especially in meaning. *The birth of Graham's first grandchild was a significant event in his life.*

Material can mean important. *"The time when the shot was fired is a most material clue," said Inspector Ochida.*

Vital can mean extremely important. *Often Kayonga must spend hours collecting the firewood vital to his family.*

Momentous means very important. *The breakup of the Soviet Union is among the century's most momentous political changes.*

SEE **value** for related words.
ANTONYMS: insignificant, unimportant

Improve
verb

Improve means to make something better, increase its value, or correct its faults. *"Your writing will be improved, Priscilla, if you use some synonyms for 'really,'" said her teacher.*

Better is a formal word that means to improve. *The United Nations was created in hopes of bettering the lives of people everywhere.*

Help can mean to make a physical ailment better. *The nurse told Kimi that glasses might help her headaches.*

Reform means to improve, especially by removing faults. *Mr. Chung suggests that we reform the village government by limiting the number of years people can hold office.*

Amend is a formal word that can mean to make a change for the better. *Proposals to amend the Constitution require approval by three-fourths of the states.*

ANTONYM: worsen

Increase
verb

Increase means to make something larger or greater. *In week three of his science experiment, Keith increased the amount of water to some seedlings and decreased it to others.*

Enlarge means to make something larger, especially in area. *The Coopers enlarged their kitchen by removing a wall and enclosing the back porch.*

Amplify means to increase the strength or amount of something. *His voice amplified by a loudspeaker, the police officer ordered the crowd to break up.*

Multiply can mean to increase the number or size of something. *Darcy tried to multiply her prizes by buying more raffle tickets, but she just lost more money.*

Build up means to make larger or stronger. *Emilia lifts weights every day to build up her muscles.*

SEE **expand** and **lengthen** for related words.
ANTONYMS: decrease, lessen, reduce

Indifferent
adjective

Indifferent means not interested or not caring. *Indifferent to the bird attracted by her flute, Maxine played on.*

Uninterested means not interested. *Chantal is uninterested in cars.*

Unconcerned means indifferent. It is often used to suggest that people should be interested. *Only twenty years ago, most Americans were largely unconcerned about pollution.*

Aloof means indifferent and keeping to yourself. *Taney seemed aloof until we realized she was just shy.*

Apathetic means totally indifferent, with no feeling or energy. *People in this neighborhood are so apathetic that nobody even bothers to vote.*

SEE **careless** for related words.
ANTONYMS: eager, enthusiastic

Indifferent to the bird attracted by her flute, Maxine played on.

Influence
verb

Influence means to make someone do or believe something without giving orders. It often suggests not showing that you want to affect someone. *The director said she hoped her new movie would influence young people to stay away from drugs.*

Sway can mean to influence someone, especially to change a decision or opinion. *The crowd's boos failed to sway the umpire's decision.*

Induce means to influence someone. It suggests an open attempt to lead or persuade. *The social workers try to induce runaway children to return to their families.*

Move can mean to cause someone to do something. *Tanya's concern for the homeless moved her to collect blankets for the shelter.*

SEE **persuade, suggest,** and **urge** for related words.

Informal
adjective

Denise was so happy that she did a **spontaneous** cartwheel.

Informal means for everyday use, not following rules of public and official behavior. *"For a family picnic, Loretta, informal clothes will do better than that good dress," said her grandmother.*

Casual can mean informal. It suggests just letting things happen. *Darshon is a fierce competitor who hates losing even a casual game with his friends.*

Offhand can mean informal. It suggests not giving something much thought. *Max really hurt Carmelita's feelings with that offhand comment about her science project.*

Natural can mean acting or done without plan or control, from impulse. *Since she retired from her law practice, Mrs. Wechsler has become much more relaxed and natural with people.*

Spontaneous means acting or done without plan or control, from impulse. *Denise was so happy that she did a spontaneous cartwheel.*

Free and easy is an idiom that means informal and natural. *"No plans," Mr. Madison told the neighbors, "just a free and easy weekend at the beach."*

WRITING TIP: Informal Language

Informal behavior is fine for everyday use, but not for official occasions or public events. Informal language is also for everyday writing and speaking, but not for really serious or important documents or speeches. When you see a word described as "informal," you know that it is all right for friendly letters or talk, but you know not to use it in a speech, a letter to someone in government, or an important report. At **joke,** for instance, *wisecrack* and *gag* are described as informal words. It would sound fine to say, "Alex makes a lot of wisecracks, and some of his gags are pretty funny." But if you were discussing Abraham Lincoln's humor, these synonyms would sound odd; *joke, witticism,* and *quip* would do better.

Information
noun

Information means things that are known. *"I need more information,"* Alfred said to the salesman, *"about your replacement parts and the guarantee."*

Data means recorded facts, often technical or scientific. *For her report on regional weather over the past year, Julia got data from the National Weather Service.*

Intelligence can mean information. It usually suggests valuable, confidential information. *The government gathers intelligence about other countries.*

News means information about recent events. *Cordelia has been home sick for a week, and she's eager for news from school.*

Word can mean news, usually of one event. *We received word this morning that Mrs. Czerny had her baby.*

> **WATCH IT!**
> ●
> **Data** is a plural noun. When you use data, think "facts."
> It may sound strange at first to say, "data are." But
> remember, you would not say, "facts is."

Innocent
adjective

Innocent means not guilty. *"Why do I get blamed for everything when I'm perfectly innocent?"* Rona sighed to herself.

Blameless means not deserving any blame. *"James was nowhere near the fight,"* Adam defended his friend. *"He's blameless, I assure you."*

Guiltless means innocent. It suggests feeling no guilt. *The bus driver insists she is guiltless of the accident.*

Irreproachable means not deserving blame or criticism. *Throughout the whole investigation, Detective Hansen's methods have been irreproachable.*

In the clear is an idiom that means free of suspicion or blame. *Flip has been suspended from school for breaking windows, but Jake is in the clear.*

ANTONYM: guilty

Intense
adjective

Intense means having strong feelings about something. *Mya's parents have an intense desire for her to do well in school.*

Emotional can mean likely to have feelings about something. *Rory gets so emotional about table tennis that many people avoid playing with him.*

Fiery can mean intense. *Patrick Henry's fiery speeches pushed the Colonies toward independence.*

Passionate means very intense. *Rosario is passionate when he describes the mistreatment of animals.*

Vehement means passionate. It suggests great energy and insistence. *Mackenzie was vehement in the defense of her friend's reputation.*

SEE **eager** for related words.

Intention
noun

Intention means what a person has in mind to do or get by doing. *Automobile companies do research with the intention of increasing fuel efficiency.*

Purpose means a strong intention. It suggests choosing to act in particular ways. *"My purpose in letting the students run the school for a week," said Mrs. Peebles, "is to let them find out how much work it really takes."*

Goal can mean something for which a person works, usually with effort. *"We have a goal," Coach Bryant yelled, "and that goal is to win this swimming meet!"*

Aim can mean a specific result or achievement that a person chooses to try for. *Rodrigo's aim is to win the school's photography prize this year.*

Point can mean a purpose. *"Right now the point is to clean up this mess, not to blame each other," Lori told her sister.*

Object can mean a purpose. *The object of this film is to alert people to the destruction of the rain forests.*

SEE **plan** for related words.

Interesting
adjective

Interesting means making you feel like paying attention and knowing more. *To a chameleon, any insect is interesting.*

Intriguing means interesting because it makes you curious. *The ads for the new movie were intriguing, but the movie itself was boring.*

Fascinating means so interesting that it's hard to stop. *Damien finds computer programming so fascinating that he'll sit at his keyboard for hours.*

Absorbing means extremely interesting. *Naoko enjoys crossword puzzles if they are hard enough to be absorbing.*

Spellbinding means so interesting that it is impossible to stop paying attention. *Both pitchers have no-hitters going into the eighth inning of this spellbinding game.*

Engrossing means so interesting that it makes you forget other things. *"When I'm painting," Frazier wrote to his pen pal, "it's so engrossing I don't think of anything else."*

ANTONYMS: dull, boring, uninteresting

To a chameleon, any insect is **interesting.**

Interfere
verb

Interfere means to get involved in somebody else's business without being asked and in an unwelcome, unhelpful way. *"Stop interfering with Lerice's homework or you're going to bed," Mom told Allen.*

Meddle means to interfere. It suggests trying to do more than you should. *When the editor changed the end of the story, the author asked her to stop meddling with it.*

Tamper means to meddle with something and spoil the way it works. It suggests idle curiosity. *The janitor says somebody has tampered with the fuse box.*

Kibitz means to interfere by giving unwanted advice. *"Young man, I was repairing cars before you were born, so I'll thank you not to kibitz!" the mechanic told his assistant.*

SEE **bother** for related words.

IDIOMS

There are many idiomatic ways of expressing the idea of interfering with someone else's concerns. We have shown some here.

Mess with means to tamper with something. *If we mess with my dad's computer files we'll be grounded.*

Monkey with and **monkey around with** mean to mess with. *"Somebody's been monkeying around with the smoke detector," Larry said, pointing to the scratches.*

Put your oar in is an idiom that means to meddle or interfere with what another person is doing. It can suggest a desire for attention. *Whatever people are talking about, Pete always puts his oar in.*

Butt in is a slang phrase that means to interfere rudely and thoughtlessly. *If I start to say something, Joey has to butt in with a wisecrack.*

Put your two cents in means to give advice where none is wanted. *Mrs. Abrams is always trying to put her two cents in at the community council meetings.*

Stick your nose in means to interfere in a nosy way. *Mrs. Runkel hates it when her neighbor sticks his nose in her business.*

Can you think of other ways of expressing this?

Intermission

noun

Intermission means a scheduled pause during a performance. *During intermission, Emma moved to a better seat in the concert hall.*

Time-out means a short pause during a game. *The basketball team called a time-out to plan their last-minute play.*

Recess means a pause during some official activity. *The judge called a recess during the trial.*

Interval means the time between two things. *The interval between World War I and World War II was only twenty-one years.*

Interlude means interval. *Two bitterly cold weeks were separated by an interlude of one warm and sunny day.*

SEE **pause** for related words.

WORDS AT PLAY

The concert had reached intermission,
But on stage there was still one musician:
    A cellist, who strained
      To stand up, then explained,
"I'm stuck in a sitting position!"

235

Job
noun

Job means work you have to do. *Getting the table upstairs to the apartment turned out to be one hard job.*

Task means a certain amount of assigned work to be done. *Once she was finished with her household tasks, Nella was able to join us for pizza.*

Chore means a regular task. *Pablo's chores include walking the dog twice a day and taking out the garbage.*

Responsibility can mean a chore. *Josey's responsibilities at the store include sweeping up and straightening items on the shelves.*

Duty can mean a task that is part of someone's position or employment. *As assistant coach of the soccer team, it's Victor's duty to lead the pregame warm-up.*

Errand means a job that includes making a trip. *Grandma asked me to run several errands before the guests arrived for the party.*

Mission means a very serious errand. *The astronauts' main mission on this flight will be to launch a new satellite.*

Assignment means a certain amount of required work, especially schoolwork. *Tim needs a math tutor to help him with his assignments.*

SEE **work** for related words.

Join
verb

Join means to put or bring things together. *More than six hundred pictures of our neighborhood have been joined in this exhibition.*

Connect means to join things together, often so they touch at one place. *The Panama Canal connects the Pacific Ocean and the Caribbean Sea.*

Fasten means to tie, lock, or otherwise make things stay joined together. *Richard doesn't just fasten his bike to the fence; he removes the front wheel and takes it inside with him.*

Attach means to fasten. *My little sister Nina has clips to attach her mittens to her coat.*

Couple means to fasten two things together. *Lyle coupled the trailer to his car.*

Link means to connect as if by the loops of a chain. *With arms linked, the rescuers pulled the woman to safety.*

Combine means to put things or people together for a special purpose. *Gail and William combined their ideas and won first prize at the science fair.*

Unite means to join into a single thing. *The school board is voting whether or not to unite the boys' and girls' high schools.*

Associate means to join things in thought. *Alma associates her grandparents with Christmas, because that's when she gets to see them.*

SEE **mix** and **tie** for related words.
ANTONYM: separate

The Great Seal of
the United States

HAVE YOU HEARD...?

You may have seen the phrase "E Pluribus Unum." This is a Latin phrase that means "one out of many." It is the motto on the Great Seal of the United States and refers to the creation of one nation out of the thirteen original states. This motto also appears on a one-dollar bill. Can you find it there?

237

Joke
noun

Joke means something said or done to make someone laugh. *Everyone laughs at her jokes, but I don't think Alane is very funny.*

Gag can mean a joke. This meaning is informal. *"That water balloon gag works every time," Chuckles told the younger clowns.*

Wisecrack is an informal word that means a clever joke or smart remark, often one that makes fun of someone else. *Spike could tell by the way Steve laughed that Delores had made a wisecrack.*

Quip means a short, clever saying. *Hector's quip made the whole class burst out laughing.*

Pleasantry is a formal word that means a good-natured joke. *The party guests were exchanging pleasantries when dinner was served.*

Jest means a joke. It is now found mostly in books. *"Say not that I shall wed Sir Lionel, even in jest!" cried Lady Pamela.*

Witticism means a clever, funny remark. *When Mom is performing at the comedy club, she can answer heckling with witticisms so fast, it's amazing.*

SEE **funny, humor,** and **laugh** for related words.

Joy
noun

Joy means great happiness. *Let's all wish the newly married couple years of joy.*

Glee means lively joy. *Imagine Sasha's glee when he learned that the saddle was his to keep.*

Bliss means complete joy and satisfaction. *"This is bliss," Emma said, munching on a freshly picked peach.*

Jubilation means joy openly shown, especially in public. *After we won the Super Bowl, there was jubilation in the streets.*

Rapture means joy so strong that it takes all of someone's attention. *"Disneyland!" murmured Pepita in rapture.*

Ecstasy means total, overwhelming joy. *Darla got the concert tickets she wanted, so she's in ecstasy.*

SEE **happy** for related words.

Jump
verb

Sarah **leaped** to catch the ball.

Jump means to move suddenly through the air. *The cat jumped onto the table and sniffed at the hamburger meat, but she saw us watching and jumped right off.*

Leap means to jump high into the air. *Sarah leaped to catch the ball.*

Spring means to jump quickly and gracefully. *When Tomás gets home, his dog springs into his arms with yips of happiness.*

Bound can mean to move quickly with many jumps. *With the wolf at its heels, the rabbit bounded for its burrow.*

Skip means to move quickly, with one jump after another. *Kenny skipped all the way to Helen's house after learning she wasn't moving away after all.*

Hop means to jump on one foot, or on both feet together. *After stubbing his toe, Shiro grabbed it and hopped around on his other foot.*

Vault means to jump over something by using your hands or a pole. *At the sound of the alarm, the prowler vaulted the fence.*

Hurdle means to jump over something while running. *Jake hurdled a bush to catch the bus.*

Gambol means to run and jump around in play. *Sergio sat on the steps and watched the second graders gamboling happily in the little park across the street.*

IDIOMS

Jump is a key word in several idioms. Here are some of them:

Jump down someone's throat means to get very angry at someone. *"I told you I'm sorry, Lena; there's no need to jump down my throat," Vera complained.*

Get the jump on someone means to have an advantage over someone. *This summer I'm going to read all the books Mrs. Nabors usually assigns, so I'll get the jump on the rest of the class.*

Make someone jump through hoops means to make a person do something embarrassing or unpleasant, to prove your power over him or her. *My cousin Joshua made me jump through hoops before showing me his secret hideout.*

Keep
verb

Keep means to have and not get rid of something. *Chris has kept his model train set and all its parts.*

Retain is a formal word that means to keep. *As food is digested, the body retains nourishing substances.*

Withhold means to keep back and refuse to give. *The police are withholding the names of people hurt in the accident until their families are notified.*

Hold can mean to keep in and not let out. *"Please hold your questions until the mayor finishes speaking," requested her assistant.*

Save can mean to keep and put away. *Joey is saving money for another game cartridge.*

Reserve means to hold back. *Dr. Tran wants to reserve comment until he sees the X rays.*

Hang on to and **hold on to** can mean to refuse to get rid of something. *Throughout the game Fernando hung on to the belief that his team could win. The other team held on to its three-goal lead until the final minutes of play.*

SEE **have** and **store** for related words.
ANTONYM: discard

Chris has **kept** his model train set and all its parts.

Kill
verb

Kill means to put to death. *The boa constrictor kills its prey by squeezing with its powerful body.*

Murder means to kill someone on purpose and against the law. *The woman confessed that she had murdered her husband.*

Slay means to kill someone with violence. It is used mostly in writing. *The villagers were fearful and prayed for a hero who would slay the monster.*

Assassinate means to murder a well-known person in a sudden attack. *Can you name the four U.S. Presidents who have been assassinated?*

Execute can mean to kill someone, obeying a court order. *Jon and Holly will debate whether any criminals should be executed.*

Massacre means to kill cruelly and in large numbers. *Massacred for their oil, blue whales were nearly extinct when protective laws were finally enacted.*

Slaughter can mean to massacre. *Under Hitler's rule, the Nazis slaughtered six million Jews.*

Butcher can mean to massacre. *"If I attack that hill, Colonel, my men will be butchered," said the lieutenant.*

Liquidate can mean to kill deliberately and ruthlessly. *The secret police liquidated all the dictator's critics.*

WRITER'S CHOICE

On November 22 Kennedy was assassinated and replaced by Lyndon Johnson.

—Don Lawson, *The War in Vietnam*

Why *assassinated?* Lawson might have written accurately that Kennedy was killed, but people can be killed in accidents. He might also have written accurately that Kennedy was murdered, but when the victim of a murder is a well-known, public figure—as was President John F. Kennedy—the best and most specific word to use is *assassinate*.

Ms. Fuchida gave Marcy a **kindly** smile and some flowers from her garden.

Kind
adjective

Kind means friendly and good to others. *It's so kind of these retired people to tutor our students in reading.*

Kindly means kind. *Ms. Fuchida gave Marcy a kindly smile and some flowers from her garden.*

Gentle can mean kindly and thoughtful, eager to avoid hurting others. *Allison's gentle manner makes her a better baby-sitter for younger children.*

Warmhearted means kind and helpful to others. *How could anyone not like a person as warmhearted as Mrs. Echohawk?*

Good-natured means kind and cheerful. *Mr. Clayton is very good-natured about letting Ardrella and Quentin watch him in his work-shop.*

Benevolent means kind and eager to do good for others. *Mrs. Pertrillo is so benevolent—she's donated one hundred books to the school library.*

SEE **friendly, nice,** and **thoughtful** for related words.
ANTONYMS: cruel, unkind

Know
verb

Know means to have knowledge of something or someone. *Michelle and her family know a beautiful picnic spot in the state park.*

Realize means to understand that something is true. *Watching Mr. Brigano work in his garden, we never realized he was almost 90.*

Recognize can mean to realize. *Matt recognizes now that he was wrong to break up with Lewsha.*

Be acquainted with and **be aware of** mean to know. *"I am acquainted with the book you want," said the librarian, "but I am not aware of any library in the city that might have it."*

SEE **understand** for related words.

Michelle and her family **know** a beautiful picnic spot in the state park.

IDIOMS

There are many idioms that mean to know something fully and thoroughly. You can **know** something:

by heart	like the back of your hand
inside out	backwards and forwards
like a book	

There are also many ways to say that someone understands the situation. You can be **in the know,** and you can **know:**

the dope	the score
the ropes	what's up
the scoop	what's what

Do you have other ways of saying this?

243

Language
noun

Language means the speech or writing of a group of people who understand each other. It includes vocabulary and grammar. *The airport announcer repeats all messages in several languages.*

Tongue can mean a language. It is used mostly in books. *The armies of Islam carried the Arabic tongue to many countries.*

Speech can mean spoken language. *Words often become common in speech before they are accepted in writing.*

Dialect means a local form of a language. *Spanish is a language with a number of different dialects that are spoken in different countries or in different areas of the same country.*

Lingo is an informal word that means speech containing unknown words and therefore not understood by the listener. *When I try to teach my dad about computers, he complains about my lingo.*

Jargon can mean the language, especially the vocabulary, of some special group. *TV shows about doctors and police are full of jargon.*

The airport announcer repeats all messages in several **languages.**

Last
adjective

Last means after all others, or coming at the end. *Christie was the last person in line, so she had to wait the longest.*

Final means last. It emphasizes that there are no more to come. *Today is the final day of the contest, so call the station now!*

Ultimate means final, especially as the last part of a process. *Thuy has not yet taken the ultimate step of mailing her application.*

Latest can mean most recent or last up to this time. *Martin keeps up with the latest music by watching MTV.*

Concluding means last. *The concluding section of the program will be a sing-along with everyone joining in.*

Closing can mean last. *The closing period of the championship game was the most exciting.*

Eventual means final. It suggests that the end is different from the previous parts. *Valaree started asking on Monday if we could go to the movies on Friday, hoping Mom's eventual answer would be yes.*

SEE **end** and **stop** for related words.
ANTONYMS: first, initial

HAVE YOU HEARD...?

You may have heard people talk about "the last straw." This phrase comes from the saying "It was the last straw that broke the camel's back." This saying means that after a lot of problems, one more can be unbearable. *After Sheela tore her dress and dropped her books and missed her bus, losing her lunch money was the last straw, and she started crying.*

Christie was the **last** person in line, so she had to wait the longest.

245

Late
adjective

Late means not on time, especially a scheduled or expected time. *Sara was so anxious not to be late for her first baby-sitting job that she got there a half hour early.*

Tardy means not arriving on time. It is often used to mean late for school. *The traffic jam made everyone on the bus tardy.*

Belated means later than should be, especially because of delay. *Uncle Griff sent me a belated birthday card with apologies.*

Overdue means promised for a particular time, but not arrived or delivered. *The drugstore clerk says the October issue of Teen Health magazine is overdue.*

Behind means late, especially in making payment or doing something else required. *"When Dad was sick and we got behind on the rent, Mr. Iglesias was very nice about it," Julie told her friends.*

Behind time means not arriving at the scheduled time. It is often used about vehicles. *"The stagecoach from Laramie is behind time, ladies, so you'll have to sleep in the barn," said the rancher.*

ANTONYMS: early, prompt, punctual

Laugh
verb

Laugh means to show joy or amusement by making certain sounds and movements. *Chris often laughs so hard at his own jokes that he's funnier than the jokes are.*

Chuckle means to laugh very quietly or softly. *Shana chuckled as she watched the kittens wrestling.*

Giggle means to laugh in a silly way, with short, high-pitched sounds. *Molly and Ellen stopped giggling when their teacher told them to stand up.*

Snicker means to laugh but try to cover it up, or laugh in a sly way. *The scouts snickered when they noticed the banner was upside down.*

Guffaw means to laugh loudly, with your mouth wide open. It is a very strong word. *Lorenzo guffawed, and his laughter echoed down the hall.*

Chortle means to chuckle and snort. *Aunt Kathryn chortles every time Uncle Bruce talks back to the television.*

CONTINUED ON THE NEXT PAGE

The photographer asked us to look serious for one picture, but we kept **cracking up.**

Cackle can mean to laugh with a sound similar to the broken, shrill chatter of a hen. *The actress playing the wicked witch cackled fiendishly.*

Titter means to laugh in a nervous way. *When Rennie's false beard came loose, the other actors began tittering.*

Howl and **roar** can mean to laugh loudly, in uncontrolled amusement. *The toddlers howl with laughter every time their father tickles them. Grandpa loves to watch, and he roars when they try to tickle their father.*

Crack up can mean to laugh long and hard. *The photographer asked us to look serious for one picture, but we kept cracking up.*

SEE **funny, humor,** and **joke** for related words.

HAVE YOU HEARD...?

You may have heard someone say, "She was laughing up her sleeve." This is a phrase that means to be secretly amused. The laughter can sometimes be mean. *Sarah helped me to clean off the mud after I fell, but I know she was laughing up her sleeve.*

You also may have heard someone say, "He who laughs last, laughs best." People usually say this when they have been the victim of a joke or prank, to warn that they are planning to get even. If they do, they will have the last—and therefore best—laugh.

247

Lazy
adjective

Lazy means unwilling to work. *Moira and Grant act lazy because this job bores them.*

Shiftless means lazy and irresponsible. *People call Uncle Max shiftless, but he works harder at his painting than they know.*

Sluggish means without energy and slow-moving. *Daisy's an old dog now and sluggish.*

Idle and **inactive** mean not doing anything. *Ethel's crew was idle today because the bakery is being inspected. Ethel hates being inactive, so she spent the day cleaning house.*

Indolent is a formal word that means lazy. It suggests that someone is unwilling to do anything that requires energy, either work or play. *The indolent actress requested breakfast, lunch, and dinner in bed.*

Slothful is a formal word that means lazy. It suggests that someone is unwilling to do anything that requires energy, either work or play. *Greedy and slothful, the nobility were hated both by peasants and by the middle class.*

ANTONYMS: industrious, hard-working

Legal
adjective

Legal means permitted by law or according to law. *Calvin said he would do anything to help his older brother—so long as it was legal.*

Lawful means legal. *Since Mr. Torres made no will, his only cousin is his lawful heir.*

Rightful means according to law. *A military government has imprisoned the rightful president.*

Legitimate means rightful. *Ms. Littledog's insurance company ruled that her claim was legitimate and paid her $2,000.*

Licensed means permitted by official license. *Only licensed boats are allowed on Lake Waupaukee.*

Constitutional can mean permitted by or according to a constitution, especially that of the United States. *The Supreme Court has ruled that the death penalty is constitutional.*

ANTONYMS: illegal, unauthorized, unlawful

CONTINUED ON THE NEXT PAGE

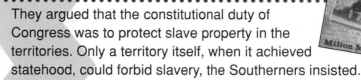

They argued that the constitutional duty of
Congress was to protect slave property in the
territories. Only a territory itself, when it achieved
statehood, could forbid slavery, the Southerners insisted.

—Milton Meltzer, *Voices from the Civil War*

Why *constitutional?* Southerners claimed that slavery was legal, and that
it was legal for slaveowners to protect their "property" (enslaved people).
Further, they claimed that Congress had a duty to help them do it. The
Southerners said that these claims were based on the Constitution of the
United States, the most basic law of the land.

Lengthen
verb

Lengthen means to make something longer. *Marge is growing so fast
this year, we have to lengthen all her skirts.*

Stretch can mean to lengthen something, usually by pulling it. *Skip
tugged on Nathaniel's sweater, stretching it.*

Extend can mean to lengthen. *The shoe store will
extend its back-to-school sale for one more
week.*

Prolong means to lengthen in time. *Sometimes
a drug can prolong the life of a sick person.*

SEE **increase** and **expand** for related words.
ANTONYM: shorten

Skip tugged on
Nathaniel's sweater,
stretching it.

Let
verb

Let means not to stop something from happening. *Mr. Kaiser will let me make up my lab work later.*

Allow means to let. *"Teeka, don't allow the boys to stay up late, and no TV after nine," Mrs. Sullivan told the baby-sitter.*

Permit means to allow. *The hospital permitted my father to be in the room when baby Saul was born.*

Consent means to give permission. *Julio wants to take dance lessons, and his parents have consented.*

Agree can mean to consent. *The bus company agreed to keep student fares at the same amount this year.*

SEE **permission** for related words.
ANTONYMS: forbid, prohibit

WATCH IT!

People sometimes mix up **let** and **leave**. *Let* means not to stop something from happening. *Leave* means to go away. Except in very relaxed conversation, it is not correct to say *"Leave her go, if she wants to"* or *"Leave me be."* In formal and informal English, these sentences should be *"Let her go, if she wants to"* and *"Let me be."*

Level
adjective

Level means with the same height all over, so that round things don't roll by themselves. *Forrest put some cardboard under one table leg to make it level with the others.*

Even means level. *Undisturbed by wind, the snow lay even on the windowsills and rooftops.*

Flat means level. It often suggests something low. *During the last Ice Age, glaciers scraped the prairies flat.*

Horizontal means level and parallel with the horizon. *The carpenter checked the windowsill to be sure that it was perfectly horizontal.*

Straight can mean horizontal. *Sally pinned the hem of the skirt and used a yardstick to see that it was straight.*

Flush can mean level with another surface. *The river is flush with its banks now, and any more rain will bring a flood.*

SEE **smooth** for related words.

Liberty
noun

Liberty means the condition of being able to do or say what you choose, without being prevented or controlled by others. *Members of the audience are at liberty to join in the dancing.*

Freedom means liberty. *Freedom of speech is guaranteed in the United States Constitution.*

Independence means the condition of not being controlled by others. *The colonists fought for independence in the American Revolution.*

The colonists fought for **independence** in the American Revolution.

Liberation means the act of freeing from control or imprisonment. *The new government promises liberation of all hostages.*

Emancipation means the act of legally declaring someone to be free. *A proclamation by President Lincoln resulted in the emancipation of millions of enslaved people.*

License can mean freedom. It often suggests that someone has made too much use of freedom, or a wrong use. *"Going off a diet isn't license to eat everything in sight, Lindsay," said her grandmother.*

SEE **free** for related words.
ANTONYM: slavery

▼ HAVE YOU HEARD...?
. . . .

You may have heard someone speak of "poetic license." This is not a permit to be a poet but freedom from precise accuracy. A poet could write:

> *Deep in the cloudless summer night*
> *A million stars make darkness bright.*

A person can't really see a million stars without a telescope, but a poet or a person using poetic license can write that because that's how it feels.

Lie

noun

Although I took pictures, people said my UFO sighting was just a **story.**

Lie means an untrue statement that is intended to deceive someone. *"I saw you take my lunch, so don't tell me any lies about it,"* said Thomas.

Falsehood means an untrue statement. It suggests less wrongdoing than *lie* does. *"I want your real opinion of my work,"* Ava told her aunt, *"not some polite falsehood."*

Fib means a little, harmless lie. It is an informal, somewhat childish word. *I forgot her call, so I used a fib, that I never got the message.*

Story can mean an untrue statement or claim, especially one used to seem important or to avoid blame. This meaning is informal. *Although I took pictures, people said my UFO sighting was just a story.*

Untruth can mean a falsehood. It is a somewhat formal word. *The lawyer suggested to the witness that her testimony contained untruths.*

Misrepresentation means a statement intended to deceive by concealing the truth. It may not be directly untrue. *"It is a misrepresentation to say that you found no dirty laundry, Margie, since you never looked,"* said Mrs. Collins.

Tall tale means an untrue and unlikely story, told for amusement. *Willie claims he receives radio broadcasts through his braces, but that's a tall tale.*

ANTONYM: truth

AROUND THE WORLD: Lying

If you sow falsehood, you reap deceit.
— **Ghanaian proverb**

One who lies for you will lie to you.
— **Arabic proverb**

A liar is easier to catch than a lame dog.
— **Hungarian proverb**

It takes a thousand lies to hide one.
—**Indian proverb**

Yesterday's liar gets no belief tomorrow.
— **Russian proverb**

Lift
verb

Lift means to push or pull something up. *Ruby lifted the baby out of his crib.*

Raise means to lift. *The deer sensed Makwokeeta's approach and raised their heads to sniff the wind.*

Elevate means to lift. It is used mostly about things that are large, heavy, or important. *The back of a dump truck can be elevated so that the dirt slides out. The bishop was elevated to the rank of cardinal.*

Heave means to lift with force or effort. *Marilyn and Dick heaved the old trap door open and stared into the darkness below.*

Hoist means to lift, especially using ropes and machines. It is sometimes used to suggest that something is very heavy or awkward to lift. *With difficulty, the locomotive was hoisted back onto the track.*

Boost means to push someone up from underneath. *Aaron couldn't get over the fence until Kyra boosted him.*

Erect is a formal word that means to lift something into an upright position. *The statue shows Marines erecting the flag at Iwo Jima.*

SEE **climb** for related words.
ANTONYMS: drop, lower

Like
verb

Like means to be pleased with someone or something. *Felipe likes baseball and electronics.*

Enjoy means to take pleasure in something. *"I've so enjoyed your visit," Grandmother said.*

Fancy can mean to like something and to want it or choose it. *Mom really fancies sweets, so the corner bakery is a favorite place.*

Relish means to like something. *Ivana relished the excitement and variety of life in the city.*

Care for means to like. It is often used in questions, or with "not." *"Would you care for more salad, Valerie?" asked her mother. "I don't care for windsurfing," said Veronica. "It messes up my hair."*

Be fond of means to like something or someone very much. *Ellen admired Jane's confidence, but it was Anna she was fond of.*

SEE **love** for related words.
ANTONYM: dislike

Likely
adjective

Likely means having a good chance of happening. *Richie is likely to spend Saturday helping his father make deliveries.*

Probable means almost sure to happen. *When she felt the first drops of rain, Ms. Porter knew it was probable that the picnic would be canceled.*

Liable means likely to have something bad happen. *Scientists know that earthquakes are liable to strike again where they've struck before.*

Apt means likely, especially because of the way someone or something is. *Tamara can do most of the problems, but she's not apt to help us.*

Prone means apt to have something bad happen. *Grace's father's illness makes him prone to periods of bad temper.*

Inclined means somewhat likely. It suggests a better chance of happening than not happening. *Mr. Montalbo is inclined to give Ignacio the job, since he asked first.*

ANTONYM: unlikely

Limit
verb

Limit means to say where or when something must stop. *Rules of the debate limited each speaker to three minutes for an opening statement.*

Bound means to limit. *Hong's enthusiasm for the game was bounded by the fact that he had a large science project due the next day.*

Restrict means to allow only certain choices. *Now that Rafael and Carmen are both in college, the Gutierrez family budget is very restricted.*

Confine means to restrict. It emphasizes control and a small number of choices. *Toby confines his TV viewing to only five hours a week.*

Circumscribe is a formal word that can mean to restrict. *"Margaret's activities must be circumscribed," said Dr. Wagner, "until her heart is stronger."*

SEE **enclose** for related words.

List
noun

List means a series of names, words, or numbers in a row. *Gail said, "First, let's draw up a list of everyone in the neighborhood whose windows we could wash."*

Table can mean a brief list, especially of numbers. *Marcena's report on George Washington Carver has a table of important dates in his life.*

Roll can mean a list of people's names. *Mr. Philpotts will call the roll after everyone finds a seat on the bus.*

Catalog means a list of things that someone sells or owns. It usually arranges items in order, with information about each item. *Isaac went through every catalog in the house, but none of them had the pants he wanted.*

Inventory means a list of items that a business owns. It is for the business to use, not for customers. *Mrs. Young hired Nelson to make an inventory of the pet supplies.*

Register means a list, especially an official one. *Mrs. Schaefer says to make sure all our parents are on the register of voters.*

Mrs. Young hired Nelson to make an **inventory** of the pet supplies.

WORD POOL

There are many special kinds of lists, each with its own name. Here are some of them (and the fields in which they are used):

agenda (business)	**manifest** (cargo)
bibliography (books)	**menu** (foods)
bill (prices)	**program** (players)
calendar (dates)	**schedule** (times)
directory (names)	**table of contents** (page numbers)
gazetteer (places)	**thesaurus** (synonyms)
glossary (words)	

Little
adjective

Little means not big, or less than normal in size. *Constanza's sister tried to reach the counter top, but she was too little.*

Small means little. *Jane likes everything about the new apartment except the small kitchen.*

Dwarf means much smaller than usual size. *Bonsai, the art of growing dwarf trees, is popular in Japan.*

Midget means very small. *Did you know that my homeroom teacher spends her weekends racing midget cars?*

Short can mean not tall. *Aaron may be short, but he can shoot baskets as well as anyone here.*

Undersized means smaller than the usual size. *The day-care center has undersized chairs and tables in the main room.*

Slight means small in amount or in importance. *Jolene said, "Thank you, but I have a slight headache, so I think I'll stay home."*

Skimpy means too little to work very well. *It's too cold for just that skimpy blanket.*

SEE **tiny** for related words.
ANTONYMS: big, large

Live
verb

Live means to have a home in a certain place. *After the fire, the Mendez family had to find a new house to live in.*

Dwell is a formal word that means to live. *People first began to dwell in cities more than 5,000 years ago.*

Reside is a formal word that means to live in one place over a period of time. *Only people who have resided in the city for at least six months may vote in local elections.*

Lodge means to live in a place for a short time. *Jamie asked if he could lodge with us until his dormitory opens in the fall.*

Stay can mean to live somewhere for a while as a guest. *Marvella's cousins are staying with her right now.*

Settle can mean to go somewhere and make a home there. *Driven from their eastern lands, the Cherokee were forced to settle in Oklahoma.*

Lively
adjective

Lively means full of life, quick motion, and cheerfulness. *Everyone was amazed that Ellen could be so lively just two days after having her appendix removed.*

Active means lively, especially in motion. *Calvin wished his little brother weren't so active early in the morning.*

Peppy is an informal word that means lively and energetic. *The doctor says that it's just a flu, and that Mi-Cha will be as peppy as ever in three days.*

Frisky means lively and playful. *The frisky colt jumped and ran around in the field.*

Perky means lively, happy, and friendly. *Better not let that perky little puppy in where your father's taking a nap.*

Spirited means lively, confident, and brave. *"Thank you, Ms. Costello, for that spirited performance of The Stars and Stripes Forever," said the principal.*

Spry means active. It is often used about older people. *Mrs. Lipshitz remains as spry at 83 as most people half her age.*

Sprightly means lively, quick-witted, and full of fun. *Alex and Jeff love it when their sprightly Aunt Alicia comes to visit.*

Feeling your oats is an idiom that means lively. *"So, Tony, you're feeling your oats today?" chuckled Gramps.*

ANTONYMS: dull, lifeless, sluggish

The **frisky** colt jumped and ran around in the field.

Lock
verb

Lock means to shut something with a special device, so that it cannot be opened except with a key or a certain combination of numbers. *"Don't forget to lock the door when you leave, Charlene," said her boss.*

Latch means to shut a door, gate, or window with a catch that holds it shut but not locked. *Faith latches the backyard gate to keep her cat, Sampson, from getting out.*

Bolt means to shut something with a small sliding rod moved by hand or by a key. *Hurry and bolt the doors before the storm reaches us!*

Bar means to shut a door or window with a pole or rod that can be moved only from inside. *"Bar the city gates!" cried the messenger. "The Roman army is upon us!"*

Secure can mean to shut something so that it cannot be opened against your will. *Mr. Frazier secured the steel grates over his windows.*

Make fast means to fasten or shut something firmly and reliably. *The captain commanded the crew to make the ship fast to the dock.*

SEE **enclose** for related words.

Faith **latches** the backyard gate to keep her cat, Sampson, from getting out.

Sampson the cat looked terribly **forlorn** when Faith left him behind.

Lonely
adjective

Lonely means feeling sad because of a need for company. *Dorothy was lonely in the new neighborhood until she met Patty.*

Lonesome means feeling sad because of being alone. *When Andrew gets lonesome, he heads for the playground.*

Forlorn means lonely and sad, usually because of being left behind. *Sampson the cat looked terribly forlorn when Faith left him behind.*

Desolate can mean very sad, lonely, and friendless. *Eliza Ann felt desolate as she heard the door of the orphanage close behind her.*

SEE **alone** and **sad** for related words.

WRITING TIP: Creating Mood

To create a scene in a reader's mind, it often helps to choose words that suggest a mood. To create a mood of loneliness, for example, you might use the words *forlorn* or *desolate,* or you could add details that suggest how desolate the scene is.

At the end of the small peninsula, a solitary tree struggled to find a foothold in the rocky soil. Wispy gray clouds obscured the horizon, with not even a seagull moving in the sky. The foamy waves that lapped the shore seemed to whisper to Karen's ear, "They're gone. . . They're gone. . . ." Forlorn as she felt then, she knew that the desolate days ahead would be harder still.

By using synonyms and carefully chosen details (such as a solitary tree) that bring out an emotional response in the reader, you can suggest a mood that is sad or happy, miserable or comfortable or filled with joy. Not every scene or piece of writing has a mood, but you can make your fiction writing more effective by thinking about when to use mood.

259

Look
verb

Look means to point your eyes at something in order to see it. *"Look! There goes a hummingbird!" Jeri called to her father.*

SEE **examine, see,** and **watch** for related words.

Look is used in phrases that have special meanings. Each of these phrases has its own set of synonyms.

look after

Look after means to pay attention in order to be sure that someone or something is all right. *"Look after our bikes, Errol, and we'll get you a soda," Jake promised.*

Tend means to look after. *Tim tends the cattle for his father in the summer months.*

Mind can mean to look after. It emphasizes paying attention. *Clara enjoys minding the baby when her mother has to go to the store.*

Watch can mean to look after and guard. *"Who'll watch the campsite while we're swimming?" asked Jamal.*

Care for can mean to look after someone, especially a person who is sick or who has trouble with daily life. *The loon cares for its babies by carrying them with it everywhere.*

Attend to and **take care of** can mean to look after. They often suggest a certain amount of time or a certain number of tasks. *Weak with hunger, the shipwrecked sailors could barely attend to their signal fire. After they were rescued, they were sent to the hospital where doctors could take care of them.*

Keep an eye on is an idiom that means to mind. *Inayuuq will keep an eye on the sled dogs while his uncle is away.*

CONTINUED ON THE NEXT PAGE

The loon **cares for** its babies
by carrying them with it everywhere.

look into

Look into means to study something in order to learn more about it. *Mr. Van den Hoek is looking into the possibility of opening a restaurant.*

Investigate means to look into something in order to learn the truth. *The cash box was gone, and, as manager, Jane had to investigate the theft.*

Explore can mean to look into something. *A committee will explore the costs of building a new stadium downtown.*

Probe means to look into something thoroughly. It suggests effort and difficulty. *Reporters probed old records and found that the factory had been polluting the river for years.*

Analyze means to investigate the details of something and how they are connected. *Sir Isaac Newton was the first to analyze the nature of color using prisms.*

look up to

Look up to means to have a very good opinion of someone and want to be like that person. *Serafina looks up to her grandparents for the way they have worked so hard and stayed so gentle.*

Admire can mean to have a good opinion of someone or something. *Everyone admires the way that Joel gets along with other people.*

Respect means to have a good opinion of someone or something. *Her friends don't agree with Adriana's decision, but they respect her courage in making it.*

Esteem is a formal word meaning to admire greatly. *Although Vincent van Gogh's paintings are widely esteemed today, during his life no one wanted them.*

Honor means to respect greatly. It is often used when respect is shown in a serious, public way. *"We are here today to honor Father Driscoll for his many contributions to the school," said Mrs. Connors.*

Put someone on a pedestal is an idiom that means to admire someone more than is reasonable. *Just because Warren can program his own video games, that's no reason to put him on a pedestal.*

Loose
adjective

Loose means not fitting tightly or not tightly fastened. *Jennifer's sandal strap was so loose, she found it difficult to dance.*

Slack means loose, especially not stretched tight. *The sail hung slack on the still, windless day.*

Lax means not firm or tight. It suggests weakness or lack of effort. *This rubber band is too lax to hold the papers together.*

Relaxed means loose after being tight. *I woke up with a stiff neck, but now that I've had a hot bath, the muscles are relaxed.*

Baggy means loose and hanging down. It is used mostly about clothes. *Into the clown's baggy pants went three fish, flowers, and a poodle.*

ANTONYM: tight

Loud
adjective

Loud means having or making a big sound. *The thunder was so loud, it seemed the storm was right over our house.*

Noisy means with a lot of loud, harsh sounds. *Elora ran past the noisy street repairs as fast as she could.*

Roaring means making a loud, deep sound. *This is no place for kids to play, with broken glass and roaring traffic.*

Thunderous can mean very loud, like thunder. *"Just listen to that thunderous applause from these hockey fans!" said the announcer.*

Blaring means making a very loud, harsh sound. *The blaring stereo in the upstairs apartment kept Pavel's family awake.*

Deafening means loud enough to hurt the ears. *Mrs. Nuñez installed a deafening siren in her new car so it wouldn't be stolen.*

Earsplitting means deafening. *The earsplitting squeal of the smoke alarm made Naomi cover her ears.*

Clamorous means loud, especially with voices. *Irene says you have to shout just to give your order because of the clamorous noise in that restaurant.*

Fortissimo means extremely loud. It is used in writing music. *The fortissimo closing notes brought the audience to their feet.*

SEE **noise** and **shout** for related words.
ANTONYMS: quiet, silent, still

Mrs. Hightower held the sleeping child with **love.**

Love
noun

Love means a strong and tender feeling of liking or being fond of someone. *Mrs. Hightower held the sleeping child with love.*

Affection means a kind, warm feeling for someone or something. It is not as strong a word as *love*. *Whitney has a special affection for the elderly couple upstairs and often visits them.*

Fondness means liking or affection. *Grandma's fondness for Pooch is obvious from the way she crawls around on the floor with him.*

Devotion means a very loyal feeling of love or affection for someone or something. *Rocco saved that puppy from drowning, and it gives him total devotion.*

Adoration means devoted love and admiration. *Allen's feeling for his favorite rock group amounts almost to adoration.*

Passion can mean a very strong love, especially between a man and a woman. *Romeo and Juliet is a tale of passion that ends with the tragic deaths of the hero and heroine.*

Crush can mean a sudden, strong liking for someone, which stops after a while. This meaning is informal. *Felix has a crush on a waitress at the taco place, so he's probably there now.*

SEE **like** for related words.
ANTONYMS: hate, hatred

Grandma Rose has been a **faithful** fan of the Dover Skylarks for forty years.

Loyal
adjective

Loyal means always having the same good feelings for someone or something and always on the same side. *Ed isn't the best debater, but he's a loyal member of the team.*

True can mean loyal. *Kwa-Mei promised her grandmother to be true to the ways of her ancestors.*

True-blue means loyal. It suggests complete honesty and sincerity. *Mr. Skerritt was a true-blue union member for forty years.*

Faithful means loyal and always acting from loyalty. *Grandma Rose has been a faithful fan of the Dover Skylarks for forty years.*

Devoted means very loyal and faithful and giving all your time and strength to someone or something. *Rosemary and Blaine are really devoted to each other.*

Staunch can mean loyal and strong. *Mexico's President Juarez was a staunch friend of the poor.*

ANTONYMS: disloyal, unfaithful

264

Luck
noun

Luck means what seems to make things happen, without anyone planning, controlling, or predicting events. *"Just my luck," Paula said, as the bus pulled away without her.*

Fortune can mean luck. *Ms. Voigt's good fortune at finding the lost ring in the wastebasket was amazing.*

Chance can mean luck. It suggests that things really happen for no reason. *It's not just chance that Manasa and Hank both showed up at the library.*

Accident can mean chance. *By accident, he caught a glimpse of his friend on the street.*

The breaks, the way the ball bounces, and **the way the cookie crumbles** are informal expressions that all mean chance. They are all used when something unpleasant happens. *"I lost my lunch," said Matt. "That's the breaks. And I forgot my wallet, but that's the way the ball bounces. Anyhow, the cafeteria's closed. I suppose that's the way the cookie crumbles."*

HAVE YOU HEARD...?

You may have heard people say that finding a four-leaf clover is supposed to bring good luck. Did you know that the things listed below are also supposed to bring good luck?

a bent coin	a coin with a hole in it
picking up a pin	a dream that you are dancing
a rabbit's foot	finding a horseshoe
picking up a penny	sleeping on your right side

Are there other things you've heard about that are supposed to bring good luck?

Mad
adjective

Mad means having lost one's temper. *It made Stephanie mad when the store clerk ignored her.*

Angry means mad. *My brother is angry with me because I took his skates without asking first.*

Sore can mean angry. This meaning is informal. *RayEarl is sore because he didn't get picked to play third base.*

Indignant means mad about something unjust or mean. *Candyce was indignant when I told her I didn't like her hair.*

Irate means seriously angry. *A group of irate tenants was shouting at the janitor.*

Boiling can mean angry and very excited. *Traffic has been stuck for an hour, and the drivers are boiling.*

Furious means wildly angry. *Ronald was furious when his little sister spilled milk on his baseball cards.*

Enraged means furious. *Queen Aubrey became enraged when she learned that an enemy army had invaded her land.*

Hot under the collar is an idiom that means annoyed and angry. *The principal is hot under the collar about the mess in the auditorium.*

Fit to be tied is an idiom that means extremely angry. *Somebody robbed Mr. Hilbert's apartment, and he's fit to be tied.*

SEE **anger** and **cross** for related words.

CONTINUED ON THE NEXT PAGE

Here are words that mean "to make someone mad." Some mean to cause mild anger, like *annoy*. Others, like *enrage*, mean to cause great anger. Which words would you group with *annoy*? with *enrage*? Use your dictionary to look up any word you don't know.

aggravate	exasperate	irritate	peeve
anger	incense	madden	provoke
annoy	infuriate	miff	rile
enrage	irk	outrage	vex

Main
adjective

The Komodo dragon is named for the island in Indonesia that is its **primary** habitat.

Main means most important. *According to Mr. Boykin, the main problem with the car is the transmission.*

Central can mean main. *The central library sends books to a branch library near our house.*

Major means more important than most others. *Houston is one of the major cities of the United States.*

Chief means first in rank. *As chief executive, the President controls the operations of the U.S. government.*

Principal means first in order of importance. *The principal idea of* Roots, *Greg said in his report, is the value of family history to personal dignity.*

Primary means most important and coming before others. *The Komodo dragon is named for the island in Indonesia that is its primary habitat.*

Leading means most important and directing others. *The city's leading citizens are calling for the mayor's resignation.*

Foremost can mean chief or leading. *Mrs. Dubose is one of the world's foremost authorities on computer publishing.*

Top can mean highest or best. *Sam "Tallman" Jones was the top scorer in last night's game.*

SEE **important** and **value** for related words.
ANTONYM: minor, subordinate

Mr. Schmidt works in a factory that **manufactures** auto parts.

Make
verb

Make means to put together or give form to something. *Lissa's brother said they could make a good gerbil cage from an old aquarium.*

Shape means to make something by giving it a form. *The bottles are shaped by pouring melted glass into molds.*

Build means to make something from materials and according to a plan. *Mr. Butler built a sandbox for the children.*

Construct means to build. *Before constructing the bridge, the engineers prepared careful drawings.*

Manufacture means to create something from materials, over and over. *Mr. Schmidt works in a factory that manufactures auto parts.*

Assemble can mean to make an object by fitting parts where they belong. *Angel's mother has a job assembling computer keyboards.*

Fashion means to make, especially by hand. *Doug fashioned a lamp out of a bowling pin.*

Form means to make, especially by hand. *Yong-Sun can form fish and flowers by folding paper.*

Fabricate means to build or assemble. *The frame of the skyscraper is fabricated of steel and concrete.*

Forge can mean to shape. It suggests difficulty and repeated changes. *Tecumseh worked to forge alliances among American Indian tribes, encouraging them to defend their land.*

Put together means to form something by combining different people or things. *The coach put together an excellent team. Mom put leftovers together to make a delicious casserole.*

ANTONYMS: demolish, destroy

Manage
verb

Manage means to plan and guide what other people do. *After school, Carmen manages the younger children because both her parents work.*

Control means to have power over something and make decisions about it. *While the queen was a girl, her uncles controlled the country and made themselves rich.*

Direct means to manage. It emphasizes planning certain results and controlling things so those results are achieved. *Luther's father directs the community hunger project.*

Conduct can mean to manage. It suggests keeping things going. *A millionaire at twenty-five, Charmayne conducts three businesses from her penthouse office.*

Oversee means to make sure that people are doing what they should. *Tong's father was gone all week, overseeing the planting of his fields.*

Supervise means to oversee. *Her mother still needs to supervise Louise when she does her homework.*

Administer is a formal word that means to manage an organization's activities. *Ms. Gower administers this department and also the sales staff.*

Regulate means to control by rules or laws. *The government regulates the employment of children to prevent the abuses of the past.*

Run can mean to manage. *Bill runs a delivery service with four helpers on bicycles.*

Handle can mean to manage. *Getting rid of the gangs was tough, but the neighborhood handled the whole job.*

Head can mean to manage. *Who would have thought that the undercover operation was headed by that quiet store clerk?*

Be in charge of means to manage. *She doesn't have time to be in charge of the work, but Andrea still wants to be on the stage crew.*

SEE **command** and **guide** for related words.

Many
adjective

Many means including a large number, not a few. *People have immigrated to the United States from many countries.*

Numerous means many. It emphasizes the large number. *On numerous occasions last year, it was impossible to get good seats at the outdoor concerts.*

Multitudinous means very many, like a crowd. *As populations increase, governments face multitudinous problems in providing necessary services.*

Countless means too many to count. *Countless pigeons all took flight at once.*

Innumerable means too many to count. *Buffalo were once innumerable in the United States, but by 1889 only 551 remained.*

Umpteen means countless. It is an informal word. *"Bianca, you've played that cartridge umpteen times," complained her sister.*

A lot of, lots of, and **quite a few** mean many. *Dad took a lot of my friends to the game for my birthday. We had lots of soda pop and quite a few hot dogs.*

ANTONYM: few

Match
verb

Match means to be equal or the same. *The burglar's fingerprints matched those on the cash register.*

Coincide can mean to be the same. *The pilot's description of the UFO coincided with the reports from the passengers.*

CONTINUED ON THE NEXT PAGE

The burglar's fingerprints **matched** those on the cash register.

270

Correspond can mean to be the same, except for minor differences. *Mrs. Suharto's background in teaching corresponds with what the school is looking for.*

Agree can mean to be very much the same. *Some readers wonder if the movie version will agree with the book.*

Check can mean to be the same when compared to something. *Mr. Hobbs was pleased when my inventory list checked with his.*

Jibe is an informal word that means to match. *Juwain's story of the winning goal jibes with Marcy's.*

SEE **copy, same,** and **similar** for related words.
ANTONYMS: differ, vary

Meaning
noun

Meaning is the idea of a word or words, which you understand when you hear or read. *Jake speaks Spanish with an accent, but he gets his meaning across.*

Sense can mean a meaning, especially one definition of a word that has several definitions. *"When Marco said my sunglasses were 'bad,' in which sense did he mean it?" asked Cynthia.*

Significance can mean a meaning of words or actions. *The significance of the mayor's comment became clear when she fired the police chief.*

Import can mean a significance. It suggests that the meaning has not been made openly clear. *Scientists are struggling tonight to understand the import of the space aliens' communication.*

Implication can mean a significance that is only suggested or hinted at. *The implication of Marjorie's silence was that she'd rather not talk about Alonzo.*

Content can mean the meaning contained in a speech or piece of writing. *The test will cover the content of Section 3, "Environment and Ecology."*

Message can mean the main idea of a speech or piece of writing. *"Ask what you can do for your country" was the message of President Kennedy's inaugural speech.*

Measure

verb

Measure means to find the size or amount of something. *When Yin measured her room, she found it was nine feet wide and ten feet long.*

Weigh means to find out how heavy something is. *Herb weighed the mixture before continuing with his science experiment.*

Survey can mean to measure land for its area, boundaries, and shape. *They needed to survey the site before the archaeologists could dig.*

Gauge means to measure. It is mostly used in discussing science. *We gauged the amount of rain that fell yesterday as half an inch.*

Quantify means to measure an amount of something. It is mostly used in discussing science. *Aboard the space shuttle, the astronauts record quantified scientific information.*

Calibrate means to check a measuring instrument by comparing it to another. It is used mostly in discussing science. *After the broken scale is fixed, it will have to be calibrated.*

SEE **estimate** for related words.

They needed to **survey** the site before the archaeologists could dig.

WORD POOL

Science and daily life both use many measuring instruments. Here is a list of some (along with what they measure):

altimeter (altitude)	**magnetometer** (magnetic force)
ammeter (electric current)	**odometer** (distance driven)
anemometer (wind speed)	**pedometer** (distance walked)
barometer (air pressure)	**photometer** (light)
calorimeter (heat)	**sphygmomanometer** (blood pressure)
chronometer (time)	**tachometer** (speed of rotation)
hygrometer (humidity)	**voltmeter** (electromotive force)

And there are dozens more.

Meet
verb

Meet means to come face to face with someone or something, usually by plan or for the first time. *Ramon's parents met all his teachers on PTA night. "Meet me outside the old tower at midnight," whispered Victoria.*

Encounter is a formal word that means to meet unexpectedly. *The explorers encountered polar bears and huge walls of ice.*

Face can mean to meet bravely. *In the movie <u>High Noon</u>, Gary Cooper faces three outlaws with no one to help him.*

Confront means to meet. It emphasizes that the meeting is face to face and suggests an unpleasant meeting. *Everado was chosen by the group to confront Paul about the missing instruments.*

Run across and **run into** mean to come face to face with someone, especially by chance. *I ran across George at the library yesterday. It was the second time I had run into him this week.*

Bump into can mean to run across. *She bumped into Josh just after leaving a message for him at the ticket counter.*

Come up against means to meet suddenly and unexpectedly. It suggests that the meeting causes a problem. *"Tell the lieutenant we've come up against five enemy tanks!" Sergeant MacKenzie called out to the radio operator.*

ANTONYM: avoid

The explorers **encountered** polar bears and huge walls of ice.

273

For people kidnapped into slavery, the voyage to America meant weeks of **agony.**

Misery
noun

Misery means great sadness or pain. *Misery at his wife's death seemed to age Mr. Friedkin overnight.*

Suffering means helpless pain of body or mind. *There is nothing we can do for that cat except put an end to her suffering.*

Torture can mean extreme pain. *Stammering was torture for Nora, but she's got it mostly under control now.*

Torment can mean extreme pain. *Hay fever is a torment for Al.*

Agony means almost unbearable pain or sadness. *For people kidnapped into slavery, the voyage to America meant weeks of agony.*

Anguish means great suffering. *Kamil watched in anguish as his escaped hawk flew away.*

SEE **care, pain, sad,** and **sorrow** for related words.
ANTONYMS: happiness, joy

HAVE YOU HEARD...?

You may have heard the phrase "Misery loves company." This can mean that unhappy people like to complain about their problems to other people. It can also mean that unhappy people may try to make others unhappy as well.

You may also have heard the phrase "Laugh and the world laughs with you, weep and you weep alone." This means that other people try to stay away from unhappy people. So, put them together and what do we have? Misery may love company, but company doesn't necessarily love misery!

Misfortune
noun

Misfortune means bad luck or an unfortunate happening. *Josleen had the misfortune to race against the city's best sprinter in the first round of the girls' 100-meter dash.*

Accident means an unfortunate happening, usually a sudden one. *Traffic is backed up because of the auto accident.*

Misadventure means an accident, usually not a serious one. *James and his friends were covered with mud after their misadventure while feeding the pigs.*

Mishap means a misadventure. *"Keep practicing the dance," the director said, "and it will go without any mishap."*

Mischance means misfortune. *Mrs. Beauford always imagines some mischance if her children are out after dark.*

SEE **disaster** for related words.

Mistake
noun

Mistake means something you do wrong. *Elana made fewer mistakes on her math quizzes after she started working with a tutor.*

Error means a mistake. *"It's a simple error," Sun-Hi's mother said. "We can fix it easily."*

Slip can mean a mistake, especially in speaking. *Tania made a slip of the tongue, calling Ms. Kaplan "Mrs."*

Blunder means a careless or stupid mistake. *I couldn't believe Jamielle's blunder—she brought the cake and balloons but forgot the birthday candles!*

WORD STORY

Many words that begin with *mis-* mean particular kinds of mistakes. For example, a ***mis**calculation* is a mistake in calculation. Other such words include

miscount	**misjudgment**	**mispronunciation**
misprint	**misspelling**	**misunderstanding**

What others can you think of?

275

Mix

verb

Mix means to put two or more things together. *Succotash is corn mixed with beans.*

Mingle means to mix, especially many things together. *The variety show will mingle songs, dancing, comedy, magic, and storytelling.*

Blend means to mix thoroughly, so that parts are changed and become something else. *Blend the eggs into the pancake batter.*

Merge can mean to become completely mixed with something else. *The Allegheny and Monongahela rivers merge at Pittsburgh to form the Ohio River.*

Dilute means to make something weaker by mixing it with something else. *The chemistry experiment called for one part ammonia diluted with three parts water.*

Scramble can mean to mix in a confused way. *The Scouts got scrambled with our marching band during the parade.*

Integrate can mean to mix parts into a whole thing, especially people of different races in an equal group. *Students from the city and the suburbs are integrated in this school district.*

SEE **join** and **tie** for related words.
ANTONYM: separate

The Scouts got **scrambled** with our marching band during the parade.

WORD STORY

Blending words already in use is one way that people make up new words. *Chortle,* for instance, blends *chuckle* and *snort.* Other blends are *bionic* (*biology* + *electronic*), *motel* (*motor* + *hotel*), and *smog* (*smoke* + *fog*).

Try making up your own blends— how about *sloring,* to describe something that is *slow* and *boring?* Or *swizzy,* for a drink that is *sweet* and *fizzy?*

Move
verb

Move means to change the position of something. *"If you move the mirror, Marta, you'll get more light in your microscope," advised her science teacher.*

Shift means to move something to a different place or position, especially one nearby. *Mr. Avila shifted the heavy suitcase from hand to hand as he walked.*

Transfer means to change the position of something. *When the moving van broke down, we had to transfer all the boxes to another one.*

Remove means to move something away from a place. *Oskar removed the hot pan from the burner.*

Budge means to move even a little. It is often used with "not." *The anchor was caught, and the crew couldn't budge it.*

Dislodge means to move something from its place, often by force. *Several bricks were dislodged from the wall after the storm.*

Displace can mean to dislodge. *War has displaced the villagers, who are living in the city now.*

Replace can mean to move something back to where it was before. *Ellen replaced all the tools after she finished fixing her bicycle chain.*

SEE **carry, pull, push,** and **put** for related words.

VERB PLUS

Sometimes when a word is added to a verb it makes a phrase with special meaning. Here are some phrases with **move:**

Move in means to bring furniture and possessions to a house or apartment and begin living there. *Shawna was excited to see that the people moving in upstairs had a piano.*

Move on means to continue traveling after a stop. *After the cowboy helped capture the bandits, he told the townspeople he would be moving on at dawn.*

Move out means to take furniture and possessions and stop living somewhere. *Emilio earns money helping the janitor clean apartments after people move out.*

Move up means to advance to something or some place better. *Mrs. Red Willow has moved up to vice president for home loans.*

Mystery
noun

Mystery means something that has not been explained or cannot be completely understood. *Faith's absence was a mystery to her classmates until Jerrold called her house. The reason for the disappearance of the dinosaurs is still something of a mystery.*

Problem means a difficult question or a mystery. *On tonight's show, Lt. Singletary catches a killer dentist in "The Problem of the Poisoned Toothbrush."*

Puzzle means a challenging problem. *Many people find it a real puzzle to set their VCR timers.*

Riddle means a trick question that requires clever thinking to answer. *"Which is heavier, a pound of feathers or a pound of lead?" is a familiar riddle.*

Secret means a mystery or something hidden from your knowledge. *Archaeologists found this tool near Timbuktu, but how it was used remains a secret.*

Enigma means a baffling mystery, seemingly impossible to solve. *The strange movements of the boy in the boat remained an enigma to everyone who watched the videotape.*

WORDS AT PLAY

Alone in the house late at night,
I had only a candle for light
But was doing my best to ignore
Shadows creeping like mice on the floor
And the wind outside howling like doom.
The clock struck; as its chime pierced the gloom,
I beheld, with a sway of the drape,
A most dreadful, mysterious shape!

"Ah, great heavens," I cried, "what a fright!
My hands shake, and my hair's turning white!
Tell me how did you get here, and where
Did you come from, and must I beware?

Is this mystery meant just for me?
Who—or *what*—is this shape that I see?"

Name
noun

Name means the word or words that you call something. *My best friend's name is Rebecca, and she hates being called "Becky."*

Title means the name of a book, movie, painting, or other work of art. It can also mean a name that shows a person's rank or work. *In spite of its title, <u>My Darling, My Hamburger</u> is not a cookbook. The Grand Duchess never uses her title—she likes to be called Suzie.*

Nickname means an informal name that a person is called by, usually instead of a first name. *Her teammates gave Jody the nickname "Slugger" because she hits so many home runs.*

Alias means a false name used by someone who wants to hide his or her true identity. *In Germany, the spy used the alias "Helma Schuler."*

Pen name means an alias used by an author. *Mark Twain is the pen name of Samuel Clemens.*

Label can mean a word or phrase that describes a thing, a place, or a person. *How did New York City get the label "The Big Apple"?*

Designation is a formal word that can mean an official name. *The island's full designation is "Commonwealth of Puerto Rico."*

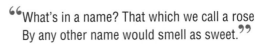

"What's in a name? That which we call a rose
By any other name would smell as sweet."
— **William Shakespeare**
(1564–1616)

279

Naughty
adjective

Naughty means not behaving well or not being nice. *Christine charges extra to baby-sit with those naughty O'Toole kids.*

Bad can mean not behaving well. *"Bad dog!" shouted Mr. Ortiz, but the puppy paid no attention.*

Disobedient means not obeying or not willing to obey. *The disobedient puppy refused to come inside.*

Mischievous means taking pleasure from behaving badly. *Some mischievous person put Rob's bicycle in a tree.*

Impish can mean mischievous. *"Who could have done that?" asked Alyx, with an impish grin.*

Disorderly can mean making trouble. *The disorderly group was put out of the concert hall by the security guards.*

Rowdy means disorderly or quarrelsome. *The rowdy class quieted down fast when the principal walked through the door.*

Unruly means disorderly and hard to control. *An unruly mob threw rocks and bottles.*

Insubordinate means disobedient and rebellious. *Terry has been angry and insubordinate since his father left home.*

SEE **wicked** for related words.
ANTONYMS: good, obedient, well-behaved

The **disobedient** puppy refused to come inside.

Near
adjective

Near means at a short distance from something. *Many early civilizations built their cities near rivers, lakes, and other bodies of water.*

Close means very near. *Tilmon's family lives in an apartment building close to the railroad tracks.*

Nearby means fairly near. *People nearby think the puppy's behavior is cute.*

Next means nearest. *The fire started after lightning struck the oak tree next to the barn.*

Neighboring means near or next. *When we open our windows in summer, we often hear stereos from neighboring apartments.*

Adjoining means next to something or even touching. *Hee-So and Young-Hee took adjoining seats on the bus.*

Adjacent means next to something or even touching. *We heard a burst of laughter from the adjacent classroom.*

Within a stone's throw is an idiom that means only a short distance away. *Mr. Boudin set up his souvenir stand within a stone's throw of the stadium.*

Cheek by jowl is an idiom that means quite close. *Automobiles are packed cheek by jowl in the parking lot.*

ANTONYMS: distant, far

People **nearby** think the puppy's behavior is cute.

281

Neat
adjective

Neat means clean and in order. *Sarah keeps her clothes neat by wearing a smock when she's painting.*

Orderly means neat. *Inside these orderly rows of test tubes are the germs of a deadly disease.*

Tidy means neat and arranged in a pleasing way. *Whenever Grandmother Willits visits, Edward has to make his room tidy.*

Trim means neat and in good condition. *When Captain Lee took over the old freighter, the crew got orders to make it trim again.*

Shipshape means trim. *Volunteers are working hard to make sure the new library is in shipshape condition for its grand opening.*

Spick-and-span means neat and completely clean. *Jeremy polished his tap shoes over and over to get them spick-and-span for his recital.*

Uncluttered means neat and without many things around. *The Avilas' house is the one with a completely uncluttered yard and garage.*

Neat as a pin is an idiom that means extremely neat, with nothing out of place. *Mom's secretary keeps his desk as neat as a pin.*

Spruce means neat, clean, and carefully arranged. It is mostly used to describe people. *Ms. Hepner looks spruce in her new mail carrier's uniform.*

ANTONYMS: cluttered, messy, untidy

Necessary
adjective

Necessary means needed. *Iron, coal, and limestone are necessary to make steel.*

Essential means completely necessary. *The keyboard is an essential part of a computer.*

Vital can mean essential. *Lt. Privac returned from her mission with the vital supplies.*

Required means necessary. It suggests that the need is a result of a decision or rule. *Lindsay did the four required book reports and one more for extra credit.*

CONTINUED ON THE NEXT PAGE

Indispensable means too necessary to do without. *A dictionary and a thesaurus are indispensable tools for a writer.*

Irreplaceable means too necessary to get another instead. *Brook is irreplaceable to our chorus, so we only sing where she can go in her wheelchair.*

ANTONYM: unnecessary

WORD STORY
· ·
Vital comes from the Latin word meaning "life."
When something is truly vital, people call it
"a matter of life and death."

New
adjective

The judges of the kite contest said Colin's five-sided design was a **novel** idea.

New means recently made, become known, or come into existence. *Jorge's family is moving into a new house that was finished just last month.*

Brand-new means very new. *The contestant on the game show won a brand-new car.*

Fresh means newly picked, made, or found, and not yet affected by time or use. *The fresh tomatoes were a real treat at the picnic.*

Novel means new or of a new kind. *The judges of the kite contest said Colin's five-sided design was a novel idea.*

Original can mean novel. *The prime minister is seeking original approaches to solving the country's economic problems.*

Modern means of the present time or not far in the past. *Some modern music is played on electronic instruments.*

Contemporary can mean modern. *Miles's grandparents plan to sell their antiques and buy contemporary furniture.*

Current can mean of the present time. *Elizabeth wakes every morning to "It's 7 A.M. on WNEW, and here's Buzz with the current news and weather!"*

Newfangled means new and in fashion. It often suggests that something is not liked as well as the older kind. *Joshua's father says he prefers the stove to the newfangled microwave oven.*

ANTONYMS: ancient, antique, old

Nice
adjective

Nice means pleasing or good. It is a general word of approval. *What a nice young man your friend Carlos is!*

Pleasant means giving pleasure and enjoyment. *Lynne spent a pleasant afternoon shopping with her friends.*

Enjoyable means giving a feeling of enjoyment and happiness. *The whole family spent an enjoyable week at the seashore.*

Delightful means very enjoyable. *"My friends, you have made these years as your pastor a truly delightful time," said Reverend Wills to his congregation.*

Lovely can mean pleasing and delightful. *"Thanks for the lovely evening, Darryl," Winona said.*

Welcome means pleasant. It suggests pleasure after discomfort or need. *Halfway through painting the room, Julia paused for a welcome lemonade.*

Agreeable means pleasant and fun to be with. *Now that Aunt Mary has a hearing aid, she's as agreeable as ever.*

Likable means pleasant and easy to like. *"You mean that likable young woman has gone off with all my money?" gasped Dr. Earnshaw.*

People often use *nice* when another word would be more precise and more interesting. There are many other synonyms for *nice* at various places in this book. Find the idea you want to describe in the list below, and then see that set of synonyms.

SEE **beautiful** and **cute** for words that mean nice to look at.
SEE **happy** and **wonderful** for words that mean having a nice time.
SEE **excellent** and **good** for words that mean high in quality.
SEE **friendly, gentle, kind, polite, thoughtful**, and **wonderful** for words to describe nice people.

CONTINUED ON THE NEXT PAGE

The word *nice* is often overused. Instead, you might use some of the synonyms for *nice* that are discussed on the previous page or at the other studies mentioned there.

"It was nice of Anna Maria to invite our whole scout

troop to her birthday party," said Michelle.

an enjoyable
"Yes, I had ~~a nice~~ time. Playing with her new puppy

delightful
was especially ~~nice~~. Don't you think Mr. and Mrs.

likable
Quinones are ~~nice~~?" asked Carol.

"Yes, but that kid brother isn't. He didn't even try

friendly
to be ~~nice.~~ Look, here's the bus," Michelle said.

pleasant
"It's such a ~~nice~~ afternoon," said Carol, "I think

good
I'll walk." "What a ~~nice~~ idea!" exclaimed Michelle.

"So will I."

Noise
noun

Noise means an unpleasant sound. *The noise of the jet engine made Gina cover her ears.*

Racket means a banging noise. *The plumber banging on the pipes downstairs made a terrible racket.*

Clatter means a loud noise of things knocking or banging together. *From the kitchen came a loud clatter of plates being put away quickly and carelessly.*

Din means a mixture of loud, confused noises that may last a long time. *"What did you say?" shouted Toni over the din of the lunchroom.*

Commotion means a noisy, excited disturbance. It suggests disorderly sounds and movement. *"What's all the commotion about?" asked Officer Jimson, as he walked up to the people clustered on the sidewalk.*

Tumult means commotion. *The tumult from the protesters drowned out the speakers on the platform.*

SEE **loud, shout,** and **uproar** for related words.
ANTONYMS: quiet, silence

AROUND THE WORLD: With a Tweet-Tweet Here and a Jikk-Jikk There

Many languages have different ways to imitate the noises that animals make. For example, in English the bird's song is *tweet-tweet.* But

in Ethiopian, it's *qa-qa*   in Japanese, it's *peechiko-pachiko*
in Finnish, it's *ti-ti-tyy*   in Korean, it's *jack-jack*
in German, it's *ti-vi-li-lie*   in Russian, it's *chic-chiric*
in Greek, it's *tsioo-tsioo*   in Turkish, it's *jikk-jikk*

In English, a rooster's crow is *cock-a-doodle-doo.* But

in Chinese, it's *wo-wo-wo*   in Indonesian, it's *ku-ku-ru-yuk*
in Danish, it's *kee-kly-ky*   in Spanish, it's *kee-kee-ree-kee*
in French, it's *coco-rico*   in Swahili, it's *koo-koo-ree-koo*
in Farsi, it's *ghoo-ghoolie-ghoo* in Thai, it's *ek-ee-ek-egg*

Do you think that songbirds and roosters really make different noises in different places? Or do people hear the same noise differently?

286

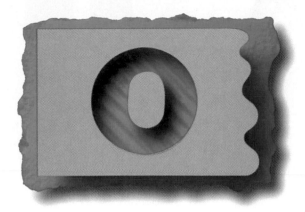

Obey
verb

Obey means to do what someone tells you to do, or to do what the rules say you must do. *"You will obey my commands," said the hypnotist.*

Follow can mean to obey and act according to rules or orders. *Kristin followed the recipe and baked a delicious cake.*

Mind can mean to obey. *The Dwyers told their children to mind the baby-sitter.*

Observe can mean to act carefully according to a rule. *Observing ancient custom, the village leader fasts and prays when the moon is full.*

Comply means to obey. It suggests agreeing with what you are told to do. *American colonists refused to comply with the Stamp Act.*

Conform to means to obey laws or rules, especially of a group that you want to be in. *"If you will not conform to the dress code, Sir, you cannot eat in this restaurant," said the headwaiter.*

Toe the line is an idiom that means to obey orders exactly. It suggests taking special care. *The parole board told the offender he'd better toe the line, or he'd go right back to jail.*

ANTONYMS: disobey, rebel

Mom's main **objection** to our plan to camp out was that it was raining.

Objection
noun

Objection means a reason or argument given to oppose some idea or action. *Mom's main objection to our plan to camp out was that it was raining.*

Complaint can mean a reason for saying that something is wrong. *Hannah's complaint about the cafeteria food is that she has to eat it.*

Opposition means statements or actions against something. *The president's plan to reduce the armed forces has met great opposition from the generals.*

Protest means a statement or action that expresses strong feeling against something. *Protest against segregation became common in the 1960s.*

Criticism can mean a statement that points out faults in an idea or action. *Jim used Mr. Cole's criticism to improve his blueprints.*

Challenge can mean a demand for proof of a statement. *Abe's challenge forced Ms. Iyasu to reconsider her claim that rock music is unimportant.*

Rebuttal means an objection answering a previous argument. It suggests a debate or legal dispute. *At the meeting, those in favor of the new school stated their case first, and then those opposed to the plan offered their rebuttal.*

Beef can mean a complaint. This meaning is informal. *All the way to the airport, the cabdriver told us about his beef with the city.*

Kick can mean a complaint. This meaning is informal. *Fernando's kick against television is that it has too many dumb commercials.*

SEE **complain** and **criticize** for related words.

288

Obstacle
noun

Obstacle means something that stands in the way and prevents or delays action. *"Not knowing how to read," confessed Mr. Fitzroy, "has been the greatest obstacle of my life."*

Obstruction means an obstacle. *An obstruction in the pipe caused the sink to overflow.*

Barrier means an obstacle. It suggests something like a long high wall. *The new treaty removes most barriers to free trade between the two countries.*

Hindrance means something that prevents or delays action. It suggests holding back or standing in the way. *Experts fear that environmental problems may be a hindrance to the country's economic progress.*

Hitch can mean a hindrance. *A slight hitch in traffic can clog an expressway for miles.*

Bar can mean an obstacle. *Heavy snow acted as a bar to the rescue of the hiking party on the mountain.*

Block can mean an obstacle. *Carey's temper is a block to his winning the sportsmanship award.*

SEE **prevent** and **stop** for related words.

WRITING TIP: Writer's Block

Here are four things to do when you can't think of what to write next:

1. Write *anything* down. To get your thoughts flowing again, keep writing and don't stop for five or ten minutes. The act of writing down your thoughts will bring you more thoughts.

2. Talk to someone. Ask a friend or family member to help brainstorm ideas. Their thoughts and the opportunity for you to express your thoughts may bring new ideas.

3. Find out more about the subject. It depends what you are writing, but you might thumb through some magazines on sports if you are writing a story about basketball, or you might try looking in an encyclopedia if you are writing a report about a visit to an art museum.

4. Make a word bank—a list of words related to your subject. If, for example, you are writing about trends in fashion, list words for clothing styles. Then try to use some of these words as you continue writing.

Often
adverb

Often means many times. *Casimir often earns a few dollars helping people carry groceries.*

Frequently means often and at short intervals. *Rain falls frequently in the tropical forest.*

Repeatedly means many times and the same each time. *Juana must go repeatedly to the stream for her family's water.*

Regularly means often and at the same interval. *"Buses should arrive at this corner regularly," said Mr. Crankshaw, "but I haven't seen one yet."*

ANTONYMS: infrequently, rarely, seldom

Old
adjective

Chet Dole may be **getting on in years,** but he still plays a great saxophone.

Old means having lived for a long time. *The old tortoise at the zoo was born during World War I.*

Elderly means old. *Maria's elderly great uncle remembers when there were no radios.*

Aged means having lived to a great age. *The aged couple still live in a small cottage near the lake.*

Getting on in years means having lived on into old age. *Chet Dole may be getting on in years, but he still plays a great saxophone.*

SEE **ancient** for related words.
ANTONYMS: young, youthful

AROUND THE WORLD: Older Is Better

Old crows are not easy to catch.
— **German proverb**

When you see an old lady run, don't ask what's the matter—you run too!
— **Jamaican proverb**

An old horse does not forget his path.
— **Japanese proverb**

An old camel is worth two young ones.
— **Sindhi proverb** (Pakistan)

Opinion
noun

Opinion means what someone thinks about something. Opinions may be supported by facts, but they can still be questioned. *Do you share Roger's opinion that Chinese food is the best food?*

View can mean a very personal opinion. *In Ms. Luchesi's view, Einstein had the wisest eyes she's ever seen.*

Judgment can mean an opinion based on carefully considering and deciding. *In Mrs. Delany's judgment, Tina is ready for music school.*

Conclusion can mean an opinion reached by reasonable thinking. *After passing the same buildings three times, the driver came to the conclusion that she was lost.*

Position can mean a set of opinions about a particular subject. *The mayors of both towns repeated their positions for and against the new highway.*

Attitude means the way that someone thinks and feels about something. *Tom finds his attitude toward school changing as he gets older.*

Consensus means an opinion that most people share. *The consensus among voters is that new leaders are needed.*

SEE **belief, feeling,** and **idea** for related words.

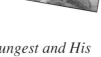

WRITER'S CHOICE

"He just doesn't care about playing in tune," said Second Sister. "I don't think there's any use practicing until his attitude is better."

—Lensey Namioka, *Yang the Youngest and His Terrible Ear*

Why *attitude?* Second Sister thinks Fourth Brother Yang's playing won't improve until he changes his thoughts and feelings about playing in tune. He must care about the results before he can learn from practice.

Pablo is my favorite **opponent,** because he's so good at the game.

Opponent
noun

Opponent means a person on the opposite side in a game, argument, or fight. *Pablo is my favorite opponent, because he's so good at the game.*

Antagonist means an opponent, especially an unfriendly one. *Captain Corcoran's antagonist in the struggle for control of the starship was a creature from Planet Omicron.*

Rival means an opponent who wants the same things as another person. *Kelly and Iona are rivals for a single opening on the softball team.*

Competitor means a rival. *The Kleen Again dry-cleaning store has survived three competitors on that block.*

Opposition can mean a group of opponents, especially in politics. *Mr. Khodai led the opposition to the plan to cut social services.*

Adversary means an antagonist. *The senator's adversary is showing some very nasty TV ads.*

SEE **argue, enemy, fight,** and **oppose** for related words.
ANTONYM: ally

Oppose
verb

Oppose means to act against something that you don't like and don't want to happen. *"Do you oppose or support the death penalty, Sam?" asked Mrs. Bissinger.*

Resist means to oppose. It may suggest that a struggle is involved. *Until 1974, Little League Baseball resisted girls' attempts to join.*

Withstand means to resist, especially successfully. *At the Battle of New Orleans, General Jackson's soldiers withstood a direct attack by the British Army.*

CONTINUED ON THE NEXT PAGE

Defy means to resist openly. It suggests a public declaration. *The protesters defied the dictator by holding a rally in the square.*

Buck can mean to work against some strong force. *Julia bucks the fashions, and she dresses however she likes.*

Stand up to means to face someone or something that you oppose. *Juan decided to stand up to the bully rather than run away.*

Take on can mean to oppose. *We are here to take on society's ignorance of the disabled and their lives.*

SEE **argue, fight, objection,** and **opponent** for related words.
ANTONYMS: aid, support

Opposite
adjective

Opposite means completely different from each other. *The ships are headed in opposite directions through the canal.*

Contrary means opposite. *The Sedlacek sisters hold contrary opinions about which of them started the fight.*

Reverse means exactly opposite, especially in direction or position. *How fast can you say the alphabet in reverse order?*

Contradictory means saying something opposite to what was said before. *The candidate has made several contradictory statements about raising or not raising taxes.*

ANTONYMS: alike, same

WRITING TIP: Oxymorons

An *oxymoron* (ok/si môr/on) is a phrase combining words with opposite meanings, such as *burning cold, sweet sorrow,* or *loud silence.* Oxymorons can emphasize ideas, get attention, describe something poetically, or express ideas that are hard to say in any other way: *bittersweet, kill with kindness,* and *sad laughter.* Sometimes they are made for humor: *a definite maybe.* Sometimes they happen because the meanings of the words are overlooked or forgotten: *jumbo shrimp.* Have you heard similar phrases in everyday conversation or in advertising?

You can use oxymorons in your writing when you need a very special phrase. Think of two words that have opposite meanings but that will create their own unique meaning when used together. If nothing else, you can play the *wise fool* and come up with some *serious nonsense.*

Origin
noun

Origin means the thing or place that something comes from. It often suggests the reasons for the new thing. *This huge traffic jam had its origin in one flat tire.*

Source means the person or place where something comes from. It often suggests a steady supply. *Rachel's new cat is a constant source of amusement.*

Root can mean a source or a cause. *The root of Lamar's interest in trains is that his grandfather was a railroad engineer.*

Spring can mean an origin. *"Our ancestors," Jae Choi told his children, "are the spring from which our whole family flows."*

Derivation can mean an origin, especially of words. *The derivation of "Halloween" is two words meaning "holy evening."*

SEE **beginning** and **start** for related words.
ANTONYMS: end, finish

WORD STORY

The story of the derivation—the origin and development—of words is called *etymology.* Many English words come from other languages, including French, German, Spanish, Arabic, Greek, and Latin. What is the etymology of *etymology?* It comes from old Greek words meaning "true" and "word." Etymologies tell the true words from which words come.

Overturn
verb

Overturn means to turn upside down. *The raft began to overturn when it hit the rapids.*

Upset means to knock something over or to turn something over. *Mrs. Jenks's cat jumped on the table and upset the vase of roses.*

CONTINUED ON THE NEXT PAGE

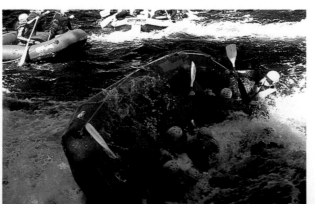

The raft began to **overturn** when it hit the rapids.

Tip can mean to upset. *The bucket got tipped over, and we had to mop the floor again.*

Flip can mean to turn something over. *Dad flipped the eggs in the frying pan.*

Invert means to turn something upside down. *The way to divide one fraction by another is to invert one and multiply them.*

Capsize means to turn upside down. It is used mostly about boats and ships. *Many lives were lost when the ferry capsized in the typhoon.*

Keel over means to turn upside down. *A gust of wind hit the beach chairs, and they keeled over.*

Overwhelm
verb

Overwhelm means to overpower completely. *The U.S. basketball team overwhelmed its opponents.*

Flood can mean to overwhelm, as if by covering with water. *Shoppers flood the malls during the holiday season.*

Swamp can mean to overwhelm and make helpless, as if by filling with water. *Mr. Evans says that part of teaching is feeling swamped by paperwork.*

Drown can mean to overwhelm finally, as if by keeping under water. *The crowd roared its agreement, drowning a few scattered protests.*

Engulf means to overwhelm completely, as if surrounding with water. *The crew of the burning tanker was engulfed in smoke.*

Deluge means to overwhelm as if by an immense flood. *The radio station was deluged with calls when it announced free concert tickets.*

WRITING TIP: Strong Verbs, Active Imagery

Strong, active verbs such as *flood, swamp,* and *drown* create pictures in the reader's mind. Compare the images created in these two sentences:

Shoppers <u>came to</u> the mall during the holiday season.
Shoppers <u>flooded</u> the mall during the holiday season.

In the second sentence, visions of rushing floodwaters communicate the idea that shoppers are everywhere, almost covering the mall, rushing and swirling from shop to shop.

When you write, create vivid pictures for your readers by using strong verbs.

Pain
noun

Pain means the bad feeling you have when you hurt yourself or when you are sick. *Lionel was in a lot of pain last night, but he's better now.*

Ache means a steady pain. *Ringing up groceries all day gives Cindi an ache in her shoulders.*

Soreness means pain. *César often experiences soreness in his wrist after playing volleyball.*

Twinge means a sudden pain. *Azim felt a twinge in his back while he was helping his father move the piano.*

Stitch can mean a sharp pain, usually along your side. *After running in the 50-yard dash, Jenna got a stitch in her side.*

Pang means a sudden, sharp, strong pain. *"If I skip breakfast, I get terrible hunger pangs in math class," said Clarissa.*

SEE **misery** for related words.

WORD STORY

Notice that many of our words for particular kinds of pain are formed by adding the word *ache* to the place where the pain occurs:

backache	headache
bellyache	stomachache
earache	toothache

But although you can have a pain in your ankle, elbow, knee, or toe, for example, you would probably *not* say:

ankleache	kneeache
elbowache	toeache

Pair
noun

Pair means two people or things that belong together. *Grandma knitted the baby a pair of booties.*

Couple means a pair. *Marisa and Sean make a great couple—they both love hiking and scary movies.*

Twosome means a group of two people. *We need another twosome for the three-legged race.*

Duo means a pair, especially two musicians playing together. *Reddins on trumpet and Ortiz on guitar— a great duo!*

Twin means one of two children born as a pair. *When the twins were born, Cerise had to give them her room and share with Paula.*

Yoke can mean two animals working together. *Darshan is proud of how much work his yoke of buffalo does every day.*

Reddins on trumpet and Ortiz on guitar—a great **duo**!

Pamper
verb

Pamper means to give or let someone have too much of whatever is wanted. *The Markovs pamper their dog with toys and food.*

Baby can mean to pamper someone as if that person were a young child. *Gramps insists on sharing the housework and errands because he hates to be babied.*

Spoil can mean to pamper someone so much that it is bad for the person's character. *The Smiths have spoiled their daughter; she cries if she doesn't get her way.*

Oblige can mean to do someone a favor or to satisfy someone's wish. It suggests something not very important or hard to do. *Mom asked Meara to oblige her by not reading during dinner.*

Humor can mean to satisfy someone's wishes or demands so as to keep them quiet or give them comfort. *Lance has a bad cold, so we're humoring him and letting him choose all the TV shows.*

Pardon

verb

Pardon means to cancel or stop someone's punishment for a wrong act. It often suggests an official decision. *The new president of the island country has pardoned all political prisoners jailed by the army.*

Forgive means to choose not to punish someone for a wrong act. *Dad has finally forgiven me for losing his tennis racquet.*

Excuse can mean to forgive someone. It suggests that there is a reason for what the person did. *Because Marlon's mother had been quite ill, Ms. Dreher excused him for not doing his homework.*

Overlook can mean to excuse or ignore some wrong act. *"I will overlook your being late this time," said Aunt Em with annoyance.*

Condone means to forgive or to overlook. *"Everyone makes mistakes," said the manager, "but we will not condone dishonesty."*

Let off means to pardon someone. *Since Mr. Knight had never been in trouble before, the judge let him off with a strong warning.*

Let bygones be bygones means to forgive and forget. *Now that they're going to different schools, Huey and Beth don't compete all day, and they can let bygones be bygones.*

ANTONYMS: blame, condemn

HAVE YOU HEARD...?

You may have heard the phrase "Turn the other cheek." It refers to an idea expressed in the New Testament (Matthew 5:39) and means to forgive and give a second chance to someone who has hurt you.

Part

noun

Part means some piece or amount that is less than the whole. *Andrea gave me part of her doughnut.*

Portion means a part. It is often used about parts that are shared among several people. *Lori gave everyone a big portion of the tuna casserole.*

Section means a part, especially one that can be considered or handled by itself. *Chandu is reading the sports section of the newspaper.*

Segment means a section. It often suggests that something has parts naturally and in every case. *"Split the oranges into segments, please, Steve, and pass them out," instructed his teacher.*

CONTINUED ON THE NEXT PAGE

298

Fraction means an equal part of a whole. It is used most about numbers. *Once the neighborhood recovery grant is divided among more than twenty groups, the fraction for each will not be large.*

Share means the part that belongs to each person. *Charlotte has already eaten her share of the blueberries.*

Division can mean one of the parts into which a thing is divided. *Mark's mother works in the repairs division of the bus company.*

Department means a part of an organization. *Mr. Leung bought a shirt in the men's clothing department.*

Ingredient means one of the parts of a mixture. *Dedication and talent are key ingredients to success as an athlete.*

Part and parcel is an idiom that means an important and necessary part. *Obeying laws is part and parcel of good citizenship.*

SEE **piece** for related words.
ANTONYM: whole

HAVE YOU HEARD...?

Perhaps you've heard someone refer to an unfairly large part of something as "the lion's share." The phrase comes from a fable by Aesop, in which a lion hunts in cooperation with a fox, a jackal, and a wolf. After the hunt, the lion refuses to share the kill with the other three animals. The fox then says, "Those who share the labors of the powerful don't always share the reward." In Aesop's fable *the lion's share* meant all of something. Now it means the biggest part.

Participate
verb

Participate means to be one of the people who do something, especially together. *Mr. Hurkel encouraged everyone to participate in the singing.*

Engage means to participate. It emphasizes the activity more than the group. *Scott and Sue, engaged in conversation, didn't notice that the bus was leaving.*

Partake can mean to be one of the people who share something, especially something to eat or drink. It is a formal word. *"Will you partake of the buffet," asked the waitress, "or shall I bring menus?"*

Cooperate means to work together, especially in order to make the work easier. *Officer Redwing told the crowd: "If everyone cooperates, we can all go home soon."*

Collaborate is a formal word that means to cooperate. *Scholars from all over the Arab world collaborated on this exhibit of Islamic art.*

Take part means to participate. *Everyone at the picnic took part in the tug-of-war at the end of the day.*

Get into the act is an idiom that means to participate. *Rennie and Miguel had almost settled their argument when Nora got into the act and made it worse.*

Have a hand in is another idiom that means to participate. *We all had a hand in making Mom's party a success.*

Everyone **took part** in the tug-of-war at the end of the day.

Patient
adjective

Patient means to be able to put up with trouble, hard work, or long delays, without complaining. *Grandpa is always patient with Grandma, even when she gets impatient with him.*

Tolerant means able to put up with people whose ideas or behavior are not what you are used to. *"We should not just be tolerant of other cultures," explained Mr. Koenig, "we should learn from them."*

Long-suffering means patient. It is an old-fashioned word, found mostly in books. *Thrifty and long-suffering, the young carpenter's apprentice grew to be a famous architect.*

Forbearing can mean patient and with strong self-control. *The struggle for civil rights was kept nonviolent by forbearing people.*

ANTONYMS: impatient, irritated, exasperated

Pause
noun

Pause means a short stop of an activity that then starts again. *After a pause while the ambulance went by, traffic soon began moving again.*

Break can mean a pause. *The painters took a break after finishing the bedroom before they started on the hall.*

Interruption can mean a pause. *After a brief interruption to warn of heavy snow, the radio station continued broadcasting the game.*

Letup is an informal word meaning a pause. *My headache lasted all day, without any letup.*

Rest can mean a period of doing nothing after some activity. *Darcy has done four loads of laundry, and she needs a rest.*

Lull means a short time of calm or inactivity. *There was a lull in the storm around eleven, but by afternoon the wind blew hard again.*

Breather means a short break while doing something, especially in order to catch your breath. *Felipe ran two more laps and then took a breather.*

SEE **intermission** for related words.

Pay
verb

Pay means to give money in return for things or work. *The Clarks pay Mika three dollars an hour for baby-sitting.*

Repay means to pay back money that is owed. *"Sorry, I can't lend you any money until Larry repays what he borrowed," said Babette.*

Settle can mean to pay a bill. *When the plant opened and Pa went back to work, he settled all our debts as fast as he could.*

Satisfy can mean to pay in full. *"It will take two years to satisfy our debt to the hospital," said Mr. Ruter.*

Compensate can mean to pay, usually in return for some loss or extra effort. *The oil company will compensate the state for damages from the oil spill.*

Fork out (or **over**) is an informal phrase that means to pay. *"Would you believe I forked out $45 for these groceries?" Steve asked.*

IDIOMS
....

Pay is a key word in a number of idioms. Here are some of them:

Hit pay dirt means to discover something that will bring success or wealth. *The reporter hit pay dirt when she interviewed a government official who was willing to give all the details about the scandal.*

Pay the piper means to bear the results of your choices or actions. The phrase comes from an old saying, "Whoever calls the tune must pay the piper." *Orrin hasn't studied for weeks, and now he has to pay the piper.*

Pay through the nose means to pay a lot. *"Be careful with this baseball card," said Stan. "I paid through the nose for it."*

Peculiar
adjective

Peculiar means unusual. It suggests that something is not normal or not as it should be. *Fred likes peculiar foods, like salted marshmallows and pickles with chocolate sauce.*

Queer means peculiar. *It's queer that this library has no books at all by Mark Twain.*

Weird can mean extremely peculiar. *What kind of weird person keeps Halloween decorations up all year?*

Odd can mean peculiar. *Chelsea's odd behavior made us wonder if something was wrong.*

CONTINUED ON THE NEXT PAGE

Funny can mean peculiar. This meaning is informal. *By 3:45, Susan had a funny feeling that her mom had forgotten to pick her up.*

Strange means peculiar. It suggests that something is hard to understand. *Marika tried to figure out where the strange crackling sound was coming from.*

Curious can mean strange. *Manny found a curious old tool in the basement.*

Eccentric means out of the ordinary. It is mostly used to describe people and what they have or do. *The artist's eccentric paintings attracted much attention, not all of it polite.*

SEE **crazy** for related words.
ANTONYMS: normal, ordinary, usual

Penetrate
verb

Penetrate means to go through the surface of something to the inside. It often suggests force. *The book bag was made of a waterproof fabric so that no rain would penetrate it.*

Pierce means to go through the surface or skin of something. It suggests a sharp point. *Before putting the potatoes in the microwave, Sun-Hi pierced them with a fork.*

Stab means to pierce with a pointed weapon. *Moon On Water raised his spear, waiting for the right moment to stab the fish.*

Puncture means to make a hole in something by piercing it. *"A tack punctured my bicycle tire,"* Jack explained to his father.

Probe can mean to explore an object or an opening by putting a long, thin tool into it. *Dr. Ong probed Jimmy's cut foot for broken glass.*

SEE **enter** for related words.

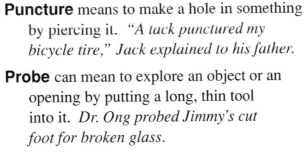

Moon On Water raised his spear, waiting for the right moment to **stab** the fish.

Perfect
adjective

Perfect means having no faults or being the best. *The swimmer made a perfect dive. Vladimir found the perfect gift for his grandmother.*

Ideal means perfect, or as wonderful as you could imagine. *When Saturday came, it turned out to be an ideal day for the carnival.*

Flawless means not having any defects. *On the slender fingers of her right hand, the countess wore two flawless diamonds.*

Faultless means flawless. *Although Javier has been in this country for only three years, he already speaks faultless English.*

Pure can mean perfect. It suggests that something contains no bad parts. *Ronald prides himself on his homemade candy, made with pure chocolate and fluffy coconut.*

Foolproof means made so that nothing can go wrong. *The prisoners thought that their escape plan was foolproof—until they found the guards waiting in the tunnel.*

Impeccable means so faultless that no one can find anything wrong. *He had such impeccable manners that no one guessed the "prince" was really a swindler.*

SEE **correct** and **excellent** for related words.
ANTONYM: imperfect

WORDS AT PLAY

I'm so bored with being perfect
But there's nothing I can do.
I'd be glad to have a weakness
But can't think of one, can you?

If you think I have a problem,
You should pass it right along;
And I'll judge if you are right or—
What is far more likely—wrong.

Mount Rushmore is a **perennial** favorite among tourists.

Permanent
adjective

Permanent means the same for a long period of time, and not expected to change. *My dentist, Dr. Faber, says that almost all my permanent teeth have come in.*

Stable can mean permanent. *After a lot of odd jobs, Kendall finally found stable employment.*

Durable can mean lasting a long time. *With so many bumps and curbs, it's a good thing Viola has a durable wheelchair.*

Perennial can mean lasting for a very long time. *Mount Rushmore is a perennial favorite among tourists.*

Endless means going on forever, the same for all time. It is often used to mean that something seems to go on and on. *Corey's endless chatter about television stars gets on my nerves.*

Eternal means going on forever. *This flame will be an eternal reminder of those who died for their country.*

Everlasting means going on forever. *Astronomers do not know whether the universe will come to an end in another few billion years or be everlasting.*

Perpetual means endless. *"Will you children stop that perpetual quarreling?" said Mr. Hooper from the front seat.*

SEE **continue** for related words.
ANTONYM: temporary

305

Permission
noun

Permission means agreement that it is all right for someone to do something. *"Who gave you permission to keep your bikes in the basement?" the janitor asked sternly.*

Consent and **leave** mean permission. *"Do I have your consent to go on the field trip, Dad?" asked Mike. "The teacher says we need to get our parents' leave."*

Authorization can mean official permission. *Only a laboratory with special authorization can experiment with these deadly germs.*

Dispensation can mean official permission to break a rule. *Pets are forbidden in public buildings, but dog guides get a dispensation.*

Go-ahead is an informal word that means permission to begin or proceed. *Mr. Marcum gave our recycling program the go-ahead.*

Blank check can mean permission to do whatever you choose. This meaning is informal. *"I'm extending your curfew tonight," Mrs. Wilson told her daughter, "but that's not a blank check for weekend evenings from now on."*

Carte blanche is a formal phrase that means permission in advance to do whatever you choose. *The architect has been given carte blanche to do whatever is necessary to make the museum accessible to the differently abled.*

SEE **let** for related words.
ANTONYMS: ban, prohibition

WORD STORY

Carte blanche (kärt′ blänch′) is French for "blank paper." If a king signed a piece of paper and left the rest of it blank, the person who had that paper could write anything on it. Whatever was written, the ruler would have signed it in advance, giving permission for whatever was done. The phrase still means permission in advance, but usually there is no actual paper involved.

Person

noun

Person means a human being. *"I'm my own person; I don't have to do what you do,"* Samantha said to her twin sister.

Human means a person. It is used when other living things are also being mentioned. *Kara, a chimpanzee, can speak in sign language to the humans in the lab.*

Individual means a person. *Our laws protect the rights of every individual.*

Fellow can mean a person. *"Poor fellow. He must not have known the forecast called for rain,"* said Mrs. Tilson sympathetically.

Guy is an informal word that means fellow. *"Dad, tell that guy to move his car from our driveway,"* Mark whined.

Being means a living thing. It often suggests something not human. *Hundreds of different beings may inhabit a small section of a coral reef.*

Creature means being. *"Gosh, Professor Vega,"* Peggy said, *"what are those weird creatures?"*

Mortal can mean a human being. *"When I look up at all those stars,"* confessed Mr. Jackson, *"I feel how little we mortals really understand."*

Personage is a formal word that means a person of importance. *At the sight of the commanding personage, a whisper swept the glittering ballroom: "It's the Duke!"*

WATCH IT!

Until recent years, *man* was used as a synonym of **person**. It was also used to mean people generally. You will find it used this way in books. Many women dislike this meaning, however, and it is much less common today. The same objection applies to using *mankind* to mean all human beings. The poet Alexander Pope wrote in the 1700s,

The proper study of mankind is Man.

Today, he might have written

*The thing we should be best at seeing
Is how to be a human being.*

Persuade
verb

Persuade means to make someone agree with you by giving reasons. *"What will it take to persuade you to give up one of those cookies?" asked Tasha with a smile.*

Convince means to make someone believe that something is true. *Irina convinced Jacob that it wasn't she who told his secret.*

Talk into means to persuade someone by speaking. *Latisha tried to talk her mother into letting her bleach her hair.*

Sell on means to convince someone of an idea as if you were selling it. *Vicky hopes to sell her parents on the idea of an after-school job at Burger Barn.*

Win over means to persuade someone in spite of objections. *At first Clint's parents said no to a skateboard, but he won them over.*

Prevail upon is a formal phrase that means to persuade. *We planned to leave early, but the Fowlers prevailed upon us to stay and meet Mr. and Mrs. Vasquez.*

SEE **influence, suggest,** and **urge** for related words.

WRITING TIP: Persuasive Writing

We all state our opinions easily to our friends and family. Usually we don't have to give reasons for what we believe. But in a written argument, you need to state and support your opinion carefully if you want to persuade your reader.

Suppose your idea is: *We should do more to help homeless people.* You need to supply facts that will convince your audience that you have a reasonable argument. Be specific when you present your supporting evidence. An unconvincing statement is: *Far too many homeless people have nowhere to sleep at night except parks and other public places.*

Instead, give your readers facts that they can verify for themselves, such as: *There are about 40,000 homeless people in New York City. With 5,400 families living in crowded city shelters, there is often no space for anyone else.*

The more evidence you provide, the more likely you'll be to convince your reader.

Piece

noun

The dirt around the rosebushes is covered with wood **chips** so that the soil stays moist.

Piece means a small part of something larger, or one thing among others like it. *Della swept the pieces of the broken glass into a pile. The platter was the largest piece of china on the Serra's dinner table.*

Bit means a small piece of something larger. *Caroline tore the letter into bits.*

Particle means a very little bit. *Dust particles from the volcano make the sunsets very colorful.*

Scrap means a little piece, especially a piece left over. *Andrea cut the picture to fit into the frame and then threw away the paper scraps.*

Lump means a small, solid piece of material. *Darryl gave the carnival pony a lump of sugar.*

Chunk means a thick lump. *Tillie's mother makes stew with chunks of meat, carrots, and potatoes.*

Fragment means a piece that has been broken off. *A fragment of the plane landed 500 yards from the crash site.*

Chip can mean a thin, small piece. *The dirt around the rosebushes is covered with wood chips so that the soil stays moist.*

Slice means a thin, flat, broad piece cut from something. *Franklyn wants a sandwich with one slice of cheese and three slices of ham.*

SEE **part** for related words.

IDIOMS

Piece is a key word in a number of idioms. Here are some of them:

Give someone a piece of your mind means to scold someone. *The stove still doesn't work right, and Mrs. Childers says she's going to give the janitor a piece of her mind.*

Go to pieces means to collapse emotionally or break down from stress. *After losing the game in double overtime, the team went to pieces and played badly all month.*

Of a piece means of the same kind, as if made from the same piece of something. *"These new accusations," the mayor told reporters, "are of a piece with previous falsehoods from my opponent."*

Pity
noun

Pity means a feeling of sorrow for someone who is suffering. *Sharon feels pity for her brother, who is stuck at home with chicken pox.*

Mercy means undeserved extra kindness, often coming from pity for someone. *Mrs. Giotta had mercy on Ray and excused him from gym until his hay fever stopped.*

Sympathy means sharing the sorrow or unhappiness of someone else. *Sympathy for animals is essential if you want to work at the animal shelter.*

Condolence means an expression of sympathy. *The class sent their condolences to Otis when they learned that his grandmother had died.*

Compassion is a formal word that means pity and sympathy. *Mother Teresa's compassion for the sick and poor has led people to call her the "saint of the gutters."*

SEE **sorrow** for related words.

Place
noun

Place means where something or someone is. *Did Arnold put the spare key back in its usual place?*

Position means a place. *Mr. Johansen has charted the position of his nephew's navy ship every week for two years.*

Location can mean a place, especially the place where something is put or built. *The new copier is bigger, so it will need a different location.*

Whereabouts means location. *Do you know the whereabouts of my glasses, Riquiña?*

Site means a place where something happened or will happen. *Los Angeles was very proud to be chosen as the site of the 1994 World Cup final.*

Locality means one place and the places near it. *Rocco's grandparents came from the locality of Naples.*

Post can mean the place where someone is on duty. *"The Foreign Legion expects its soldiers to die at their posts," growled the sergeant.*

CONTINUED ON THE NEXT PAGE

Pia's favorite **spot** for sketching is in the desert about two miles outside of town.

Station means post. *"Please go to the nursing station, Clive, and see if they have my pills," Mrs. Rivers requested.*

Spot can mean a place. *Pia's favorite spot for sketching is in the desert about two miles outside of town.*

IDIOMS

Place is a key word in many idioms. Here are some:

Give place means to be replaced by someone or something else. *As the sun rose, darkness gave place to day.*

Know your place means to understand how important you are— or aren't —in comparison to other people, and to act accordingly. *"I know my place," Mom said to Dad, "but the boss was wrong, so I had to tell her."*

Put someone in his or her place means to remind someone that he or she should act less important. *When Rae kept trying to score instead of passing the ball, Coach put her in her place by taking her out of the game.*

Take place means to happen. *This story takes place in Egypt, three thousand years ago.*

Plan
noun

Plan means a carefully thought-out way of doing or making something. *Plans for the church picnic are threatened by a forecast of rain.*

Program can mean a plan going from one step or event to the next. *The health club's program for weight control has helped Gene a lot.*

Outline can mean a general plan, especially in the form of a list. *A publisher has paid $5,000 for the outline of Mr. de Leon's new novel, Love in Acapulco.*

Project means a plan, usually for doing something on a large scale. *The city announced a project to cut air pollution by using streetcars.*

Proposal can mean project. *Proposals to tunnel between England and France first emerged in the 1800s.*

Enterprise means a plan of danger or difficulty. *Amelia Earhart's last enterprise was an attempt to fly around the world.*

Undertaking means enterprise. *Collecting all the baseball cards for the 1975 Red Sox team may be a costly undertaking.*

Design means a plan, especially a drawing for making something. *Derrek is working hard on a design for the cover of our magazine.*

Strategy can mean skillful planning and management, especially in war. *Allied strategy was to bomb Iraq and follow with a surprise ground attack.*

SEE **idea, intention,** and **plot** for related words.

> "Make no little plans. They have no magic to stir men's blood."
>
> — **Daniel Hudson Burnham (1846–1912)**

WRITER'S CHOICE

Jimmy was already late for school. But he was trying to figure out a strategy. He needed to know what to do, how to get things together to get him through the year. It was March, and he only had a few months to go.
If he could get it all together just one more time, just for a few months, he could get out of the tenth grade and then maybe be straight for the eleventh.

— Walter Dean Myers, *Somewhere in Darkness*

Why *strategy?* Jimmy has bad grades and a bad attendance record. He knows that he needs to make changes soon, or he won't get into the eleventh grade. To succeed will take careful planning and self-control. It will be a difficult, serious job, almost like winning a war.

The sandwich shop has a **plentiful** supply of meat, cheese, and other ingredients to choose from.

Plentiful
adjective

Plentiful means more than enough, but not too much. *The sandwich shop has a plentiful supply of meat, cheese, and other ingredients to choose from.*

Ample means plentiful. It suggests more than enough for some particular purpose. *The Peking Inn has ample parking.*

Bounteous can mean plentiful. It suggests generosity on the part of the provider. *Mrs. Oliphant's bounteous gift to the recreation center includes six new basketball hoops!*

Bountiful can mean bounteous. *Eric had never seen such a bountiful picnic meal: three kinds of pie, two dozen sandwiches, eggs, tomatoes, and a watermelon.*

Galore means plentiful. It always comes after the noun it describes. *When the neighbors gather for the celebration of the Kwanzaa Karamu, there will be food and fun galore.*

Abundant means very plentiful. *Emily is always threatening to give up her abundant curls and get a pixie cut.*

Inexhaustible means so plentiful that it cannot be used up. *Brian meets the challenges of his hearing impairment with inexhaustible determination and humor.*

Dime a dozen is an idiom that means so abundant that the worth is lowered. *Elvis impersonators are a dime a dozen.*

SEE **generous** for related words.
ANTONYM: scarce

Plot
noun

Plot means a secret plan, especially to do something evil. *The newspapers have uncovered a plot to rig the next election.*

Scheme can mean a plot. *In this movie, the crooks have a scheme to steal the original Declaration of Independence.*

Intrigue means secret plots and crafty dealing. *Marlynn wants to join the CIA and lead a life of intrigue.*

Conspiracy means secret plotting with other people to do something wrong. *José thinks there's a conspiracy to keep him off the soccer team, but he's really just a bad player.*

Connivance means secret agreement to do something evil. *With the connivance of a bribed inspector, the landlord got a city license for the unsafe building.*

SEE **plan** for related words.

Polite
adjective

Polite means having or showing good manners. *You may not like what Ebony says, but she's always polite in the way she says it.*

Courteous means polite and thoughtful. *"How courteous!" Mrs. Taylor exclaimed, when the bus driver got out to help her lift the stroller.*

Gracious means courteous, pleasant, and kind. *Even with the nine unexpected guests, Ms. Nuñez remained calm and gracious.*

Obliging means polite and helpful. *Mr. Spotted Dog was the most obliging salesman in the store.*

Tactful means able to say and do the things that are best suited to other people's feelings. *Richard wondered if there were a tactful way to tell John he should wash his hair more often.*

Diplomatic can mean tactful. *Even when she's criticizing someone, Debbie remembers to be diplomatic.*

Suave means polite and smoothly agreeable. *It's Janna's favorite game show because the host is so handsome and suave.*

SEE **thoughtful** for related words.
ANTONYMS: ill-mannered, impolite, rude

CONTINUED ON THE NEXT PAGE

HAVE YOU HEARD...?

You may have been told to "mind your p's and q's." This phrase means to be polite, be careful of what you do, and not make careless mistakes. The phrase may come from printing, in the days when each letter was a separate piece of metal type. Because *p* and *q* look like reflections of each other, it was easy to confuse them unless people were careful. Or the phrase may have come from businesses that sold liquids. The *p*'s and *q*'s may have stood for pints and quarts. Since a quart costs more than a pint, it would be important not to get the two amounts mixed up.

Pollute
verb

Aunt Alma says the city air is so **polluted** that the birds should wear gas masks.

Pollute means to make something filthy and unfit for human use. It is used mostly about the environment. *Aunt Alma says the city air is so polluted that the birds should wear gas masks.*

Contaminate means to pollute, especially by contact with something unclean. *"Once a needle has been used, it's contaminated, so we use a new needle for every shot,"* the nurse explained.

Soil means to make something dirty. *Before automobiles, dirt from thousands of horses soiled the streets of every city.*

Foul means to make something extremely dirty. *The Riveras' cabin was fouled by raccoons who spent the winter there.*

Taint means to make something impure and unhealthy, especially with decay. *Curt was hospitalized after he ate the tainted meat.*

Poison can mean to put something dangerous to life into something else. *The chemical factory is poisoning the river with toxic wastes.*

SEE **dirty** for related words.
ANTONYMS: cleanse, purify

Poor
adjective

Poor means having little or no money. *Many poor people cannot afford doctors if they get sick.*

Penniless means without any money, even if only temporarily. *Whoever stole Mrs. Feld's purse left her penniless and miles from home.*

Broke can mean without money. This meaning is informal. *"Oh, no," moaned Sam, "all jeans are on sale, and I'm flat broke."*

Needy means very poor and not having enough to live on. *"Remember the needy," the newspaper urges its readers at holiday time.*

Poverty-stricken means poor and not able to do anything about it. *Homeless and poverty-stricken, the refugees in these camps wonder if their futures will be any better.*

Bankrupt means unable to pay debts. Someone can have much money but still be bankrupt if debts are large. *"How can a bank go bankrupt?" Juana demanded.*

Hard up is an informal phrase that means needing money badly. *We were hard up when Mom was laid off from the battery factory.*

ANTONYMS: rich, wealthy, well-to-do

Power
noun

Power means the ability to do something or to make something happen. *Paul has the power to motivate people with his eloquent speeches.*

Energy can mean power. It often suggests power stored up, ready to be used. *The creative energy of the students really comes out in the school's weeklong Festival of Brazil.*

Force means active power. It suggests effort and work. *The force of the blast leveled the building and took out the side of the mountain.*

Strength means the amount of power that someone or something has. *Most ants have enough strength to lift ten times their own weight.*

Might means great power or strength. *Janek took a deep breath and flung himself at the locked door with all his might.*

Vigor means strength and force. *Imagine Miss Henderson's vigor, to run a marathon at 73!*

SEE **force** for related words.
ANTONYM: weakness

Most ants have enough **strength** to lift ten times their own weight.

CONTINUED ON THE NEXT PAGE

You may have heard the phrase "with vim and vigor." This means with much strength, force, energy, and eagerness. *Vim* has the same meaning as *vigor,* but it is not used much except in this phrase.

You may also have heard the phrase "with might and main." This means with all your strength. It is mostly used when people try hard to do something, but don't succeed. It suggests that they made their best effort. *Main* can mean force or strength, but it is rarely used, except in this phrase.

Why do these phrases use two words that have very similar meanings? One reason is for increased effect by repeating the idea (see the Writing Tip "Repetition for Emphasis" at **calm**).

Another important reason is that the phrases contain *alliteration* (ə lit′ə rā′shən). Alliteration is repeating the beginning sounds of words, like the sounds in the phrases "might and main" and "vim and vigor." Like rhyme (repeating the ending sounds), alliteration pleases the ear. It calls attention to itself and is easy to remember. That's why you find alliteration in so many product names and advertising slogans.

You too can use alliteration to make your writing livelier and more interesting.

Powerless
adjective

Powerless means unable to do something in particular, or anything at all. *Days of a high fever left Tawanda powerless even to get out of bed.*

Helpless means powerless to help yourself. *Some baby birds are helpless, but others can walk and swim soon after being born.*

Defenseless means unprotected and helpless against danger, harm, or attack. *"If that dam breaks, Colonel, the whole valley is defenseless!" said the mayor.*

Vulnerable means weak and easy to attack. *"You swing at everything, Pollín, so you're vulnerable to the curve ball," said the coach.*

Weak can mean with little strength and unable to do much. *A bout of food poisoning left Dan weak and tired.*

Feeble means weak. *My dad made some feeble excuse about why I can't stay with him this weekend.*

SEE **weak** for related words.
ANTONYMS: powerful, strong

Practice

noun

Practice means doing something over and over in order to increase skill. *You can tell from Boris's juggling act how much practice he's had.*

Drill can mean training by doing something over and over in the same ways. *There will be fire drills every week until we get them right.*

Review means studying something again in order to be sure of knowing it. *The class will spend all next week on a review of decimals.*

Rehearsal means practice of something that will be performed in public. *"Remember, tomorrow's rehearsal is at 4:30 in the concert hall!" said Mr. Umiker.*

Run-through means a rehearsal or a review. *It was the final run-through before the performance, and Gloria and June were still bumping into each other.*

Exercise means practice, especially physical activity to increase skill and strength. *The therapist says that after three months of exercise Pete can dance again.*

Workout means a period of physical exercise. *The workout was long and tough, and Joe left the aerobics class exhausted.*

Dry run means doing something as if for real, but actually for practice. *Howard injured his ankle during a dry run of the band's homecoming halftime show.*

SEE **go over** (at **go**) for related words.

You can tell from Boris's juggling act how much **practice** he's had.

Praise
verb

Praise means to say or write nice things about someone or something. *The cookies were barely done and oddly shaped, but Mrs. Collins praised her son enthusiastically.*

Compliment means to praise someone, especially in speech. *"If you want to compliment Sarah," her dad said, "talk about her skill with a coping saw."*

Acclaim means to praise highly and loudly. *This widely acclaimed musical tells the story of Harriet Tubman.*

Flatter means to praise someone too much. *Don't pay any attention to Marty; he just flatters people so they'll do things for him.*

Commend means to praise in a formal way. *The judges sent a letter commending Lisbet's science fair project.*

Butter up is an informal phrase meaning to flatter someone. *The detective buttered up the clerks at the car rental place so they would let her see the files.*

ANTONYMS: condemn, criticize, insult

HAVE YOU HEARD...?

You may have heard someone say that a person gave "a left-handed compliment." This is a compliment that is really an insult, such as "That was a good catch for someone as clumsy as you!" or "That's a good picture—if you don't care whether the horses look real or not."

Why *left-handed?* Because most people are more skillful with their right hand than their left hand, "left-handed" is sometimes used to mean "not well done" or "not properly meant." When a lefty insults someone in this manner, should it be called a "right-handed compliment"?

Prejudice
noun

Prejudice means an unfair and usually bad opinion formed because of personal feeling. *George grew up with a prejudice against anyone from other countries.*

Intolerance means unwillingness to let other people think or act differently from you. *Abby is getting over her intolerance of people who disagree with her.*

Narrow-mindedness means intolerance. *Arnie's narrow-mindedness is all that keeps him from admitting that people in wheelchairs can be top athletes.*

Bigotry means an unreasonable belief in your own prejudices. *The refusal to let women vote was the result of bigotry.*

Bias can mean a tendency to favor some people over others because of prejudice. *For decades, a bias toward immigrants from northwest Europe was shown in United States law.*

Discrimination can mean an unfair difference in the treatment of someone or some group, compared to others. *The newspaper says that discrimination against hiring older people is still common.*

Racism is prejudice and discrimination according to race. *"When we tell ourselves racism is finished," Reverend Davis told the crowd, "we only help it live."*

The refusal to let women vote was the result of **bigotry.**

Pretend

verb

Pretend means to make yourself seem to be doing something that you are not really doing. *Gerry knew that Grandpa was only pretending to be asleep.*

Make believe means to pretend to be someone or something else. *"OK, now we'll make believe I'm the movie star and you're the TV reporter," said Stephen.*

Act can mean to pretend you are feeling something when you really are not. *Jody is really stuck-up, even though she tries to act nice and friendly.*

Pose can mean to pretend something and try to fool people into believing it. *Sandra and her mom like to go into fancy stores and pose as rich people.*

Bluff means to try to fool someone by pretending you are confident. *Glinda is just bluffing when she claims that she's sure to make the team.*

Suppose can mean to pretend something, in order to play with the idea. *"Suppose you owned a big ranch," Hank said to Joan. "Would you let wolves live there?"*

Play possum is an idiom that means to try to fool someone by pretending to be weak, inactive, or dead. *In the movie, the crooks thought they'd killed the police officer, but she was just playing possum.*

Go through the motions is an idiom that means to pretend to do something without really trying to do it. *Evan made noises as if he were cleaning his room, but he was just going through the motions.*

SEE **imaginary, imagine,** and **imitate** for related words.

WORD STORY

The idiom *to play possum* comes from an unusual behavior of the opossum. When threatened, the opossum appears to play dead by lying on its side. Some scientists have wondered if the opossum is really fainting from fear. However, careful tests do not show the bodily changes that normally go with fainting. So it seems likely that an opossum does pretend, in order to save its life.

Prevent
verb

Prevent means to stop something from happening. *Brushing and flossing help to prevent cavities.*

Block means to stop the progress of someone or something. *Tina leaned out the car window, trying to see what was blocking traffic.*

Avert means to prevent something bad from happening. *By making a backup copy, Jo averted a disaster when her computer crashed.*

Thwart means to prevent someone from doing something, usually something planned. *"I hope the weather doesn't thwart our cookout," said Milada nervously.*

Be a dog in the manger is an idiom that means to prevent something, even though you gain nothing by it. *By refusing to rent these empty apartments, the landlord is being a dog in the manger.*

Throw a monkey wrench into is an idiom that means to prevent something by interfering with it or sabotaging it. *Our lead singer joined another band, which threw a monkey wrench into our plans.*

SEE **forbid, obstacle,** and **stop** for related words.
ANTONYMS: allow, permit

WORD STORY

The idiom *to be a dog in the manger* comes from a fable by Aesop. In this fable, an ox goes to a manger to eat and finds a dog lying on the straw there. Of course, the dog doesn't want to eat the straw. But he is unwilling to budge, so the ox gets no dinner. *Manger,* a feeding box for animals, comes from a Latin word meaning "to chew."

Previous
adjective

Previous means coming or happening earlier than something else. *Marco hopes the new owner of the hardware store will sponsor his soccer team, as the previous one did.*

Prior and **preceding** mean previous. *This puzzle requires no prior knowledge and can be solved by anyone. You'll find the answer to the puzzle on the preceding page.*

Foregoing is a formal word that means previous. It is often used about ideas and information. *When you have reviewed the foregoing material, proceed to the chapter on verb tenses.*

CONTINUED ON THE NEXT PAGE

Recent means happening not long ago. *Mark and Julio's recent fight has left them both feeling bitter.*

Past can mean just gone by. *As she was leaving, Greta said, "I've had a lot of fun these past couple of days."*

Former can mean of long ago. *My sister's former boyfriend says he still loves her.*

Preliminary means coming or happening before something more important. *The preliminary steps for making the casserole are to heat the oven and gather all the ingredients.*

ANTONYMS: following, later

Price
noun

Price means the amount of money needed to buy something. *What's the price of this antique train set?*

Charge means the money asked in return for a service. *There's no extra charge if you want a green seat instead of black on that bicycle.*

Fee means a charge. *We have to pay a fee each time we use the city pool.*

Rate can mean price or charge. *After Dad's accident, our car insurance rates went up.*

Bill means a record of money owed for something. *Mom nearly fainted when she read the mechanic's bill.*

Check can mean a written bill for money owed in a restaurant. *"Check, please," Ms. Ortiz said to the waiter.*

Tab can mean a bill or check. *If long-time customers run out of money near the end of the month, the grocer lets them buy things on a tab.*

SEE **cost** for related words.

Prize
noun

Prize means something won in a contest or game. *Kendall jumped for joy when his science project won first prize.*

Jackpot can mean the big prize of a game. *Mr. O'Latry won the jackpot at this week's Bingo game.*

Trophy means a prize, often a small statue or a plaque, given to the winner in a sports competition. *The old trophy had a little bowler on it and said "Hutchinson Titans."*

Cup can mean a large metal vase given as a trophy. *The Stanley Cup goes to the best ice hockey team every year.*

Award means something given as a prize after an official decision. *My favorite movie didn't win the award for best picture.*

Decoration can mean a medal, ribbon, or badge, given as a sign of honor. *"This decoration," explained Ralph's grandfather, "was for the time I saved three people's lives during a fire."*

Ribbon and **medal** can mean an award or decoration. *Our cat, Puma, won a blue ribbon for best Siamese in show. We put it on the shelf where we keep medals she has won in other shows.*

WORD POOL

Here are some names for awards (and the fields in which they are awarded):

Clio (advertising)	**Nebula** (science fiction)
Edgar (mystery novels)	**Nobel** (literature, science, peace, economics)
Emmy (television)	**Oscar** (motion pictures)
Grammy (recordings)	**Pulitzer** (literature, music, journalism)
Hugo (science fiction)	**Tony** (theater)

Can you think of the names of other awards?

Oscar

Promise
verb

Promise means to give your word to someone that you will or will not do something. *The hotel clerk promised to hold a room for us.*

Agree can mean to promise to do something that someone else wants. *Miriam agreed to wait for me if I was late.*

Pledge means to promise something in a sincere, solemn way. *Next, we will pledge allegiance to the flag.*

CONTINUED ON THE NEXT PAGE

324

Vow means to pledge. *After the accident, Sampson vowed that he would never again horse around in the car.*

Swear can mean to make a serious pledge or vow. The word is often used about a person who makes an official oath. *During inauguration ceremonies, the new President swears to support the Constitution.*

Guarantee means to promise, especially to fix, replace, or take back an item sold. *On this used tape deck, everything is guaranteed for ninety days.*

Undertake is a formal word that can mean to promise to do something. *The city undertakes to build new roads to the area if the company will open a factory there.*

Vouch for means to promise that someone or something is good, true, or valuable. *The auto dealer vouches for the good condition of the used car's engine and brakes.*

Promote
verb

Promote means to help something toward success. *UNICEF promotes the welfare of the world's children.*

Further means to promote. *Kevin is studying Spanish to further his career plans.*

Advance can mean to promote. *The breakup of the Soviet Union has advanced the cause of democracy.*

unicef

UNICEF **promotes** the welfare of the world's children.

Foster means to help the growth or development of something. *The circus's Clown College continually fosters a search for new forms of silliness.*

Boost can mean to promote something by speaking well of it. *Business leaders met with the mayor to boost a light-rail transportation system.*

SEE **encourage** and **help** for related words.
ANTONYMS: obstruct, prevent

Proud
adjective

Proud means pleased with yourself and with what you have done. *Congresswoman Martinez ended her victory speech by telling her election workers that they should all be proud of themselves.*

Haughty means too proud and too scornful of others. *Mara regretted her haughty words when no one asked her to the dance.*

Arrogant means haughty. *The arrogant general gave his soldiers no credit for the victory.*

Conceited means having too high an opinion of yourself or your good qualities. *The conceited actor stopped bragging after he forgot his lines.*

Vain means conceited, especially about good looks. *"Well, if Miguel is vain, he's sure got good reasons," said Tom wistfully.*

Boastful means fond of talking about yourself and how good you are. *The boastful man went on and on about what a great fisherman he was.*

Cocky is an informal word that means conceited and boastful. *"That team from Warren Harding Middle School won't be so cocky when we finish with them—right, kids?" said the coach.*

Stuck-up is an informal word that means conceited and haughty. *Patricia is so stuck-up that she has no friends at all.*

On your high horse is an idiom that means haughty. It is usually used with "not." *"Don't get on your high horse with me, young lady —spelling bee winners still have to set the table," declared Dad.*

SEE **brag** for related words.
ANTONYMS: humble, modest

Pull
verb

Pull means to make something move toward you, or follow along behind you. *Enrique pulled the wagon along the sidewalk, giving his little sister a ride.*

Jerk means to pull quickly and suddenly. *The cook jerked his hand away from the hot stove.*

Tug means to pull hard, sometimes stopping to rest between pulls. *Kata and Miki had a good laugh when they realized they'd been trying to tug an anchored boat to shore.*

CONTINUED ON THE NEXT PAGE

Mr. Rivera **yanked** on the cord to start the boat's engine.

Yank is an informal word that means to pull hard with a sudden motion. *Mr. Rivera yanked on the cord to start the boat's engine.*

Drag means to pull something along the ground. *"The way you drag your jacket around, it's no wonder that it's tattered and torn," Eric said to his brother.*

Haul means to pull something large or heavy for a long distance. *The Black Diamond Trucking Company hauls oranges from Florida to Cleveland.*

Draw means to pull, drag, or haul. *"That old mule drew our wagon all the way from Oklahoma," Pa announced proudly.*

Tow means to pull something along behind a car or boat or whatever you're riding in. *After breaking down on the highway, Mr. Belen's car had to be towed to a gas station.*

SEE **move** for related words.
ANTONYMS: push, shove

Punish
verb

Punish means to cause pain or loss to a person who has done something wrong. *The soldiers were punished for sleeping on duty.*

Penalize means to punish, especially with a particular loss or pain. *The referee penalized the Mammoths 15 yards for unnecessary roughness.*

Discipline can mean to punish, especially to control people. *Mr. Berman finds disciplining his students one of the hardest parts of his job.*

Correct can mean to punish, in order to make someone better. *Mom says she must correct our new puppy so he'll stop chewing furniture and shoes.*

Fine means to make a person pay money for doing something wrong. *The library fines people only five cents a day for late books but a dollar a day for late videos.*

Ground can mean to punish a young person by not letting him or her go out for fun. This meaning is informal. *Because he came home two hours after curfew, Chung-Ho knew his parents would ground him.*

Throw the book at someone means to punish someone severely. *"If I catch you cheating," warned Ms. Otoya, "I will throw the book at you."*

Give someone just deserts means to punish someone in an especially suitable way. *Kris was given her just deserts when Ms. Poston made her write a book report on each of the library books she had damaged.*

WORD STORY

Discipline comes from two Latin words meaning "to learn" and "a boy or girl." Together, they meant "a pupil." *Disciple* also comes from these words, because a disciple is one who follows and learns from a great teacher. If you are trying hard to learn something, you need to control your efforts. Teachers may discipline students to keep them under control, and therefore to help them learn.

Push
verb

Push means to move something away from you. *Kevin pushed the door open and stepped into the hall.*

Nudge means to push gently. *When Gail's horse Ruffian knows it's mealtime, he nudges her as if to say, "Feed me now, please."*

Shove means to push hard. *Julita shoved the garbage cans to one side, clearing the alley for the ambulance.*

Propel means to push something forward with a steady force. *This experimental car is propelled by an electric motor.*

Thrust means to push hard and quickly. *Max thrust his hands into his coat pockets and turned away.*

Roll means to push something so that it turns over and over. *"Don't lift the tire; roll it over here," Papá said to Luis.*

SEE **move** for related words.
ANTONYMS: drag, pull, tug

When Gail's horse Ruffian knows it's mealtime, he **nudges** her as if to say, "Feed me now, please."

Put
verb

Put means to move something to some place. *Mickey put a note in the book before he handed it to Ellen.*

Put is also in phrases that have special meanings. Each of these phrases has its own set of synonyms.

put back

Put back means to move something to where it was before. *Mr. Stoll poured a glass of milk and put the bottle back in the refrigerator.*

Replace can mean to put something back. *When his mother said "Just one," Yanni sadly replaced all but one of the videotapes on the store shelves.*

Restore can mean to give something back or put something back. *Police hope to restore the parrot to its owner, who left it in a taxi.*

Return can mean to bring something back or put something back. *If you don't return library books on time, you have to pay a fine.*

Reinstate is a formal word that means to put something or someone back. It suggests a return to a former condition or state of being rather than to a physical place. *The government has ordered the company to reinstate all workers fired during the strike.*

put down

Put down means to give information in written form. *The landlord asked the Guptas to put down their last three addresses.*

Note means to put down in order to use the information in the future. *Researchers who note violence in TV shows say that it is increasing.*

Record means to note. *As early as the 1300s B.C., Chinese astronomers were recording eclipses of the sun and moon.*

Jot means to write briefly and quickly. *Sally jotted a list of errands on the back of an old envelope.*

List means to write down brief pieces of information, often in a special order. *On the first day of school, Mr. Connelly asked us to list our expectations for his class.*

Register means to put down information, especially in a list. *Dr. del Pino's receptionist registers all her patients in the appointment book.*

CONTINUED ON THE NEXT PAGE

Inscribe means to put down information in a careful, formal way, often by carving it into stone or metal. *Mom and Dad had my initials inscribed on the back of the watch they gave me for graduation.*

Enter can mean to put down information. It is often used about numbers. *Mrs. Myung enters every sale into the store's computer.*

Write down means to put down. *She gave Alan her phone number, but he was so happy he forgot to write it down.*

put on

Put on means to act or sing or play some work for an audience. *For publicity, the dancers put on part of their show outside the theater.*

Perform can mean to put on. *"Tonight our choir will perform songs of hope from popular music," announced Reverend Samuels.*

Produce can mean to put on. It is used about all the work connected with a performance, not just what happens for an audience. *The work of producing a movie starts months before the filming and years before the movie appears.*

Give can mean to produce. *The class is giving a recital, and Darla's job is to sell ads for the program.*

Present can mean to produce. *The Metro Theater is proud to present a Festival of African Dance.*

Stage means to put on. It is used mostly about plays, and especially about the way they are planned for performance. *Ms. Benes has staged the work very simply, with few props and no scenery.*

For publicity, the dancers **put on** part of their show outside the theater.

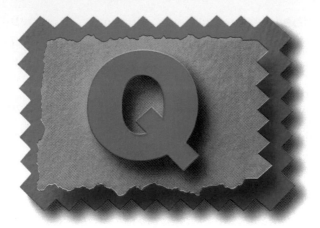

Quality
noun

Quality means something special you can describe about a person or thing. *Humor and modesty are among Eric's best qualities, but he doesn't show much ambition.*

Attribute can mean a quality. *The ability to listen and observe is an important attribute for a doctor.*

Feature can mean a quality, especially a very noticeable one. *Corn meal has been the major feature of Mexican diet since people in Mexico first discovered how to grow corn thousands of years ago.*

Property can mean a permanent quality, especially of a thing. *One property of the metal mercury is that it is liquid at room temperature.*

Aspect means a quality. The word is mostly used about a thing or a situation, when someone is examining it. *The thieves had considered almost every aspect of the bank robbery plan.*

SEE **characteristic** and **disposition** for related words.

Quick
adjective

Quick means moving, happening, or done in a short time. *Graciella made a quick grab and got her purse back from the thief.*

Fast means moving with much speed. *Young Raven hurled his fish spear, but the salmon was too fast.*

Rapid means fast. It is used mostly to describe motion or action. *Rapid work by the paramedics saved Mr. Thayer's life.*

Swift means very fast. *This train is so swift that we'll be in Los Angeles tomorrow.*

CONTINUED ON THE NEXT PAGE

Speedy means very quick. It is often used to describe things that you want to happen or be finished. *The bank robbers could not make a speedy getaway because of the parade.*

Brisk means quick and lively. *Deshon and his grandmother meet every Wednesday afternoon for a brisk game of tennis.*

Hasty means quick and with not enough time or thought. *Courtney's hasty reply started a quarrel.*

Hurried means hasty. *"Gone jogging, back soon," read Darla's hurried note to her mother.*

SEE **hurry** and **suddenly** for related words.
ANTONYM: slow

The bank robbers could not make a **speedy** getaway because of the parade.

Quiet

verb

Quiet means to make someone or something less noisy and more peaceful. *Desi quieted his younger brothers when they were frightened by the thunderstorm.*

Calm means to make someone less excited or nervous. *The police officer calmed the crowd following the bomb scare.*

Soothe means to make quiet and comfortable. *"I do enjoy a soothing cup of tea," said Mr. Benson.*

Settle can mean to soothe. *After the argument, Paolo took a long walk to settle his nerves.*

Hush means to make someone or something less noisy or silent. *"Could there be ghosts here?" Clara asked in a hushed voice.*

Still means to calm or to quiet. It is used mostly in books. *"Hear me!" cried Caesar, and his manner stilled the mob.*

Tranquilize means to calm. *Tranquilized by the music, Mr. Jacobi stopped worrying about his hard day.*

Pacify means to quiet. It emphasizes peacefulness after being upset. *Tracy has a way of pacifying the baby when no one else can.*

SEE **calm** and **comfort** for related words.
ANTONYMS: disturb, excite, stir up

WRITER'S CHOICE

But once out at sea, there came the steady sound of an engine, and the ship began to sway in the water, up and down, and also from side to side. . . . When there was a good stiff breeze, the captain hoisted sails, stilled the engines, and then we skimmed over the water without a sound.

—Elizabeth Borton de Treviño, *El Güero*

Why *stilled?* The ship has both steam engines and sails. On days with little breeze, the ship uses its engines to move through the water. These engines can be heard and felt throughout the ship. When there is enough breeze to move the ship using the sails, the captain has the engines turned off, restoring calm and quiet to the ship.

Random
adjective

Random means for no reason and with no pattern. *Ms. O'Donnell is afraid to live in the housing project, where random violence occurs every day.*

Haphazard means random. *Because the break-ins are so haphazard, police do not believe that experienced burglars are involved.*

Hit-or-miss means random. *After two hit-or-miss answers, Phil admitted he hadn't done the reading.*

Chance means not planned or expected. *Amy's chance visit surprised Joel, who had just gotten out of the shower.*

Accidental means not on purpose. It often suggests something bad. *In his accidental meeting with the rattlesnake, Far Thunder nearly fell from his horse.*

SEE **luck** for related words.
ANTONYMS: deliberate, intentional, planned

In his **accidental** meeting with the rattlesnake, Far Thunder nearly fell from his horse.

Rare
adjective

Rare means not often found. *The city zoo has a program to help keep rare frogs from extinction.*

Scarce means hard to get because not plentiful. *Uncle Jack is still out of work because jobs are scarce today.*

Infrequent means happening seldom. *Aunt Debbie's visits are too infrequent and always wonderful.*

Uncommon means rare and different from normal. *Teresa's uncommon patience with tough customers won her the Employee of the Month award.*

Unfamiliar and **unusual** mean rare and different from normal. *Rachel saw an unfamiliar bird on her birdwatching trip. She later discovered that it was unusual to see that kind of bird in her area.*

Unique can mean very uncommon or unusual. This meaning is informal. *The combination of accordions and bagpipes gives our band a unique sound, I think.* (See the Watch It! at **single**.)

Exceptional means unlike most others or unlike the standard way. *We all agree that Max is an exceptional piano player.*

Extraordinary means very remarkably unusual. *The church's after-school programs have produced extraordinary gains in some students' grades.*

SEE **peculiar** and **special** for related words.
ANTONYMS: abundant, common, plentiful

Real
adjective

Real means not false or artificial or made-up. *Ms. Lorber asked Shirrel to give her the real reason why she was late.*

Genuine means being what it seems or is said to be. *I thought Clara's friendliness was genuine, until she asked to copy my math homework.*

True can mean genuine. *"Oh, Reginald—" Priscilla hugged her pillow—"my one true love!"*

Actual means existing in fact or really happening. *"There's been an actual tornado sighting, so everyone go into the basement—now!" said Mr. Landau.*

CONTINUED ON THE NEXT PAGE

Authentic is a formal word that can mean genuine. *An authentic Inuit sculpture may be worth hundreds or thousands of dollars.*

Factual means containing facts. *This movie about a one-legged distance runner has a solid factual basis.*

SEE **correct** for related words.
ANTONYMS: artificial, false, imaginary

WRITING TIP: Redundancy

We all do it: use two or more words that say the same thing. Have you ever said, "This is the *real* truth"? If it's real, then of course it's the truth, and if it's the truth, it's real.

There are dozens of phrases like this, called *redundancies*, that you hear every day. Sometimes you may choose to repeat ideas to make them stronger (see the Writing Tip "Emphasis by Repetition" at **calm**). Redundancies rarely make ideas stronger, however. When you repeat an idea for no clear reason, it suggests that you aren't thinking about what you're writing. Which word in each of the phrases below might you choose to eliminate?

advance reservation	free gift	plan ahead
all complete	I myself personally	repeat again
continue on	join together	same identical
drop down	natural instinct	subjective opinion
end result	past history	unintentional mistake
false pretenses	personal friend	verbal discussion

What others can you think of?

Reason
noun

Reason means an explanation of why something happened. *Doug says his reason for quitting the job is that he didn't respect the boss.*

Cause can mean a reason. *The "A" on Jaleel's history final was cause for celebration!*

Occasion can mean a reason. It suggests a particular single event. *The Coyas' twenty-fifth anniversary was the occasion of a family reunion.*

Grounds can mean a reason. It suggests serious thinking about facts. *Too many unexcused absences from school are grounds for being suspended.*

Motive means a thought or feeling that makes someone do something. *The high cost of city living was Mr. Poole's motive for moving to a small town.*

Incentive is a formal word that means motive or cause. It suggests giving someone encouragement to make a choice. *The city offers reduced taxes and other incentives to companies that open factories here.*

SEE **excuse** for related words.

Recover
verb

Recover means to get back something that has been lost or given up. *Mrs. Tallant got her TV back, but her stolen necklace will probably never be recovered.*

Retrieve means to recover, usually after much effort or after a search. *After hours of diving, the police retrieved the weapon from the river.*

Redeem means to get something back by giving up something else. *With money from the corn crop, Farmer Simms redeemed the land he had mortgaged to the bank.*

Reclaim means to claim something back that has been temporarily given up or lost. *This treatment plant reclaims sewage water by filtering it until it is clean again.*

Recycle means to put something through a process that makes it useful again. *Jim collects cans that can be recycled for their aluminum.*

CONTINUED ON THE NEXT PAGE

During all those long years of wandering among humans, I had known I would return to my own kind some day—even if I hadn't been sure of how. It wouldn't be long now before I would reclaim my proper place among dragons.

—Laurence Yep, *Dragon Steel*

Why *reclaim?* The dragon Shimmer, who tells the story, once had a place among the other dragons. Now she is going to claim her place again—to *re*-claim what she has temporarily lost.

Reliable
adjective

Reliable means worthy of being counted on or trusted. *Mr. Koenig told us to use only reliable sources for our research papers—no supermarket tabloid newspapers.*

Dependable means reliable. *Ms. Bailey says that Tomás is dependable enough to manage the store on Sundays.*

Sure can mean reliable. *With her speed and sure hands, Tessa should be a great volleyball player.*

Responsible can mean reliable and sensible in making decisions. *We always make Tazu referee because we need the most responsible person for that job.*

Steady can mean responsible and having good habits. *Is Jerome steady enough to take care of the other three children until Mrs. Waters gets home from work?*

Tried and true means known by experience to be reliable. *With his tried and true dog guide, Buck, Mr. Nulty walks fifteen blocks to and from work each day.*

With his **tried and true** dog guide, Buck, Mr. Nulty walks fifteen blocks to and from work each day.

Religious
adjective

Religious means devoted to God. *My grandmother is so religious that she goes to church every single morning.*

Godly means caring much for the worship of God. *"We left England," Mr. Fulton told Judith, "to live a godly life in the New World."*

Pious means godly. *The pious ways of the Amish make them unusual in today's world.*

Devout means active in worship and prayer. *Devout Muslims pray five times every day.*

Spiritual can mean caring much for the life of the spirit. *We honor Lincoln for his spiritual quality.*

SEE **holy** for related words.

AROUND THE WORLD: Religion

Judaism

Islam

Shinto

Christianity

Buddhism

340

Reluctant
adjective

Reluctant means not wanting to do something. It suggests trying to avoid or resist. *Austin has been wrong so often that his friends are reluctant to follow his advice.*

Hesitant means holding yourself back from doing something. It suggests doubt or fear. *Peering over the edge of the diving board, Janice felt hesitant about jumping.*

Unwilling means not willing to do something. It suggests an attempt to refuse. *"I am unwilling to spend seventy dollars just because you think the shoes are cool," May's father said.*

Grudging can mean given or done by someone who does not want to. *Harold said a grudging "Hi" to his sister's date.*

ANTONYM: eager

Remember
verb

Remember means to call something back to mind. *"Remember!" shouted the captain. "We meet tomorrow in Spyglass Bay!"*

Recall means to remember. It is often used when an effort is required. *Can you recall when we asked the janitor to fix the sink?*

Recollect means to recall something, especially something from long ago. *"I can recollect when this neighborhood was mostly woods," Mr. Rosewater told his granddaughters.*

Reminisce means to remember and talk about people and events from the past. *Mom and her brothers like to reminisce about their childhood in Cuba.*

Review can mean to go through memories of something. *"Reviewing the strange events of the Cold Storage Murder Case, I marvel again at the criminal's daring," said Inspector Douglass.*

Memorize means to learn something so well that you can remember all of it at will. *LuAnne memorized the street names by chanting them over and over as she walked.*

Retain can mean to hold something in mind. *As people grow older, they often find it harder to retain new information.*

Think of can mean to remember. *Walking through the apartment, Mrs. Droseh tried to think of all the places she might have left her keys.*

ANTONYM: forget

341

Repair
verb

Repair means to put something that is broken or that doesn't work back into good condition. *"I've got to get this thing repaired,"* thought *Colleen, when another tape jammed in her player.*

Fix can mean to repair. *"Lester, will you help me fix my bike seat?" asked his younger brother.*

Mend means to make something whole again that was torn, broken, or worn out. It is often used about things that have holes in them. *"There's a hole that needs mending in the west pasture fence," Joe reported to the ranch foreman.*

Patch means to mend something by putting a new piece of material in a hole or worn place. *Someone patched all those broken windows with cardboard.*

Service can mean to put something into good working condition, especially a machine. *Ms. Delgado has a job servicing air conditioners.*

Restore can mean to bring back something to a former condition. It suggests making something as good as new. *Restored after almost 500 years, Michelangelo's painting once again glows with the original colors.*

Overhaul means to examine something carefully and fix whatever needs fixing. *Mrs. Imura's car has traveled 50,000 miles, and it needs to be overhauled.*

HAVE YOU HEARD...?

You may have heard people say, "If it's not broken, don't fix it." But you may also have heard people say, "A stitch in time saves nine." You can see that these proverbs say opposite things. There are many other contradictory sayings:

"Absence makes the heart grow fonder," but
"Out of sight, out of mind."

"Haste makes waste," but
"He who hesitates is lost."

"Many hands make light work," but
"Too many cooks spoil the broth."

Can you think of any others?

Report
verb

Report means to tell or write about something in a detailed, organized way. *"Remember how much we spend,"* Maria said, *"because we'll have to report it all to Mom when we get back."*

Describe means to tell or write about something in a way that makes clear what it is like. *"Close your eyes and describe what I'm wearing,"* Eva challenged her friend.

Relate means to report something fully and in order. It is used mostly about reporting a series of events. *Nathan thought back and related the movie's most important scenes.*

Narrate means to relate. It suggests a story in a book, or an attempt to sound like one. *"The reason I knew Kitty would survive the shipwreck is that she's the character narrating the novel,"* explained Patrick.

Recount means to relate events one after another as they happened, in very full detail. *Hour by hour, this article recounts one day in the life of a paralyzed veteran.*

Request
verb

"Well," said Mr. Minn,
"if no student wants to
claim this water pistol,
I guess it's mine now."

Request means to try to get something by politely stating your desire. *"The librarian requests that you be quiet or leave,"* whispered the library monitor.

Ask can mean to request. *Asking Grace to go out with him was easier than Hank had expected.*

Appeal means to request earnestly. *The President appealed for calm during the riots.*

Apply can mean to request. It is often used about jobs and other official situations. *Tina's parents have applied to adopt a baby.*

Demand means to request very strongly, and to insist on getting what you want. *"I was here first, and I want you to take my order first,"* Arnold demanded.

Claim means to request something as a right or as legal property. *"Well,"* said Mr. Minn, *"if no student wants to claim this water pistol, I guess it's mine now."*

SEE **beg, command,** and **urge** for related words.

343

Revolt
noun

Revolt means a refusal to obey people who are in charge. It may suggest the use of force against authority. *The first Mexican revolt against Spanish rule occurred in 1810.*

Mutiny means revolt, especially against military authority. *Thirteen sailors were charged with mutiny for taking control of the ship.*

Uprising means a sudden revolt. It is often used about the acts of a few people, but it may suggest the beginning of a broad action. *When the government soldiers entered the town and arrested the very popular mayor, there was an uprising among some of the younger townspeople.*

Rebellion means open warfare against a government in order to get rid of it. It is used mostly about unsuccessful attempts. *In 1831, Nat Turner led the most famous slave rebellion in the history of the United States.*

Revolution means a complete and usually violent change in a government. It suggests success by organized force. *During the American Revolution, British soldiers were surprised to find themselves sometimes facing armed fighting women.*

Coup can mean a sudden, illegal replacement of one government by another, usually with little violence. *One officer after another fled the coup, so a corporal now runs the country.*

WORD STORY

Revolution is used about complete changes in society as well as in government. *The Industrial Revolution depended on machine power, and the Computer Revolution came from electronics.* Originally *revolution* meant a complete turn—and in *RPM*, revolutions per minute, it still does.

Rich
adjective

Rich means having a lot of money or a lot of expensive things. *Scrooge was rich, but lonely and poor in spirit.*

Prosperous means successful, especially with money. It does not suggest as much money as *rich* does. *The Aguilars live in a prosperous middle-class neighborhood.*

Well-off and **well-to-do** mean having enough money that you don't have to worry. *Mr. Henderson is very well-off. He comes from a well-to-do family.*

Well-heeled is an informal word that means prosperous and not needing more money. *That resort is for well-heeled vacationers.*

Moneyed means having a lot of money, especially in contrast to others who don't. *With the help of moneyed relatives, Michiko was able to study engineering in college.*

Wealthy means very rich, with great status and influence. *Several wealthy families in the city have contributed to the Museum of African American Art.*

Affluent means having and spending a large amount of money. *"The Sans Souci jewelry store, Madame, is for customers affluent enough not to consider the cost," said the haughty salesman.*

SEE **wealth** for related words.
ANTONYMS: poor, poverty-stricken, penniless

IDIOMS

There are many idioms that mean someone has a lot of money. Here are some of them:

made of money	born with a silver
on easy street	spoon in your mouth
rolling in dough	in clover

Can you think of other expressions that people use to say that someone is rich?

"The Sans Souci jewelry store, Madame, is for customers **affluent** enough not to consider the cost," said the haughty salesman.

345

Ridicule
verb

Ridicule means to make fun of someone or something. *"Just because I'm taller than anybody in my school,"* Alice sighed, *"do people have to ridicule me all the time?"*

Mock means to ridicule, especially by imitating. *The clown mocked the lion tamer by pretending a trained poodle was ferocious.*

Kid means to tease someone playfully. *"Bill kids you about your clothes because it's the only way he knows how to be friendly,"* said Mrs. Fredriks.

Josh is an informal word that means to make fun of someone in a good-natured way. *Aunt Prue joshes Uncle Al about what a mistake she made in marrying him.*

Razz is a slang word that means to make fun of someone, especially with rude noises. *After Joanne tripped and was tagged out between first and second, her teammates razzed her all the way back to the dugout.*

SEE **scoff** for related words.

Rigid
adjective

Rigid means not changing or not willing to change. *The company has a rigid rule against smoking at work.*

Unyielding means determined and firm in purpose. *Ms. Banks was unyielding in her claim that she had been treated unfairly by her supervisor.*

Inflexible means rigid or unyielding. *LaDonna has an inflexible practice schedule: two hours every single day but Sunday.*

Demanding means requiring a lot, and not changing requirements with circumstances. *Gene's summer art class was very demanding.*

Grim can mean unyielding despite suffering. *With grim determination, Lieutenant Roxas searched the burning apartment house.*

Relentless means without pity and unchangingly harsh. *Relentless poverty grips many Indians who live on reservations.*

Set in your ways means used to doing things by habit, and not wanting to change. *Our dog, Compañero, is so set in his ways, he won't even eat early.*

SEE **severe** for related words.

As the hot-air ballons **lifted** into the sky, their colors were beautiful against the clouds.

Rise
verb

Rise means to get up or go up. *"All rise," said the court officer as the judge entered.*

Arise is a formal word that means to get up, usually from a seat or a bed. *As an apprentice, Sam had to arise while it was still dark to start the blacksmith's fire.*

Ascend means to go upward steadily. *"We are now ascending to an altitude of twenty thousand feet," the airplane captain announced.*

Lift can mean to go up slowly. *As the hot-air balloons lifted into the sky, their colors were beautiful against the clouds.*

Soar means to fly upward quickly and smoothly. *Keithla gave her kite more string, and it soared up toward the clouds.*

Rocket can mean to rise very fast. *When the recess bell rings, Yuen rockets from her seat and rushes out to claim a basketball court.*

SEE **climb** and **lift** for related words.
ANTONYMS: descend, fall

Room
noun

Room for one more!"
cried Arnie, crowding
into the elevator.

Room means a place big enough for something. *"Room for one more!" cried Arnie, crowding into the elevator.*

Space can mean room. *The old kitchen had no space for a dishwasher.*

Expanse means a large spreading area of something. *Somewhere in the huge expanse of this parking lot is our little car.*

Extent means a large area, or the distance to the limits of something. *Some scientists define a desert as an extent of land receiving an average of less than ten inches of rain a year. The extent of the polar ice cap changes with the seasons.*

Range means extent. *The range of view from Ravi's window includes the street and part of the marketplace.*

Elbowroom means plenty of room in which to do something. *Mr. Miklaus cleared off the table, saying, "We need elbowroom to build model airplanes."*

Clearance can mean the distance needed for two things to pass without touching. *Be sure there's clearance for Althea's wheelchair to get onto the bandstand.*

Leeway can mean clearance, or an extra amount of something necessary. *Flora saw with dismay that there was not leeway for the stroller to go through the door.*

WORD STORY

Where does the word *leeway* come from? The *lee* side of a ship is the side away from the wind. Because the wind is pushing in that direction, a ship tends to drift in that direction. Moving or at anchor, ships need extra room on the lee side, so that they don't drift onto rocks or hit other ships. This extra room is called leeway. An extra amount of any kind is also called leeway, even by people who don't know where the word came from.

Rotate
verb

Rotate means to turn around a central point. *The gas station has a tall rotating sign so that drivers will notice it.*

Revolve means to go in a curve around some place. *The moon revolves around the Earth once about every 27⅓ days.*

CONTINUED ON THE NEXT PAGE

Turn means to go around like a wheel. *The turning fan blades sent a cool breeze through Jared's room.*

Circle means to move in a circle. *The wolves circle the elk, waiting for a sign of weakness.*

Wheel means to turn quickly and gracefully. *Bharati wheeled, jumped, and shot the ball right into the basket.*

Roll means to move along by turning over and over. *The huge boulder rolled down the mountain toward the cabins.*

Swivel means to turn around a connecting part. *The TV antenna swivels in all directions to pick up broadcast signals.*

Pivot can mean to turn on a point where the weight rests. *Pivoting on second base, Luisa threw to first for the double play.*

> **WATCH IT!**
> ....
> People sometimes mix up **rotate** and **revolve,** especially when they are talking about planets and moons. Remember, an object *rotates* around its own center (as the Earth rotates on its own axis); an object *revolves* around another object (as the Earth revolves around the sun).

Rough
adjective

Rough means having a surface that is not smooth. *Frank snagged his sweater on the rough wall of the basement.*

Uneven means not smooth or level. *Our car bounced along the uneven gravel road.*

Bumpy means having a lot of bumps. *The sidewalk was too bumpy for good skateboarding.*

Harsh means unpleasantly rough to the touch. *These towels get harsh and scratchy after they've been washed a lot.*

Rugged means having a rough, uneven surface. *The slope looked easy, but the ground became rugged toward the top.*

Coarse can mean rough and heavy. *Silas used coarse sandpaper to smooth the sides of the bookshelf.*

Shaggy means rough and hairy. *Wild pigs have shaggy hides suited to life in the forests.*

ANTONYMS: even, level, smooth

Rude

adjective

Rude means showing bad manners and acting in an unpleasant way, especially on purpose. *The cab driver shouted something rude at the driver who had cut in front of him.*

Boorish means rude. *We couldn't enjoy the movie because the boorish people behind us kept talking.*

Offensive means rude and annoying. *"I'm sorry," Jennifer said, "I didn't mean to be offensive."*

Impertinent and **insolent** are formal words that mean boldly rude. *"Such an impertinent question does not deserve an answer," the senator said. With an insolent shrug, the reporter turned away.*

Blunt can mean to the point, without concern for other people's feelings. *Ceretha was blunt in her analysis of my handwriting.*

Crude can mean without any understanding of good manners. *Joan was disgusted by Randy's crude table manners.*

Vulgar means crude. *"Your father and I don't find such vulgar jokes funny," said Mom.*

Gross can mean crude and disgusting. *"Society will not tolerate such gross racism," said Judge Faber.*

SEE **sassy** for related words.

ANTONYMS: courteous, polite, respectful

WATCH IT!

Some expressions are offensive to particular ethnic groups or nationalities and should be avoided. For example, the phrase *paddy wagon* was once used for a police patrol wagon, which the police still use to take arrested people to the station. *Paddy* is a nickname for *Patrick,* a common Irish name.

Expressions like *paddy wagon, Dutch treat,* and *Indian giver* are offensive to Irish, Dutch, and Native American people. Names like *Dutch elm disease* and *Indian corn* are not offensive. If in doubt, ask!

Ruin
noun

Ruin means very great damage or complete spoiling. *"This means ruin," sighed Komo, as the blazing roof fell in.*

Destruction can mean ruin. *Destruction of the buffalo herds meant the end of Plains Indian culture.*

Demolition means tearing something down. *Architects and historians hope to prevent demolition of the landmark hotel, now closed.*

Disintegration means the breaking up of something into small, useless pieces. *Acid rain is causing the disintegration of many statues.*

Devastation means widespread and complete ruin. *After four months of battle, the city was a scene of devastation.*

Annihilation means ruin so complete that nothing remains. *The general swore he would see the annihilation of his entire country before he would surrender to the rebels.*

Rule
verb

Queen Liliuokalani **reigned** in Hawaii from 1891 to 1893.

Rule means to have political power over others. *Mexico's ruling party, founded in 1929, has had two different names.*

Govern means to rule. It is often used about the work done by people with political power. *Many American cities are governed by a council and a city manager, without a mayor.*

Reign means to be a queen, king, or other monarch. *Queen Liliuokalani reigned in Hawaii from 1891 to 1893.*

Preside means to be in charge. It is mostly used about meetings. *The Vice-President is the presiding officer of the U.S. Senate.*

Tyrannize means to use political power cruelly and unjustly. *A military government tyrannizes that unfortunate country.*

> **HAVE YOU HEARD…?**
> •
> You may have heard people say that someone "rules the roost." This is an expression that means to be in control of a group, especially a family. The phrase comes from chicken roosts (nesting places), where one bird is more powerful than all the others. *Kelly's grandmother rules the roost in their house.*

351

Run
verb

A giraffe can **run** almost twice as fast as a human being.

Run means to go fast by moving the legs quickly. *A giraffe can run almost twice as fast as a human being.*

Trot means to run steadily and not very fast. *When Amelia rides her bike to the playground, her dog trots along behind her.*

Jog can mean to trot, especially as a form of exercise. *Elena jogs two miles every day.*

Lope means to run with a long, easy stride. *Loping behind the buffalo herd came a pack of wolves.*

Scamper means to run quickly with small steps. *At the park, little Anna scampers from one swing to another.*

Scurry means to scamper. *When it gets dark, Harry's gerbils start to scurry around in their cage.*

Sprint means to run at full speed for a short distance. *Mr. Carter always ends gym class by having us sprint around the track.*

Gallop means to run at top speed, with the largest possible steps. *With the finish line in sight, the horses are galloping as hard as they can.*

Canter means to gallop gently at less than top speed. *High Cloud's riderless horse cantered into camp two days after the battle.*

SEE **hurry** and **walk** for related words.

VERB PLUS

Sometimes when a word is added to a verb, it creates a phrase that has special meaning. Here are some phrases with **run:**

Run across means to meet by chance. *At the grocery store, Mom ran across a high-school classmate.*

Run down means to stop working. *Laird's cassette player ran down, and he had to buy new batteries.*

Run off can mean to make copies of something written. *The photocopy shop isn't going to charge us for running off ads for the Saturday car wash; it's their contribution to our fund.*

Run out means to be used up and come to an end. *We came to a town just as the gas was about to run out.*

Run through means to use up. *Damian takes such careful notes that he runs through a pencil in a week.*

Sad
adjective

Sad means not happy or not pleased. *Loni is sad because her goldfish died.*

Unhappy means sad. *Tori was unhappy when she learned that her best friend, Simka, would be moving away.*

Gloomy can mean sad and hopeless. *Floyd is feeling gloomy today because his team has lost four games in a row.*

Glum means gloomy. *"Well, of course no one likes you if you're always glum and sorry for yourself," Mom told me.*

Depressed means gloomy. *Depressed at that time by personal problems, Mozart nevertheless wrote sparkling music.*

Blue can mean gloomy. *Shawn was so blue that not even his puppy could cheer him up.*

Miserable means extremely unhappy. *Steve lost his new watch, and he's miserable.*

Sorrowful means full of sadness. *Ada enjoyed the movie until it came to a sorrowful ending.*

Mournful means sorrowful. *Grampa spent a mournful year after Grandma's death, but he's been more cheerful lately.*

Down in the mouth is an idiom that means gloomy. *Three months out of work have left Mrs. Rollins pretty much down in the mouth.*

SEE **discouraged, hopeless,** and **sorrow** for related words.
ANTONYMS: happy, glad, joyful

The sling holds the baby **snug** and happy on her father's chest.

Safe
adjective

Safe means out of any danger. *Constanza always keeps her glasses in a safe place.*

Secure means safe and without fear. *My little brother feels more secure when the hall light outside his bedroom is on.*

Protected means kept safe from danger. *Freedom of the press is protected by the First Amendment in the Bill of Rights.*

Snug means safe and comfortably protected. *The sling holds the baby snug and happy on her father's chest.*

Out of harm's way is an idiom that means away from danger. *Captain Smith had two soldiers take the children to a friendly town, out of harm's way.*

HAVE YOU HEARD...?

You may have heard people say that someone or something is "safe and sound." It means out of danger and in good shape, not injured or damaged. *The tornado turned away, leaving the trailer park safe and sound.* The two ideas are connected, and alliteration connects the sounds of the two words as well, so the phrase is common (see the Writing Tip "Using Alliteration" at **power**).

Same
adjective

Same means exactly alike. *Much to our surprise, Rita and I wore the same dress to the party.*

Identical means same. *When the machine is working right, the copies and the originals are identical.*

CONTINUED ON THE NEXT PAGE

Equal means same in number, size, or some other amount. *The recipe calls for equal parts of flour and water.*

Even can mean equal. *Gil and Lois have won an even number of games.*

Equivalent means same in value, meaning, or effect. *When Mom says, "We'll see," it's equivalent to her saying "no."*

Uniform means always the same or all the same. *Mass production systems manufacture uniform products in large numbers.*

Synonymous means having the same or nearly the same meaning. *In the phrase "calm, cool, and collected," the three main words are synonymous.*

SEE **similar** for related words.

HAVE YOU HEARD...?
. . . .
You may have heard people say, "Six of one, half a dozen of the other." This means that the two items or ideas are enough the same that there is little reason to choose between them. The phrase is usually an answer to a question. *"Shall we go now or later?" "Six of one, half a dozen of the other."*

Sassy
adjective

Sassy means showing no respect and talking back a lot. *"I'm never baby-sitting with those sassy kids again!" exclaimed Gavin.*

Fresh is an informal word that means sassy. *Samantha got fresh with the restaurant manager, so she's gone.*

Bold can mean too free in manner and not careful of good behavior. *The bold little boy marched up to the fountain and jumped right in.*

Forward can mean bold and too sure of yourself. *Amy Lou is so forward that she invited herself to my party!*

Flippant means bold and not properly serious. *When Alma asked Roy for advice, he made a flippant remark that hurt her feelings.*

Pert means bold in an amusing, harmless way. *Suzy acts pert, but her grandfather likes it.*

Impudent is a formal word that means very bold and rude. *As the hero's impudent servant, young actor Phil Williams is very funny.*

SEE **rude** for related words.
ANTONYMS: respectful, well-behaved

Satisfy
verb

Satisfy means to grant a desire or make someone happy by giving what is needed. *The store promises it will do anything it can to satisfy the customers.*

Content means to satisfy. *If Shonna apologizes in front of everyone, will that content Gail?*

Please means to make someone happy. It suggests being or giving what is wanted. *That waitress always pleases her customers with good service and a friendly manner.*

Gratify means to give someone strong pleasure. It suggests something more than what is needed. *Gratified by all the attention from her family, Great-Grandma had the best birthday ever.*

Gladden means to make someone happy, especially after worry or sadness. *We were gladdened to hear that Uncle Xavier's house was spared by the storm.*

Hit the spot is an idiom that means to satisfy someone perfectly. *Angela had been shoveling snow for an hour, and the hot chocolate really hit the spot.*

Warm the cockles of your heart is an idiom that means to please and encourage you. It is a phrase used mostly in writing and speeches. *This movie shows real characters overcoming real problems, and it will warm the cockles of your heart.*

WORD STORY

What are *cockles,* anyway? The cockle is a kind of shellfish. The Romans thought that these shellfish resembled the largest parts of the human heart. They believed that these parts of the heart were the center of people's feelings.

Angela had been shoveling snow for an hour, and the hot chocolate really **hit the spot.**

Save
verb

Save means to make safe or keep safe from danger. *Smoke alarms save many lives.*

Rescue means to save with quick or strong actions. *The Coast Guard rescued the crew from the burning freighter.*

Deliver can mean to save from a danger or suffering. *Education delivers more people from poverty than athletics can.*

Ransom means to save a captive by paying a price. *The knights ransomed the kidnapped princess with two large sacks of gold and a small sack of gems.*

Salvage means to save property from fire, flood, or other disaster. *Very little could be salvaged from the homes destroyed by the flood.*

Bail someone out is an idiom that means to save someone who is in trouble. *When Mr. Gordon was out of work and needed money, Dad bailed him out.*

Say
verb

Say means to make words with the voice. It is also used about written words. *"Let's go to the store," said Dad. What time does the invitation say the party starts?*

Express means to put an idea or feeling into words. *Rae expresses her innermost feelings in her poetry.*

Utter means to say or express. *Reverend Slater was so moved that he could barely utter his thanks.*

Comment means to say an opinion or something that helps to understand. *Mr. Maxwell will comment on the proposal to have school all year.*

Remark means to say in a few words. *"A great science project—very imaginative and thorough," remarked Ms. Samuels.*

Mention means to remark or to say something about a subject. *Reshard mentioned that he liked that movie. Did Connie mention our argument?*

Saying
noun

Saying means a brief common statement generally believed to be true. *You know that old saying, "An elephant never forgets."*

Proverb means a usually old, often-repeated saying. It gives advice or states a general truth. *As often as I recite the proverb, "A penny saved is a penny earned," I never have any money!*

Moral can mean a short statement that sums up the meaning of a story. *The moral of the story is, "Treat people as you want to be treated."*

Motto means a word or phrase chosen to express what a person or a group believes in most deeply. *"All for one and one for all" was the motto of the Three Musketeers.*

Slogan means a motto. *Mr. Rosario is offering a prize to the employee who thinks of the best company slogan.*

Expression can mean a familiar word or phrase with a particular meaning. *If Jason uses the expression "totally awesome" again today, I'll scream!*

"All for one and one for all" was the **motto** of the Three Musketeers.

Months of **scanty** rainfall have dried up the fields and ruined the crops.

Scanty
adjective

Scanty means not enough or barely enough. *Months of scanty rainfall have dried up the fields and ruined the crops.*

Skimpy means scanty. It may suggest unwillingness to give or spend. *"How can I have any fun," Cora complained, "on such a skimpy allowance?"*

Measly can mean scanty. It suggests scorn. This meaning is informal. *Orin sent four letters to his pen pal and got back only one measly postcard.*

Bare can mean just enough. *Mahal's piano teacher says three hours' practice a week is the bare minimum to improve her playing.*

Inadequate means not as much as is necessary. *In poor neighborhoods, the number of parks and hospitals is often inadequate.*

Insufficient means inadequate. *The amount of clothes collected in the clothing drive was still insufficient for the town's homeless.*

Deficient is a formal word that means lacking something. *Many American diets are deficient in fresh fruits and vegetables.*

Meager is a formal word that means scanty. *"This year's meager sales," said the company president, "make bonuses impossible."*

SEE **rare** for related words.
ANTONYMS: abundant, plentiful, sufficient

Scare
verb

Scare means to make someone afraid. *Reba's loud laughter scared the baby.*

Frighten means to fill someone with sudden fear. *Angel was only playing, but his sudden rush toward them frightened Stephanie.*

Alarm means to cause someone to worry about possible danger. *When the dog started barking late at night, it alarmed Poppa.*

Horrify means to make someone feel weak with fear. *Molly was horrified when she realized she had left her cat out overnight.*

Terrify means to fill someone with very great fear. *One look down from the high balcony terrified Gaston.*

Terrorize means to cause great fear in someone on purpose. *The gang members terrorized the people in their neighborhood.*

Bully means to control someone through fear. *Conchita is brave, and no one tries to bully her.*

Intimidate means to control someone through fear. *Jay's angry threats intimidated his brother.*

Make your flesh creep means to scare you so much that you feel it all over your body. *Just talking about the stitches she had gotten made Anna's flesh creep.*

Make your hair stand on end means to scare you so much that you feel it all over your body. *"Honestly, Valerie," said her father, "I don't see why you watch movies that make your hair stand on end."*

SEE **afraid, fear,** and **terrifying** for related words.

WORD STORY

Alarm comes from two Italian words that mean "to arms!" If danger threatened a city or military camp, soldiers were given this order to get hold of their weapons. *Alarm* became the name of this order in English, as in "give the alarm." Then it was used as a verb meaning to warn someone of danger, and now it means to cause worry about possible danger.

Scatter
verb

Scatter means to throw or spread things without aiming, so that they become far apart. *Raoul scattered bread on the water, hoping to attract the ducks.*

Strew means to throw, drop, or put things across a surface in no order. *To find her keys, Jane turned her purse upside down and strewed the contents over the kitchen table.*

Shed can mean to strew. *Linda shed her winter hat, gloves, and boots all over the apartment.*

Sprinkle means to scatter tiny things, such as drops of water or crystals of sugar. *Before adding milk, Therese sprinkled raisins and nuts on her cereal.*

Sow means to scatter seeds so that they will grow. *When she is finished sowing, Mwaka must carry water to the fields.*

ANTONYMS: gather, collect

Raoul **scattered** bread on the water, hoping to attract the ducks.

Scoff
verb

Scoff means to make rude fun of something in order to show scorn or disbelief. *Justin scoffed at Victor's claim that he did all the math problems in thirty minutes.*

Jeer means to laugh in a rude, scornful way at someone or something. *The fans jeered when the umpire threw the manager out of the game.*

Pooh-pooh means to make fun of something in order to treat it as unimportant. *Armond pooh-poohs the Lane Tech team, but he's practicing hard for the game against them.*

Sneer means to show scorn by insulting words or looks. *The villain in the movie is so boring—all he does is sneer and shoot.*

SEE **ridicule** for related words.

Scold
verb

Scold means to speak sharply and angrily to someone who has done wrong. *We could hear our neighbor scolding her children for leaving their backyard without permission.*

Lecture can mean to scold. *My mom caught me using lipstick, and she lectured me for a week.*

Reprimand is a formal word that means to express official disapproval. *Sydney was reprimanded and made to apologize for printing gossip in the class magazine.*

Bawl out means to scold loudly. *Once Phil's parents were sure he wasn't hurt, they both started bawling him out together.*

Chew out means to scold loudly. *The coach chewed the whole team out the day they lost 20 to 3.*

Tell off means to scold someone in a full, deliberate way, saying everything you want to. *When Mr. Rivera finished telling off the rude clerk, everyone in the store applauded.*

Give someone a piece of your mind is an idiom that means to scold someone in a full, deliberate way, saying everything you want to. *"If that kid throws sand at us one more time," Earlene said, "I'm going to give him a piece of my mind."*

SEE **blame** and **criticize** for related words.
ANTONYM: praise

Scorn
noun

Scorn means a feeling that someone or something deserves to be insulted and rejected without any respect. *Grandma and Grandpa felt that the shopkeeper treated them with scorn because they were dressed in old work clothes to help clean our attic.*

Contempt means a strong feeling of scorn, combined with anger and deep dislike. *Mrs. Sosa's face showed her contempt for the people who had littered the park.*

Snobbishness means a feeling of being better than other people and of wanting to know only certain superior people. *Heidi is fed up with Jacquelyn's snobbishness about clothes and money.*

Disdain means a feeling that someone or something is worthless. *The old violinist speaks of modern music with disdain.*

Search
verb

Search means to look for something. *The shepherd searched for his lost lamb all night.*

Seek means to search for. It suggests something not lost but unknown. *Mrs. Dawkins drove through the snowstorm, seeking a place to park until visibility improved.*

Hunt can mean to search for something. *Kai hunted everywhere for his bicycle, but it had vanished.*

Rummage can mean to search for something in a disorderly way. *Ellen rummaged through every drawer, looking for her lost locket.*

Ransack means to treat a place in a rough, disorderly way while searching. *Police found that burglars had ransacked the apartment.*

Pry means to look curiously, especially at things that aren't your business. *"I don't mean to pry," Mr. Walters said to his neighbor, "but I wondered if those birds in your garage are chickens?"*

Beat the bushes is an idiom that means to search as thoroughly as possible. *Dexter can't find his library book, so he's beating the bushes for it.*

Leave no stone unturned is an idiom that means to search as thoroughly as possible. *Police promise to leave no stone unturned in their effort to find the counterfeiters.*

SEE **examine** for related words.

Police found that burglars had **ransacked** the apartment.

363

Secret
adjective

Secret means kept from the knowledge of others. *The spy stole the company's secret soft drink formula.*

Confidential means told or written as a secret. *She started to open the letter but saw that it was addressed to her brother, and the envelope was marked "confidential."*

Private can mean secret or confidential. *"How dare you read my private diary?" Tim asked angrily.*

Hush-hush is an informal word that means very secret. *"The surprise party for Lara is on," Flora said, "and it's still hush-hush."*

Undercover means working or done in a secret way. *An undercover insurance investigator found out who started the fire.*

Classified can mean kept secret from most people by government or military orders. *"All troop movements," Col. Dawkins told reporters questioning her, "are classified information."*

Under your hat means not told to anyone. *"I know what Tom said to Ellie when he called her, but I'm keeping it under my hat," announced Gloria.*

The spy stole the company's **secret** soft drink formula.

See
verb

See means to know something by using your eyes. *Chantal saw long lines for the movie and walked on by.*

Behold means to see. It is an older word, usually found in writing. *The emperor Montezuma first beheld Cortes in November 1519.*

Observe means to see and give attention to. *Mai observed a flock of geese flying southward.*

Notice means to see and give attention to. *Mary pointed out the new billboard, which her mother had not noticed.*

Perceive is a formal word that can mean to see and understand. *Some artists perceive beauty in common household objects.*

Witness means to see or be present at something. *Elana witnessed the whole robbery from her window across the street.*

Sight means to see something, usually something far off. *"We should sight whales," said Captain Lopes, "an hour or so out of port."*

Glimpse means to see something briefly. *Roberto glimpsed the porpoise in the water, but it was gone before Janet could see it.*

SEE **watch** for related words.

VERB PLUS

Sometimes when a word is added to a verb it creates a phrase that has special meaning. Here are some phrases with **see.**

See about means to take care of something or attend to something, especially a problem or a responsibility. *Mr. Rodriguez is at the store seeing about some deliveries, but he'll be here in time to coach the game.*

See off means to go with someone to the place where a journey will start. *Every school morning, Shonna's dog walks down to the bus stop to see her off.*

See out means to finish something, especially a job. *Mom's receptionist is going to work for another dentist but will see out this month at Mom's office.*

See through means to understand the real purpose or nature of something. *Joan saw through Dick's unfriendliness and realized that he was lonely and shy.*

Send
verb

Send means to cause to move from one place to another. *Mother sent Vanessa on an errand to the store.*

Ship means to send by ship or some other vehicle. *Many countries shipped food and supplies to the area damaged by the volcano.*

Mail means to send by the post office and letter carriers. *When she goes on a trip, Tasha always mails postcards to her friends.*

Transmit can mean to send signals or programs from one place to another. *Communications satellites transmitted television coverage of the Olympics around the world.*

Dispatch means to send quickly. *The hospital dispatched an ambulance as soon as the news of the accident came in.*

Forward can mean to send on further. *The post office will forward the Jiangs' mail to their new address.*

Export means to send something out of one country to be sold in another. *Honduras exports bananas, coffee, timber, and other products.*

SEE **carry** and **move** for related words.
ANTONYM: receive

WATCH IT!

People sometimes mix up **import** and **export**. *Import* means to bring something into a country. *Export* means to send something out of a country. One way to keep these words straight is to remember that *im-* looks like *in* and *ex-* is in *exit*.

Separate
verb

'A house divided against itself cannot stand.' I believe this government cannot endure permanently half slave and half free.**"**

— Abraham Lincoln (1809–1865)

Separate means to keep things apart or take something apart. *The highway separates these apartment buildings from the neighboring houses. Separate dark and light clothes before you wash them.*

Divide means to separate. It is often used about equal parts or sharing. *Ms. Polanak divided the class into teams for a softball game.*

Part means to separate. It is often used about things that were strongly joined. *Parted by war, the sisters met again by accident, years later.*

Split can mean to divide something as if by cutting. *Tom and Dave split the money they got for the empty cans.*

CONTINUED ON THE NEXT PAGE

Segregate can mean to separate people of different races. *The people of South Africa were the last in the world to be officially segregated.*

Sever can mean to break a connection or to separate a part from the rest. *Mr. Dankworth's finger was severed in a farming accident.*

Partition means to divide something as if by walls. *The Louisiana Purchase was eventually partitioned among fifteen states.*

ANTONYMS: unite, join

WRITER'S CHOICE

At the time, the armed forces were highly segregated. The only military jobs available for blacks were menial, like mess [food] attendants and ditch diggers and latrine cleaners.

—James Haskins, *Thurgood Marshall: A Life for Justice*

Why *segregated*? There are many different kinds of jobs in the armed forces, from fighting to washing dishes. When World War II started, United States soldiers were not given different kinds of jobs according to what they'd be good at, but were separated according to their race.

Series
noun

Series means several things one after another. It suggests that the things are similar. *After a series of robberies, shopowners are nervous.*

Sequence can mean a series. It suggests a clear pattern, in which each thing leads to or causes the next. *For the spacecraft to have the right orbit, its engines must fire in the proper sequence.*

Succession means several things or people that happen in order. It emphasizes that they are all parts of one process in time. *A succession of great African American artists has enriched this country's culture.*

Round can mean a familiar series of events or activities. *Grandma's day is a round of visits with her friends in the neighborhood.*

String can mean several things in a line or row. *The movie's plot is just a string of car chases and unbelievable stunts.*

Chain can mean a connected group of things. It suggests things that are thought of together. *The Mendozas own a chain of stores.*

Serious
adjective

Serious means showing deep thought and purpose. *"I am the man of the family now," said Tom in a serious voice.*

Earnest means serious and full of strong feeling. *The governor made an earnest appeal for help from the federal government after his state was struck by a hurricane.*

Sober can mean serious and not playful. *The story of the UFO sounds strange, but witnesses insist that it's the sober truth.*

Solemn means serious, formal, and impressive. *The President takes a solemn oath to uphold the Constitution.*

Grave can mean very serious and dignified. *What makes Ernesto's jokes so funny is the grave face he uses to tell them.*

Staid means serious and settled in your way of doing things. *Ms. Welles seems staid, but she's the oldest person who ever bungee-jumped from Larkin Bridge.*

SEE **firm** and **formal** for related words.
ANTONYMS: frivolous, lighthearted

Severe
adjective

Severe means following the rules without gentleness or sympathy. *Mr. Turner's severe boss refused to let him leave work early on the day of his daughter's piano recital.*

Strict means very careful of the rules. *A space shuttle launch is carried out with strict attention to detail.*

Stern means severe and firm in control or judgment. *The vice-principal is stern with students who make trouble.*

Harsh can mean severe and pitiless or even cruel. *"Turning away sick poor people?" asked Mrs. Palmer. "How can a hospital be that harsh?"*

With an iron hand is an idiom that means stern or harsh in power. *For more than 20 years, dictator Joseph Stalin ruled the Soviet Union with an iron hand.*

SEE **rigid** for related words.
ANTONYMS: considerate, good-natured, kind

Shake
verb

Shake means to move quickly up and down or back and forth. *Their old washing machine always began to shake during the spin cycle.*

Tremble means to shake because of fear or excitement. *When Fluffy sees a pigeon at the window, she trembles all over and meows.*

Shiver means to shake because of cold or fear. *Evonne got caught in the rain and came home soaked and shivering.*

Shudder means to shake because of horror or fear. *Marguerite shuddered when she saw the rat in the garbage.*

Quiver means to shake slightly and quickly. *The dart continued to quiver for a moment after it landed in the target.*

Vibrate means to move rapidly a short distance back and forth, like a guitar string. *When the subway goes by underneath, this whole building vibrates.*

Quake means to shake violently. *The tunnel collapsing under the street made the whole building quake.*

Teeter means to shake as if about to fall. *"Look out!" yelled Avram as the ladder teetered.*

Totter can mean to teeter. *The tottering Oxner administration cannot win this election.*

Wobble means to shake or tremble. *Dora looked at the canyon below and felt her legs wobble.*

WORDS AT PLAY

My brother had quite an ambition:
To fix his car's awful condition.
    It would shiver and shake,
    It would quiver and quake,
Before he turned on the ignition!

369

The race was so close that the losers felt no **disgrace**.

Shame
noun

Shame means the painful unhappiness caused by knowing that you have done something wrong or stupid. *When she forgot her lines for the third time, the actress burst into tears of shame.*

Humiliation means shame and loss of pride. *Already losing by six goals, the team spent halftime in a silence of humiliation.*

Disgrace means loss of other people's approval and respect. *The race was so close that the losers felt no disgrace.*

Dishonor means disgrace and loss of self-respect. *When Uncle Ranee's business failed, he avoided any sense of dishonor by paying every debt, even though it took him years.*

SEE **ashamed, embarrassed,** and **sorry** for related words.
ANTONYM: pride

Shape
noun

Shape means the outward appearance of something, including its length, width, and thickness, but not its color or material. *Myra's grandfather gave her a locket in the shape of a heart.*

Form means shape. *Luisa shaped the clay into the form of a horse.*

Figure can mean shape. *Archaeologists found figures of birds carved on the ancient tombs.*

Outline means a line that shows the shape of something. *The scenery for the play showed only outlines of buildings with no details.*

Contour means an outline. *The contour of Italy on a map looks like a boot.*

CONTINUED ON THE NEXT PAGE

Profile means a view of someone or something from one side, showing its shape. *The biology book includes pictures of the profile of a child's head at various ages from birth to ten years old.*

Silhouette means a picture that is cut out of black paper, or a dark shape on a light background. *Raydell's prize drawing shows the silhouettes of chimneys and water towers against the sunset.*

WORD STORY

Silhouette comes from Étienne de Silhouette, a French government official in the 1700s. There are two stories explaining why. Some books say that his hobby was cutting out profile portraits in black paper. Other books say that this kind of portrait was inexpensive and popular at the time and named after him because he was so good at cutting government costs. Whatever the truth was, the word is now the main reason for remembering him.

Share
verb

> "Grief can take care of itself, but to get the full value of joy you must have somebody to divide it with."
>
> — **Mark Twain (1835–1910)**

Share means to divide something into parts and give part to each person. *Ricardo and his brothers shared the peanut brittle.*

Portion means to share. *The counties agreed to portion water from the reservoir for their irrigation projects.*

Divide can mean to share. *After selling all the cans they had collected, Roy and Shirley divided the money.*

Divvy is a slang word that means to share. *"Come on, Flora, divvy up that pie!" said her friend Hideyo.*

Ration means to give out limited amounts of something because there isn't much. *The government was forced to ration gasoline during World War II.*

SEE **distribute** for related words.

Sharp
adjective

Sharp means quick-witted and clever in noticing and taking advantage of things. *Even Tabitha, sharp as she is, has never scored enough power points in this computer game to reach level seven.*

Keen can mean quick to notice and understand things clearly. *A keen observer, Swift Horse immediately sensed the silent presence of the mountain lion.*

Acute can mean able to notice and understand things that others miss. *Because Jamal is so acute, his photographs catch the details that make the neighborhood special.*

Knowing can mean noticing and understanding a great deal. *Hardware Warehouse is popular with knowing shoppers because of its broad range of merchandise and bargain prices.*

Shrewd means sharp and keen. *Mrs. Kellers is a shrewd businesswoman and rarely makes a bad deal.*

Canny means shrewd and cautious. *Canny Ms. Jenkins noticed the check was forged.*

SEE **smart** and **wise** for related words.
ANTONYMS: dull, slow

Shelter
noun

Shelter means something that covers or protects from the weather or from danger. *During the rain, the church picnic continued under the shelter of the tents.*

Cover can mean shelter. *The baby crane took cover between the long legs of its mother.*

Haven can mean a place of shelter and safety. *The Drama Club is Loretta's haven from problems at home.*

Refuge means a shelter or a place of safety. It suggests escape from trouble. *The first National Wildlife Refuge was created by Theodore Roosevelt to protect pelicans.*

Asylum can mean refuge. *The refugees asked for political asylum in a nearby country.*

CONTINUED ON THE NEXT PAGE

Sanctuary can mean a refuge or place of protection, especially one where animals are protected from hunters or other dangers. *Behind the zoo is a bird sanctuary, closed to people.*

Preserve can mean a place where animals and plants are protected. *This whole area within the bend of the river is a wildlife preserve.*

SEE **guard** for related words.

> **WORD STORY**
> . . . .
> *Sanctuary* comes from a Latin word meaning "a holy place." In the Middle Ages, people could avoid arrest by staying in a church. Because a church is a holy place, the laws at that time said that a person could be protected there.

Shine
verb

Shine means to send out or reflect bright light. *The sun has been shining for about five billion years.*

Gleam means to shine. It often suggests light with darkness around it, or light from a hard surface. *Every weekend, Ms. Timkins washes and waxes her car until it gleams.*

Glow means to shine steadily because of heat, or as if with heat. *Paolo blew softly on the lighted charcoal until it began to glow.*

Beam means to shine very brightly. *Kids play long after dark under the beaming lights of the playground.*

Glare means to shine so brightly that it hurts the eyes. *We shaded Rex's eyes from the glaring sun.*

Glisten means to shine because wet, or as if wet. *Ramon's eyes glistened with tears, but his voice was firm and strong.*

Shimmer means to shine faintly and perhaps unsteadily. *The clouds in the painting seem to shimmer with moonlight.*

SEE **bright** and **flash** for related words.

We shaded Rex's eyes from the **glaring** sun.

Short
adjective

Short means taking only a small amount of time. *"This was supposed to be a short assignment, but it's taking forever,"* Regina sighed.

Brief means taking a small amount of time. *Ken gave a brief talk about collecting beetles.*

Thumbnail means very short. *Dario gave a thumbnail description of the baseball game: "They got the runs; we didn't."*

Concise means brief and clear in meaning. *Oliver's report was so concise that he covered the subject in less than fifteen minutes.*

Summary means brief and limited to main ideas. *Mr. Perrera has his classes hand in summary outlines of each week's reading.*

Crisp can mean short and sure. *"Buy the company," read Mrs. Newton's crisp telegram.*

Curt means very brief and abrupt. *The third time Brady asked Rachel out, she gave him a curt reply.*

ANTONYMS: lengthy, long, wordy

Shorten
verb

Shorten means to reduce the length of something. *Megan's mother shortened Megan's old dresses to fit little Cassie.*

Abbreviate means to shorten a word by leaving out some of its letters. *My grandfather abbreviated his name from Orlovsky to Orr.*

Summarize means to shorten something by giving only its main ideas. *To summarize, the meaning of Mrs. Hanley's talk was, "Just say no."*

Prune means to shorten something, by cutting out unnecessary or undesirable parts. *The senator pruned his speech by cutting out three anecdotes.*

Abridge means to shorten something, especially by using fewer words. *Even abridged, the talking book edition of this novel is on six tapes.*

Boil down can mean to shorten something to its most basic form or parts. *Boiled down, the letter says that the building has been sold.*

Put in a nutshell is an idiom that means to boil down. *"Let me put it in a nutshell," said Barbara. "No!"*

SEE **decrease** and **shrink** for related words.
ANTONYMS: extend, lengthen

Leah **shrieked** so much on the rollercoaster, she can barely talk.

Shout
verb

Shout means to speak out in a loud voice to get someone's attention. *"Watch out!" Joshua shouted.*

Holler is an informal word that means to shout. *If you kids don't stop hollering, there's going to be trouble.*

Bellow can mean to shout in a deep, angry voice. *"You will pay for this treachery!" bellowed Shaka.*

Yell means to shout as loud as you can when you are excited. *The crowd yelled when the race began.*

Call means to speak in a louder voice than usual. *"Andrea, call your mother to dinner, please," said Grandma.*

Cry means to call out, with or without words. *"Ouch!" cried Keith when he hit his arm on the door.*

Scream means to cry out in a very loud voice, especially because of fear, anger, or excitement. *"I won! I won!" Scott screamed.*

Shriek means to cry out in a shrill voice, especially because of fear, anger, or excitement. *Leah shrieked so much on the rollercoaster, she can barely talk.*

> **WRITING TIP: Personification**
>
> A writer might say that "the wind shrieked through the trees" or "the storm screamed through town." In these examples, the wind and the storm are given qualities that make them seem human. When something that isn't human is given human qualities, this is called *personification* (per son′ə fə kā′shən). Writers often use personification to present things or ideas in a more vivid and understandable way. For example, "Democracy stands hand in hand with Freedom" is more effective than "Democracy and freedom go together."

375

Show
verb

Show means to cause something to be seen. *Patrick wants to show his new shoes to Saburo.*

Display can mean to show things in a way that gets people's attention. *Thalia yawned widely, displaying her braces.*

Exhibit can mean to show something publicly. *Tara exhibited her paintings at the arts and crafts show.*

Parade can mean to show something as openly as possible. *I hate the way Leslie parades her new jewelry.*

Demonstrate means to show something in a way that helps people understand. *The company rented a booth at the county fair and demonstrated its new milking machine.*

Expose means to show something openly where anyone can see. It suggests previous concealment. *Low tide at the beach exposed seaweed and shells.*

Point out means to show where something is or to call attention to something. *Manuel pointed out all the sights of Chicago to his relatives.*

SEE **guide** and **turn up** (at **turn**) for related words.
ANTONYMS: conceal, hide

At school today, Caitlin **showed off** her trophy from the wheelchair race.

VERB PLUS
. . . .
Sometimes when a word is added to a verb, it creates a phrase with special meaning. Here are some phrases with **show:**

Show off means to display something you are proud of. *At school today, Caitlin showed off her trophy from the wheelchair race.*

Show out means to lead someone to an exit. It suggests a formal or official situation. *"I was showing out Mr. Derby's guest," the butler told police, "when I heard the shot."*

Show up can mean to come to a place. *Raul always shows up for dance rehearsals on time and well prepared.*

Showy
adjective

Showy means attracting attention by being very easy to see, especially in a bright way. *Tropical forest birds often have showy feathers.*

Loud can mean showy in dress or manner. This meaning is informal. *Lonnie gets embarrassed when her dad wears loud clothes.*

Flashy can mean showy. It suggests something that gets more attention than it deserves. *The store windows are flashy, but the stuff they sell there isn't any good.*

Gaudy means too bright and colorful. It suggests something cheap and in bad taste. *In the motel lobby hung a gaudy red and gold painting of a crying clown.*

ANTONYM: drab

Tropical forest birds often have **showy** feathers.

Shrink
verb

Shrink means to become smaller or make smaller. *Luke's shirt shrank in the wash, but it still fits him.*

Miniaturize means to make something very much smaller. *A miniaturized radio in the wolf's collar tells naturalists where it is.*

Compress means to make something smaller by pressure. *A hay baler compresses alfalfa into bales and binds them with twine.*

Condense means to shrink by increasing thickness. *You have to add water to condensed soup before you heat it.*

Narrow means to shrink, especially across. *"Put it down," growled Walt, his eyes narrowing in anger.*

Contract means to shrink, especially lengthwise. *When the humidity decreases, the doors will contract, and we'll be able to shut them all the way.*

Shrivel means to shrink by drying up. *Without water, the rosebuds shriveled into little brown balls.*

SEE **decrease** and **shorten** for related words.
ANTONYM: expand

Shut
verb

Shut means to move something so that it stops being open. *"Shut the gate so that the dog won't get out,"* Rachel called to her little brother.

Close means to shut. It emphasizes that no opening remains. *"Let's close the windows before we leave—it looks like rain,"* said Mrs. Torres.

Slam means to shut something hard, especially a door. *Dad told Fern not to slam the door, or she'll have to stay inside.*

Draw can mean to close curtains or window shades. *"It's time to look at our vacation slides!" cried Mr. Benson, drawing the blinds.*

Seal can mean to close something tightly and everywhere. It often suggests using glue or some other substance. *"Don't seal that envelope, Lara," said her father, "I want to put in a photograph."*

Plug means to close an opening by filling it with a wad or block of some substance. *The Heimlich maneuver can remove an object plugging the windpipe and save someone who is choking.*

ANTONYM: open

VERB PLUS

Sometimes when a word is added to a verb, it creates a phrase that has special meaning. Here are some phrases with **shut:**

Shut down means to stop activities. *It is always sad to see the amusement park shut down at the end of the summer.*

Shut in means to keep inside. *The twins have chicken pox and will be shut in all week.*

Shut off means to turn something off. *Mom told Nial to shut off the TV and do his homework.*

Shut out means to exclude. *Because Tan hadn't seen the movie they were talking about, he felt shut out of the conversation.* **Shut out** can also mean to defeat a team without allowing it to score. *The Cougars shut out Wilson Junior High, three goals to none.*

As soon as we brought it home, the **timid** pup crawled under the sofa.

Shy
adjective

Shy means lacking confidence and uneasy in the presence of others. *Jeff was too shy to try out for the chorus.*

Bashful means shy and easily embarrassed. *Can you believe that Ajani used to be bashful?*

Timid can mean shy and frightened. *As soon as we brought it home, the timid pup crawled under the sofa.*

Modest can mean unwilling to call attention to yourself. *Hank is so modest, he doesn't want to run for class president.*

Retiring means shy and tending to keep to yourself. *Helen's such a quiet and retiring person, you don't notice her much at first.*

Demure means pretending to be shy, in order to seem good. *"The maid acts demure, but she's really an undercover cop," said Cindy, explaining the plot of the movie.*

Coy can mean pretending to be shy in order to appear charming or meek. *It's time for Chantal to stop being coy and tell Darrell that she likes him.*

ANTONYMS: assured, confident

HAVE YOU HEARD...?

You may have heard people say "Once bitten, twice shy." In this saying, *shy* means frightened and timid. Someone who has been hurt learns to be afraid of whatever caused the pain. Another saying with the same idea is "The burned child fears the fire." Both sayings suggest that people may not be careful enough until they get hurt.

Sick
adjective

Sick means in poor health. It suggests a temporary condition and expected recovery. *No, Leo's not sick; that's his allergy making him sneeze.*

Ailing can mean sick. *Mrs. Diaz is ailing today, so the meeting has been postponed.*

Unwell means sick. It often suggests a sickness that is not serious, or that is not yet diagnosed. *"I cannot accompany you to the ballet as I am, most unfortunately, unwell," said Mr. Gleason's small, handwritten note.*

Ill means sick. It may suggest a serious condition and a slow recovery. *"Grandfather was ill for months," Stacey told her friends, "but he's a lot better now."*

Diseased means having a disease or showing signs of disease. It is not often used about individual people. *Scientists suspect that whales beach themselves because they are diseased.*

ANTONYMS: well, healthy

IDIOMS

There are many idioms that mean sick. Here are some:

laid up	out of sorts	under par
not yourself	run down	under the weather

Can you think of others?

Sign
noun

Sign means an indication of something that will happen. *The first red and yellow leaves are a sign that summer is over.*

Indicator can mean a sign. *A sudden drop in air pressure may be an indicator of an approaching storm.*

Symptom means a sign, especially of illness or suffering. *Symptoms of neighborhood poverty include closed stores and empty buildings.*

Omen means a sign or something believed to be a sign. *Daniel thinks it's an omen of good luck if he sees an all-white pigeon.*

Warning means something that tells of possible trouble or danger to come. *"Let that be a warning to you," Alejandro told the sobbing bully.*

CONTINUED ON THE NEXT PAGE

Premonition means a strong feeling that something in particular will happen, usually something bad. *Judith's grandmother had a premonition that the train would crash, so she drove instead.*

Straw in the wind is an idiom that means a sign. *Dana's mom hasn't said anything about quitting her job, but there are plenty of straws in the wind.*

SEE **emblem** and **evidence** for related words.

Silent
adjective

Silent means without noise. *At night, the house was dark and silent.*

Quiet means with little noise or no noise. *At the library, Lani tried everything to keep the baby quiet.*

Still means without noise or motion. *After the swimmers left, the lake grew still.*

Noiseless and **soundless** mean making no sounds. *Dr. Ribera tried to be noiseless as she moved from bed to bed. One patient's yellow light was blinking in a soundless call for a nurse's attention.*

Inaudible means impossible to hear. *Kyra was so afraid of being overheard that her whispers to Grace were almost inaudible.*

SEE **quiet** for related words.
ANTONYM: noisy

"Silence is golden."
— Thomas Carlyle
(1795–1881)

After the swimmers left, the lake grew **still.**

Similar means much the same, but not completely the same. *The twins have similar haircuts, but Andy's hair is a bit longer than Jack's.*

Like and **alike** mean similar. *Like* is used before or after things it describes. *Alike* is used only after the things it describes. *Marcy's wheelchair is like Ted's, but smaller. If they were any more alike, it would be hard to tell them apart.*

Comparable means similar enough to be compared. *The two cars are comparable in many ways—it's the price that makes the difference.*

Corresponding means similar. It suggests that two people or things have related places in their separate systems. *Plug the cord from your CD player into the corresponding sockets on your stereo.*

Parallel can mean corresponding. *Though Pike is a city school and Moran is in the suburbs, the two schools have parallel funding problems.*

Of a piece is an idiom that means similar, as if cut from the same piece of fabric. *"We are tired," stormed Mrs. Cowan, "of having millions of widely different senior citizens treated as if they were all of a piece."*

SEE **match** and **same** for related words.

WRITING TIP: Simile and Metaphor

Writers often say that two things are similar, comparing them in order to add liveliness and interest to their writing. A *simile* compares two things by the use of "as" or "like."

> *As quick as a panther, Don Miguel leaped to pull the children from the path of the angry stallion. Like steel, his powerful arms held them against his chest.*

A *metaphor* compares two things without using "as" or "like."

> *The palomino was frozen sunlight, rearing defiantly in the corral.*

Similes and metaphors make writing lively by adding feelings that come from the things that are compared to the main ideas. Here we feel that the man has more than human speed and strength, and that the horse is so shining that it makes light. But too many similes and metaphors, especially in a row, can distract your reader from your main ideas. Use them when you want to make a strong point, not just because you can.

A **solitary** horse stood on the horizon.

Single
adjective

Single means one and no more. *Felipe was the single student with a perfect test score.*

Only means single. *"I locked my only set of keys inside the house," moaned Tad.*

Sole means single. It emphasizes that there are no others. *Until the 1992 election of Carol Moseley-Braun to the Senate, Edward Brooke was the sole African American to serve there since the 1800s.*

Lone means single. It suggests that others may exist, but that this one is alone. It is often used in poems and stories. *As night fell, the travelers directed their steps toward the lone house in the empty valley.*

Solitary means lone. *A solitary horse stood on the horizon.*

Unique means one of a kind, unlike any other. *Lola likes the unique sweaters her grandmother knits for her.*

Singular is a formal word that can mean unique. *Weather records prove that our Fourth of July snowstorm was a singular event.*

SEE **alone** and **rare** for related words.

WATCH IT !

Sometimes people say that something is "very unique" or "the most unique" of all. This use of the word is informal. Many people object to it, because *unique* already means one of a kind. You can't have something that is "very one of a kind" or "the most one of a kind." A thing either is unlike any other, or it isn't. If you are writing for a serious purpose, use the word *unique* only to mean that something is unlike anything else, and use the word without any modifiers.

Size
noun

Size means the amount of space something takes up. *The entertainment center was such a large size that it seemed to take over the family room.*

Proportions means size. It suggests that the space has been or could be measured. *The Flexners are delighted with the large proportions of their new apartment.*

Volume can mean size. It is used especially when height, breadth, and width are all considered. *The sheer volume of the landslide is difficult to comprehend.*

Area means the amount of surface something takes up. *Lily's snow fort covered half the area of the front yard.*

Extent means how far something stretches out. *Opened to its fullest extent, the dining room table could comfortably seat twelve people.*

Dimensions can mean extent. *The land of the Navajos has the largest dimensions of any American Indian territory.*

SEE **room** for related words.

Slant
verb

Slant means to go up or down at an angle. *My handwriting always slants to the left.*

Slope means to slant, usually gradually. *The sand dunes slope towards the ocean.*

Incline can mean to slope. *The road inclines upward from the railroad tracks.*

Tip means to slant, often so much that something falls over. *The way Mr. Simpson tips back in his chair while talking makes his classes very nervous.*

Lean means to stand at an angle. *This postcard shows the Leaning Tower of Pisa, in Italy.*

Tilt means to slant or lean. *Beau tilted the hologram back and forth to see the changing picture.*

The leopard spends much of the day **drowsing** in a tree.

Sleep
verb

Sleep means not to be awake. *The brothers sleep in the same bed.*

Slumber is a formal word that means to sleep lightly and peacefully. *Gently, Mr. Hendricks pulled a blanket over his slumbering son.*

Nap means to sleep for a short time, especially in daytime. *Grandma always naps after lunch.*

Catnap means to take a nap or a series of naps. It suggests sleeping very lightly. *By catnapping in the evening, Gianetta stays up later to work on her drawings of the moon.*

Drowse means to be half asleep but still partly awake. *The leopard spends much of the day drowsing in a tree.*

Doze means to be barely asleep. It suggests sleeping without meaning to. *Tim dozed on the bus and missed his stop.*

Snooze means to rest or nap for a short time only. It suggests day-time rest, not a full sleep. *Ms. Bristol warned her students, "In my classroom, whoever snoozes, loses!"*

IDIOMS

There are many informal and slang expressions meaning to sleep. Here are some of them:

catch forty winks	hit the hay
crash	hit the sack
get some shuteye	zonk out
grab some Zs	

Are there other expressions you and your friends use?

Slide
verb

Slide means to move along smoothly and easily on a surface. *Dad fixed my dresser, and now the drawers slide in and out properly.*

Skid means to slide sideways, out of control of where you are going. *The dog raced onto the wet floor and skidded helplessly across the room.*

Skate means to slide on wheels or blades. *Meera wears a helmet and kneepads whenever she goes skating.*

Glide means to move along with an easy, graceful movement. *I love to watch my grandparents glide across the floor in a tango.*

Skim can mean to slide or glide. *As her canoe skimmed over the lake, Calling Crow's thoughts were full of the adventures ahead.*

Coast can mean to glide, without any work or moving power. *Jawan can coast on his bike downhill most of the way to school.*

Slip means to move smoothly and quickly. *The wet glass slipped through Irina's hands, crashing to the floor.*

Sail can mean to move smoothly and steadily. *Miranda sailed through her homework, doing all fifteen problems in just under an hour.*

Slither means to slide along a surface with a twisting, wavelike motion. *The boa constrictor slithered down the tree limb.*

Slow
adjective

Slow means taking a long time to go or do or happen. *When traffic is this slow, downtown seems far away.*

Leisurely means relaxed and without hurry. *Sandra and her father spent a leisurely afternoon at the beach.*

Poky means slow and without energy. *The pony Antonio had chosen was poky and wouldn't go faster.*

Sluggish means slow and tired. *After a sluggish first inning, the team began to pick up.*

Gradual means happening little by little. *There was a gradual decline in temperature throughout the day.*

Deliberate can mean slow and careful. *Mrs. Morales painted the chairs with deliberate strokes of her brush.*

ANTONYMS: fast, quick

Continued on the next page

My friend Milwaukee Joe is nice enough, but oh so slow.
Not just relaxed, without a sense of bustle to-and-fro.
No—he's slow.
Not gradual, say, like a plant that needs some time to grow.
No—he's slow.
Not careful and deliberate, like walking tippy-toe.
No, he's a guy who takes a leisurely hour to walk a block,
   who barely finishes his lunch before it's dinner time,
   and when you greet him, who waits until tomorrow
   to say, "Hello."
See?—That's *slow!*

Sly
adjective

Sly means able to trick or fool people in order to get what you want. *Our dog Max is so sly, he eats his dinner and then acts as if he never got it.*

Slick can mean sly. *People call Mayor Davies a slick politician—but they keep voting for her.*

Cunning means sly and clever. *Coyote, the cunning hero of many Native American myths, shows the success of brains over force.*

Tricky means sly and clever at cheating people. *The spies had a tricky plan to get at the navy's code book.*

Crafty and **foxy** mean skilled at fooling or tricking people. *It's a standard TV comedy: two crafty kids, a foxy grandpa, overworked parents, and a parrot that makes wisecracks.*

WORD STORY

Like *foxy,* many other words come from the names of animals. Often these words use an idea of what the animal is like to describe a person. *Foxy* is one example; *sheepish* and *mulish* are others. Sometimes names of animals are used in new ways but without changing the word. To *dog* someone, for instance, means to follow that person the way a dog follows a trail. And a *mammoth* problem seems as big as a huge fossil elephant.

Smart
adjective

Smart means able to learn easily and to solve problems quickly. *Enzo is the smartest student in our class and deserves the prize.*

Intelligent means able to think clearly and make good decisions. *Kimama's report discusses the question of how intelligent dolphins and whales are.*

Alert can mean very quick to understand and respond. *Smelling smoke, the alert baby-sitter called 911 and got the children out of the house.*

Clever means quick to think of good ideas. *Hannah is so clever, we think she's going to become a successful inventor.*

Quick-witted means clever and alert. *A quick-witted waitress performed the Heimlich maneuver on the choking customer and saved the man's life.*

Bright can mean smart in an active way. *Mr. Ko commended us for our bright ideas about saving energy at school.*

Brilliant can mean having great mental ability. *The brilliant criminal Professor Moriarty presented the greatest challenge of Sherlock Holmes's career.*

Brainy is an informal word that means very smart. It is sometimes used as an insult. *"For a brainy kid," Lori told Jeff as she looked at the mess, "you've got no sense at all."*

Gifted means having special ability. It is often used about unusual intelligence. *To Be Young, Gifted, and Black is a selection of Lorraine Hansberry's writings.*

SEE **sharp** and **wise** for related words.
ANTONYMS: dull, dumb, stupid

AROUND THE WORLD: Think Smart
• •
Smart is better than strong.
—**Spanish proverb**

The smart person knows when to look stupid.
—**Kikuyu proverb** (Kenya)

Louder isn't smarter.
—**Irish proverb**

People who tell you how smart they are, aren't.
—**Jewish proverb**

Smell
noun

The lilac has a
sweet **perfume.**

Smell means the quality of a thing that is sensed by the nose. *Harold loves the smell of bacon cooking.*

Odor and **scent** mean smell. *What I remember best about my grandparents' apartment is the odor of furniture polish and the scent of Grandma's homemade bread.*

Aroma means a pleasant, often spicy smell. It is often used about food. *The aroma of ginger drifted from the Hunan House restaurant into the street.*

Fragrance means a sweet, pleasing smell. *The bush in the Solers' garden grows huge yellowish-white roses, but they have almost no fragrance.*

Perfume can mean fragrance. *The lilac has a sweet perfume.*

Stink means a very bad smell. *When we became aware of the terrible stink, Marion guessed that our bicycle ride had taken us near the garbage dump.*

Smooth
adjective

Smooth means having a surface with no roughness or uneven spaces. *Denise loves to pat her dad's smooth cheeks after he finishes shaving.*

Polished means made smooth and shiny by rubbing with a cloth. *For the ceremony, Tino wore his best suit and a new tie and brightly polished shoes.*

Slippery means so smooth that it causes slipping. *"Careful, Trang, the floor is wet and slippery," said his dad.*

Slick means smooth or slippery. *Rena steered her bike around the slick oil spot on the road.*

Glossy means smooth and shiny. *Spencer varnished the table he made to give it a glossy finish.*

Sleek means glossy and soft. *Caitlin's dog, Ebony, has a sleek black coat of hair.*

SEE **level** and **soft** for related words.
ANTONYMS: coarse, rough

Sneak
verb

Sneak means to move in a secret way, trying to hide. *The kitten likes to sneak up and pounce on people's feet.*

Slink means to sneak. *We heard something fall, and then our dog, Buttons, came slinking out of the kitchen.*

Prowl means to sneak around looking for a chance to get something. *Ms. Williams saw this man prowling around the building, so she called the police.*

Lurk means to sneak or to wait in ambush. *When the geese see the fox lurking near their nest, they drive him away.*

Creep can mean to move slowly and secretly. *Making no sound, Oluwa crept toward the antelopes.*

Tiptoe means to walk very quietly, on your toes only. *Late that night, the girls tiptoed into the kitchen.*

Soft
adjective

Soft means easy to bend or push into, not hard or stiff. *After two weeks of sleeping on a hard camp cot, Phil is glad to get back to his own soft bed.*

Floppy means easy to bend and hanging or swaying in a loose way. *After a long week in her squad car, Mom spends Saturday morning in her floppy old bathrobe, reading and relaxing.*

Limp means so easy to bend that it cannot stay straight. *The noodles were limp when Tessa lifted them from the boiling water.*

Yielding means easy to push into. *These fossil footprints were made in yielding mud that turned to stone.*

ANTONYMS: firm, hard, rigid, stiff

These fossil footprints were made in **yielding** mud that turned to stone.

WORD POOL

Many words that mean soft come from the names of soft things. Here are some:

doughy	fluffy	pulpy
downy	mushy	spongy
flabby	fleecy	woolly

Sorrow
noun

Sorrow means strong unhappiness about something in particular. It often suggests a loss of something precious. *Although excited at moving all the way across the country, Kiefer felt sorrow for all the friends he was leaving behind.*

Grief means a deep feeling of sorrow and mental suffering. *Tears of grief streamed from the eyes of the refugees as they described how the invaders destroyed their town.*

Mourning means grief, especially because of someone's death. It also means a period of time spent in grief because of someone's death. *In the past, members of the families of people who had died wore black armbands every day as a sign of mourning.*

Heartbreak means crushing and long-lasting sorrow. *The country and western performer sang about the heartbreak of having his girlfriend leave him.*

Woe is a formal word that means extreme distress and sorrow. It suggests grief so great that it cannot be comforted. *The play showed the deep woe of people who had survived the plague but had lost their families and loved ones.*

SEE **misery** and **sad** for related words.
ANTONYMS: delight, happiness, joy

Sorry
adjective

Sorry means feeling bad about something you did. *Scott told Ms. Bowers he was sorry for running over the flowerbed with the lawnmower.*

Apologetic means saying or wanting to say that you feel bad about hurting someone or disappointing someone. *In his apologetic note to Sandy, Mark said he did not mean to hurt her feelings.*

Regretful means sorry and wishing that you had acted differently. *"I should have stayed in school," the beggar said in a regretful voice.*

Remorseful means deeply and painfully sorry. *The remorseful prime minister resigned because of the tax scandal.*

Repentant means sorry and wanting to make up for what you did. *"If you were really repentant, Michael, you'd help the Nortons clean up that mess," said his grandmother.*

SEE **ashamed** for related words.

Sour
adjective

Sour means tasting like lemons, without sweetness. *Grapefruit is sour, but Sophie loves it.*

Tart means pleasantly sour. *Aunt Ruth says that tart apples are better than sweet ones for making pies.*

Acid can mean sour. *Plain yogurt's slightly acid taste always makes Genny thirsty for a glass of water.*

Sharp can mean with a strong, biting taste. *Julio's Restaurant is famous for its sharp cheese sauce.*

ANTONYM: sweet

HAVE YOU HEARD...?
••••••••••••••••••••••••••••••••
You may have heard people use the phrase "sour grapes." It comes from Aesop's fable of a fox who wanted a bunch of grapes but couldn't reach them. To make himself feel better, the fox decided the grapes were probably sour. In the same way, someone who can't have something may claim not to want it. *"She says she didn't want to go to the party, anyway—sounds like sour grapes to me," said Sally.*

Special
adjective

Special means of a kind different from others. *Today is a special day for Ray because he starts competing in the national spelling bee.*

Individual can mean of or for a single person or thing. *Every box of this pudding holds twelve individual servings in plastic containers.*

Particular can mean belonging to one person or thing. *There are many Spanish-speaking countries, each with its own particular culture.*

Specific can mean belonging to some particular thing or group of things, as a characteristic. *Each chemical element has a specific number of protons in the nucleus of every atom.*

SEE **peculiar, rare,** and **single** for related words.
ANTONYMS: common, general, ordinary

Speech
noun

Speech means a set of words spoken in public by one person, often for many minutes or hours. *The principal's speech was filled with quotations from Shakespeare and Thomas Jefferson.*

Talk means an informal speech, usually to a small audience. *Shambala gave a brief talk to the class about her family in India.*

Lecture means a talk planned to teach a particular subject. *The famous scientist will present a lecture this Friday on why dinosaurs became extinct.*

Sermon means a speech given as part of a religious service. *"My sermon," Reverend Lambert told her congregation, "will be about our duty to the poor."*

Address means a formal speech at a serious public event. *Lincoln's Gettysburg Address took only a few minutes to deliver.*

Oration is a formal word that means an address. It is often used when the speech is very good, or the event is very important. *In his stirring oration before the Interplanetary Commission, Ambassador Grog warned that war could lead to the destruction of the entire galaxy.*

Spend
verb

Spend means to use money or something else valuable. *Environmental groups urged the government to spend more time and money to fight pollution.*

Expend is a formal word that means to spend. It often suggests large amounts. *The cyclists must expend more energy pedaling up the steep hill than coasting down it.*

Invest means to spend in a way that will bring benefits in the future. *Jorge has invested weeks of work in making that old bike like new.*

Splurge can mean to spend a lot or too much. *Jared decided to splurge and buy both CDs.*

Squander means to spend foolishly. *Belinda squandered her babysitting money on candy.*

SEE **pay** for related words.

The magician **twirled** the scarf and a dove appeared.

Spin
verb

Spin means to turn rapidly, many times. *Casja can spin her jump rope so fast it becomes a blur.*

Twirl means to spin. It suggests speed and gracefulness. *The magician twirled the scarf and a dove appeared.*

Whirl means to spin. It suggests great speed and force. *The whirling propeller lifted the helicopter into the air.*

Swirl means to move in a twisting motion. It suggests complicated movements. *As they stirred the frosting, Lani and Eunice watched the caramel and chocolate swirl in the bowl.*

Pirouette means to turn on your toes, once or several times. It is a word from dance. *"Now Wright gets the ball—he pirouettes, he shoots—he scores!" the sportscaster shouted.*

SEE **rotate** for related words.

WORD STORY

Swirl, twirl, and *whirl* look very much alike and sound alike too. You might suspect that they come from the same word—but they don't! *Swirl* comes from an old English word meaning "little whirlpool." *Whirl* comes from an old Scandinavian word meaning "to turn." *Twirl* doesn't come from either one of these sources. But no one knows where it does come from.

Spot
noun

Spot means a point that is different in color or texture from the surface around it. *Manasa got ink spots on her blue jacket.*

Mark means a spot or other trace left by one thing on another. *Her mother's kiss left a red lipstick mark on Jane's cheek.*

Dot means a small, round spot. *Alex's favorite tie is bright red with large blue dots.*

Blemish means a spot that hurts something's appearance. *Mrs. Volmer says the best way to control skin blemishes is to wash your face three times a day.*

Speck means a tiny spot, especially one that is only touching a surface. *Ramiro cleans every speck of dirt or dust off his bike each night before dinner.*

SEE **stain** for related words.

Stain
noun

Stain means a mark that hurts something's appearance and is hard to get out. *The twins had spilled so much grape juice that the tablecloth was covered with stains.*

Blot means a stain, especially one made by ink. *"Neatness counts," Mr. Schneider told his class. "Make sure your papers have no blots on them."*

Smear means a stain or other mark made by spreading or rubbing. *Edna tried to clean the peanut butter off the piano, but she only made a worse smear.*

Smudge means a dirty mark, especially a smear. *After making the posters for the election campaign, Anna had several dark paint smudges on her face.*

Blotch means a large, irregular stain or other mark. *You can still see the blotches on the carpet where the pitcher of root beer spilled.*

Splotch means a blotch like a splash mark. *The broken water balloon left a dark splotch on the sidewalk.*

SEE **dirty** and **spot** for related words.

Standard
noun

Standard means something used to judge what a thing is worth, or how well a person has done. *Joseph was glad to have Ms. Frazier, who kept very high standards, as his teacher.*

Measure can mean a standard. It may be used when no real measuring is done. *The students trying out for the cross-country team are in good physical condition, but what measure can we use to judge their spirit?*

Yardstick can mean a standard. Like *measure*, it may be used when no real yardstick is involved. *Ms. Zeyda's smile and nod were the yardstick by which her piano students measured the success of their playing.*

Mark can mean a standard that someone or something should match. *Khari wants to play on the volleyball team, but she is afraid she won't reach the mark.*

Gauge can mean something used to judge the size or force of something else. *A wet finger held in the air is an easy gauge of the wind's direction and strength.*

WORD POOL

There are many measures of length. Here are some:

angstrom	foot	meter
block	hand	micron
centimeter	inch	mile
chain	kilometer	rod
decimeter	league	yard
ell	light-year	

The smallest in this list is the *angstrom*, a unit of measurement for the wavelength of light. It is equal to one ten-millionth of a millimeter. The largest in this list is the *light-year*. It is a measure of the vast distances between stars and galaxies. It is equal to the distance light can travel in one year, about six trillion (6,000,000,000,000) miles.

Can you put the rest of these in order from small to large? Your dictionary will help you.

Start

verb

❝A journey of a thousand miles begins with a single step.**❞**

— Lao-tzu
(604–c. 531 B.C.)

Start means to do the first part of something. It suggests that you will continue to do it. *Jan finally opened her book and started to do her homework.*

Begin means to start. *"Who would like to begin the lesson?" asked Mr. Suarez.*

Commence is a formal word that means to begin, especially officially or publicly. *The court proceedings commence at ten o'clock.*

Initiate is a formal word that means to start an activity. It suggests that the activity is expected to continue into the future. *Clara was responsible for initiating the after-school tutoring program at the Neighborhood Club.*

Launch can mean to start something. *The store launched a new advertising program for the fall clothes.*

Inaugurate is a formal word that can mean to start something of serious public importance. *Thousands of people can stop driving to work, once the city inaugurates the new subway line.*

Embark can mean to start something new such as a trip or job. *After graduation, D'Neesha decided to embark on a career in broadcasting.*

SEE **beginning** for related words.
ANTONYMS: end, finish, stop

A journey of a thousand miles **begins** with a single step.

IDIOMS

There are many idioms that mean to get started. Here are some of them:

dive right in
get down to business
get your feet wet
get the show on the road
plunge in
roll up your sleeves
set the ball rolling
take the first step

Can you think of other ways to say this?

State
verb

State means to tell clearly and openly, in speech or writing. *"State your name and occupation," ordered the judge.*

Declare can mean to state strongly. *"No matter what they say, I still believe we'll win this game!" Arnetta declared.*

Affirm means to state firmly and as the truth. *Despite efforts to change his mind, Reverend Witherspoon affirms his intention of retiring next year.*

Insist means to state something and refuse to change it. *Hector insists that his father makes the best barbecue in town.*

Maintain can mean to affirm. With this meaning, it is a formal word. *The city government maintains that it cannot afford to build a new stadium.*

SEE **announce** and **tell** for related words.

Stay
verb

Stay means to continue to be in a place for a while. *Monty asked whether Elisabeth could stay for supper.*

Remain means to stay, especially after others have gone. *Dad will meet us at the park, but he has to remain home until the groceries are delivered.*

Wait means to stay until someone comes or something happens. *A good nature photographer waits for the right moment to take each picture.*

CONTINUED ON THE NEXT PAGE

A good nature photographer **waits** for the right moment to take each picture.

Linger means to remain, especially because you do not want to go. *Han lingered after saying goodnight, knowing he would not see Emmeline again for many months.*

Loiter means to stay for no reason or to move along aimlessly. *"I waited so long for you outside the restaurant," Angel said to Dottie, "they must have thought I was loitering there."*

Stick around is an idiom that means to stay or wait nearby. *James asked us to stick around while he tried to talk Dave into coming along.*

ANTONYMS: go, leave

> **WORD STORY**
>
> *Loiter* comes from a Dutch word meaning "to be loose." That word was used to describe loose teeth, or anything else that was not firmly attached. A person who loiters is not really going, not really staying, just sort of wobbling around.

Steady
adjective

Steady means strongly supported so that there is no swaying or shaking. *The girls' tree house is steady in that big oak.*

Firm can mean strong and solid, not easily moved. *After gluing the chair leg, Keith clamped it to keep the joint firm.*

Stable means firm. *Our new kitchen table is more stable than our old folding one.*

Substantial can mean firm. It suggests something that is well-built. *Even substantial houses were leveled in the hurricane.*

Fixed means fastened in place and firm. *Mrs. Haskell tugged on the safety belt to make sure the baby's car seat was securely fixed.*

Secure can mean fixed so strongly that there is no reason to worry. *Once the concrete sets, the post for the birdhouse will be secure in the ground.*

Fast can mean secure. *The door of the bank vault is shut fast by three locks and a massive bolt.*

Immovable means permanently in place, not able to be moved. *Since the boulder is immovable, the architect planned the garden around it.*

ANTONYMS: shaky, unstable, unsteady

Steal
verb

Steal means to take something that belongs to someone else. It suggests secret, usually nonviolent taking. *This vase was badly chipped in an attempt to steal it from the museum.*

Rob means to take money or property from a person or place. *The convenience store over on 27th Street was robbed twice last weekend.*

Shoplift means to steal things from a store while pretending to be a customer. *Since the Trans installed a lot of mirrors and cameras, nobody shoplifts from their store.*

Hold up means to stop by force and take money or property. *Bandits held up the stagecoach outside Bitterroot Springs.*

Stick up is a slang expression that means to rob. *She stuck up a couple of banks, so she's in jail for fifteen to twenty years.*

Rip off is a slang expression that means to rob or to steal. *"Anyone who asks you to give money so that you can get more money back is trying to rip you off,"* explained Sheila.

SEE **crime, criminal,** and **thief** for related words.

WATCH IT!
· ·

Steal and **rob** have related meanings, but they are not really synonyms, because of the way they are used. The object of *steal* is the thing that is taken. The object of *rob* is the person or place that something is taken from. *They robbed the store and stole the money.*

Stick
verb

Stick means to touch something and stay touching. It is often used about things that are gummy or about wet things that have dried. *On a rainy fall morning, wet leaves stick to everyone's feet.*

Cling means to stick. It suggests that something hangs on in spite of efforts to get it off. *Marcy brushed her skirt to remove the cat hairs clinging to it.*

Adhere means to stick. It is used mostly about flat things. *Mrs. Olivares asked her class how electricity made the paper adhere to the glass.*

Cohere means to stick together. *Powdery snow does not cohere well.*

SEE **join** for related words.

Every muscle was **tense** as the runners waited for the race to start.

Stiff
adjective

Stiff means not easy to bend or move. *Grandpa prefers a hairbrush with stiff bristles.*

Rigid means very stiff. *The wet clothes became rigid overnight in the frosty air.*

Inflexible can mean stiff. It suggests that something is impossible to bend. *We tried to bend the branch to get at the apples, but the branch was inflexible.*

Hard means not bending or moving when pushed. *After three days, the loaf of bread was stale and hard.*

Firm means hard. *The butter is still cold and too firm to spread.*

Solid can mean hard. It is used to show a difference from liquid or gas. *"Thank heaven," said Monique when the ferry ride ended, "back on solid ground again."*

Tense means stretched tight. *Every muscle was tense as the runners waited for the race to start.*

Taut means tense. *If guitar strings are too taut, they may break.*

ANTONYMS: flexible, soft

The twins **interrupted** Celia when she started to play.

Stop
verb

Stop means to keep from doing or happening. *Uncle Henry patched the roof to stop the rain from leaking in.*

Halt means to force to stop for a time. *The police halted traffic until the fallen tree was removed from the road.*

Cease means to stop something that has been going on for a while. *The two countries have ceased fighting, and peace is near.*

Discontinue means to stop something that has been happening for a long time. *We discontinued our subscription to the newspaper when we moved.*

Interrupt means to stop something in the middle. *The twins interrupted Celia when she started to play.*

Check means to stop forcefully, if only for a short time. *The wall of sandbags has checked the flood—for now.*

Arrest can mean to stop. This meaning is formal. *This city's economic development has been arrested by its pollution problems.*

SEE **end** and **prevent** for related words.
ANTONYMS: begin, continue, start

IDIOMS

There are many informal idioms that mean to stop an activity. Here are some of them:

crack down on	**lay to rest**	**nip in the bud**
cut short	**lower the boom on**	**put the kibosh on**

Can you think of others?

Store
verb

Store means to put something away for later use, especially in a safe place. *Cooked leftovers should be stored promptly in the refrigerator.*

Stockpile means to collect a supply of necessary things and store them. *The Langfords stockpile vegetables from their garden for the winter.*

Hoard means to store something that you think will become scarce. It suggests selfishness. *The shipwrecked sailors were horrified when they caught the captain stealing food and hoarding it.*

Deposit can mean to store money in a bank. *Pam deposits five dollars in her savings account every month.*

Stock up on means to stockpile. *As the hurricane approached, people hurried to stock up on candles and batteries.*

Set aside means not to use something so that you can store it. *The Romulos set aside money each week for their retirement.*

Lay away means to set aside. *Karen asked the store to lay away the jacket so that she could pay for it gradually.*

SEE **hide** and **keep** for related words.

Story
noun

Story means a set of events told in words. *William wrote a story about two farmers who found a treasure in a cave.*

Narrative is a formal word that means a story. *Description of the World is Marco Polo's narrative of his travels in Asia.*

Tale means a story, usually of imaginary events. *Mr. Shaunessy often delights the children with fairy tales from Ireland.*

Yarn can mean a long story that goes on and on, about unbelievable events. *While the four boys walked home, they repeated the story of their bicycle accident until it grew into a long and elaborate yarn.*

Account means a report of events or of a situation. *Grace enjoyed the museum trip and wrote an account of it for the class.*

Anecdote means a short story, often of one event happening in a person's life, or of a funny event. *Mr. Washington often begins his classes with anecdotes about famous people.*

Strong
adjective

Strong means having great power or strength. *The strong man lifted a huge weight over his head.*

Powerful means full of power and force. *The school's program to send books to Mozambique is the result of Ms. Masire's powerful speech about her country's needs.*

Sturdy means strong and solidly built. *This sturdy table will not wobble.*

Stout can mean sturdy. *The stout walls of the fort saved the soldiers inside.*

Tough can mean strong and able to resist wear and tear. *"That Houston Diggs is one tough football player," remarked Coach Myers.*

Robust means strong and healthy. *Andy looks so robust now, it's hard to believe that just last year he was dangerously ill.*

Hardy means strong enough and healthy enough to overcome all difficulties. *Cockroaches are so hardy that they have been a successful form of life for 250 million years.*

ANTONYM: **weak**

The **strong** man lifted a huge weight over his head.

Stubborn
adjective

Stubborn means insisting on an idea or plan and not willing to change it. *Because Shelby was stubborn about which movie to see, his friends went without him.*

Hard-headed can mean stubborn. *Dad says his boss is too hard-headed to listen to Dad's good ideas.*

Obstinate means stubborn. *Both the company and the union are obstinate, and a strike appears likely.*

Headstrong means foolishly determined to have one's own way. *Lindsey's headstrong insistence on skating too fast has cost her a broken knee.*

Stiff-necked can mean stubborn and proud. *Carl is too stiff-necked to admit that he needs help with his Spanish.*

SEE **firm** and **rigid** for related words.

CONTINUED ON THE NEXT PAGE

. . . .

The differences in meaning among synonyms are important to writers. Words create favorable or unfavorable impressions in the minds of readers. Notice how different the mayor seems in these sentences:

> *The mayor is <u>firm</u> in his refusal to consider the arguments against building a new airport.*

> *The mayor is <u>stubborn</u> in his support for building a new airport in spite of the arguments against it.*

> *The mayor is <u>headstrong</u> in his refusal to consider the arguments against building a new airport.*

When you write, consider the impressions given by the words you choose. Do you intend to show your own opinions? If not, try to avoid using words that are slanted toward one point of view. On the other hand, if you do want to persuade your readers to think in a certain way, using loaded language is one way to do that.

Stuff
noun

Stuff means what a thing is made of. It often suggests that someone does not know or care exactly what that is. *The outside of the television is made of some stuff that looks like wood but isn't.*

Material means stuff. It is mostly used about kinds of stuff that are made into things for sale. *Mr. Lanza's business sells lumber, bricks, and other building materials.*

Substance means a particular kind of stuff. The kind can be general or very specific. *Ice, water, and steam are the same substance in different forms.*

Matter means anything that takes up space and has weight. With this meaning, the word is used mostly in science. *"Identify the three different types of matter," began the science test.*

WORD STORY

. . . .

If you stuff a turkey, what sort of stuff do you use for stuffing? Any stuff—because that's where the word *stuff* came from. First it was a French verb, meaning to fill a space by packing it with something. Then it became a French noun, too, meaning the something you stuff with. Both forms came into English. Then people started using the word *stuffing* to mean stuff made to stuff with.

Stupid
adjective

Stupid means very slow to learn or understand. *"Because I don't speak Spanish," Neal told the class, "I felt stupid many times during my family's trip to Mexico."*

Dull can mean not quick to think, learn, or act. *The dull dog was no match for the squirrel that went scurrying by.*

Slow can mean dull. *Tory may have been slow when she started flute lessons, but she's a whiz now.*

Dumb can mean stupid or silly. *That dumb cat hisses at her own reflection in the mirror.*

Dense can mean stupid. *I felt dense when Tim had to explain his pun to me.*

Shortsighted can mean not thinking ahead. *Lakwonda's report ended by saying that it would be shortsighted not to conserve our natural resources.*

ANTONYMS: bright, intelligent, smart

That **dumb** cat hisses at her own reflection in the mirror.

Subject
noun

Subject means what something is about, as in a book, a picture, a talk, or a movie. *"The American Revolution will be the subject of today's discussion,"* announced Mr. Leffer.

Theme means a subject. *"Fighting Pollution" was the theme of the science fair.*

Topic means the subject of a speech or piece of writing. It is often used when the subject is happening now. *The main topics of conversation at Gregg's party were music videos and the new gym teacher.*

Text can mean a subject, especially a quotation from the Bible as the subject of a sermon. *The minister took "I will fear no evil" as the text for her sermon.*

Matter can mean what a speech or piece of writing says. It is often used in the phrase *subject matter.* *"The author's subject matter is quite interesting," said the book review, "but his writing makes that matter hard to understand."*

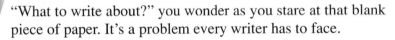

WRITING TIP: Selecting a Topic

"What to write about?" you wonder as you stare at that blank piece of paper. It's a problem every writer has to face.

If you've been keeping a writer's journal, you can look through your list of possible subjects there and choose one that looks interesting.

If you haven't been keeping a journal, here are some guidelines for something to write about:

> something you're familiar with, or
> something you'd like to learn about, or
> something you feel strongly about.

Here's a further word of advice: Phrase your topic as specifically as possible. "Garbage in the Nugget River" makes a better topic than "The Environment" or even "Pollution." If you have a specific topic, you can make sure that it gives you enough to write about. Also, it will keep you from rambling on and on.

P.S. Make your problem easier by starting to keep a writer's journal—now!

Substitute
verb

Substitute means to put someone or something in another's place, or to take another's place. *The recipe says you can substitute honey for sugar when making these cookies. When Mrs. Jackson had her baby, Mr. Klinkowitz substituted for her as our math teacher.*

Change can mean to put in another's place. *When Jonathan changed partners during the square dance, he found himself face to face with his old girlfriend, Amber.*

Replace means to take another's place. *Han will replace Gil in left field next inning.*

Displace means to replace. *In the experiment, neon is pumped into the glass tube and displaces the oxygen that was in there originally.*

Relieve can mean to replace someone on duty. *The guards at the Tomb of the Unknown Soldier are relieved frequently.*

Pinch-hit can mean to take another's place in an emergency. *Cindy got sick, so her sister pinch-hit for her at the science fair exhibit.*

Stand in for can mean to replace. *The mayor will be unable to attend the opening of the new library, but her son will stand in for her.*

Spell can mean to relieve. *Mom said to Dad, "If you're getting tired of driving, I could spell you for a while."*

The guards at the Tomb of the Unknown Soldier are **relieved** frequently.

HAVE YOU HEARD…?

You may have heard people say, "He's robbing Peter to pay Paul." This does not really mean to steal. It describes using something in one way that was meant to be used another way. It suggests that this substitution will solve a problem, but only for a little while. *"I can catch up with my math assignments if I don't do my English homework tonight," thought Bruce, "but that's only robbing Peter to pay Paul."*

408

Subtract
verb

Subtract means to take a part away, especially with numbers. *Dad subtracted the money I owed him from my allowance.*

Deduct means to subtract an amount, often for a particular reason. *Ms. Lezak deducts points from your math test score if you don't show your calculations.*

Discount means to make the price of something smaller by a part. *Because the movie was a flop, stores have discounted all the related merchandise.*

Detract means to take away a part of something's value. It is not used about money. *All that make-up Fiona wears detracts from how pretty she is.*

Knock off is an informal phrase that means to take a certain amount from a price. *The salesman has offered to knock off 15 dollars if I buy the bike today.*

SEE **decrease** and **shrink** for related words.
ANTONYM: add

Succeed
verb

Succeed means to do what you planned and hoped, with a good result. *The doctors succeeded in finding a cure for the disease.*

Prosper is a formal word that means to succeed for some time. It often suggests a gain in wealth. *Some computer manufacturers have prospered, but some have gone out of business.*

Flourish means to succeed openly and happily. It suggests rapid, vigorous growth. *Mr. Lyon's garden is flourishing—he has enough tomatoes to feed the neighborhood.*

Thrive means to flourish, often for a particular reason. It may suggest overcoming difficulty. *Once he makes some friends, Ernie should thrive in his new school.*

Win means to gain victory in competition. *Derek Walcott of the West Indies won the Nobel prize for literature in 1992.*

Triumph means to gain a great victory. *Jim Thorpe triumphed in the 1912 Olympic Games.*

ANTONYM: fail

Suddenly
adverb

Suddenly means quickly and without being expected. *Suddenly the sky became dark, and a fierce storm began.*

Unexpectedly means without any sign that something is going to happen. *The phone rang unexpectedly in the middle of the night.*

Abruptly means suddenly. *The road ends abruptly about a mile west of town.*

Short can mean suddenly. *The bike rider stopped short when a car turned in front of her.*

Instantly means at once, with no delay. *"When I realized she wasn't breathing," Deanna explained, "I began CPR instantly."*

Immediately means instantly. *When he missed the bus, Gavin immediately called his mother to let her know he would be late.*

Pronto is an informal word that means right now, as fast as you can. *"Claire!" her father yelled up the stairs, "I want to see you pronto!"*

All of a sudden and **all at once** mean suddenly. *All of a sudden Korinne realized that she was falling. All at once Tony jumped up and caught her arm.*

On the spur of the moment is an idiom that means suddenly, without planning or considering what to do. *Marissa decided, on the spur of the moment, to buy the book.*

SEE **quick** for related words.
ANTONYM: gradually

Suggest
verb

Suggest means to offer an idea to someone. *"I suggest we vote on what movie to rent," said Margaret.*

Propose means to suggest an idea for someone to consider and then decide about. *Mr. Ortiz has proposed we take a lunch break and meet back here in an hour.*

Advise means to suggest an idea and say that it should be used. *It was supposed to rain that afternoon, so Aunt Lovella advised Tim to take an umbrella.*

Recommend can mean to advise. *"I recommend you think twice about wearing those shoes to school," Mom told me.*

CONTINUED ON THE NEXT PAGE

Hundreds of people have **put forward** names for the zoo's new baby hippopotamus.

Advance can mean to suggest. This meaning is formal. It is often used about public business. *At this morning's meeting, Ms. Engelbrecht advanced a plan for repairing the parking lot.*

Put before can mean to propose an idea at a meeting. *A proposal to start a school magazine was put before the Student Council.*

Put forward can mean to propose an idea, usually publicly. *Hundreds of people have put forward names for the zoo's new baby hippopotamus.*

SEE **hold out** (at **hold**) and **urge** for related words.

Sullen
adjective

Sullen means silent, unhappy, and angry. *In a sullen mood, Joe lowered his head and refused to speak.*

Sulky means sullen. It suggests childish pouting. *David banged around the kitchen feeling sulky and sorry for himself because he had to stay home.*

Moody can mean sullen. It suggests a feeling that goes on for some time, without a clear reason. *"Michelle's not mad at you," Toni told Paul, "she just gets moody sometimes."*

Brooding means thinking over and over about things that make you unhappy or angry. *The actor stood in brooding silence with a mirror in one hand.*

SEE **cross, mad,** and **sad** for related words.
ANTONYMS: cheerful, pleasant

411

Support
verb

Support means to hold something up and keep it from falling. *Workers put up scaffolding to support the crumbling wall.*

Bear means to support. It emphasizes the weight of what is held up. *This bridge was designed to bear the weight of dozens of cars.*

Carry can mean to bear. *Jana climbed into the basket with her parents and six brothers, wondering how the balloon could carry them all.*

Sustain can mean to support. *The roof of this building isn't strong enough to sustain a garden.*

Prop means to hold something up by putting something else underneath or behind. It suggests a temporary arrangement. *Daniella propped up the clothesline with a pole to make it taut.*

Brace means to give support to something by adding some strong extra part to it. *It's a rickety old table, but I've braced its legs so that it's sturdy enough.*

Buttress means to brace. As a verb, it is used mostly about ideas or arguments. *The debater buttressed her argument with quotations and statistics.*

> **WRITER'S CHOICE**
> ●
>
> His mother lifted him to prop him up on pillows to ease his labored breathing, then pulled down the blankets so that Dr. Louise could listen to his heart with her stethoscope.
>
> —Madeleine L'Engle, *A Wind in the Door*

Why *prop?* Being in an upright position makes it easier for the boy to breathe, but he cannot rest comfortably in that position. His mother uses pillows to help support him in that position temporarily.

Sure
adjective

Sure means having no doubt. *Are you sure you turned out the lights?*

Positive means sure, without any second thoughts. *Eric is positive that he had ten dollars when he started shopping.*

Certain means sure, based on the facts. *After looking at the map, Donna was certain that she was heading in the wrong direction.*

CONTINUED ON THE NEXT PAGE

Confident means sure, with a hopeful feeling. *Joaquín studied hard for the social studies test and is confident he did well on it.*

Convinced means made sure by proof or persuasion. *Supposedly, an experiment on the Leaning Tower of Pisa left Galileo convinced that objects of different weights fall at the same speed.*

Assured can mean convinced. It emphasizes that someone or something has made you sure. *Listening to the debate, Branford felt assured that his candidate would win the election.*

Satisfied can mean convinced. It emphasizes that you had doubts but have given them up. *The jurors were completely satisfied that the defendant was guilty.*

ANTONYMS: unsure, uncertain

WRITING TIP: Sounding Sure

You can make your writing stronger by sounding positive about what you say. One way to do this is to leave out words that suggest you are only partly right. If you describe someone as "sort of timid," "a bit confused," "a little depressed," or "somewhat annoyed," you don't appear sure of what you are saying. Let your characters be timid, confused, depressed, or annoyed. Eliminate the feelings of doubt.

Sometimes, however, you need to use words like "almost" or "perhaps" to show that you are being carefully accurate.

> *About 500 people attended our school's science fair last Saturday. Our principal said it was one of the most successful science fairs we've ever had at George Washington Carver School*

In the first sentence, *about* shows that no one knows exactly how many people came. In the second sentence, *one of the most* avoids the problem of proving just how successful it was.

Do you want to sound positive or careful? Make up your mind, then choose your words to fit your purpose.

Supposedly, an experiment on the Leaning Tower of Pisa left Galileo **convinced** that objects of different weights fall at the same speed.

Surprised
adjective

Surprised means filled with wonder because of something unexpected. *"Marceea, I'm surprised to find you here!" exclaimed Grandpa.*

Amazed means greatly surprised. *His parents were amazed when Eldred began composing music at such an early age.*

Astonished means amazed. *"Vernon, I'm speechless!" said Mrs. Alvarez, astonished at her student's carefully handcrafted gift.*

Astounded means completely surprised and unable to understand what has happened. *"I'm astounded that you would send the Fitzroys another invitation after that last disaster," Mom told Dad.*

Flabbergasted is an informal word that means astounded. *Al stood in flabbergasted silence as the magician gave back his watch and keys.*

Thunderstruck means so surprised that you cannot think or do anything. *Dr. Wilkerson, thunderstruck by the sight of the treasure, did not hear the heavy stone roll into place behind him.*

Startled can mean caused to jump in surprise and fright. *Kazuo is such a light sleeper that once he woke up, startled by a noisy goldfish.*

Shocked means surprised and very upset. *Jamaine was shocked to find her ordinarily quiet dog barking and snapping at the mail carrier.*

Dumfounded means amazed and speechless. *The lawyer was dumfounded when his client suddenly confessed to the crime.*

Swing
verb

Swing means to move back and forth, usually in a regular, even way. It is often used about things that hang down. *At the zoo, Laurel likes to watch the monkeys swing from branches.*

Dangle means to hang and swing loosely. *Wires dangled from the telephone pole after the fierce thunderstorm.*

Rock means to swing. *Arturo gets his baby sister to go to sleep by holding her in his arms and rocking from side to side.*

Sway means to rock in an unsteady way. It is often used about things that stand on something else. *The conductor warned the passengers that the train would sway a bit as it crossed the stretch of rough track.*

CONTINUED ON THE NEXT PAGE

Reel means to sway and nearly fall over. *Brooke reeled after running into the door.*

Seesaw can mean to move up and down or back and forth. *The score seesawed during the game, but the Maroons finally won.*

Waver means to move back and forth like a wave. It is often used about weak or soft things. *The curtains wavered in the gentle breeze.*

SEE **shake** for words that mean to tremble.

WORDS AT PLAY

"Take your partner and swing her!" the caller began,
And the square dancers did, every woman and man,
Except Jerry and Jenny, who spun round the floor.
They had lost all control! They sailed straight out the door!
And we heard, as they vanished off into the night,
"Did we swing too far left? or too far to the right?"

Take
verb

Take means to make something your own or to get hold of something. *Everyone may take some cookies. Jeff took his umbrella from the closet.*

SEE **carry** for related words.

Take is also used in phrases that have special meanings. Each of these phrases has its own set of synonyms.

take after

Take after means to be like someone or something else. It is often used about members of the same family. *Unlike his brother, who moved to the city, Garth takes after his father and wants to stay on the farm.*

Resemble means to be like someone or something else. It is used about any people or things. *The actor playing Thomas Jefferson strongly resembles portraits of the President painted from life.*

Suggest means to cause a thought to occur. It is used when someone or something is partly like another. *As we lay on the grass, Caroline remarked that the shapes of the clouds suggested buildings.*

Simulate can mean to act like or look like something else. It is used about active imitation. *Astronauts prepare for shuttle flights by training in devices that simulate the weightless conditions of space.*

Call to mind means to suggest. *"Your problem," Uncle Orville told Brent, "calls to mind my own difficulties at your age."*

take back

Take back means to say that something you said before was not right. *After Florence won the race, Jackie had to take back her claim that she could beat anyone.*

416

Continued on the next page

Withdraw can mean to take back something, or to say that something is no longer working or active. *The band withdrew its application for a permit to perform in the park when it got another job.*

Retract can mean to withdraw. *The city has retracted its offer to buy Mr. Benson's land.*

Recall can mean to withdraw. *The order to attack was recalled when heavy rain began.*

take up

Take up means to be busy doing something because you are interested in it. *Mrs. Oster has taken up skydiving and does it every weekend.*

Engage means to keep yourself busy with something. *Martina helps at Sunday School, sings in the choir, and engages in many other activities at the church.*

Apply can mean to put yourself to work at something. *Felix has applied himself to his exercises, and now he weighs just what he wants to.*

Study means to try to learn. It can be used as a synonym for *take up,* suggesting serious effort to gain a skill. *Jenny is studying the tuba.*

Turn your hand to is an idiom meaning to direct your efforts at. *After completing this novel, the author turned her hand to poems.*

Jenny is **studying** the tuba.

WORD POOL

People who are studying something often like to talk about it. This may be why the English ending *-ology,* meaning "a subject to study," comes from a Greek word meaning "word" or "speech." This ending combines with other Greek and Latin words to name many of the subjects that people take up in a serious way. Here are some of those subjects (and what they mean):

anthropology (study of people)

archaeology (study of old things)

chronology (study of time)

dermatology (study of skin)

etymology (study of word stories)

graphology (study of handwriting)

ichthyology (study of fish)

meteorology (study of weather)

ornithology (study of birds)

pharmacology (study of medicines)

psychology (study of the mind)

seismology (study of earthquakes)

toxicology (study of poisons)

zoology (study of animals)

And there are dozens more. When you see *-ology,* you know that some people have been interested and busy.

Talk
verb

Talk means to make words with the voice. It suggests that this goes on for a while. *"OK, let's not stand here talking when there's work to be done!" exclaimed Uncle Brevis.*

Speak means to say words. *Mrs. Chalmers doesn't allow us to speak in class without raising our hands first.*

Chat means to talk with others in an easy, relaxed manner. *After school, my friends and I often get together at the Huddle to chat over soft drinks.*

Converse is a formal word that means to talk with others, sharing ideas and opinions. *The ambassador and his guests were conversing about world affairs when dinner was announced.*

Gossip means to talk about people's private lives. *Mr. Thiel is a shut-in, but he knows what's going on from gossiping with his neighbors.*

P.S.   Getting Your Words' Worth

This is a book about words. What makes words important? How much you can do with them—that's what. If you can talk well, and write well, you have a real advantage over other people. To see what words are good for, look at the lists of synonyms in this book. More than thirty of the entries are about different things to do with words. With words, you can do all these—and more!

admit	brag	discuss	report	state
announce	call	encourage	request	suggest
answer	command	explain	ridicule	talk
argue	complain	forbid	say	tell
ask	consult	persuade	scoff	urge
beg	criticize	praise	scold	warn
blame	describe	promise	shout	whisper

Words make stories: books, movies, television. Words make news. Words are basic to law, to religion, even to science and computers. The better you are with words, the more money you're likely to make. So use this book!

This has been, we hope, a word to the wise.

Tame
adjective

Tame means obedient to people and not wild anymore. It is used about animals. *The tame bears at the circus ride on motorcycles.*

Domesticated means living with people and raised by people. It is used about animals and plants. *Cats probably became domesticated about 5,500 years ago, long after dogs and other animals.*

Broken can mean trained from being wild to being tame. It is used mostly about work animals, especially horses. *"Don't go near that gray horse," warned Mrs. Sleeping Bear. "He isn't broken yet."*

Housebroken means trained not to make messes indoors and able to live in a house. It is used mostly about dogs. *Mom says we can only get a dog that's already housebroken.*

ANTONYM: wild

Tasty
adjective

Tasty is an informal word that means tasting good. *For supper last night, Todd made a tasty meat loaf.*

Flavorful means having a strong, pleasant flavor. It is used mostly in writing. *More and more Americans are discovering the flavorful food of Thailand.*

Appetizing means tasting good enough to make people want more. It is used mostly in writing. *Every morning, the shopkeeper arranges a colorful display of appetizing fruit.*

Spicy means tasting strongly of spices. *Durond helped his father make spicy barbecue sauce.*

SEE **delicious** for related words.
ANTONYMS: flavorless, tasteless, unappetizing

Every morning, the shopkeeper arranges a colorful display of **appetizing** fruit.

419

The parcel is full of **shredded** paper to protect the vase from damage.

Tear
verb

Tear means pull apart by force. *Luis tore a ligament in his left knee while playing soccer.*

Rip means to tear something, especially along a seam. *Lily saved the largest present for last and then ripped the paper open.*

Shred means to tear something into small pieces. *The parcel is full of shredded paper to protect the vase from damage.*

Snag means to catch something on a sharp point and tear it. *Ann snagged her dress while climbing over the fence.*

Rend is a formal word that means to tear violently. *When their headman dies, the villagers will rend their clothing in grief.*

SEE **cut** for related words.

VERB PLUS
Sometimes when a word is added to a verb, it creates a phrase that has special meaning. Here are some phrases with **tear:**

Tear around means to move hastily and carelessly from place to place. *"I want you to stay with me," Mom told us, "and not go tearing around the mall."*

Tear away means to make someone leave, against strong feeling. *It was hard for the children to tear themselves away from the zoo in time to catch the bus.*

Tear into means to attack violently. *At the neighborhood meeting, Mrs. Curtis tore into the plan to widen the street for more traffic.*

Tear off means to remove quickly or forcefully. *The woman tore off her coat and shoes, jumped into the river, and saved the child.*

Tell
verb

Tell means to make something known to someone by using words. *Tell your sister dinner's ready.*

Inform means to tell someone facts. *Ted closed his letter by asking the company to inform him of the steps it was taking to decrease its smoke emissions.*

Advise can mean to inform someone. *"Well, why didn't the printer advise us of the missing pages?" asked the yearbook editor.*

Acquaint means to inform someone. It suggests making the facts familiar. *Managers are expected to acquaint all new employees with Burger Barn procedures.*

Communicate means to tell and be told by messages. *The Student Council communicated students' concerns to their faculty advisor. It was clear that both teachers and students need to communicate with each other more.*

Notify means to tell a person something in an official way. *There are signs on all the buses notifying riders of changes in service.*

Confide means to tell something as a secret. *Darren confided his feelings to Gloria.*

Impart is a formal word that can mean to share knowledge by telling. *The judge has asked witnesses not to impart their stories to anyone until the trial.*

VERB PLUS

Sometimes when a word is added to a verb, it creates a phrase that has special meaning. Here are some phrases with **tell:**

Tell of means to show or indicate. *The peeling paint and broken windows tell of this neighborhood's decay.*

Tell off can mean to scold someone fully. *When Thea learned what Neal had done, she really told him off.* (SEE **scold** for more words that mean to tell off.)

Tell on means to report what someone has done wrong. *Who told on Neal to Thea?*

421

Terrible
adjective

Terrible means very bad. *Cathy had a terrible scrape on her knee.*

Awful can mean very bad or unpleasant. *There was an awful crash on the highway last night.*

Ghastly can mean very bad. This meaning is informal. *"Are you listening to that ghastly music again?" Dad asked.*

Nasty can mean very unpleasant. *Sammy fell on the ice and got a nasty cut on his forehead.*

Horrible can mean very bad or foul. *The rotten fish left a horrible odor in the kitchen.*

Rotten can mean extremely bad. *Milly has a rotten cold and will have to miss the class trip to Kansas City.*

Horrid can mean extremely bad or unpleasant. *"Tomorrow's going to be horrid," announced the TV weatherwoman cheerfully.*

Wretched can mean very bad in quality. *"Oh!" cried Aunt Lavinia, "this wretched umbrella is simply no use at all!"*

SEE **bad** for related words.
ANTONYMS: excellent, great, wonderful

WORD WORKSHOP

The word *terrible* is often overused. Instead, you might use some of the synonyms for *terrible* shown here.

Last week, Mr. Webster's sixth-grade class learned just how terrible it is to be homeless. At Welcome Shelter, people told us about eating ~~terrible~~ *horrible* food, wearing ~~terrible~~ *wretched* old clothes, and sleeping outside in ~~terrible~~ *awful* weather. "You feel rotten a lot," said one man. The shelter takes in fifty men and women every night. The really terrible thing is, many others still have no place to go.

Terrifying
adjective

Terrifying means causing great fear. *As people ran for the basement, they heard the terrifying roar of the tornado.*

Fearful means terrifying. *The rider brought a fearful message: the prairie is on fire!*

Bloodcurdling means terrifying, especially in a spooky way. *At the bloodcurdling scream, Barron ran out of the Spook House in terror.*

Hair-raising means terrifying, especially because of great risk. *The audience watched the acrobat's hair-raising stunt in complete awe.*

Scary means likely to scare you. *Suki doesn't like to watch scary movies alone.*

Frightening means likely to scare you very badly. *"There is a frightening possibility of plague," the doctor told reporters.*

Frightful means frightening. *The campers woke to the frightful sound of a grizzly bear outside their tent.*

Dreadful means causing fear that something bad is about to happen. *Dreaming that a friend has died is a dreadful experience.*

Horrifying means causing fear and disgust. *The book tells about the horrifying conditions in city slums 100 years ago.*

Hideous means horrifying. It often suggests something especially ugly. *The movie monster looks hideous but turns out to be friendly.*

Appalling means causing so much fear that it is hard to think or do anything. *Even the ambulance crew were shocked by the appalling accident.*

SEE **afraid, fear,** and **scare** for related words.

The movie monster looks **hideous** but turns out to be friendly.

Then
adverb

Then means following in time or place. *To get to the concert, Miles and Tyrone had to ride the subway first and then transfer to a bus.*

Next means immediately following. *First Aunt Julia arrived; next Uncle Bill came; and finally Grandpa and Grandma showed up.*

Later means at a following time. It suggests that time has passed. *Later the detective realized that the suspects had been telling the truth all along.*

Afterwards means later. *Miguel and Luisa went to a movie, and afterwards they stopped for ice cream.*

Whereupon can mean at the time of something else. It suggests that one event causes another. *On December 7, 1941, the Japanese bombed Pearl Harbor, whereupon the United States declared war on Japan.*

Subsequently is a formal word that means later. It suggests some connection between earlier and later events. *Archaeologists first discovered bones at the ancient burial site in 1961, and they have subsequently found tools and pottery there.*

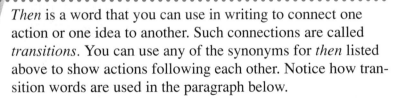

WRITING TIP: Making Transitions

Then is a word that you can use in writing to connect one action or one idea to another. Such connections are called *transitions.* You can use any of the synonyms for *then* listed above to show actions following each other. Notice how transition words are used in the paragraph below.

> *Yesterday, my friends and I played ball until late afternoon. <u>Afterwards</u> Dad asked me to help him clean out the garage. This kept me busy until nearly supper. <u>Later</u> some friends came over, and we all watched TV and ate popcorn. <u>Then</u> it was time for bed.*

Another kind of transition shows cause and effect. Transition words include *consequently, therefore,* and *as a result.*

People often use *then* when one of these other words—or just *and*—would be better.

Thick
adjective

Thick means close together, or with its parts close together. *The lilies were so thick that they covered the water in the pond.*

Dense means thick. It suggests a lot in a small space. *The underbrush is so dense that it makes hiking difficult.*

Compact means closely packed together. *Blanche and Mabelle keep their old magazines in a compact pile in the closet.*

Heavy can mean dense. *After the autumn rain, a heavy layer of bright leaves covered the sidewalks.*

Lush means growing thick and green. It is used about plants. *The lush grass in the park is like a piece of green velvet.*

Thief
noun

Blackbeard the **pirate** was a terror to sailors.

Thief means a person who steals, especially in secret. *Some thief got the radio out of Mr. Manilow's car.*

Robber means a person who steals by force. *Unlike most robbers, Robin Hood stole from the rich to give to the poor.*

Mugger means a person who assaults people in order to rob them. *A policewoman will speak at assembly on how to avoid muggers.*

Burglar means a person who breaks into a building in order to steal. *Mr. Gaston chased off the burglar who had broken into his house.*

Shoplifter means a person who steals from stores while pretending to be a customer. *"Shoplifters will be prosecuted," said the sign in the hobby shop.*

Pickpocket means a person who steals from people's pockets or purses. *"Look out for pickpockets in crowds," warned Grandpa.*

Pirate means a person who attacks ships at sea and steals from them. *Blackbeard the pirate was a terror to sailors.*

Rustler is an informal word that means a cattle thief. *Rustlers got fifty head of cattle from the Bar None Ranch last night.*

Hijacker means a person who steals a vehicle, or goods from a vehicle. *A hijacker seized control of the plane shortly after takeoff.*

SEE **criminal** and **steal** for related words.

425

Thin

adjective

Thin means not having much flesh. *Compared to a beagle, a greyhound is a thin dog.*

Lean means not fat. *The basketball player is tall and lean.*

Slender and **slim** mean pleasingly thin. *The slender model wore one of the latest fashions. Lauren thought the dress would look good on her sister, who was also slim.*

Slight can mean slender and small. *John is so slight that his mother worries about his playing on the soccer team.*

Willowy means slender and graceful. It often suggests that someone is tall. *In only a year, Half Moon had grown from plump to willowy, so she needed a complete set of new clothes for school.*

The basketball player is tall and **lean.**

Lanky means thin and tall and awkward-looking. *As a young man, Lincoln was lanky but very strong.*

Skinny means too thin. *After eight weeks in a cast, Joe's leg is pale and skinny.*

Scrawny means skinny. *How can Julie's cat eat all the time and still be so scrawny?*

Gaunt means very thin and not healthy-looking. *Mr. Smythe looked gaunt for many weeks following his operation.*

All skin and bones is an idiom that means very thin. *Alice grew so fast and ate so little that she was all skin and bones.*

ANTONYMS: fat, plump

Thing
noun

Thing means any single part of all there is. *"What's that thing called that hangs down in the back of your throat?" asked Tammy.*

Object means a thing that can be seen or touched. *Christine believes that the unidentified object in the picture is a balloon.*

Article can mean a particular thing, often a thing of a certain kind. *After the fire, not one article of furniture was undamaged.*

Item means a thing that is part of a group or a list. *The other item Jerry wants to buy is not sold in this store.*

Body can mean a large object. It is often used in science. *Mars is a heavenly body. No bodies of water are thought to exist there.*

SEE **gadget** and **tool** for related words.

▼ WORD WORKSHOP

The word *thing* is often overused. See what happens in the paragraph below when we replace *thing* with more precise words.

Dad showed me some of the ~~things~~ *equipment* in his office, where he writes his newspaper stories. On his desk is a keyboard and a ~~thing~~ *mouse* that he clicks to control his computer screen. Right next door are a laser ~~thing~~ *printer* and a ~~thing~~ *fax machine* for sending and receiving copies instantly to and from anywhere in the country. I asked Dad if all these new ~~things~~ *devices* were fun to use. He told me that, as with any ~~thing,~~ *tool* the important thing is that it helps you do the job better and faster than before.

Think
verb

Think means to use the mind in order to form ideas or understand something. *What does Rosa think the author's message is in this book?*

Reason means to think carefully in order to make a judgment or solve a problem. *Chet and Lonnie reasoned that they could get the wheelchair up the steps if they could find a big enough board.*

Ponder means to think about something long and very hard. *Albert Einstein spent his life pondering the deepest problems of science.*

Deliberate means to think slowly and carefully about something. *The honor council deliberated for two hours before deciding on a punishment for the students who cheated.*

Meditate means to think quietly and seriously about something. *Dov stared at the chess board, meditating his next move.*

Speculate means to think very carefully about something, often using imagination as part of thinking. *Astronomers speculate about how the universe began.*

CONTINUED ON THE NEXT PAGE

Albert Einstein spent his life **pondering** the deepest problems of science.

Concentrate can mean to pay special attention and think really hard. *After she was hit by a pitch, Sujata found it difficult to concentrate while batting.*

Brood can mean to think for a long time about one particular thing that worries you. *Jennifer brooded for days about the mistakes she made at her recital.*

Use your head is an idiom that means to think. *"Use your head in sorting out the stockroom," Mr. Grace told Henry, "and don't stack boxes of books on top of boxes of glass ornaments."*

SEE **consider, decide, imagine,** and **plan** for related words.

Thoughtful
adjective

Thoughtful means careful of other people's feelings. *"How thoughtful!" said Angelique. "You brought my favorite flowers!"*

Considerate means thoughtful. It suggests thinking of people's feelings without having to be told. *They tried to be considerate of the downstairs neighbors by walking quietly in the hallway.*

Sympathetic means thoughtful, kind, and able to understand how someone else feels. *When he saw my braces, Emilio showed his own in a sympathetic smile.*

Sensitive can mean quick to understand how someone else feels, or able to understand someone's feelings especially well. *Dana says that her friend from the Big Sister program is sensitive and easy to be with.*

Attentive means steadily thoughtful. It suggests making an effort to be sure of being kind and pleasant. *Michael is attentive to Mrs. Lao's needs, and he shovels the snow from her walk whenever he does his own.*

Caring means attentive. It suggests that someone else's feelings are important to you. *Everyone in class made a fuss when Jacob first broke his leg, but only Amanda was caring enough to visit him often.*

Concerned can mean thoughtful and interested. It suggests some worry. *A concerned neighbor spotted the smoke and called the fire department in time.*

SEE **kind** and **polite** for related words.
ANTONYMS: inconsiderate, thoughtless

Threatening
adjective

Threatening means giving a warning that something bad is about to happen. *The little dog let out a threatening snarl and looked as fierce as it could.*

Menacing means threatening. *The two boxers stared at each other in a menacing way.*

Sinister means threatening in a way that suggests wicked power. *The villain gave a sinister laugh.*

Forbidding means seeming dangerous or very unpleasant. *The overgrown entrance to the cave looked forbidding.*

Ominous is a formal word that means threatening. It often suggests that the particular danger is not clear or not known. *An ominous quiet hung over the battlefield, and the soldiers grew tense and watchful.*

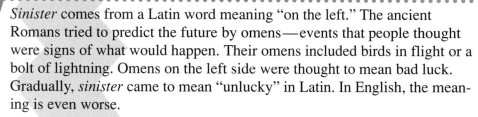

WORD STORY

Sinister comes from a Latin word meaning "on the left." The ancient Romans tried to predict the future by omens—events that people thought were signs of what would happen. Their omens included birds in flight or a bolt of lightning. Omens on the left side were thought to mean bad luck. Gradually, *sinister* came to mean "unlucky" in Latin. In English, the meaning is even worse.

Ominous comes from *omen*. The Romans believed that some omens meant good luck, but that idea has been lost in English.

Throw
verb

Throw means to make something go through the air by moving your hand and arm. *The shortstop threw the ball to first base.*

Toss means to throw easily or gently. *I tossed a pencil to Dawna.*

Pitch means to throw something and try to make it go to a certain place. *Nancy pitched a wad of paper into the wastebasket.*

Heave can mean to throw, especially something heavy. *Danny heaved the bag of garbage into the bin behind the store.*

Cast means to throw with some force. *Linda cast her fishing line far out into the water.*

Fling means to throw forcefully and carelessly. *Aline's mother said, "I do wish you wouldn't fling your clothes all over the floor."*

CONTINUED ON THE NEXT PAGE

Hurl means to throw with much force. *At the track meet, Jacob hurled the discus for a new school record.*

Sling can mean to fling, especially with a long curving motion. *The skater slung a scarf around her neck.*

Tie
verb

Tie means to fasten something with string or something like string. *Mom and I tied several bundles of newspapers with twine so that we could take them to the recycling center.*

Bind means to tie, especially to tie things close together. *The magician asked for someone in the audience to bind his hands together before he was locked in the trunk.*

Lash means to tie tightly and firmly. *Sam and Kendra lashed the canvas over the boat before the storm arrived.*

Strap means to fasten things together with narrow strips of leather, metal, or other material. *Mali watched with fascination as the machine strapped bundles of hay.*

Hitch means to fasten something with a rope, strap, ring, or other connection. *A young woman at the rental office helped us hitch the trailer to our car bumper.*

Tether means to fasten an animal to a post with a rope or chain, so that the animal can move around a bit. *Their pet goat, tethered in the backyard, has eaten the grass in a circle.*

SEE **join** for related words.
ANTONYMS: free, unfasten, untie

Their pet goat, **tethered** in the backyard, has eaten the grass in a circle.

Tiny
adjective

Tiny means very small. *The baby wrapped its tiny hand around its mother's finger.*

Wee means tiny. It is used mostly in stories, songs, and poems. *The wee elves danced under the toadstools.*

Teeny is an informal word that means tiny. *"There can't be many calories in that teeny piece of cake," Mitch told himself.*

Miniature means very much smaller than usual. *Ron collects miniature soldiers in historical uniforms.*

Minute means very tiny. It is pronounced mī nüt′. *Some chemicals are dangerous even in minute amounts.*

Microscopic means so tiny that it can be seen only by using a microscope. *Looking through the microscope, we were amazed at the number and variety of microscopic creatures in one drop of pond water.*

SEE **little** for related words.
ANTONYMS: enormous, gigantic, huge, immense

Tired
adjective

Tired means having little energy or strength left. *The twins cleaned out half the garage and then decided they were too tired to do any more work.*

Weary means feeling very tired and unable to do more. *Kelly studied her history assignment until nearly bedtime and then felt just too weary to attempt reading the short story for English class.*

Fatigued means very tired after hard work or effort. *After completing the 10-mile walk for charity, we felt fatigued but happy.*

Exhausted can mean having no strength or energy left at all. *After days of fighting the forest fire, the crews were exhausted.*

Worn-out can mean exhausted. *Jeremy claims he feels worn-out after just watching that exercise video.*

Bushed is an informal word that means exhausted, often after much physical activity. *"I finished shearing all the sheep in the pen," said Uncle Silas, "and I'm bushed!"*

Sleepy means tired and ready to sleep. *The baby always gets sleepy in the middle of the afternoon, so we put her in her crib for a nap.*

Tool

noun

Tool means something used to make work easier, especially something used by hand. *Fine carving requires a number of tools, from powerful chisels to delicate scrapers.*

Device means a tool used for a special job. *The cotton gin, a device to remove seeds from raw cotton, changed the history of the United States.*

Instrument means a tool used for a special job that requires exactness. *The surgical instruments lay in order on the cart beside the operating table.*

Utensil means a tool or container, especially one used in cooking. *Aunt Julienne claims she doesn't need a lot of fancy utensils, and her meals are wonderful.*

Appliance means a machine that does a particular job, especially in the home. *We have so many electrical appliances in the kitchen that there's almost no counter space left.*

Implement means a tool used to farm or garden. *Mr. Gorsuch keeps his rake, shovel, and other large implements under his porch.*

SEE **gadget** for related words.

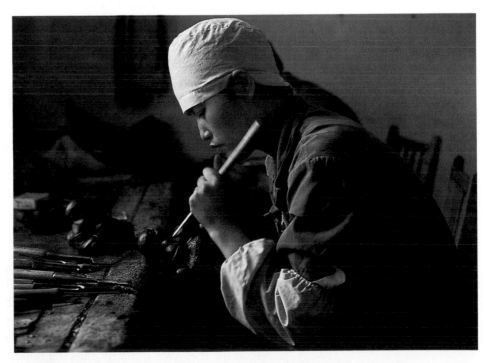

Fine carving requires a number of **tools,** from powerful chisels to delicate scrapers.

Top
noun

Top means the highest point or part of something. *There are TV broadcasting antennas on the top of that skyscraper.*

Crown can mean the top of something. *A line of trees runs along the crown of the hill.*

Summit means the very top of something, especially a mountaintop. It emphasizes that this is the very highest point. *The summit of Mount Rainier is 14,410 feet above sea level.*

Peak means a pointed top, especially of a mountain. *Van took a photograph of the sun setting behind the jagged mountain peaks.*

Crest can mean a summit or a peak. *Kainoa guided her surfboard across the smooth water just under the crest of the big wave.*

Acme means the highest point, or a perfect example. It is not used about physical objects. It is used about skills, plans, processes, or qualities. *Pete thinks his jokes are the acme of wit.*

ANTONYM: bottom

Trade
verb

Trade means to give something and receive something else in return for what you gave. *The baseball team traded a pitcher for a shortstop.*

Swap means to trade. It is an informal word. *"Nelson," asked his brother, "will you swap your old cap for three candy bars?"*

Barter can mean to trade one kind of goods or service for another. It emphasizes that money is not used. *Our zoo has bartered two lion cubs for a rare lizard.*

Exchange means to give one thing and get another thing back. It is often used when the two things are similar. *Mrs. Ryoo's new toaster didn't work right, so the store exchanged it for another one.*

Switch can mean to exchange. *Edie switched bus seats with Jaime.*

WORD STORY

Swap comes from an old English word meaning "to hit." It may have begun as an imitation of the noise made by a hand hitting something. How did it get to mean "trade"? In old days, two people who had settled on a trade would strike each other's hands as a sign that they had made a deal. Today, people show the same thing by shaking hands. Someday, perhaps *shake* will mean "trade."

After repeated **trials,** the boys have discovered how to make fudge just the way they like it.

Trial
noun

Trial means a process of learning the facts about something by attempting to do or use it. *After repeated trials, the boys have discovered how to make fudge just the way they like it.*

Try can mean a trial. *The mechanic gave the engine another try, but it still didn't work.*

Proof can mean a trial. *Today's game will be a proof of the plays the team practiced this week.*

Experiment means a carefully planned trial, especially to learn scientific facts. *Lydia and Carmen are doing an experiment to see how strong their electromagnet is.*

Test means a thorough trial, often an official one. It suggests very definite results. *Government tests show that the meat is safe to eat.*

Audition means a trial to see how well a person performs, especially an actor, singer, or musician. *"Auditions for the choir are open to all members of the congregation," announced Reverend Parkton.*

HAVE YOU HEARD...?

You may have heard people say that "the proof of the pudding is in the eating." This means that the real test of a plan or project is not how good it looks or sounds, but how well it works. The phrase comes from Miguel de Cervantes' book *Don Quixote.*

Trick

noun

Trick means something done to cheat or deceive someone, especially by making a person believe something that is not true. *"Look out behind you!" shouted the detective, but the criminal knew that trick and didn't turn around.*

Device can mean a trick. *By the device of letting the enemy capture false plans, the general made sure that the attack was a surprise.*

Dodge can mean a trick, especially to avoid a responsibility. *When his tax dodges didn't work, Mr. Brady ended up owing the government $800.*

Maneuver can mean a clever or skillful trick. It suggests planning and a series of actions. *Lisbet went out a couple of times with Dale as a maneuver to make Vince jealous.*

Hocus-pocus means confusing talk or actions, meant to deceive. *Amid much hocus-pocus, the short clown stole the tall clown's hat and hankie.*

Gimmick means a clever or tricky idea or device. It can mean a way of getting something from someone. *I can't believe I fell for his gimmick of offering to pay me back on the 30th of February.*

SEE **cheat** and **deceive** for related words.

Amid much **hocus-pocus,** the short clown stole the tall clown's hat and hankie.

436

Trip
noun

Trip means the act of going some distance. *Eric and his family went on a trip to Dallas.*

Journey means a long trip. *Krystal hopes to make a journey to Africa someday.*

Tour means a trip, often to see many places. *The President stopped in five countries during his tour of South America.*

Voyage means a long trip, especially by ship. *Columbus made four voyages to the Western Hemisphere.*

Cruise means a voyage for pleasure that takes you to several places. *Dario's parents celebrated their twenty-fifth anniversary with a Caribbean cruise.*

Expedition means a trip for some special purpose. *Explorers have gone on expeditions to the South Pole to learn more about the earth.*

Outing means a short trip taken for enjoyment. *The Lal family's outing to the park was cut short by rain.*

Jaunt means an outing. *Cassie has plans for a jaunt downtown this weekend.*

Excursion is a formal word that means an outing, especially of a group. *The company excursion to Lake Lewis is open to all full-time employees and their families.*

Trek means a long and difficult trip. *In 1849, thousands of people made the trek to California to search for gold there.*

Pilgrimage means a journey to a holy place as an act of devotion. *The Koran commands every Muslim to make a pilgrimage to Mecca.*

WORD STORY

Pilgrimage comes from two Latin words meaning "outside the country" or "foreign." These were combined into one Latin word meaning "foreigner" or "wanderer." Hundreds of years ago, people did not travel as often as they do now, because travel was very difficult. People who did travel were often going to visit religious centers and holy places. Religious pilgrims were the only foreigners that many people saw, and so the two words became connected.

The young trapeze artist **relies** on his father to catch him in midair.

Trust
verb

Trust means to believe firmly that a person will do exactly what he or she says. *Bob loaned Allie the money because he trusts her to pay it back.*

Rely means to trust. It suggests making decisions or doing things based on firm belief. *The young trapeze artist relies on his father to catch him in midair.*

Count can mean to rely. *Dr. Thunderstone counts on her nurse to deal with patients who are not seriously ill.*

Depend can mean to rely. It suggests a need that you believe someone will satisfy. *Kelly depends on her dog guide, Scout, to take her everywhere.*

Confide can mean to show trust in someone by telling secrets. *The boys have been friends for years and confide in each other completely.*

Bank on means to depend. *Because Pablo banks on getting his old summer job back, he's not looking for another one.*

ANTONYMS: distrust, mistrust

WATCH IT!

Trust and **entrust** look alike. But *trust* means to believe that someone will do what he or she says. *Entrust* means to give something to someone who will keep it safe. *I trust Phyllis completely. Therefore, I have entrusted my kitten to her while I'm away next week.*

438

Try
verb

Try means to make an effort to do something. It often suggests lack of success. *The driver tried to stop, but the car skidded on the ice.*

Attempt means to try. It suggests willingness but some doubt of success. *Doctors will attempt to transplant a new heart into the sick baby.*

Undertake means to try. *Myron and April undertook to clean the whole apartment while their parents were at the game.*

Endeavor is a formal word that means to attempt very strongly to do something. *"And now," called the ringmaster, "Kardak the Magnificent will endeavor to raise this horse into the air!"*

Strive means to try very hard to get something done. It suggests hard work. *Representatives of the two governments are striving to negotiate a peace treaty between their countries.*

ANTONYMS: abandon, give up, quit

WATCH IT!

People sometimes say that they will "try and" do something. This phrase is very informal, not correct for writing. The correct phrase is "try to" do something. The trying is part of the same idea as the doing. They are not two ideas to be joined by "and." Try to be careful about this phrase when you write.

IDIOMS

There are many idioms that mean to try to do something. Here are some of them:

give something a whirl

take a crack at something

have a fling at something

take a shot at something

make a stab at something

try your hand at something

What others can you think of?

Turn
verb

Turn means to go around like a wheel. *As the propellers turned more quickly, the helicopter rose into the air.*

SEE **rotate** for related words.

Turn is used in phrases that have special meanings. Each of these phrases has its own set of synonyms.

turn down

Turn down means to say no to an offer or suggestion. *Wally asked Lola to go to the party with him, but she turned him down.*

Refuse means to turn down. *The team has refused the quarterback's request for a million-dollar raise in salary.*

Reject means to refuse to take something. It suggests a blunt, complete refusal. *Embarrassed by falling on the ice, Petra angrily rejected people's helping hands.*

Decline is a formal word that means to refuse. It suggests a polite refusal. *"I fear I must decline to be on your city's library committee," wrote the author.*

turn into

Turn into means to change from one thing to a different one. *"Next," the magician told her audience, "I shall turn these roses into tulips."*

Transform means to change the form or appearance of something so that it seems to be a different thing. *With a new belt and hat and a different pair of shoes, Ms. Ortiz transformed her office clothes into an evening outfit.*

Transfigure is a formal word that means to transform. It often suggests a very complete change, much for the better. *A new roof and new siding completely transfigured the old house.*

Convert means to turn something into something else, so that it can be used in a different way. *The new landlord converted the basement into a laundry room.*

Mutate means to change, especially in physical nature. *As germs mutate, they may become able to resist medicine.*

Evolve means to change gradually. *The government of the United States has evolved since 1787 to the system we know today.*

CONTINUED ON THE NEXT PAGE

turn over

Turn over means to let someone else have what was yours. *When Patty outgrows these sweaters, she will turn them over to her younger sister.*

Transfer means to turn over. It suggests an official change. *The Seventeenth Amendment transferred the election of senators from state legislators to voters.*

Pass can mean to turn over. *Dad has to stay late at the office because his boss went out of town and passed a lot of work to him.*

Give can mean to turn over. It suggests willingness. *Randall dried half the dishes and then gave Terry the towel.*

Yield can mean to turn over. It suggests some unwillingness that is overcome. *Rosa finally yielded the video game controls to Paul.*

Entrust can mean to turn something over for safekeeping. *Shabila entrusts her guppies to the people upstairs when she goes to camp.*

turn up

Turn up means to find something that was not in plain sight or well known, as if by digging. *Joyce turned up Dad's glasses behind the sofa.*

Uncover can mean to turn up. It suggests letting other people know. *Uncovered in an attic, the painting has now been sold for $14,000.*

Reveal means to make something known that was not known before. *X rays will reveal whether Mrs. Crow broke any bones when she fell.*

Disclose can mean to reveal. It suggests that something was hidden or secret until made known. *Both candidates have disclosed details of their business activities.*

Expose can mean to reveal. It suggests making public something bad. *Television reporters exposed the polluted condition of state parks.*

Bring to light means to uncover. It suggests that something has been unknown for a long time. *"Frozen Bigfoot Brought to Light!" said the supermarket newspaper headline.*

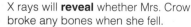

X rays will **reveal** whether Mrs. Crow broke any bones when she fell.

Type
noun

Type means a group of things or people that are alike in some way or ways, and different from other things. *Iris likes the type of carnival ride that spins around fast and makes her dizzy.*

Kind means a type. *"What kinds of bird did you see?" Mr. Mendoza asked Raul.*

Sort means a type. *My brother Ethan is at the age where he likes spiders, snakes, and things of that sort.*

Class means a type. *Mrs. Waller always complains about how there used to be a better class of people in her building.*

Variety can mean a type. *Ned claims he's eaten every variety of ice cream they sell here.*

Category means a group of things that are alike in some particular way that is easy to describe. *Kenny sorts his CDs into three categories: wonderful, good, and OK.*

Breed can mean a type. *Beagles, St. Bernards, and collies are three well-known breeds of dog. Dog-lovers are a different breed from cat-lovers.*

Brand and **make** mean a group of manufactured items that are alike and have the same name. *Mr. Wu always buys the same brand of coffee, but he keeps trying new makes of coffeepots.*

WORDS AT PLAY
. . . .

I went to buy a pair of shoes—
So many kinds! Which ones to choose?
I didn't want the hype type,
or the bland brand,
or the fake make,
or the society variety.

But I liked the look of the sport sort—
you know, the speed breed!
I counted the money that I earned cutting grass
and looked for some shoes in the fastest class.
But—shoes cost a bundle in that category,
so I need to earn more. That's my shoe-buying story.

Ugly
adjective

Ugly means unpleasant to look at. *Vandals have covered the wall with ugly spray paint marks.*

Unsightly means ugly. It is a milder word. *The neighbors all joined in and got rid of the unsightly garbage from the vacant lot.*

Homely means not good-looking. It is also not as strong a word as *ugly. Amid the crowds in the railway station, Lise was delighted to see the smiling, homely face of her beloved Uncle Frank.*

Plain can mean not pretty or not handsome. *Grandma says that plain people should be proud because their looks are honest.*

Unattractive means not likely to attract people because of an ugly appearance. *The landlord is having difficulty renting the apartment because it is painted such unattractive colors.*

Hideous means very ugly and horrible to look at. *Butch loves movies with hideous monsters, but I think they're mostly boring and stupid.*

Monstrous can mean hideous. *The monstrous faces stared at Mr. Williamson and chanted, "Trick or treat!"*

ANTONYMS: attractive, beautiful, good-looking

WORD STORY

Ugly comes from an old Scandinavian word meaning "fear."
Hideous comes from an old French word meaning "fear."
One reason we have synonyms is that sometimes the same
idea came into English from different languages.

443

Uncertain
adjective

Uncertain means not known for sure. *It is still uncertain which of the candidates won the election.*

Unsettled means uncertain because something may change. *Experts say that business conditions are still unsettled.*

Touch-and-go means uncertain and risky. *Grandpa's operation was a success, but the doctors admitted that it was touch-and-go for a while.*

Indefinite means not clear or not exact, and therefore uncertain. *Kishi's mother has a job that requires her to travel an indefinite number of days every month.*

Vague means indefinite. *The store owner promises to hire people from the neighborhood, but he's vague about when and how many.*

Debatable can mean uncertain and open to discussion. *Many people think the facts of President Kennedy's assassination are debatable.*

ANTONYMS: certain, definite, sure

IDIOMS

There are a number of idioms that mean "uncertain." Although they all have the same general meaning, you can see from the sample sentences that you cannot always substitute one for the other.

in the balance: *The fate of the Union hung in the balance when the armies of Lee and Meade clashed at Gettysburg.*

up in the air: *"Cardozo Middle School has a one-goal lead, but the outcome of the game is still up in the air," said the announcer.*

neck and neck: *The race between the forest fire and the firefighters remained neck and neck until the rain came.*

nip and tuck: *It's nip and tuck whether the construction of the new gymnasium will be finished in time for the start of school.*

Under
preposition

Under means with something else on top or over. *Flo put a saucer under each cup. Tom set down the shopping bag under the hall table.*

Below means lower than something else. It can mean right under something, or at a lower level somewhere else. *Far below the top of the skyscraper, the cars on the streets look like toys.*

CONTINUED ON THE NEXT PAGE

Beneath means under or below. It often suggests being covered. *On hot summer days, the cows lie in the shade beneath the trees.*

Underneath means under. It suggests being hidden from sight. *Paul keeps his diary in a locked box underneath his bed.*

At the bottom of and **on the bottom of** mean at the lowest part of something. *At the bottom of the box was an old roll of film. On the bottom of the film package were the words, "Use by Dec. 1972."*

ANTONYMS: above, over

Understand
verb

Understand means to get the meaning of something. *After years of work, scientists are beginning to understand the writing carved on this stone by an ancient people.*

Comprehend means to understand. It suggests complete understanding. *Mr. Dunne says his kids comprehend their computer programs so much better than he does that he has to ask for advice.*

Grasp can mean to understand. It suggests taking hold of an idea with the mind. *Most people have trouble grasping how far it is from the sun to even the nearest star.*

Realize means to understand something clearly and be fully aware of it. *Realizing that he had hurt Pedro's feelings, Bart quickly apologized.*

Catch on is an informal phrase that means to understand. It often suggests not understanding at first. *Once Mrs. Park caught on to what we were planning, she offered to help with all the phone calls.*

Take in can mean to understand. It suggests complete understanding of something complicated. *As he studied the tracks, Standing Elk took in the whole story of what happened among the wolves, the buffalo, and the coyote.*

After years of work, scientists are beginning to **understand** the writing carved on this stone by an ancient people.

Unimportant
adjective

Unimportant means not mattering much. *"It's a good story, Macky,"* *said Ms. Lee, "but you've included a lot of unimportant details."*

Small can mean unimportant. *We had a small problem with the new VCR, but the store fixed it right away.*

Petty means unimportant. It often suggests a lack of generosity or too much concern for small things. *Amber isn't much fun to be with because of her constant petty complaints.*

Pointless can mean without purpose and unimportant. *Deron says the movie has too much pointless music.*

Trifling means too unimportant to be worth attention. *"A trifling problem," said the great detective. "Anyone could have solved it."*

Insignificant means so unimportant that it is meaningless. *The couch is like new except for an insignificant stain near the bottom.*

Immaterial means unimportant. The word suggests that something matters so little that it barely exists. *As long as the gloves are warm, the color is immaterial.*

ANTONYMS: important, significant

HAVE YOU HEARD...?

You may have heard people talk about "fiddling while Rome burns." This means to do something very unimportant in the middle of an emergency. The Roman emperor Nero is supposed to have played music during a terrible fire instead of doing anything to stop it. Violins hadn't been invented then, so he actually played an instrument like the one shown in this movie scene, but "fiddling" sounds even more pointless.

Unkind
adjective

Unkind means hurting others' feelings, not friendly or good to others. *The county humane society works to keep people from being unkind to animals.*

Unfriendly means hostile and showing dislike for others. *We thought the new student was unfriendly, but it turns out that he's just very shy.*

Mean means unkind on purpose in a selfish way. It suggests contempt. *Dick's jokes aren't funny, and they're often mean.*

Nasty means very mean. It suggests an active desire to cause pain. *It's a science-fiction story about a girl who stops a nasty villain from enslaving some gentle space aliens.*

Spiteful means filled with a desire to hurt or annoy others. *Aunt Flo doesn't like that movie critic because she thinks he just tries to be spiteful.*

Insensitive can mean slow to notice or care how others feel. *Shelly apologized for her insensitive and thoughtless remark.*

Hardhearted and **cold-hearted** mean lacking pity or sympathy. *The hardhearted general ordered the farmers to give their grain to his soldiers. When the farmers resisted, he gave a cold-hearted order to burn their barns.*

Heartless and **unfeeling** mean completely without pity or sympathy. These words suggest an absence of normal human qualities. *"Massive pollution such as this is a heartless crime," the lawyer told the jury. "It is your duty to punish this unfeeling attack on public health."*

SEE **cruel** for related words.
ANTONYM: kind

Uproar
noun

Uproar means the loud yelling of a crowd. *The union meeting ended in uproar without a vote.*

Rumpus is an informal word that means a noisy disturbance that someone makes. *Every time we go past Allie's house, her dogs make a big rumpus.*

Ruckus means rumpus. It is also an informal word. *"Your mother had to bring work home tonight," Mr. Santos told the children, "so I don't want to hear any ruckus."*

Hubbub means a loud, confused noise, especially of voices. *With everyone in the class talking at once, the hubbub is deafening.*

Hullabaloo means hubbub. *The hullabaloo of the neighbors' party made it hard to sleep.*

Outcry means a loud noise, especially of angry voices. *Despite an outcry from the passengers, the bus driver went past the stop.*

Clamor means outcry. *When the singer refused to perform, the clamor of people in the audience was fierce.*

Row means a noisy quarrel. *The coach took Barry out of the game after he got in a row with another player.*

SEE **loud, noise,** and **shout** for related words.

When the singer refused to perform, the **clamor** of people in the audience was fierce.

Upset
adjective

Upset means nervous and feeling out of control. *Jerome is upset because his jacket is missing.*

Flustered means upset and confused. *Boos from the fans got the pitcher flustered, and he walked the next two batters.*

Rattled can mean flustered. *Jena was so rattled when she fell off her bike on the busy road that she couldn't ride home.*

Fazed means upset and worried. It is an informal word, mostly used with "not." *Mrs. Aragon is not fazed by having lost the election, and she will run again.*

Agitated can mean upset and very excited. *"Why on earth won't you perform?" asked the singer's agitated manager.*

Perturbed means upset and afraid. It suggests a feeling that lasts for some time. *Perturbed by her dropping grades, Leigh went to talk to the school counselor.*

Shaken can mean badly upset and afraid. It suggests a feeling so strong that it produces physical weakness. *Mr. Watkins was shaken by his fall, but not injured.*

Ruffled can mean upset and angry. *Neal has learned not to get ruffled when people try to help by pushing his wheelchair.*

Troubled means upset. It suggests not knowing what to do. *Doctors say they are troubled by the increase in cases of tuberculosis.*

SEE **confused** and **worried** for related words.

"Why on earth won't you perform?" asked the singer's **agitated** manager.

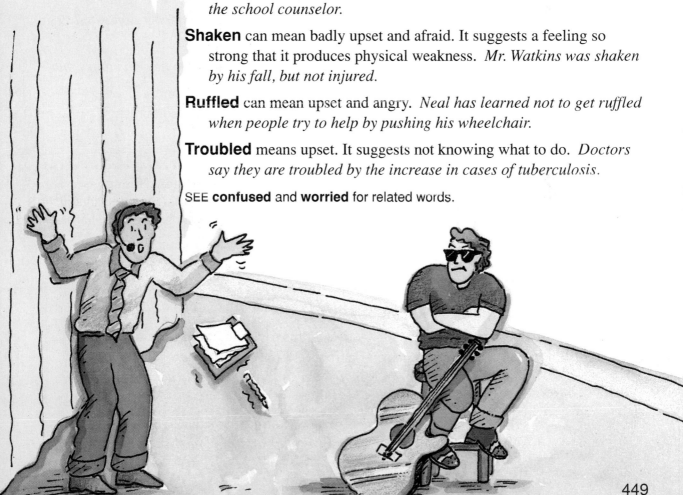

449

Urge
verb

Urge means to try to get someone to do something by saying to do it. *Highway police are urging people not to drive during this blizzard.*

Press can mean to urge by asking strongly several times. *Since it was so late, the Douglasses pressed us to stay for supper.*

Incite means to urge, especially by arousing emotion. *The cattle ranchers incited each other to attack the rustlers' hideout.*

Coax means to urge in gentle, pleasant ways. *"Just a little chicken soup," Mr. Greer coaxed his sick daughter.*

Tempt means to urge someone to do something wrong. *Theo knows he's not allowed down by the tracks, but his buddies tempted him to go.*

Spur can mean to urge, especially by causing emotion. *His family's pride in him has spurred Myung-Dae to study hard.*

Exhort is a formal word that means to urge strongly. *The speaker exhorted students to take pride in their cultural backgrounds and to learn more about them.*

Egg on means to urge or encourage. *If Donna is too nervous to try out for cheerleading with us, we'll have to egg her on.*

SEE **beg, command, encourage,** and **persuade** for related words.

WORD STORY

Egg on does not mean to urge someone by using eggs. This *egg* is another word, spelled the same way, that comes from an old Icelandic word meaning "edge." If you "egg someone on," it is as if you sharpen that person's will and put an edge on it.

Use
verb

Use means to put something into practice or service. *In Ghana, men and women use brightly colored kente cloth for all kinds of clothes.*

Employ can mean to use. With this meaning, it is a formal word. It suggests a particular purpose. *"The city will keep roads open during the blizzard," said the mayor, "by employing hundreds of snowplows and salt trucks."*

Utilize means to use something or to find a practical way of using something. *Recycling utilizes many tons of paper that used to be thrown away.*

CONTINUED ON THE NEXT PAGE

Exercise means to make use of something. It often suggests using a right or a quality of mind. *"Exercise some patience," Ms. Ramos advised Hilda, "and your drawing will improve."*

Apply can mean to make use of something in a practical way. It often suggests using knowledge. *Since she retired, Mrs. Lindstrom has applied her teaching skills in the adult literacy program.*

Wield means to hold something firmly and use it effectively. *When it comes to pie crust, nobody wields a rolling pin like Mr. Dawkins.*

Useful
adjective

Useful means able to be used easily and in many ways. *Mrs. Montale bought a computer for her hardware store, and she says it's very useful.*

Helpful means giving a lot of help. It suggests helping you do something you couldn't do by yourself. *Thanks to many helpful suggestions from the employees, the company has had much higher profits.*

Handy means useful in simple ways that do not require much work. *Lovanna got one of those handy penknives with all the extra tools.*

Convenient means saving trouble, time, and work. *Many people find tape-recorded books more convenient than Braille books.*

Functional and **serviceable** can mean useful. They suggest a lack of decoration or style. *These pre-owned snow boots are scuffed, but they're still perfectly functional. There's a lot of other serviceable winter clothing at the thrift shop.*

Applicable means suitable to use for a particular purpose. It usually describes ideas, not things. *An eagle carried the baseball off, and the umpire is trying to find an applicable rule.*

ANTONYM: useless

> **"**In mathematics, . . . whatsoever is most beautiful and regular is also found to be the most useful and excellent.**"**
> — Sir D'Arcy Wentworth Thompson (1860–1948)

WORD STORY

Applicable comes from *apply,* of course, and *apply* comes from two Latin words meaning "to fold on." Whenever you see *-plic* or *-ply,* it's likely that the word story starts with folding. An implied idea is folded in. A complicated problem feels all folded together.

Useless
adjective

Useless means not worth using or doing, or not able to be used. *It's useless arguing with Bill, because he never admits it when he's wrong.*

Worthless means having no use or value. *If the broken leg on that table can't be fixed, the table is really worthless.*

Needless means useless and without purpose. It suggests a waste of time. <u>*Whisper of Death*</u> *would be a much better mystery if it omitted needless attempts at humor.*

Inefficient means not worth using or doing because work is wasted. *Copying whole pages of the textbook is an inefficient way to study the lesson.*

Fruitless means producing poor results or no results. *After a fruitless search outside for their cat, the Benoits saw him watching them through the living room window.*

Futile means useless because not successful. *After a few hours, Dan and Julio gave up their futile attempt to build a treehouse by themselves.*

Vain can mean completely futile. *"Even if we do not see any results,"* preached Reverend Tilmon, *"no good deed is vain or wasted."*

ANTONYM: useful

Usual
adjective

Usual means most commonly seen, found, or happening. *In Chicago some snow is usual in winter. We'll meet for lunch at the usual time.*

Customary means usual or according to custom or habit. *It is customary for me to get up at seven o'clock. For the Bedouins of Saudi Arabia, the customary way to travel is by camel.*

Traditional means customary because it has been handed down from generation to generation. *Acupuncture, which relieves pain by inserting needles into certain parts of the body, is a traditional Chinese medical treatment.*

Regular means usual and according to custom or rule. *Sarah was late and missed her regular bus.*

Ordinary means usual and regular. *Visiting and helping out friends who are sick is an ordinary part of my grandmother's life.*

CONTINUED ON THE NEXT PAGE

452

Accustomed means customary. *The cat sat in its accustomed place by the fireside.*

Habitual can mean usual or customary. *"All right, let's get to business!" is our teacher's habitual way of starting class.*

SEE **common** and **general** for related words.
ANTONYMS: peculiar, rare, unusual

WORDS AT PLAY

A habitual life pleases Lester,
With each day very much like the last.
He likes custom and values tradition,
And he judges what's new by what's past.

And that's why last Tuesday at sundown
When the crocodiles flew overhead
And the trees started clapping their branches,
And the sun headed northward instead,
When the clouds sang old comedy theme songs,
And the sidewalks grew bright purple fuzz,
Lester cried in a voice of annoyance:
"Now I want everything as it *was!*"

Valuable
adjective

Valuable means worth very much. Something may be valuable because it costs a lot, or because people care a lot about it. *Even more valuable than the silver prize cup is the pride in his talent that Darnell has gained.*

Precious means specially valuable. It is often used about things that people care about. *"These pictures are precious to me," Mr. Spencer told his class, "because I never saw my grandfather's face except in them."*

Prized means valuable. It is often used about one thing that is more important than other valuable things. *The museum is happy to report that the minor fire did not damage its prized 600-year-old Nigerian carvings.*

Inestimable is a formal word that means valuable beyond estimating. *The National Park System has conserved lands of inestimable beauty and importance.*

Priceless means too valuable for any price. *The little plane battled fierce storms to bring priceless medicine to the Arctic town.*

Invaluable means priceless. *Now that Mr. Orozco no longer walks well, he finds the church's service van invaluable.*

SEE **expensive** and **important** for related words.
ANTONYM worthless

CONTINUED ON THE NEXT PAGE

Normally, words that start with *in-* have meanings opposite from the rest of the word. For example, *indivisible* means not divisible. But **valuable** and **invaluable** both mean that something is worth a lot. Why? Because *value* has two meanings. It can mean:

1) to think that something is worth a lot. *Lisa values her friendship with Yuying.*
2) to judge how much something is worth. *The antique store values the vase at five hundred dollars.*

If you think that something is really worth a lot (definition 1), then the amount may be so big that you cannot judge its value (definition 2). So the more valuable something is, the more likely it is to be invaluable too.

Two more words that look like opposites but mean the same thing are *flammable* and *inflammable*. They each mean easily set on fire.

Value
noun

Value means what something is good for or how much people want it, usually thought of as its price. *Harvey bought the lamp in the antique store for ten dollars, but its actual value is at least fifty dollars.*

Importance means how much something matters to people. *The discovery of penicillin was of great importance to medicine.*

Worth means value, especially something's usefulness or importance. *The owners recognized Delgado's worth to the team and gave him a salary of a million dollars.*

Merit means value, but it points to the goodness of something, not to its price. *The merit of Lien's plan is that it includes so many people.*

Account can mean value. It is often used in negative sentences. *Mom thinks my large collection of comic books is of little account.*

SEE **cost** and **price** for related words.

Mom thinks my large collection of comic books is of little **account.**

Very
adverb

Very means more than usually. *A very tall boy like Hank may have trouble buying clothes.*

Awfully can mean truly and deeply. *When Mrs. Marston's dog was hurt, she got awfully upset.*

Extremely means much more than usual. *It has been extremely hot this week.*

Exceedingly means extremely. *In the past, it was often exceedingly difficult for people with disabilities to enter buildings and vehicles.*

Terribly can mean awfully. *"This mission," the captain told Sergeant Slovitz, "is terribly dangerous."*

Highly means fully and actively. *Parents in this neighborhood are highly involved with school activities.*

Mighty can mean very. Used this way, it is an informal word. *Estrella's pink dress is mighty pretty.*

WORD WORKSHOP

The word *very* is often overused. Instead, you can use one of the synonyms for *very* shown here, or you can use stronger synonyms for the words that *very* modifies. See what happens in the paragraph below when we replace *very* with these kinds of words.

It was ~~very hot~~ *sweltering* in the city. It was so hot that our clothes became ~~very wet~~ *drenched* only minutes after we put them on. Roddy suggested that if we ran ~~very~~ *extremely* fast the breeze would cool us, but (surprise!) that didn't work. There was ~~a very good~~ *an excellent* movie downtown, but we didn't have enough cash. Then Mary Lynn came up with ~~a very cheap~~ *an economical* suggestion. So we spent a cool, comfortable afternoon at the public library.

Victory
noun

Victory means complete success and defeat of an opponent in a contest, game, or war. *Washington's victory at Yorktown convinced the British that they could not prevent American independence.*

Conquest means total victory by force. It suggests taking control of the loser's property. *The Spanish conquest of the Aztecs was made possible when thousands of other Indians rebelled against Aztec rule.*

Triumph means supreme victory and joy. *Ms. Walton gained a triumph in the city seniors' golf tournament.*

Win means a victory, especially in sports. With this meaning it is an informal word. *A win today means that Lofaro will wrestle Jackson for the championship.*

Landslide can mean an election victory won by a very large majority of the votes. *Elected in a landslide, the new mayor promised that she would deserve the voters' confidence.*

Sweep can mean a complete victory, winning all the games in a series, or all the prizes in a competition. *Best Cat, Best Pet, Most Personality—the neighborhood pet show was a sweep for Queenie!*

Walkover means an easy victory. *The game ended 5 to 4 in overtime, so you know it wasn't a walkover.*

SEE **conquer** and **defeat** for related words.

Ms. Walton gained a **triumph** in the city seniors' golf tournament.

457

From the boat on Lake Michigan, we had a great **view** of downtown Chicago.

View
noun

View means what can be seen from a particular place. It often suggests something enjoyable to look at. *From the boat on Lake Michigan, we had a great view of downtown Chicago.*

Sight can mean something worth looking at. *Lonnie's class will spend two days touring the Alamo and other sights of San Antonio.*

Scene can mean a view. It suggests that several parts have combined to create the view. *The painting Harris is working on now is a scene of the sun setting behind a mountain lake.*

Outlook means what can be seen by looking out of something such as a window or a room. *Our motel advertised a "scenic outlook," and from our window we could see the mountains.*

Panorama means a very wide view, especially of an area seen from one point. It suggests a variety of things to see. *Ernesto wheeled his chair to the railing and gazed at the panorama of Niagara Falls.*

SEE **display** for related words.

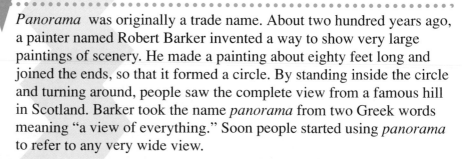

WORD STORY

Panorama was originally a trade name. About two hundred years ago, a painter named Robert Barker invented a way to show very large paintings of scenery. He made a painting about eighty feet long and joined the ends, so that it formed a circle. By standing inside the circle and turning around, people saw the complete view from a famous hill in Scotland. Barker took the name *panorama* from two Greek words meaning "a view of everything." Soon people started using *panorama* to refer to any very wide view.

Visitor
noun

Visitor means someone who goes to be with someone or something. It often suggests spending some time. *Visitors to the United States from overseas often go to see Washington, D.C.*

Guest means a visitor who is welcomed and entertained. It suggests someone who is invited. *How many guests were at Cassie's party?*

Company can mean one or more visitors, usually invited ones. *The Kovals have company tonight, and the hall is full of wonderful cooking aromas from their apartment.*

Caller means a person who makes a short visit, often without an invitation or advance notice. *"Were there any callers while I was at lunch?" Mrs. Lamas asked her secretary.*

Visitors to the United States from overseas often go to see Washington, D.C.

WORDS AT PLAY

We're all washed, and we're brushed, and we're looking our best:
Mom and Dad are expecting a mystery guest!
Though they won't tell us when, and they won't tell us who,
Still I think it might be Uncle Rick from Peru.

Here are dozens of cousins and great-aunts—the dears!—
Plus some people we haven't laid eyes on in years,
Not to mention our friends and our schoolmates from home,
And our old next-door neighbors, who now live in Rome.

So the crowd racks its brains, and the crowd strains its eyes,
All in search of a guest we may not recognize!
Do you know? Can you guess? You say what? Is that true?
You're the mystery guest! Are you sure? Who are *YOU?*

Walk
verb

Walk means to move on foot. *Megan walked to the store for a carton of milk.*

Step means to walk, especially a short distance. *Hariko stepped up to the counter and ordered a cheeseburger.*

Pace means to walk back and forth. *Pacing the deck, Salvator hoped the voyage to America would go quickly.*

Stride means to take long steps. *High Cloud strides proudly as he carries his drum to the dancing place.*

March means to walk steadily, with a regular step. *The band marched down the street to the tune of "God Bless America."*

Hike means to go for a long walk for fun or exercise. *Next summer, Grandma and two friends plan to hike in Vermont for a week.*

Stroll means to walk at an easy, slow speed. *"Let's stroll through the whole mall," Mr. Wallop told Sid, "and then come back to shop."*

Amble means to stroll. *We were ambling through the park and had no idea it had gotten so late.*

Trudge means to walk, especially in a tired, heavy way. *The soldiers trudged into camp and set down their packs and rifles.*

Plod means to walk slowly and heavily. *The horse plodded up the steep hill.*

Shuffle means to walk without taking your feet from the ground. *Shuffling carefully, Oren crossed the slick ice.*

CONTINUED ON THE NEXT PAGE

Sometimes when a word is added to a verb, it creates a phrase that has special meaning. Here are some phrases with **walk:**

Walk away from means to make progress faster than others. *Juwon has walked away from everyone else in the reading race again this summer.*

Walk away with or **walk off with** means to win something easily. *Bonita thinks that her favorite actress will walk away with the Oscar.*

Walk out on is an informal phrase that means to desert someone or something. *Mr. McArthur walked out on his job and his apartment, and no one knows where he's gone.*

Walk over or **walk all over** mean to treat someone or something roughly or badly. *The tenants' lawyer says that the landlord walked all over the housing laws.*

Want
verb

Want means to feel an urge to have or do something. *Peter wants a pair of in-line skates for his birthday.*

Wish means to want or hope for something. *"If you wish to become a ballerina," Madame Claire told Ramona, "you must work as hard as you can."*

Desire is a formal word that means to wish seriously and very much. *Many people desire to conserve the environment but wonder what they personally can do.*

Long means to desire. It suggests thinking about something over and over. *Exiled to Fort Sumner, New Mexico, in 1864, the Navajos longed for their ancestral home in Arizona.*

Yearn means to long. *Evan yearns for Trish to notice him.*

Crave means to want something badly, so that the feeling of need is sharp and hard to bear. *After a year in Florida, Grampa Hendricks says he craves falling leaves and snow.*

Have your heart set on means to want something and not be able to imagine not getting it. *Wanda has her heart set on playing in the marching band.*

Wanda **has her heart set on** playing in the marching band.

461

Warn
verb

Warn means to tell of possible danger. *The lifeguard warned Zack not to dive off the rocks.*

Caution means to urge someone to be careful to avoid danger. *Barb's father has cautioned her to wear safety glasses in their workshop.*

Alert means to warn, usually against serious danger that is approaching fast. *Sirens will alert the townspeople if a tornado approaches.*

Forewarn means to warn in advance. *Forewarned by the radio of rain in the afternoon, Hernán and Yolanda took their raincoats to school.*

Tip off is an informal phrase that means to warn. *To avoid tipping off the poachers, park rangers arrived on foot and camped without a fire.*

SEE **forecast** for related words.

HAVE YOU HEARD...?

You may have heard people say that someone has "cried wolf once too often." To cry wolf means to give a false alarm. In Aesop's fable, a shepherd boy calls for help to save his flock from a wolf. When the other shepherds come to help him, he admits it was a practical joke. After he's done this several times, a wolf really does attack. But people don't believe the boy anymore and so don't come to his aid.

Watch
verb

Watch means to keep your eyes on something carefully for a period of time. *The burglars tied up the guard, so all he could do was watch as they emptied the warehouse.*

Our cat **regards** the birds on the fire escape with longing.

Look means to turn your eyes to something. *"Look at the sea lions!" Darseea called to her mother.*

Eye means to look. *Mustafa eyed each camel carefully as it approached the starting line.*

Regard can mean to watch. *Our cat regards the birds on the fire escape with longing.*

View means to watch for a reason. *"Remember to go outside," Ms. Silber told her class, "and view tonight's lunar eclipse."*

Gaze means to watch steadily. It suggests a strong attraction to what is watched. *Mr. Thurman gazed fondly at his newest grandchild.*

CONTINUED ON THE NEXT PAGE

462

Scan can mean to look over quickly. *Dad scanned the parking lot, trying to spot where he had parked our car.*

Stare means to watch steadily and directly, usually without blinking. *The first time Rachel got a pimple, she felt that everyone in school was staring at her.*

SEE **examine** and **see** for related words.

▼ **WRITER'S CHOICE**

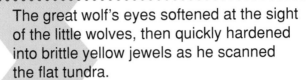

The great wolf's eyes softened at the sight of the little wolves, then quickly hardened into brittle yellow jewels as he scanned the flat tundra.

—Jean Craighead George, *Julie of the Wolves*

Why *scanned?* The wild wolf needs to feed and protect himself and the little wolves. He looks quickly to see if there is anything that he can hunt or that he may have to fight. Because tundra is flat and treeless, it is easy to see anything important there right away.

Way
noun

Way means how something is done. *Art has a book called "150 Ways to Make Paper Airplanes."*

Manner means a way. *Judy Littledog's grandmother is teaching her to make pottery in the traditional manner.*

Fashion means a way. *"I was an athlete once, in my fashion," said Mr. Sanhueza, gesturing at his trophies.*

Style can mean way. *Fara has her own style of shooting baskets, and it works for her.*

System can mean an orderly, logical way of getting things done. *Ms. Chee wants us to organize our class notes according to her system.*

Method means a way. It suggests planning a careful step-by-step action. *The scientific method is to collect information, form a theory, and test the theory with more information.*

Procedure means a method. *Mr. and Mrs. Sheppard are studying the procedure required to adopt a child.*

Routine means a method that is always the same. *Owen's morning routine gets him from bed to school in forty-two minutes.*

Weak
adjective

Weak means lacking strength to stand, bear weight, or resist force. *The roof collapsed because it was too weak to carry the heavy snow.*

Flimsy means thin, light, and weak. It often suggests something poorly made. *Sam's kite was so flimsy that it wouldn't fly.*

Insubstantial is a formal word that means flimsy. *In many countries, poor people live in insubstantial shelters made of cardboard and tin.*

Unsound means in poor condition and weak. *The unsound old building on Mickey's block will be torn down next month.*

Rickety means so weak that it is shaky and likely to fall down. *Dad took one look at the rickety table and told us to save our money.*

SEE **fragile** and **powerless** for related words.
ANTONYMS: powerful, strong, tough

Wealth
noun

Wealth means a very large amount of money or things. *Charmayne likes novels about people of wealth and power.*

Riches means wealth. *The lonely millionaire died and left his riches to his six cats.*

Money can mean wealth. *The da Silvas made their money in the pineapple business.*

Fortune means a huge amount of money. *The museum bought these paintings years ago at low prices, and today they're worth a fortune.*

Treasure means wealth that has been stored up, especially precious objects. *The tomb contains a treasure of Inca gold and jade.*

Mint can mean a very large amount of money. *"I could invent something that everyone wants," Lal daydreamed, "and make a mint."*

Capital can mean money that a company or a person can invest to make more money. *The Sampsons have mortgaged their house to get capital for their African imports business.*

SEE **rich** for related words.
ANTONYM: poverty

CONTINUED ON THE NEXT PAGE

Here in the United States, we use the *dollar*. But did you know that the word *dollar* comes from the name of a coin in central Europe? The Dutch brought the word to the New World.

Argentina uses the *austral*, which means "southern," and Argentina is the southernmost country in the world.

Guatemala uses the *quetzal*, which was named for a beautiful bird that lives there. A picture of this bird appears on the bill.

Japan uses the *yen*, which comes from a Chinese word that means "circular." Korea's *won* comes from the same Chinese word.

Poland uses the *zloty*, which originally meant "golden."

South Africa uses the *rand*, which comes from the name of a major gold-mining region.

Venezuela uses the *bolivar*, which was named after Simón Bolívar, a Venezuelan who liberated much of South America from Spanish rule.

And the currency of Zaïre is called the *zaire*. Guess why.

quetzal

picture of a quetzal on a five-quetzal bill

465

The heroine of the movie has to save her friend from some **creepy** villains.

Weird
adjective

Weird means very strange and mysterious. *From deep in the forest, She Walks Away heard a weird croaking rumble.*

Uncanny means weird. *In "The Hound of the Baskervilles," Sherlock Holmes pursues an uncanny giant dog.*

Spooky is an informal word that means strange enough to make you nervous. *It's spooky how quiet the street gets at night when traffic stops.*

Creepy can mean weird and frightening. *The heroine of the movie has to save her friend from some creepy villains.*

Ghostly means like a ghost. *Sometimes, when Obadele walks homeward across the fields at evening, mist rises in ghostly shapes around him.*

Supernatural means beyond the power of science to explain. *Tales of supernatural beings and powers are found in every culture, all over the world.*

SEE **peculiar** for related words.
ANTONYMS: natural, normal

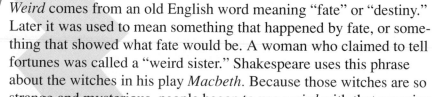

WORD STORY

Weird comes from an old English word meaning "fate" or "destiny." Later it was used to mean something that happened by fate, or something that showed what fate would be. A woman who claimed to tell fortunes was called a "weird sister." Shakespeare uses this phrase about the witches in his play *Macbeth*. Because those witches are so strange and mysterious, people began to use *weird* with that meaning. Today the older meaning is gone. Only Shakespeare's use remains.

466

Welcome
verb

Welcome means to be glad to let someone or something in. *The Drama Club welcomes new members.*

Accept can mean to let in with approval. *Raquel's sister has been accepted by a medical school.*

Admit can mean to allow to enter. *One hundred lucky contest winners will be admitted early and introduced to the band.*

Receive can mean to admit. *After the play, the actress received her fans backstage for an hour.*

Entertain can mean to have someone as a guest. *The Doyles are entertaining students from Tanzania this week.*

Take in means to admit, especially as part of business. *The animal shelter takes in stray dogs and cats.*

Well
adverb

Well means in a good way. *Eric uses sign language very well for a new student.*

Satisfactorily means in a good enough way. *The gardener answered police questions satisfactorily and is no longer a suspect.*

Properly means in the way it should be. *Joel was late today because his building's elevator isn't working properly.*

Right can mean properly. *Gloria wasn't sure how to set the VCR, but she managed to do it right.*

Successfully means in a good enough way to get the result you want. *Mrs. Mukherjee has completed all steps successfully and will become a United States citizen next week.*

Skillfully means in a way that shows talent, training, and understanding. *Pine Hill used the colored sands skillfully as she created her traditional painting.*

Ably means skillfully. *Ramona swims ably and hopes to compete for the school team.*

Efficiently means without wasting energy, time, money, and so on. *After forty years at the post office, Mr. Robinson works faster and more efficiently than people half his age.*

ANTONYMS: badly, poorly

The laundry on the line got **soaking wet** during the rainstorm.

Wet
adjective

Wet means covered with or full of liquid. *"It's too cold for you to go outside with wet hair," said Del's father.*

Soggy means heavy with liquid. *Jane eats her breakfast quickly, because she doesn't like her cereal to get soggy.*

Soaked means thoroughly wet from being in liquid for a while. *After a few minutes of playing with the hose, Aidan and Pia were soaked.*

Saturated is a formal word that means soaked. *Governor Diaz told reporters that the fields are saturated and that any further rain will run off as floodwater.*

Drenched means completely wet. *The drenched golfers hurried into the clubhouse to get out of the rain.*

Soaking wet and **dripping wet** mean completely wet. *The laundry on the line got soaking wet during the rainstorm. The window was open, and the curtains are dripping wet too.*

SEE **damp** for related words.
ANTONYM: dry

HAVE YOU HEARD...?

You may have heard people say that someone is "still wet behind the ears," meaning inexperienced. *Don't ask him for advice—he's still wet behind the ears.* It often suggests that someone is new to a job or activity. The phrase comes from the fact that baby animals are wet when they are born. It takes a while before they dry off. If a baby animal is still wet behind the ears, it is new in the world.

Whisper
verb

Whisper means to speak very softly, so that only someone nearby can hear. *Mira leaned across the table to whisper to Dominick.*

Murmur can mean to speak softly and unclearly, so that it is very difficult to hear you. *My brother Ernesto sometimes talks in his sleep, but he murmurs so softly that I can't understand what he's saying.*

Mumble means to speak without completely forming the words, with the mouth partly closed. It often suggests embarrassment. *"I'm sorry I acted that way," mumbled Dick, his face red with shame.*

Mutter means to mumble. It suggests impatience or anger. *I heard Mr. Harrison muttering, "Those darn pigeons!" while he washed his car.*

Breathe can mean to whisper. It suggests making as little noise as possible. *"Quiet," breathed Lionel, pointing to the sleeping puppies.*

Sigh can mean to say something with a long, slow release of breath. It suggests wishing for something, or sadness. *"If only I had a real best friend," sighed Ernestine.*

Say under your breath means to whisper. *"Beautiful!" said Keisha under her breath, so as not to startle the hummingbird.*

Speak in hushed tones means to talk very softly. It suggests that something makes you feel like being quiet. *As soon as we came to the mummy cases, we all began speaking in hushed tones.*

WRITING TIP: Using Onomatopoeia

Try a little experiment. Stand a few yards away from someone as you quietly say *"Mumblemumblemumble."* Now say *"Murmurmurmurmurmur."* Then say *"Whisperwhisperwhisper."* Did the other person hear you mumbling, murmuring, and whispering?

The use of words that sound like their meanings is called *onomatopoeia* (on′ə mat′ə pē′ə). Onomatopoeia also means the creation of words to imitate sounds. Some words formed this way are *buzz, clang, cuckoo, hiss, hum, sizzle, smack, splash,* and *whir.*

You can use onomatopoeia in your writing to strengthen your meaning, to dramatize events, and to add liveliness. For example, consider the difference between a *knock* on a door and a *rat-a-tat* on a door. Or the difference between a pig *eating* its food and a pig *gulping* and *slurping* it down.

Whole
adjective

Whole means with all its parts and with nothing left out. *Adam watched the whole movie, but Bert left when it got scary.*

Complete means whole. *Consuela gave complete instructions for making a piñata.*

Entire means whole. *Did Lucy and Calvin eat the entire batch of cookies?*

Full can mean whole. *Jimmy can't do the full set of exercises because of his sore elbow.*

Total means all added together. *The total bill was $81.16.*

Unabridged means without any parts taken away. It is used about books, especially dictionaries. *Ingrid finally found the rare word in an unabridged dictionary.*

ANTONYM: partial

WRITER'S CHOICE

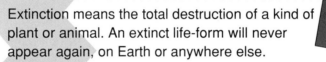

Extinction means the total destruction of a kind of plant or animal. An extinct life-form will never appear again, on Earth or anywhere else.

— Dr. Les Kaufman, *Do Fishes Get Thirsty?*

Why *total?* Extinction is the word we use when all the members of a species die. This does not happen all at once. Some die at one time or place, some at another. Eventually, all these deaths added together mean that the destruction is total. Not even one member of the species is left.

Wicked
adjective

Wicked means doing wrong things on purpose. *In this story, the wicked king is defeated by a poor shepherd girl.*

Immoral is a formal word that means wicked. *Many people believe that the use of animals for scientific research is necessary, but many other people think it is often immoral.*

Bad can mean wicked. *"Bad thoughts are the seeds that grow bad deeds," Reverend Johnson told her congregation.*

Evil means wicked and causing great harm. *At the end of the book, Carlotta destroys the death ray before the mad scientist can carry out his evil plan.*

CONTINUED ON THE NEXT PAGE

Villainous means very wicked. It suggests that someone does wrong things often. *The villainous terrorists kidnapped a bus of tourists.*

Sinful means doing wrong things, as judged by the laws of a religion. *The Koran says it is sinful to murder or steal.*

ANTONYMS: good, moral, virtuous

HAVE YOU HEARD...?

You may have heard people refer to "an ill wind." This comes from the phrase "It's an ill wind that blows nobody good." This means that even bad things are usually helpful to someone, somewhere. If a flood destroys crops in one place, farmers in other places can sell their crops at higher prices. If a factory closes, pigeons have more places to build their nests. If no one at all gets anything good from an event, it must be really very bad. Why a wind? Perhaps because weather is something that hurts some people and helps others, and people can't control it.

Wide
adjective

Wide means spreading a long distance from side to side. It is used about things or spaces. *Main Street is wide and lined with old oak trees.*

Broad means wide. It is used about things. *The river was broad but shallow and easy to cross on horseback.*

Roomy means having plenty of room. It suggests ease and comfort. *Marina borrows her brother's sweaters because she likes her clothes roomy.*

Spacious means having much space. It suggests large size. *Jafar's spacious backyard is the best for playing football.*

Boundless means having no limits but spreading outwards in all directions. *The sailors searched the boundless ocean for signs of land.*

Extensive means filling or covering a great distance. *The airport is surrounded by extensive parking lots.*

Far-flung means happening or found over a wide area. *The balloons that the class released came down in some far-flung places: Miami, Kansas City, and Montreal!*

ANTONYM: narrow

When Rita kicked the goal that won the championship, the fans went **wild.**

Wild
adjective

Wild means extremely excited and out of control. *When Rita kicked the goal that won the championship, the fans went wild.*

Frenzied means too wild to think. *In his frenzied dash for the school bus, Maksim forgot his glasses and his lunch.*

Frantic means wild with rage, fear, pain, or grief. *From the burning building came frantic cries for help.*

Disorderly can mean wild and causing trouble, especially in public. *Ushers asked the disorderly group to be quiet or leave the concert.*

Unruly means hard to control. *Lamar's puppy has so much energy that she is sometimes unruly.*

Riotous can mean excited, energetic, and hard to control. *This movie is extremely funny, and it will keep any audience in riotous laughter.*

Beside yourself is an idiom that means frenzied, especially with worry or grief. *After Grampa died, Grandma was beside herself.*

ANTONYMS: calm, tranquil

Wise
adjective

Wise means having or showing knowledge and good judgment. *It was wise of Annalie not to tell the stranger who telephoned that her parents weren't home.*

Judicious is a formal word that means wise, especially in making decisions. *Judicious treaties avoided problems between William Penn and his Indian neighbors.*

CONTINUED ON THE NEXT PAGE

Sensible means having or showing good judgment and common sense. It does not suggest so much knowledge as *wise* does. *Kelvin was sensible and went to bed early the night before the big field trip.*

Reasonable means sensible. *Witnesses say that both cars were going at a reasonable speed.*

Levelheaded means sensible. It suggests staying calm and not getting too excited to think straight. *This book is a thorough and levelheaded examination of arguments for and against the death penalty.*

Sane can mean sensible. It suggests that other ideas or other people are foolish. *Mrs. Almarado's sane speech about the need to cooperate calmed down tempers at the neighborhood meeting.*

SEE **sharp** and **smart** for related words.
ANTONYM: foolish

AROUND THE WORLD: Wisdom

You don't need to give a wise person instructions.
— **Russian proverb**

The wise person doesn't say that the fools are wrong.
— **Chinese proverb**

A wise person who knows many proverbs can solve problems.
— **African proverb** (Niger)

Withdraw
verb

Withdraw means to remove from inside something. *The jeweler opened a safe and withdrew a diamond necklace.*

Draw can mean to withdraw. It is often used in connection with weapons. *Sir Lancelot drew his sword and fought the villain.*

Extract means to get or take from inside something. It is a formal word, and it suggests hard work. *If a tooth is beyond repair, the dentist will extract it.*

Uproot can mean to tear something or someone from a place, suddenly and forcefully. *Uprooted by war, refugees streamed toward the borders of the country.*

Take out means to withdraw. *Vijay took out his wallet to buy the T-shirt.*

Wonderful
adjective

Wonderful means surprising, strange, and very good. *Doretha's triple chocolate peanut butter cherry cake sounds weird but tastes wonderful.*

Marvelous means wonderful. It suggests that something is so unusual that it is hard to believe. *Mariko made a marvelous recovery from her injury and was able to play in the last game.*

Stupendous means marvelous. *Lou Gehrig played in 2,130 consecutive major-league baseball games, a stupendous achievement.*

Fantastic can mean fabulous. *"Uncle Herman is taking us all to Florida? That's fantastic news!" said Mrs. Vogel.*

Incredible means almost impossible to believe. *This movie is about a lost girl's incredible journey alone in the Amazon rainforest.*

CONTINUED ON THE NEXT PAGE

This movie is about a lost girl's **incredible** journey alone in the Amazon rainforest.

Fabulous means hard to believe. It suggests that something is very attractive and exciting. *Our teacher, Mr. Seferis, went on a game show and won some fabulous prizes, including a sports car.*

Sensational means causing excitement, especially by unusual excellence. *In the game's final seconds, Dolores made a sensational kick and scored the winning goal.*

Phenomenal means very unusual. It suggests exceptional skill or success. *Alex has a phenomenal memory: he can learn fifty words by heart in two minutes.*

Terrific can mean wonderful. It suggests that something is very unusual and remarkable. This meaning is informal. *Grandma and Grandpa won prizes years ago, and they're still terrific tango dancers.*

Awesome means wonderful and somewhat frightening or overwhelming. It suggests great power or size. *"The Grand Canyon is a really awesome place," Sebastian told the class, "even better than the pictures I'd seen."*

WRITING TIP: Connotations

Connotations are the ideas or feelings that a word suggests without exactly meaning them. At many places in this book, we say that a word suggests something. Those suggestions are connotations. Connotations help us to choose one synonym instead of another. The two synonyms may mean the same thing while suggesting different things.

The synonyms for *wonderful* have many different connotations. Some people use *wonderful* over and over. Other people use the synonyms, without being careful about the connotations. A cake may be wonderful, but it probably isn't marvelous; cakes aren't hard to believe. A prize may be fabulous, but it probably isn't awesome; prizes don't often have great power or size.

Good writers think about the connotations of the words they use. At times, when you read good writing, you feel that it makes you excited in ways that are hard to understand. Often that excitement comes from the power of suggestion. Be careful about the connotations of the words you use, and the success of your writing may be phenomenal.

Wordy
adjective

Wordy means using too many words to get your idea or ideas across to another person. *"A Possible Problem That Could Perhaps Happen" is a wordy title.*

Long-winded means talking at great length when it isn't necessary to do so. *The mayor made such a long-winded speech that one of the reporters fell asleep.*

Talkative means in the habit of talking a lot, often without much to say. *Jane is so talkative that it's difficult to get away from her.*

Rambling can mean talking or writing in a disorganized way, often with too many words or ideas. *Yuri left a rambling message, but I think the point is that he needs a ride.*

SEE **eloquent** for related words
ANTONYMS: brief, concise

WRITING TIP: To the Point

People are often wordy in their writing because they repeat the same idea in different words. You can improve your writing by avoiding deadwood — words that just say again what you've already said. Good writers read and reread what they've written, and they prune their sentences.

Mavella's new T-shirt shrank ~~to a smaller size~~.

Lucy's ~~unexpected~~ arrival came as a surprise to us.

Grant noticed an abandoned building ~~that no one was living in at the time~~.

Your doctor's appointment is for 3:30 P.M. Monday ~~afternoon~~.

Work
noun

Work means effort in doing or making something. *After weeks of work by dozens of students, the play was a big success.*

Labor can mean work that takes a lot of strength. *Many fruits and vegetables are still harvested by human labor.*

Toil means long and tiring work. *Mr. Sefins has put a lot of money and toil into the apartment house he bought.*

Industry can mean steady, hard work. It suggests self-discipline. *Laverne's industry and dedication have already gained her three Girl Scout Pathfinder emblems.*

Drudgery means dull, unpleasant work. *The only job Lee could find was drudgery, so he's taking computer courses this summer.*

Elbow grease is an informal phrase that means hard work, especially physical work. *By pure elbow grease, Damian and Nohea have made the old sled look like new.*

SEE **job** for related words.

AROUND THE WORLD: People at Work

Zambia—soybean harvest

France—grape harvest

Japan—television production

Australia—opal mining

477

Worn
adjective

Worn means damaged from being used a long time. It is used to describe clothing, tools, books, and furniture. *Our old science books are dirty and worn, but the school can't afford new ones.*

Shabby means worn and unattractive. It often suggests that something has not been carefully tended. *Dalton was upset to think that the homeless man had only a thin, shabby coat in such cold weather.*

Frayed means worn and coming into separate bits or threads. It usually describes cloth or rope. *Max's cut-off shorts have frayed edges, almost like fringe.*

Faded means with much less color than at first, usually from long use or wear. *The drapes on the south side of the Roxas's house are faded because of the sunlight.*

Ragged means so badly worn or torn that it is in rags. *"This ragged flag was carried by soldiers at the battle of Gettysburg," the guide told the class.*

Tattered means ragged. *Coach Henkel wears his tattered lucky shirt to every game.*

Threadbare means so worn that threads show through. *In the gloomy old house, the lonely servant sat darning her threadbare stockings by candlelight.*

Beat-up means badly worn and almost used up. It is used mostly about solid objects, not often about clothes. *Lonny works on his beat-up old car every chance he gets.*

Lonny works on his **beat-up** old car every chance he gets.

Worried
adjective

Worried means uncertain what will happen and afraid of what may happen. It suggests thinking about something over and over. *Willie Don is worried because his dog won't eat and might be sick.*

Nervous can mean afraid that things will not go well. It suggests restlessness. *Before the race, Emma was nervous and wheeled her chair around the block to calm herself down.*

Uneasy means having a strong feeling that trouble is coming. It suggests not knowing for sure what the trouble will be. *Changes in the Earth's atmosphere make scientists uneasy about possible climate changes.*

Disturbed can mean uneasy, but it suggests a particular reason for the feeling. *Aurelio was disturbed by the sadness in his grandmother's voice.*

Anxious means convinced that something bad will happen, and busy thinking about it. It suggests painful excitement. *After an anxious search, Nancy found her contact lens under the seat of the car.*

SEE **care** and **upset** for related words.
ANTONYMS: calm, relaxed

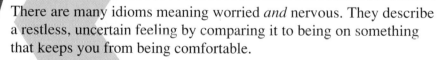

IDIOMS

There are many idioms meaning worried *and* nervous. They describe a restless, uncertain feeling by comparing it to being on something that keeps you from being comfortable.

on edge: *It's been two months since Dad had any work, and he's on edge most of the time now.*

on pins and needles: *Afraid of missing the fireworks, the children were on pins and needles until they reached the park.*

on tenterhooks: *Until the engineers examine the dam, people in the valley will be on tenterhooks.*

like peas on a hot griddle: *When the cat appeared at the window, the birds at the feeder were like peas on a hot griddle.*

X marks the spot,
But X is not
What many words begin with.

So here's a place
With empty space.
What can it be filled in with?

If xylophones
And X-rayed bones
Should come to your attention,

Remember, please,
That each of these
Lacks synonyms worth mention.

Young
adjective

Young means in the early part of life. *Some young birds can walk and swim soon after they hatch from eggs.*

Youthful means young or like young people. It suggests hope, energy, and imagination. *Grandma Salazar dances with a youthful enthusiasm that makes her seem half her age.*

Juvenile means young or youthful. It suggests that something is not suitable for older people. *Duval used to like this show until he heard Trish say it's juvenile.*

CONTINUED ON THE NEXT PAGE

Immature means not completely grown. It is often used to suggest that feelings or behavior are not grown-up enough. *Justin apologized to the substitute teacher for his immature behavior.*

Infantile can mean like an infant. It suggests extremely immature behavior. *Harriet's brother lost to her at checkers and had an infantile tantrum.*

Teenage means in the years of life from thirteen to nineteen. *With two teenage sons, a job, and night school, Mrs. Chee is always busy.*

Adolescent means in the time of life following childhood. *Adolescent girls and boys must face many changes and problems in their lives.*

ANTONYMS: adult, elderly, mature, old

WORDS AT PLAY

My brother's in his teenage years
And has some adolescent fears.
He says he won't be seen with us.
If we're around, he makes a fuss.
He calls us "twerps" and "infantile;"
He says, "You youngsters cramp my style."
He likes to brag about his car,
About his friends—how cool they are—
About his band (he plays guitar),
And how he's going to be a star.
When he's not on the telephone,
He's sulking in his room alone.
At least we're sure that time's a cure
For someone who's so immature!

Zone
noun

Zone means a particular part of the world, large or small, that has something special about it. *Bananas grow in the tropical zone.*

Region means a place that can be described in some way so as to tell it from other places. *The region north of the river contains most of the state's farmland.*

Area can mean a region. *Curvin's family traces its history back to ancestors in the New Orleans area.*

District means a region that is part of some larger place. It often suggests a special activity. *The city's old business district is now mostly antique and souvenir stores.*

Neighborhood means a district of a city or town, small enough that its parts are close together and its people know each other. *Most of the people in Suma's class live in her neighborhood.*

Vicinity means a region that is described by its nearness to some place. *Police told everyone within a two-mile vicinity of the chemical spill to leave the area until the danger passed.*

WORDS AT PLAY

Patrolling the vast desert region
Was work for the French Foreign Legion.
    So over the sands
    Marched men of all lands:
Dutch, German, Swiss, Czech, and Norwegian.

Resources

An essay on creativity,
a writer's guide,
and detailed indexes

Being Creative

Everyone is creative. You may not have realized this, but every time you have an idea, you create something. When you say something you haven't said before, you've created a new sentence. You're creative when you invent games, when you solve math problems, when you find a new route to a friend's house. Even daydreaming is a kind of creativity!

Creativity is a great thing to have and to use, and it's one of those things that gets better the more you use it. Just as people practice things like playing the piano, diving, ice-skating, painting, or baseball to improve their skill, you can improve your creativity with practice. Try some of these ideas. Think of them as mental gymnastics.

INVENTING STORIES

Open this book to any page and put your finger on that page. Now try creating a story around the sentence you are touching. The kind of story you invent is up to you. It could be a tall tale or it could be something realistic. Whatever it is, you can be sure it will be creative!

JOINING THOUGHTS

This one works best with a partner. Think of a subject for your partner. Then have him or her turn to any two pages in this book and pick a word from each page. Tell your partner the subject and have him or her write a paragraph about it, using the two words chosen from this book.

MAKING THE USUAL UNUSUAL

An important part of creativity is the ability to think about everyday things in a new and different way. Take a look at the world around you. Choose something that you see or something that you use every day. Think about a different way to use it, some way other than what it was meant for. For example, a bicycle could be a musical instrument, if you tap it, rub it with a card, scratch the seat, and make a kazoo using wax paper and its spokes. Think of some other everyday objects—a clock, a comb, a cardboard box—and imagine new uses for them.

Writing Creatively

Writing is an important creative activity. Any writing that you do, whether it's for fun or for work, is creative. Stories, poems, journal entries, even the reports that you write for school—they all use and build on your creativity.

Sometimes what you say doesn't require as much creativity as how you say it. When an author presents facts in nonfictional writing, the way the facts are presented involves creativity. What is the author saying about insects in this passage?

At our very feet, often unnoticed in the rush of daily events, is the wonder world of insects. Among the tangled weeds of the roadside or in the grassroot jungles of your own back yard, you encounter strange and incredible forms of life.

— from *Grassroot Jungles*
    by Edwin Way Teale

This is a creative way of saying, "Interesting insects are all around us."

Creativity Tips

You can help yourself develop new and interesting ideas to use in your own writing. Here are some simple ways. You may have some of your own to add to this list.

WRITE THINGS DOWN
Keep a notebook of interesting ideas. Write down the interesting things you see and hear. When you think of something interesting or funny, write it down. Keep your notebook handy so that you can write things down while you still remember them.

COPY GOOD WRITING
Use your notebook to write down interesting things that you read. If you like a poem or a joke or a way of saying something, copy it. These things you read and jot down will help you have your own ideas.

IMAGINE IT YOURSELF
If something interests you, imagine it yourself and then write down what you imagined in your notebook. Have you ever put yourself into a story you were reading? What did you do when you were in the story? Have you ever thought about how you would have written something you were reading? Have you ever wondered about the characters in a movie or a book—what were their lives like before the movie or book started? What did they do after it ended?

MAKE WRITING FUN
Play writing games with your friends. Start a poem or a story, and let someone else go on with it while you go on with theirs. Then change again.

Use the line below as the first line of a limerick. Write the second line. Have a friend write the third line and so on until the limerick is finished.

There once was a man from New York

Use the sentences below as the start of a story. Take turns writing paragraphs.

The man in the trench coat pulled his hat down over his face so that he could not be recognized. With a wave of his hand, he summoned the big black car.

CHANGE YOUR WAYS

You can exercise and strengthen your creativity by doing things differently from your normal way. Walk to school a different way every morning next week. When you watch television, turn the sound off and imagine what the characters are saying. Think about how different your life would be if you were only one inch tall. Read a library book by an author you've never heard of before.

Imagine what the world is like for animals. A dog tells more by smell than by sight. If you close your eyes, how many smells can you notice? What do they tell you? How many places can you recognize by smell?

If you were an ant, what would the grass look like to you? The writer Edwin Way Teale calls his book *Grassroot Jungles* because the grass is as big as a jungle to an insect. Find some grass or other plants and look very closely. What kinds of bugs do you see? What would be good names for them? What are they doing, and why are they doing it? Imagine what it would be like if you were as small as a bug, and you lived in the jungle of these plants.

When you do any of these things, remember to write down in your notebook whatever you think of or find out. When you want to do some writing, you can look back at your notes and see which ideas will help with the writing. For example, things you've noticed can make your writing interesting if you use them to make comparisons. Suppose you are on the bus and you see an ant on the floor. It must be a long way from its home. Later, in your writing, you could describe a character's feelings by saying that the character felt as lonely as an ant on a city bus.

Starting Up

▼ •

Sometimes you want to write, but you just can't seem to get started. Try using your creativity to help you begin. Here are some ways to try:

Time for Rhyme Pick a word and think of two or three words that rhyme with it. Write a poem that uses these words.

Start a Story Take a history book or a science book or an encyclopedia. Open it to any page, put your finger down, and start a story with the sentence you touch. Invent a character who is saying the sentence. Like this:

> *"The United States of America is the fourth largest country in the world in area and in population," said the mysterious woman in the red dress to the French border guard.*

Where will a story like this go? Work on it yourself or with a partner.

End a Story Choose another sentence the same way, and write your story to make that sentence the ending.

WRITE A PHOTO CAPTION

Photo captions explain what is going on in a picture. Find an interesting picture in a newspaper or magazine and write a caption for it. Think of something else that could be happening in the picture. Write another caption about it.

GET RIDICULOUS

If you can't think of a good idea, then think of bad ones. Brainstorm—alone or with others—a list of the silliest, most ridiculous ideas you can think of. You may find that some writing ideas come out of your list.

Sometimes writing is easy. Sometimes writing is work. Either way, writing can strengthen your creativity. And when you write, you make something that will always be yours.

Writer's Guide

People have found a number of ways to make writing easier. This guide will teach you some of those ways. If you follow its advice, you should find that writing is simpler and more interesting to do.

So have a look at these suggestions now.

Plan It

Builders have blueprints. Cooks have recipes. Shoppers have shopping lists. Teams have plays. Things go better if you think about them first. It's the same with writing. The more you plan, the less time you waste, and the fewer mistakes you make. You have the ideas you need. The words come faster. Writing without a plan is like traveling without a map.

Always write down your plan. Whatever form it takes—list, outline, diagram, anything—get it onto paper. Nothing is worse than a plan you can't remember anymore.

Three questions will help you make your plan:

1. Why are you writing?
2. What are you writing about?
3. How will you get from beginning to end?

WHY?

Writing always has a purpose. It persuades or amuses, argues or apologizes, soothes or informs. The reason you are writing tells you what sort of plan you need.

Suppose you want to write a letter to a tennis star, telling her how much you admire her, and asking her for an autographed picture. This letter will be very different from a letter to your friend Pat, all about the latest news of events at school. The differences come from the different purposes. The first letter persuades and explains; the second amuses and informs.

WHAT?

When you know why you are writing, you have a better idea of what to say. You want the tennis star to believe that you care a lot about the way she plays tennis, and that sending you her picture is a good idea. So you will need to give details about what you admire and where you will put the picture.

You want Pat to feel as though you were talking together and having a good time. You also want to remember everything you've been meaning to write about. It will help you to have a list of news and ideas. It would be a good idea to put the important details in the list. That way you won't have to write in the margins something like "Oh, I forgot to tell you—this is funny because Mrs. Morgan didn't know we saw her!"

HOW?

"Begin at the beginning," says the King of Hearts in *Alice in Wonderland*, "and go on till you come to the end: then stop." That sounds like a good idea, but it doesn't say how to know where the beginning is, or how to go on. Of course you stop at the end—but what if you think of something else later on?

This is where your plan can help. If you organize your thoughts before you start writing, the writing is much easier. Instead of always having to decide what comes next, you will have your subjects and information already in order. You can concentrate on how to say things, without having to worry about other questions.

For your letter to Pat, you would need only a list of subjects and some details. You might look over the list and change the order to make it as interesting as possible, or to tell first what happened first, or some other method of organizing. Even a friendly letter can be hard to read if it keeps changing the subject for no clear reason.

A last word about plans: they tell you what you'll need. A plan for a bookshelf says how much lumber to buy. A plan for writing says how much information you'll have to put in. If you can see that it will take many pages, or that you'll be finished in a few sentences, then you may want to change your plan. If you can see that the plan looks right, then you know what information to go find out.

Reporters don't write news stories until they've asked a lot of questions. When they know what's going on, then they start writing. With a plan, you can learn most of what you need before you sit down to start writing. If you think that makes writing easier, you've got the idea.

Write Away!

Now you are ready to roll. You've got a plan. You've looked up the facts you need. You know what you want to say. It's writing time! Here are some tips to help you:

GETTING STARTED

Pick a place to write, and get that place ready. You'll need sharp pencils or pen, paper, your plan and your notes, a dictionary, and this thesaurus. Make sure you have enough light. It's best to work somewhere quiet. A radio, television, or tape player won't help you write. And it's hard to write if people are talking around you. If you have trouble finding a quiet place, ask your family or your teacher for help. Remember, the library at school or in your neighborhood is a quiet place.

Start early. If you wait until the last day, or the last hour, you will probably be so nervous that you won't write well. And you won't have time to rewrite. So your writing won't be as good as if you start when there's still plenty of time.

When you sit down to write, make sure that you have the time you need to get something done. It's wise to set aside at least 20 or 30 minutes whenever you write. That way you have enough time to concentrate, to solve any problems that come up, and to make some progress you'll feel happy with. You can't do this during a set of commercials, or when you're supposed to be going to bed.

First thing, look over your plan. That way the whole project is in your head at the start. Then look at the part that comes first, and remind yourself why it comes first. Think of an interesting first sentence, something that will get your reader's attention right away, like "Dear Pat, The vice-principal told us yesterday that she has started taking flying lessons!"

Now start! Write as fast as you can. Leave extra space between the lines. Later on you can use that space to make changes. For now, don't worry about saying things exactly right, or being sure that the spelling is correct, or anything else that slows you down. Move ahead. After you've got your ideas down on paper, you can fix whatever needs fixing.

MOVING AHEAD

Every now and then, writing gets hard. The words don't come easily, or they don't sound right. What can you do when you feel stuck? Try these tips.

Back up Reread what you've written so far. Maybe you'll get an idea for what to say next. Read your last paragraph aloud and just keep talking. If you like what you're saying, write it down.

Review Go back over your plan and your notes. Look for a thought, a fact, a word that will help you start again.

Revise Try writing the last paragraph over differently and see if that gets you going.

Skip ahead Look at your plan and choose a later section. Try working on that. You can come back and fill in the missing parts after you're done.

Start over Use a completely different first sentence. Go in a different direction from there. Later on you can see which parts of your first draft can still be used.

Replan Sometimes you may discover while you're writing that your original plan doesn't work as well as you thought. You don't have to follow it regardless. Maybe the third section of your plan really would be better as the second section. Like starting over, replanning often lets you use parts of your first draft, in different places or different ways.

Don't just sit there, staring at the empty page. Stand up and turn around. Wash your face. Use your dictionary to look up the last word you wrote. Choose any word from the dictionary and use it in the next sentence.

DON'T QUIT! This is all a normal part of writing. Part of being a good writer is learning how to keep going. You can too.

Fix It

You've been writing quickly and steadily, not worrying about getting everything right. Now you're finished, and it's time to fix up your writing. You may not think anything needs fixing, but don't be too sure. People who write for a living know, any writing can be improved. For some authors, the hardest part is to stop trying to make their work bet-ter. Now is your chance to make your writing as good as you can. Keep these thoughts in mind as you revise:

First, wait. Don't try to start revising as soon as you finish writing. You're still thinking the same way that you have been. Take some time, and come back to your writing with a fresh viewpoint.

Second, do your revising in a different color of pencil or ink than you used for writing the first time. That way, you can see easily what changes you want to make.

Third, be sure to have your plan with you when you look at your writing. Ask yourself questions about your organization. Have you followed your plan? Did you use all the ideas that are in your plan? Does it look as if you need more ideas? Do your ideas come in an order that makes them easy to follow? There's still time to change your plan if it didn't work the way you thought.

Fourth, ask yourself questions about your writing. Does your first sentence really seize attention? Have you used specific details? Have you used words that your reader knows? Did you check this thesaurus to find synonyms, so that you don't use the same words over and over?

It's always a good idea to let someone read what you've written before you revise. Ask someone in your class, someone in your family, a friend, or your teacher to tell you what you can improve. You know what you want to say, so it's hard to tell whether you've been clear in your writing. A reader can let you know when there are problems.

Check It

When you finish revising, make a new copy. You will notice how much easier this is because you did your revising in a different color. If you had used the same color, it would be hard to tell what to copy. When the new copy is done, it's time for proofreading. When you proofread, you are checking for mistakes of any kind and fixing them. You are making sure that spelling and punctuation are right, and that no words are left out. Proofreading is like waxing a car after it's washed, to make it bright and shiny all over.

Proofreading your own writing is hard. If possible, exchange papers with someone else in your class, and proofread each other's. Or ask someone to look over your writing for mistakes. If you have to check your own writing, it can help to do pages and paragraphs backward, from the end to the beginning. If you can, try reading aloud what you've written.

When you proofread, have a dictionary with you. Check how to spell any word you're not sure of. Check for capitalization. Check punctuation. Make any changes you need to, and use a colored pencil again, so that it is easy to see everything you fix.

One way to make your proofeading easy to see, and to keep it neat, is to use some signs that professionals use. Here are some of the most common:

Make a capital.	
Change from a capital.	
Add something.	
Take something out.	
Add quotation marks.	
Add a period.	
Add a comma.	

You can find more proofreading signs in a dictionary or encyclopedia.

Finished proofreading? Congratulations! You're done!

One last thought: it's a very good idea to keep your old copy, the one you did your revising on. If your writing was for school, you'll get the final copy back from your teacher. Otherwise, the old copy may be your only way of remembering what you wrote. When you do get a paper back from your teacher, study the comments and corrections. They're on your paper to help you write better. What parts of your writing worked well? How could you fix what didn't work so well?

Writing is like sports, or music, or acting. You don't get good unless you remember what you did and practice to make it better. If you work at writing, you can be good enough that people will notice what you say and think about it a long time later. That kind of skill is worth having.

Indexes

Synonym Index

Entry words are shown in darker type.

B

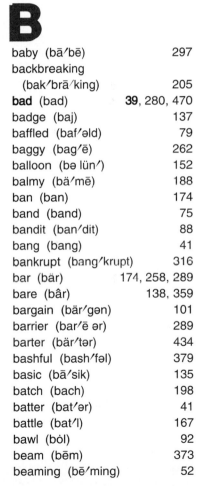

a	hat	â	care	ė	term	o	hot	ô	order	u	cup	ch	child	th	thin		a in about
ā	age	e	let	i	it	ō	open	oi	oil	ù	put	ng	long	ŦH	then	ə	e in taken
ä	far	ē	equal	ī	ice	ȯ	saw	ou	out	ü	rule	sh	she	zh	measure		i in pencil
																	o in lemon
																	u in circus

C

cabin (kab′ən) 223
cache (kash) 211
cackle (kak′əl) 247
calamity (kə lam′ə tē) 115
calculated (kal′kyə lā′tid) 107
calibrate (kal′ə brāt) 272
calisthenics (kal′is then′iks) 151
call (kȯl) **55**, 375
caller (kȯ′lər) 459
calm (käm) **56**, 334
camouflage (kam′ə fläzh) 210
candid (kan′did) 178
canny (kan′ē) 372
canter (kan′tər) 352
capability (kā′pə bil′ə tē) 22
capacity (kə pas′ə tē) 22
capital (kap′i təl) 464
capsize (kap sīz′) 295
capture (kap′chər) 60
carbon copy (kär′bən kop′ē) 84
care (kâr) **57**
careful (kâr′fəl) **58**
careless (kâr′lis) **58**
caring (kâr′ing) 429
carry (kar′ē) **59**, 412
cart (kärt) 59
carve (kärv) 94
cascade (ka skād′) 161
case (kās) 148
cast (kast) 430
casual (kazh′ü əl) 230
catalog (kat′l ȯg) 255
catastrophe (kə tas′trə fē) 115
catch (kach) **60**
category (kat′ə gôr′ē) 442
catnap (kat′nap′) 385
cause (kȯz) **61**, 338
caution (kȯ′shən) 462
cautious (kȯ′shəs) 58
cease (sēs) 402

celebrate (sel′ə brāt) 62
celebrated (sel′ə brā′tid) 162
censure (sen′shər) 90
center (sen′tər) **62**
central (sen′trəl) 267
certain (sèrt′n) 412
chain (chān) 367
challenge (chal′ənj) 288
chance (chans) 203, 265, 335
change (chānj) **63**, 408
chaperon (shap′ə rōn′) 24
char (chär) 53
character (kar′ik tər) 122
characteristic (kar′ik tə ris′tik) **64**
characterize (kar′ik tə rīz′) 108
charge (chärj) 36, 47, 323
charitable (char′ə tə bəl) 187
charming (chär′ming) 95
chase (chās) 172
chat (chat) 418
cheap (chēp) **64**
cheat (chēt) **65**
check
(chek) 66, 147, 271, 323, 402
cheerful (chir′fəl) 204
chief (chēf) 267
chilly (chil′ē) 70
chip (chip) 309
chivalrous (shiv′əl rəs) 176
chock-full (chok′fùl′) 183
choose (chüz) **66**
chop (chop) 94
chore (chôr) 236
chortle (chôr′tl) 246
chubby (chub′ē) 164
chuckle (chuk′əl) 246
chummy (chum′ē) 162
chunk (chungk) 309
circle (sèr′kəl) 349
circumference
(sèr kum′fər əns) 133
circumscribe
(sèr′kəm skrīb′) 254

circumstance
(sèr′kəm stans) 77, 146
claim (klām) 343
clamber (klam′bər) 68
clammy (klam′ē) 96
clamor (klam′ər) 448
clamorous (klam′ər əs) 262
clap (klap) 213
clarify (klar′ə fī) 156
clasp (klasp) 197
class (klas) 442
classified (klas′ə fīd) 364
clatter (klat′ər) 286
clear (clir) **67**
clearance (klir′əns) 348
clear-cut (klir′kut′) 106
clench (klench) 197
clever (klev′ər) 388
climb (klīm) **68**
cling (kling) 400
clip (klip) 94
clone (klōn) 84
close (klōz) 141, 378
close (klōs) 162, 281
close to (klōs′ tü) 23
closing (klō′zing) 245
clothes (klōz) **69**
clothing (klō′тнing) 69
clue (klü) 146
clump (klump) 198
clumsy (klum′zē) 38
cluster (klus′tər) 198
clutch (kluch) 197
coarse (kôrs) 39, 349
coast (kōst) 386
coax (kōks) 450
cocky (kok′ē) 326
coerce (kō èrs′) 174
cohere (kō hir′) 400
coincide (kō′in sīd′) 270
cold (kōld) **70**
cold-blooded (kōld′blud′id) 92
cold-hearted (kōld′här′tid) 447

a	hat	â	care	ė	term	o	hot	ô	order	u	cup	ch	child	th	thin		a in about
ā	age	e	let	i	it	ō	open	oi	oil	ù	put	ng	long	тн	then		e in taken
ä	far	ē	equal	ī	ice	ȯ	saw	ou	out	ü	rule	sh	she	zh	measure	ə	i in pencil
																	o in lemon
																	u in circus

cooperate (kō op′ə rāt′) 300
copy (kop′ē) **84**, 226
cordial (kôr′jəl) 181
core (kôr) 62
correct (kə rekt′) **85**, 328
correspond (kôr′ə spond′) 271
corresponding
  (kôr′ə spon′ding) 382
corroborate (kə rob′ə rāt′) 78
corrupt (kə rupt′) 118
cost (kȯst) **86**
costly (kȯst′lē) 154
count (kount) 438
counterfeit (koun′tər fit) 84, 160
countless (kount′lis) 270
coup (kü) 344
couple (kup′əl) 237, 297
courageous (kə rā′jəs) 50
courteous (kėr′tē əs) 314
courtly (kôrt′lē) 176
cover (kuv′ər) 199, 372
coy (koi) 379
cozy (kō′zē) 72
crabby (krab′ē) 90
crack (krak) 51, 134
crafty (kraf′tē) 387
crammed (kramd) 183
cranky (krang′kē) 90
crave (krāv) 461
craze (krāz) 158
crazy (krā′zē) **86**
create (krē āt′) **87**
creation (krē ā′shən) 44
creature (krē′chər) 307
creep (krēp) 390
creepy (krē′pē) 466
crest (krest) 434
crew (krü) 75
crime (krīm) **88**
criminal (krim′ə nəl) **88**
crisis (krī′sis) 138
crisp (krisp) 374
criticism (krit′ə siz′əm) 288

criticize (krit′ə sīz) 90
crook (krük) 88
crooked (krük′id) 118
cross (krȯs) **90**
crow (krō) 49
crowd (kroud) **91**
crowded (krou′did) 182
crown (kroun) 434
crude (krüd) 350
cruel (krü′əl) **92**
cruise (krüz) 437
crumble (krum′bəl) 51
crunch (krunch) 138
crush (krush) 263
cry (krī) **92**, 375
cultivated (kul′tə vā′tid) 176
cumbersome (kum′bər səm) 209
cunning (kun′ing) 387
cup (kup) 324
curb (kėrb) 66
curious (kyŭr′ē əs) **93**, 303
curl (kėrl) 45
current (kėr′ənt) 283
curt (kėrt) 374
curve (kėrv) 45
custom (kus′təm) 202
customary (kus′tə mer′ē) 452
cut (kut) **94**
cute (kyüt) **95**
cut-rate (kut′rāt′) 116

D

dainty (dān′tē) **96**
damage (dam′ij) 206
damp (damp) **96**
danger (dān′jər) **97**
dangerous (dān′jər əs) **98**
dangle (dang′gəl) 414
dank (dangk) 96
daring (dâr′ing) 50
dark (därk) **99**

data (dā′tə *or* dat′ə) 231
dawn (dȯn) 44
daydream (dā′drēm′) 226
dazzling (daz′ling) 52
dead (ded) **100**
deafening (def′ən ing) 262
deal (dēl) **101**
debatable (di bā′tə bəl) 444
debate (di bāt′) 118
deceased (di sēst′) 100
deceitful (di sēt′fəl) 118
deceive (di sēv′) **102**
decide (di sīd′) **102**
decided (di sī′did) 106
declare (di klâr′) 398
decline (di klīn′) 440
decorate (dek′ə rāt′) **103**
decoration (dek′ə rā′shən) 324
decrease (di krēs′) **104**
deduct (di dukt′) 409
defeat (di fēt′) **104**
defeatist (di fē′tist) 217
defect (dē′fekt) **105**
defend (di fend′) 199
defense (di fens′) 151
defenseless (di fens′lis) 317
deficient (di fish′ənt) 359
definite (def′ə nit) **106**
defraud (di frȯd′) 65
defy (di fī′) 293
dehydrated (dē hī′drā′tid) 126
dejected (di jek′tid) 117
delay (di lā′) 214
delectable (di lek′tə bəl) 107
delete (di lēt′) 143
deliberate
  (di lib′ər it) 58, **107**, 386
deliberate (di lib′ə rāt′) 81, 428
delicate (del′ə kit) 96, 177
delicious (di lish′əs) **107**
delighted (di lī′tid) 204
delightful (di līt′fəl) 284
delirious (di lir′ē əs) 223

a	hat	â	care	ė	term	o	hot	ô	order	u	cup	ch	child	th	thin	a in about
ā	age	e	let	i	it	ō	open	oi	oil	ů	put	ng	long	ŦH	then	e in taken
ä	far	ē	equal	ī	ice	ȯ	saw	ou	out	ü	rule	sh	she	zh	measure	ə { i in pencil / o in lemon / u in circus }

E

a hat	**â** care	**ė** term	**o** hot	**ô** order	**u** cup	**ch** child	**th** thin	a in about
ā age	**e** let	**i** it	**ō** open	**oi** oil	**ù** put	**ng** long	**ᴛʜ** then	e in taken
ä far	**ē** equal	**ī** ice	**ȯ** saw	**ou** out	**ü** rule	**sh** she	**zh** measure	ə { i in pencil / o in lemon / u in circus }

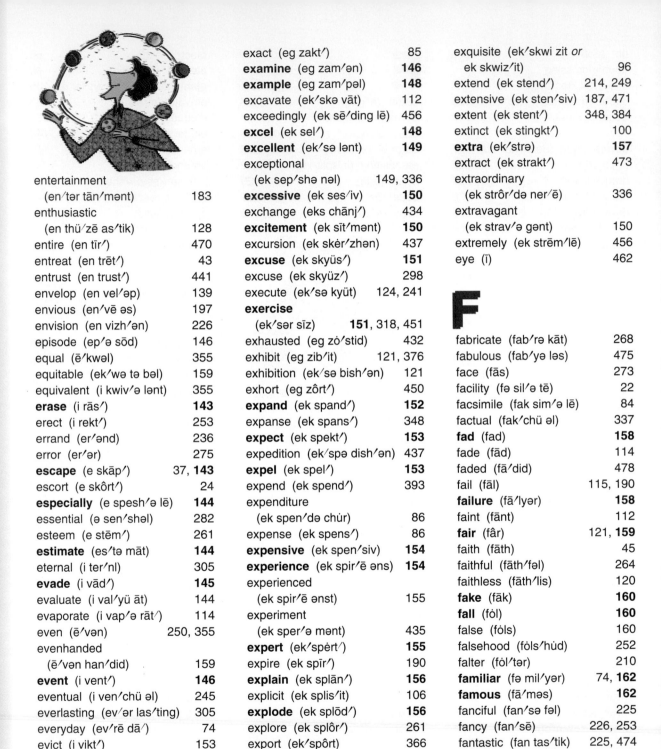

far-off (fär′of′)	123
far-reaching (fär′rē′ching)	187
fascinating (fas′n ā′ting)	233
fashion (fash′ən)	158, 268, 463
fast (fast)	332, 399
fasten (fas′n)	237
fat (fat)	**164**
fatigued (fə tēgd′)	432
fault (fȯlt)	105
faultless (fȯlt′lis)	304
favor (fā′vər)	215
fazed (fāzd)	136, 449
fear (fir)	**164**
fearful (fir′fəl)	27, 423
fearless (fir′lis)	50
feast (fēst)	131
feature (fē′chər)	332
fee (fē)	323
feeble (fē′bəl)	317
feed (fēd)	131
feel (fēl)	154
feeling (fē′ling)	**166**
fellow (fel′ō)	307
felony (fel′ə nē)	88
ferocious (fə rō′shəs)	166
fetch (fech)	188
feud (fyüd)	34
fiasco (fē as′kō)	159
fib (fib)	252
fictitious (fik tish′əs)	225
fierce (firs)	**166**
fiery (fī′rē)	218, 232
fight (fīt)	**167**
figure (fig′yər)	370
filthy (fil′thē)	114
final (fī′nl)	245
find (fīnd)	**167**
fine (fīn)	96, 149, 328
finish (fin′ish)	140
fire (fīr)	120
firm (fėrm)	**168**, 399, 401
first-class (fėrst′klas′)	149
first-rate (fėrst′rāt′)	149

fit (fit)	**169**, 208
fix (fiks)	342
fixed (fikst)	399
flabbergasted (flab′ər gas′tid)	414
flap (flap)	171
flash (flash)	**169**
flashy (flash′ē)	377
flat (flat)	250
flatter (flat′ər)	319
flavorful (flā′vər fəl)	419
flaw (flȯ)	105
flawless (flȯ′lis)	304
flee (flē)	**170**
flexible (flek′sə bəl)	**170**
flicker (flik′ər)	169
flimsy (flim′zē)	464
fling (fling)	430
flip (flip)	295
flippant (flip′ənt)	355
flit (flit)	171
flock (flok)	91
flood (flud)	295
flop (flop)	158
floppy (flop′ē)	390
flourish (flėr′ish)	409
flow (flō)	**171**
fluent (flü′ənt)	135
flush (flush)	250
flustered (flus′tərd)	136, 449
flutter (flut′ər)	150, 171
fly (flī)	170, **171**
focus (fō′kəs)	62
foe (fō)	141
follow (fol′ō)	**172**, 287
fond (fond)	**172**
fondness (fond′nis)	263
fool (fül)	102
foolish (fü′lish)	**173**
foolproof (fül′prüf′)	304
for (fȯr)	42
forbearing (fȯr bâr′ing)	301
forbid (fər bid′)	**174**

forbidding (fər bid′ing)	430
force (fȯrs)	**174**, 316
forecast (fȯr′kast′)	**175**
foregoing (fȯr′gō′ing)	322
foremost (fȯr′mōst)	267
foresee (fȯr sē′)	153, 175
foretell (fȯr tel′)	175
forewarn (fȯr wôrn′)	462
forge (fȯrj)	268
forgive (fər giv′)	298
forlorn (fȯr lôrn′)	259
form (fôrm)	268, 370
formal (fôr′məl)	**176**
former (fôr′mər)	323
fortissimo (fôr tis′ə mō)	262
fortune (fôr′chən)	265, 464
forward (fôr′wərd)	355, 366
foster (fȯ′stər)	325
foul (foul)	114, 315
foxy (fok′sē)	387
fraction (frak′shən)	299
fracture (frak′chər)	51
fragile (fraj′əl)	**177**

fragment (frag′mənt)	309
fragrance (frā′grəns)	389
frail (frāl)	177
frank (frangk)	**178**
frantic (fran′tik)	472
frayed (frād)	478

a	hat	â	care	ė	term	o	hot	ô	order	u	cup	ch	child	th	thin		a in about
ā	age	e	let	i	it	ō	open	oi	oil	ủ	put	ng	long	ᴛʜ	then	ə	e in taken
ä	far	ē	equal	ī	ice	ȯ	saw	ou	out	ü	rule	sh	she	zh	measure		i in pencil / o in lemon / u in circus

503

free (frē)	179	garnish (gär′nish)	103	glower (glou′ər)	182
freedom (frē′dəm)	251	gather (gaᴛн′ər)	**186**	glowing (glō′ing)	52
freezing (frē′zing)	70	gauche (gōsh)	38	glum (glum)	353
frenzied (fren′zēd)	472	gaudy (gȯ′dē)	377	go (gō)	**192**
frequently (frē′kwənt lē)	290	gauge (gāj)	272, 396	go-ahead (gō′ə hed′)	306
fresh (fresh)	283, 355	gaunt (gȯnt)	426	goal (gōl)	232
friend (frend)	**180**	gawky (gȯ′kē)	38	gobble (gob′əl)	131
friendly (frend′lē)	**181**	gaze (gāz)	462	godly (god′lē)	340
fright (frīt)	164	general (jen′ər əl)	**187**	good (gu̇d)	**194**
frighten (frīt′n)	360	generate (jen′ə rāt′)	61	good-looking (gu̇d′lu̇k′ing)	42
frightened (frīt′nd)	27	generous (jen′ər əs)	**187**	goodly (gu̇d′lē)	47
frightening (frīt′n ing)	423	genial (jē′nyəl)	181	good-natured	
frightful (frīt′fəl)	423	gentle (jen′tl)	**188**, 242	(gu̇d′nā′chərd)	181, 242
frigid (frij′id)	70	genuine (jen′yü ən)	336	gorgeous (gôr′jəs)	42
frisky (fris′kē)	257	get (get)	**188**	gossip (gos′ip)	418
frosty (frȯ′stē)	70	ghastly (gast′lē)	422	govern (guv′ərn)	351
frown (froun)	**182**	ghostly (gōst′lē)	466	grab (grab)	60
fruitless (früt′lis)	452	giant (jī′ənt)	219	grabby (grab′ē)	197
fulfill (fu̇l fil′)	124	gift (gift)	**189**	gracious (grā′shəs)	314
full (fu̇l)	**182**, 470	gifted (gif′tid)	388	gradual (graj′ü əl)	386
full-grown (fu̇l′grōn′)	26	gigantic (jī gan′tik)	219	grand (grand)	**195**
fun (fun)	**183**	giggle (gig′əl)	246	grasp (grasp)	197, 445
function (fungk′shən)	24	gimmick (gim′ik)	436	grasping (gras′ping)	197
functional (fungk′shə nəl)	451	give (giv)	190, 331, 441	gratify (grat′ə fī)	**195**, 356
fundamental (fun′də men′tl)	135	gizmo (giz′mō)	185	grave (grāv)	368
funny (fun′ē)	**184**, 303	glacial (glā′shəl)	70	graze (grāz)	131
furious (fyu̇r′ē əs)	266	glad (glad)	204	great (grāt)	46, **196**
further (fėr′ᴛнər)	325	gladden (glad′n)	356	greedy (grē′dē)	**197**
fury (fyu̇r′ē)	31	glare (glâr)	182, 373	grief (grēf)	391
fuss (fus)	150	glaring (glâr′ing)	52	grim (grim)	346
futile (fyü′tl)	452	gleam (glēm)	373	grimy (grī′mē)	114
fuzzy (fuz′ē)	112	gleaming (glē′ming)	52	grip (grip)	**197**
		glee (glē)	238	gripe (grīp)	76
		glib (glib)	135	gross (grōs)	350
		glide (glīd)	386	grouchy (grou′chē)	90
G		glimmer (glim′ər)	169	ground (ground)	328
		glimpse (glimps)	365	grounds (groundz)	338
gadget (gaj′it)	**185**	glisten (glis′n)	373	group (grüp)	**198**
gag (gag)	238	glitch (glich)	105	grow (grō)	**199**
gain (gān)	27, 71, 189	glitter (glit′ər)	169		
gallant (gal′ənt)	50	glittering (glit′ər ing)	52		
gallivant (gal′ə vant)	192	gloat (glōt)	49		
gallop (gal′əp)	352	global (glō′bəl)	187		
galore (gə lôr′)	313	globe (glōb)	129		
gambol (gam′bəl)	239	gloomy (glü′mē)	99, 353		
game (gām)	**186**	glorious (glôr′ē əs)	195		
gang (gang)	75	glossy (glȯ′sē)	389		
gangster (gang′stər)	89	glow (glō)	373		
garb (gärb)	69				

a	hat	â	care	ė	term	o	hot	ô	order	u	cup	ch	child	th	thin	ə	a in about
ā	age	e	let	i	it	ō	open	oi	oil	ù	put	ng	long	ᴛʜ	then		e in taken
ä	far	ē	equal	ī	ice	ò	saw	ou	out	ü	rule	sh	she	zh	measure		i in pencil
																	o in lemon
																	u in circus

a	hat	â	care	ė	term	o	hot	ô	order	u	cup	ch	child	th	thin		a in about
ā	age	e	let	i	it	ō	open	oi	oil	u̇	put	ng	long	ᴛ́ʜ	then	ə	e in taken / i in pencil
ä	far	ē	equal	ī	ice	ȯ	saw	ou	out	ü	rule	sh	she	zh	measure		o in lemon / u in circus

M

a	hat	ä	care	ė	term	o	hot	ô	order	u	cup	ch	child	th	thin		a in about
ā	age	e	let	i	it	ō	open	oi	oil	ù	put	ng	long	ᴛʜ	then	ə	e in taken i in pencil
ä	far	ē	equal	ī	ice	ȯ	saw	ou	out	ü	rule	sh	she	zh	measure		o in lemon u in circus

a hat	**â** care	**ė** term	**o** hot	**ô** order	**u** cup	**ch** child	**th** thin	a in about
ā age	**e** let	**i** it	**ō** open	**oi** oil	**ù** put	**ng** long	**тн** then	e in taken
ä far	**ē** equal	**ī** ice	**ȯ** saw	**ou** out	**ü** rule	**sh** she	**zh** measure	ə i in pencil, o in lemon, u in circus

a hat	â care	ė term	o hot	ô order	u cup	ch child	th thin	a in about
ā age	e let	i it	ō open	oi oil	ů put	ng long	ᴛʜ then	e in taken
ä far	ē equal	ī ice	ò saw	ou out	ü rule	sh she	zh measure	i in pencil
								o in lemon
								u in circus

The vowel reduction symbol ə represents the sounds: a in about, e in taken, i in pencil, o in lemon, u in circus.

a	hat	â	care	ė	term	o	hot	ô	order	u	cup	ch	child	th	thin		a in about
ā	age	e	let	i	it	ō	open	oi	oil	ù	put	ng	long	ᴛʜ	then	ə	e in taken i in pencil
ä	far	ē	equal	ī	ice	ò	saw	ou	out	ü	rule	sh	she	zh	measure		o in lemon u in circus

speedy (spē′dē) 333
spell (spel) 408
spellbinding (spel′bīnd′ing) 233
spend (spend) 393
spick-and-span
  (spik′ən span′) 282
spicy (spī′sē) 419
spin (spin) 394
spirited (spir′ə tid) 257
spiritual (spir′ə chü əl) 340
spiteful (spīt′fəl) 447
splendid (splen′did) 195
splinter (splin′tər) 51
split (split) 51, 94, 366
splotch (sploch) 395
splurge (splėrj) 393
spoil (spoil) 110, 195, 297
spontaneous (spon tā′nē əs) 230
spooky (spü′kē) 466
sport (spôrt) 186
spot (spot) 167, 311, 395
sprightly (sprīt′lē) 257
spring (spring) 239, 294
springy (spring′ē) 170
sprinkle (spring′kəl) 361
sprint (sprint) 352
sprout (sprout) 199
spruce (sprüs) 282
spry (sprī) 257
spunky (spung′kē) 50
spur (spėr) 450
spurt (spėrt) 171
squabble (skwob′əl) 34
squander (skwän′dər) 393
squawk (skwȯk) 76
stab (stab) 134, 303
stable (stā′bəl) 305, 399
stage (stāj) 331
staid (stād) 368
stain (stān) 395
stained (stānd) 114
stand (stand) 40
standard (stan′dərd) 74, 396

star (stär) 46
stare (stâr) 463
start (stärt) 44, 397
startled (stär′tld) 414
stash (stash) 210
state (stāt) 77, 398
station (stā′shən) 311
status (stā′təs or stat′əs) 77
staunch (stȯnch) 264
stay (stā) 256, 398
steady (sted′ē) 339, 399
steal (stēl) 400
steep (stēp) 113, 154, 211
steer (stir) 201
step (step) 460
stern (stėrn) 368
stick (stik) 400
stiff (stif) 401
stiff-necked (stif′nekt′) 404
still (stil) 334, 381
stink (stingk) 389
stir (stėr) 150
stitch (stich) 296
stockpile (stok′pīl′) 403
stop (stop) 402
store (stôr) 403
storm (stôrm) 36
story (stôr′ē) 252, 403
stout (stout) 164, 404
straight (strāt) 178, 250
straightforward
  (strāt′fôr′wərd) 178
strain (strān) 57
strange (strānj) 303
strap (strap) 431
strategy (strat′ə jē) 312
stray (strā) 192
stream (strēm) 171
strength (strengkth) 316
strenuous (stren′yü əs) 205
stretch (strech) 249
strew (strü) 361
strict (strikt) 368

stride (strīd) 460
strike (strīk) 213
string (string) 367
strive (strīv) 439
stroll (strōl) 460
strong (strȯng) 404
struggle (strug′əl) 167
stubborn (stub′ərn) 404
stuck-up (stuk′up′) 326
study (stud′ē) 81, 147, 417
stuff (stuf) 405
stuffed (stuft) 182
stunning (stun′ing) 42
stupendous (stü pen′dəs) 474
stupid (stü′pid) 406
sturdy (stėr′dē) 404
style (stīl) 158, 463
suave (swäv) 314
subdue (səb dü′) 80
subject (sub′jikt) 407
submerge (səb mėrj′) 113
submit (səb mit′) 214
subsequently
  (sub′sə kwənt lē) 424
substance (sub′stəns) 405
substandard (sub stan′dərd) 39
substantiate
  (səb stan′shē āt) 78
substantial (səb stan′shəl) 399
substitute (sub′stə tüt) 408
subtract (səb trakt′) 409
succeed (sək sēd′) 409
successfully (sək ses′fəl ē) 467
succession (sək sesh′ən) 367
sucker (suk′ər) 65
suddenly (sud′n lē) 410
suffer (suf′ər) 40, 154
suffering (suf′ər ing) 274
suggest (səg jest′) 410, 416
suitable (sü′tə bəl) 169
sulky (sul′kē) 411
sullen (sul′ən) 411
sultry (sul′trē) 218

a	hat	â	care	ė	term	o	hot	ô	order	u	cup	ch	child	th	thin		a in about
ā	age	e	let	i	it	ō	open	oi	oil	ů	put	ng	long	ᴛʜ	then	ə	e in taken, i in pencil
ä	far	ē	equal	ī	ice	ȯ	saw	ou	out	ü	rule	sh	she	zh	measure		o in lemon, u in circus

a hat	â care	ė term	o hot	ô order	u cup	ch child	th thin	a in about
ā age	e let	i it	ō open	oi oil	u̇ put	ng long	ŦH then	e in taken
ä far	ē equal	ī ice	ȯ saw	ou out	ü rule	sh she	zh measure	i in pencil
								o in lemon
								u in circus

(ə)

U

V

W

XYZ

a	hat	â	care	ė	term	o	hot	ô	order	u	cup	ch	child	th	thin		a in about
ā	age	e	let	i	it	ō	open	oi	oil	ù	put	ng	long	ᴛн	then	ə	e in taken
ä	far	ē	equal	ī	ice	ȯ	saw	ou	out	ü	rule	sh	she	zh	measure		i in pencil / o in lemon / u in circus

Idiom Index

Phrasal Verb Index

Feature Index

Language Arts

These features support the development of language arts and writing skills.

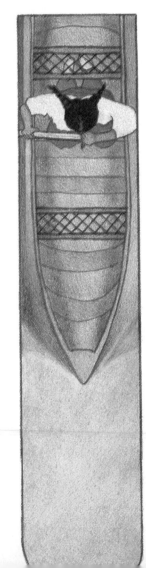

WORD WORKSHOP

VERB PLUS

IDIOMS

know: backwards and forwards, by heart, inside out, like a book, like the back of your hand, be in the know, know the dope, know the ropes, know the scoop, know the score, know what's up, know what's what   243

pay: hit pay dirt, pay the piper, pay through the nose   302

piece: go to pieces, give someone a piece of your mind, of a piece   309

place: give place, put someone in his or her place, know your place, take place   311

rich: born with a silver spoon in your mouth, in clover, made of money, on easy street, rolling in dough   345

sick: laid up, not yourself, out of sorts, run down, under par, under the weather   380

sleep: catch forty winks, crash, get some shut-eye, grab some Zs, hit the hay, hit the sack, zonk out   385

start: dive right in, get down to business, get your feet wet, get the show on the road, plunge in, roll up your sleeves, set the ball rolling, take the first step   397

stop: crack down on, cut short, lay to rest, lower the boom on, nip in the bud, put the kibosh on   402

try: give something a whirl, have a fling at, make a stab at, take a crack at, take a shot at, try your hand at   439

uncertain: in the balance, neck and neck, nip and tuck, up in the air   444

worried: on edge, on pins and needles, on tenterhooks, like peas on a hot griddle   479

Language History

▼ ● ● ● ● ● ● ● ● ● ● ● ● ● ●

These features broaden students' command of language and stimulate interest in the background and context of words and phrases.

● ● ● ● ● ● ● ● ● ● ● ● ● ● ● ●

Literature

These features use authentic literature and well-known quotations to showcase word choice.

WRITER'S CHOICE

NOTABLE QUOTABLE

Enrichment

These features enrich and extend vocabulary development.

WORD POOLS

brave: bravery, boldness, courage, daring, gallantry, guts, heart, heroism, nerve, pluck, spunk, valor   50

clothes: burnoose, caftan, cheongsam, dashiki, kilt, kimono, muumuu, parka, poncho, sari, sarong, serape   69

confused: anarchy, bedlam, chaos, clutter, disarray, disorder, jumble, mess, tangle, turmoil, uproar   79

crowd: clowder of cats, charm of finches, dray of squirrels, drift of hogs, exaltation of larks, flight of swallows, gaggle of geese, gang of elk, knot of toads, labor of moles, leap of leopards, nest of rabbits, pace of asses, pride of lions, rag of colts, school of fish, shrewdness of apes, skulk of foxes, tribe of goats, watch of nightingales, wedge of swans   91

enclose: cage, coop, corral, fence, hedge, jail, pen, stable   139

fear: ailurophobia, ballistophobia, clinophobia, doraphobia, eisoptrophobia, gephyrophobia, harpaxophobia, ichthyophobia, kakorraphiaphobia, linonophobia, logophobia, myxophobia, nephophobia, oikophobia, phronemophobia, rhabdophobia, sciophobia, triskaidekaphobia, teratophobia, xenophobia, zelophobia   165

foolish: boneheaded, cockeyed, dippy, dizzy, goofy, harebrained, inane, loony, loopy, tomfool, witless, wacky, zany   173

gadget: dingus, doodad, doohickey, dojigger, gigamaree, hootmalalie, thingumabob, thingumajig, whatchamacallit   185

list: agenda, bibliography, bill, calendar, directory, gazetteer, glossary, manifest, menu, program, schedule, table of contents, thesaurus   255

mad: aggravate, anger, annoy, enrage, exasperate, incense, infuriate, irk, irritate, madden, miff, outrage, peeve, provoke, rile, vex   267

measure: altimeter, ammeter, anemometer, barometer, calorimeter, chronometer, hygrometer, magnetometer, odometer, pedometer, photometer, sphygmomanometer, tachometer, voltmeter   272

prize: Clio, Edgar, Emmy, Grammy, Hugo, Nebula, Nobel, Oscar, Pulitzer, Tony   324

soft: doughy, downy, flabby, fleecy, fluffy, mushy, pulpy, spongy, woolly   390

standard: angstrom, block, centimeter, chain, decimeter, ell, foot, hand, inch, kilometer, league, light-year, meter, micron, mile, rod, yard   396

take up: anthropology, archaeology, chronology, dermatology, etymology, graphology, ichthyology, meteorology, ornithology, phar-

Art Credits

Unless otherwise credited, all photographs are the property of Scott Foresman.

534

535

Acknowledgments

Conrad, Pam, PRAIRIE SONGS. New York: HarperCollins, 1985, p. 8. 128

George, Jean Craighead, JULIE OF THE WOLVES. New York: Harper & Row, 1972, p. 9. 463

Hamilton, Virginia, THE HOUSE OF DIES DREAR. New York: The Macmillan Company, 1968, p 217. 99

Haskins, James, THURGOOD MARSHALL: A LIFE FOR JUSTICE. New York: Henry Holt & Co., 1992, p. 65. 367

Kaufman, Dr. Les, DO FISHES GET THIRSTY? New York: Franklin Watts, 1991, p. 33. 470

Lawson, Don, THE WAR IN VIETNAM. New York: Franklin Watts, 1981, p. 23. 241

L'Engle, Madeleine, A WIND IN THE DOOR. New York: Farrar, Straus, & Giroux, 1973, p. 146. 412

Meltzer, Milton, VOICES FROM THE CIVIL WAR. New York: Thomas Y. Crowell, 1989, p. 7 249

Myers, Walter Dean, SOMEWHERE IN THE DARK- NESS. New York, Scholastic, 1992, p. 12. 312

Myers, Walter Dean, THE MOUSE RAP. New York: Harper & Row, 1990, p. 26. 163

Namioka, Lensey, YANG THE YOUNGEST AND HIS TERRIBLE EAR. Boston: Little, Brown & Co. 1992, p 13. 291

Paulsen, Gary, WOODSONG.New York: Bradbury Press, 1990, p. 21. 177

Soto, Gary, TAKING SIDES. San Diego: Harcourt Brace Jovanovich, 1991, p. 18 124

Spinelli, Jerry, MANIAC MAGEE. Boston: Little, Brown & Co. 1990, p. 155. 193

Wilson, Johnniece Marshall, POOR GIRL, RICH GIRL. New York: Scholastic, 1992, p. 17. 145

Yep, Laurence, DRAGON STEEL. New York: Harper & Row, 1985, p. 39. 339